KARL BARTH AND REFORMED THEOLOGY

Karl Barth and Reformed Theology

Tradition, Dialogue, and Construction

Edited by PAUL T. NIMMO

CASCADE *Books* · Eugene, Oregon

KARL BARTH AND REFORMED THEOLOGY
Tradition, Dialogue, and Construction

Copyright © 2025 Wipf and Stock Publishers. All rights reserved. Except for brief quotations in critical publications or reviews, no part of this book may be reproduced in any manner without prior written permission from the publisher. Write: Permissions, Wipf and Stock Publishers, 199 W. 8th Ave., Suite 3, Eugene, OR 97401.

Cascade Books
An Imprint of Wipf and Stock Publishers
199 W. 8th Ave., Suite 3
Eugene, OR 97401

www.wipfandstock.com

PAPERBACK ISBN: 979-8-3852-3726-5
HARDCOVER ISBN: 979-8-3852-3727-2
EBOOK ISBN: 979-8-3852-3728-9

Cataloguing-in-Publication data:

Names: Nimmo, Paul T. [editor].

Title: Karl Barth and Reformed theology : tradition, dialogue, and construction / edited by Paul T. Nimmo.

Description: Eugene, OR: Cascade Books, 2025 | Includes bibliographical references.

Identifiers: ISBN 979-8-3852-3726-5 (paperback) | ISBN 979-8-3852-3727-2 (hardcover) | ISBN 979-8-3852-3728-9 (ebook)

Subjects: LCSH: Barth, Karl, 1886–1968. | Reformed Church—Theology. | Reformed Church—Doctrines.

Classification: BX4827.B3 N564 2025 (paperback) | BX4827.B3 (ebook)

VERSION NUMBER 12/02/25

Scripture quotations are taken from the New Revised Standard Version Updated Edition. Copyright © 2021 National Council of Churches of Christ in the United States of America. Used by permission. All rights reserved worldwide.

Contents

Acknowledgments | vii

List of Contributors | ix

Abbreviations of Works by Karl Barth | xi

Introduction by Paul T. Nimmo | xiii

PART ONE   **TRADITION**

Chapter 1   Karl Barth and the Reformed Tradition | 3
KATHERINE SONDEREGGER

Chapter 2   Karl Barth and Huldrych Zwingli | 17
PAUL T. NIMMO

Chapter 3   Revisiting Calvin and Barth on Natural Theology and Soteriology | 44
MICHELLE C. SANCHEZ

Chapter 4   Schleiermacher, Barth, and a Future for Reformed Theology | 65
KEVIN W. HECTOR

PART TWO   **DIALOGUE**

Chapter 5   On *Sacra Doctrina* and the *Analogia Entis*: Karl Barth and Roman Catholicism | 87
THOMAS JOSEPH WHITE

Chapter 6	"His claim upon our whole life": The Revelational-Exegetical Politics of the Barmen Declaration and the Declaration on the Russian World Teaching | 112 BRANDON GALLAHER
Chapter 7	Karl Barth's "Farewell" and the Challenge of Christian Nationalism in America | 142 KEITH L. JOHNSON

PART THREE CONSTRUCTION

Chapter 8	"In your light, we see light": The Scripture Principle in Karl Barth's *Göttingen Dogmatics* | 165 BEVERLY ROBERTS GAVENTA
Chapter 9	Going Medieval with Karl Barth: Divine Agency in Karl Barth's Doctrine of Election and His Dialogue with Medieval Scholasticism | 181 MATTHEW J. ARAGON BRUCE
Chapter 10	"The abasement of the flesh was like a veil, by which the divine majesty was covered": The Theme of Kenosis in Book 2 of Calvin's *Institutes* | 203 RINSE H. REELING BROUWER
Chapter 11	"The Princeton Creed": Expanding the Underlying Romanticism in Bruce McCormack and Karl Barth—on Dogmatics, Trinity, Kenosis | 223 ALEXANDRA PÂRVAN
Chapter 12	"Doch was geht uns die Kirche an?": A Response to Alexandra Pârvan | 259 BRUCE MCCORMACK

Bibliography | 283

Acknowledgments

This volume would not have been possible without the assistance and encouragement of a number of people. Kaitlyn Dugan, director of the Center for Barth Studies at Princeton Seminary, was the catalyst, the strategist, and the organizer of the conference at which these papers were first delivered: she has been a tireless advocate and enabler of Barth studies for many years, and my sincere thanks go to her for her long-standing support and for her work on that conference in particular. The speakers at the conference, all now contributors to this volume, have been patient and professional at every turn, and I would like to express my great appreciation to them. The people at Cascade Books—particularly Robin Parry, Matt Wimer, Mike Surber, and George Callihan, as well as a terrific copyeditor, Elisabeth Rickard, a meticulous proofreader, Rebecca Abbott, and a wonderful typesetter, Jonathan Hill—have been wonderfully helpful in bringing this project to fruition, and I am deeply grateful to them for their willingness to work with me. Here in Aberdeen, my dear colleagues Declan Kelly and Paula Duncan have been supremely diligent in preparing the manuscript for publication, and my warm thanks to them. And finally, there are those friends around me who are there for both the brightest and the darkest of days, and without whom I could do almost nothing: you know who you are, and you are much loved.

Professor Paul T. Nimmo
King's College, University of Aberdeen
March 2025

List of Contributors

MATTHEW J. ARAGON BRUCE is the director of the Cultivating the Gift of Preaching Initiative, a ministry of the Synod of the Covenant in the PC(USA), and an affiliate faculty member at Western Theological Seminary in Holland, Michigan.

BRANDON GALLAHER is associate professor of systematic theology at the University of Exeter.

BEVERLY ROBERTS GAVENTA is Helen H. P. Manson Professor of New Testament Literature and Exegesis Emerita at Princeton Theological Seminary.

KEVIN W. HECTOR is Naomi Shenstone Donnelley Professor of Theology and of the Philosophy of Religions at the University of Chicago.

KEITH L. JOHNSON is professor of theology at Wheaton College.

BRUCE MCCORMACK holds the chair in modern theology at the University of Aberdeen.

PAUL T. NIMMO holds the King's Chair of Systematic Theology at the University of Aberdeen.

ALEXANDRA PÂRVAN is senior lecturer in the Department of Psychology at the National University of Science and Technology Politehnica Bucharest, Pitești University Centre, in Romania.

LIST OF CONTRIBUTORS

RINSE H. REELING BROUWER is Professor Emeritus on the Miskotte/Breukelman Chair for Theological Hermeneutics of the Bible at the Protestant Theological University (Amsterdam).

MICHELLE C. SANCHEZ is professor of theology at Harvard Divinity School.

KATHERINE SONDEREGGER holds the William Meade Chair in Theology at Virginia Theological Seminary.

THOMAS JOSEPH WHITE is the rector magnificus of the Pontifical University of St. Thomas (Angelicum) in Rome.

Abbreviations of Works by Karl Barth

CD   *Church Dogmatics*. Edited by Geoffrey W. Bromiley and T. F. Torrance. 4 vols., in 13 parts. Edinburgh: T&T Clark, 1956–75

KD   *Die Kirchliche Dogmatik*. 4 vols., in 13 parts. Munich: Kaiser, 1932 (vol. I/1). Zurich: EVZ, 1938–65

Introduction

Paul T. Nimmo

In June 2022, the Center for Barth Studies at Princeton Theological Seminary hosted an international and ecumenical conference under the title "Karl Barth and Reformed Theology: Tradition, Dialogue, and Construction." The primary aim of the event was to explore some of the ways in which Karl Barth as a Reformed theologian interacted with the Reformed and other traditions, along paths both expository and critical, and to reflect upon the possibility—and reality—that his creative engagement might encourage and resource generative work in theology in the contemporary era. A wide range of speakers entertaining diverse perspectives assembled for the event, brought together by their common interest in the work of Karl Barth and the Reformed tradition in particular, and their shared commitment to constructive theological dialogue around substantive issues affecting church and world in general. The large number of attendees present in Princeton for the event—as well as the online participants from around the globe—were rewarded by a rich and varied range of papers on the conference theme.

The theme of Barth's relationship to Reformed theology is particularly compelling, for Barth engaged with the inheritance of Reformed theology and its representatives throughout his life, from his student days to his final conversations. Yet it is fair to say that this engagement had a slow start. In his student days in Bern, he attended a course of lectures on the history of the Reformation period and wrote a paper on Huldrych Zwingli for a church history class,[1] and during his semesters in

---

1. "Zwingli's Sixty-Seven Articles," in Barth, *Early Barth*, 72–83.

INTRODUCTION

Germany he bought and read the *Speeches* of Friedrich Schleiermacher;[2] but in truth there was little else besides. However, during his time as assistant pastor at the German church in Geneva, Barth not only continued to read Schleiermacher, but also—naturally, given the location—read an increasing amount of John Calvin, including in the commentaries and the *Institutes*, and began to develop a more contoured picture of the tradition.[3] During his ten years as pastor in Safenwil, his reading in the Reformed tradition (with a growing preference for Calvin over Zwingli) continued at points, as he sought not so much to repristinate this theology of the past but to reappropriate it creatively for the present.[4]

On becoming an honorary professor of Reformed theology in Göttingen, a broadly Lutheran faculty, Barth took on an extraordinary amount of work in order to immerse himself in the theology of the Reformed tradition so as to be able to lecture upon it—and defend it.[5] Intensive lecture courses followed semester by semester, taking as successive themes the theology of the Heidelberg Catechism, of Calvin, of Zwingli, of the Reformed Confessions, and of Schleiermacher.[6] There then followed four series of lectures of constructive theology, commonly known as the "Göttingen Dogmatics" (though the last series was delivered in Münster).[7] The lectures drew heavily on these earlier studies in the Reformed tradition, as well as on the compendium of post-Reformation Reformed theology edited by Heinrich Heppe,[8] though always with a view to making his own response to the luminary teachers of his tradition.[9] His move to Münster in 1925 led to new conversation partners,

---

2. Tietz, *Karl Barth*, 31.

3. "Das reformierte Erbe," in Freudenberg, *Reformierter Protestantismus in der Herausforderung*, 299–305.

4. "Das reformierte Erbe," in Freudenberg, *Reformierter Protestantismus in der Herausforderung*, 306–13.

5. Freudenberg, *Karl Barth und die reformierte Theologie*, 15–83. For a wider diachronic survey of Barth's reception of Reformed theology, see also Freudenberg, "Nach Gottes Wort Reformiert."

6. Barth: *Theology of John Calvin*; *Theologie Zwinglis 1922/1923*; *Theology of the Reformed Confessions*; *Theology of Schleiermacher*.

7. Barth, *Göttingen Dogmatics* (trans. Thomas Herwig).

8. Heppe, *Reformed Dogmatics*. For details of this ressourcement, both in the 1920s and later, see Reeling Brouwer, *Karl Barth and Post-Reformation Orthodoxy*.

9. Barth, *Theology of John Calvin*, stands as a classic articulation of Barth's approach to the work of his teachers—whether from his tradition (such as Calvin) or not: "We listen, we learn, and then we go our own way and in so doing we give evidence of respect, of doing the teacher justice" (5).

INTRODUCTION

given the largely Roman Catholic character of his new surrounds, and in the period that followed, Barth offered not only a fresh series of dogmatics lectures,[10] but also seminars covering themes in Luther and Thomas.[11] Yet even as his constructive positions developed ever more tangibly and explicitly, his interest in and commitment to the Reformed tradition remained strong.

During his time in Bonn (1930–35) and on into his final position in Basel, as he wrote *Church Dogmatics*,[12] Barth's engagement with Reformed theology became ever deeper, ever more informed, and arguably ever more critical. As he wended his own dogmatic way through successive loci, engaging a whole library of figures from across the denominational spectrum, Barth remained discernibly Reformed by instinct. One might mention in this regard his practical attention to the Scripture principle, his foregrounding of themes of covenant and election, his strong insistence on the distinction of the natures in Christology, his hesitation regarding certain forms of creaturely mediation, and his changing position on the sacraments, which all remained thoroughly Reformed. He recognized this Reformed inheritance and its existential importance to his work explicitly.[13] At the same time, he also distanced himself from the inherited resources of the Reformed tradition in respect of his formulation of several doctrines—from revelation to predestination, from providence to Christology.[14] At times he offered creative adjustments to the tradition; at other times, he engaged in rather more critical departures. And all this served the freedom of his theology to attend to the Word of God, his unwillingness to be unduly fettered by any particular

---

10. Barth, *Christliche Dogmatik im Entwurf.*

11. McCormack, *Karl Barth's Critically Realistic Dialectical Theology*, 378.

12. The first part-volume of *Church Dogmatics* was published in 1932, with the lectures which were the foundation of that text beginning in Bonn in the summer semester of 1931.

13. For Barth, the ultimate result of the fact that "the real Christian faith can be recognized, lived and expressed only in the relativity and determinateness of a specific place within the visible Church" is that "for us, therefore, Church dogmatics is necessarily Reformed dogmatics" (*CD* I/2, 824, 831).

14. For details of Barth's response to the Reformed tradition in respect of each of these particular doctrines, see the following texts: Kenneth Oakes, "Revelation and Scripture," 246–62; Matthew J. Aragon Bruce, "Election," 309–24; David Fergusson, "Providence," 373–88; and Rinse H. Reeling Brouwer, "Jesus Christ," 277–93, all in Jones and Nimmo, *Oxford Handbook of Karl Barth*. See also the treatments of Scripture, election, and Christology in MacDonald and Trueman, *Calvin, Barth, and Reformed Theology.*

INTRODUCTION

tradition, and his sense that to write constructive dogmatics was to write *for the church* as a whole rather than one constituency of it.[15] Ultimately, Barth's Reformed identity was central to his character and significant for his work; indeed it is impossible to understand Barth's writing and legacy without acknowledging its material impact. Yet in another sense, this identity was accidental rather than essential—a license to reform theology in response to its living Lord rather than a compulsion to tread again the ways of the past.

This book explores in its three sections the relation between Karl Barth and Reformed theology by way of a series of soundings of some of its most significant aspects.

In its first section, entitled "Tradition," it offers both contemporary insights and historical perspectives on the topic of Barth as Reformed theologian. The opening chapter, by Katharine Sonderegger, offers a striking approach to the question of the way in which Barth is a Reformed theologian. Arguing that Barth's identity as Reformed is not a matter of de facto fulfillment, Sonderegger suggests that what makes Barth Reformed is a particular mode of theological working in which the Lordship of Almighty God is acknowledged and enacted. The following chapter by Paul Nimmo attends to the relationship between Barth and the earliest Reformed theologian, Huldrych Zwingli, surveying the historical course of Barth's interactions with Zwingli and detailing the resonances between their theologies. Despite Barth's ambivalence toward Zwingli, Nimmo affirms the significance of Zwingli's impact upon Barth, and identifies a crucial resonance between their positions that has thus far not been attended. In her chapter, Michelle C. Sanchez turns to the relationship between Barth and John Calvin, the most influential Reformed theologian, focusing on the topic of natural theology and contextualizing both Calvin and Barth in their historical-scientific imaginative settings. Against the common reading of Barth as diverging from Calvin in his appraisal of the natural world, Sanchez sees both as united in rejecting a kind of specialized natural knowledge of God attached to salvation. Meanwhile Kevin Hector writes on the relationship between Barth and the quintessential Reformed and modern theologian Friedrich Schleiermach and construes both to approach the theological task in a similar way, moving from theological interpretation of context

15. In this way, Barth writes that "where dogmatics exists at all, it exists only with the will to be a Church dogmatics, a dogmatics of the ecumenical Church" (*CD* I/2, 831).

INTRODUCTION

to theological intervention into it. Following their examples in greater detail, Hector proceeds to outline possible constructive consequences for contemporary work in theology.

The second section, "Dialogue," presents the fruits of a series of encounters between Barth as Reformed theologian in the world and other ecclesiastical movements. In the first essay in this section, Thomas Joseph White draws Barth into conversation with Roman Catholic theology by way of an exploration of the Thomistic understanding of theology as *sacra doctrina*, focusing particularly on its deployment of philosophy and the implications for ecumenism. White argues against Barth that the use of philosophy within *sacra doctrina* should not be church dividing, and presents the doctrine of kenosis as a case study for ongoing theological dialogue. In his chapter, Brandon Gallaher draws Barth into dialogue with Eastern Orthodoxy, focusing on the relationship between the Barmen Declaration of 1934 and the Orthodox text "A Declaration on the Russian World (*Russkii Mir*) Teaching" of 2022. His careful analysis reveals an array of similarities between the texts, culminating in the claim that both advance a form of revelational, exegetical, and eschatological political theology. Keith Johnson turns in similarly political vein to the relationship between the German Christian nationalism that Barth faced in Germany and the contemporary resurgence of nationalist movements in the United States. Johnson examines in particular Barth's active resistance to National Socialist influence upon the German Church, and how this can inform Christians seeking to resist the recent rise in Christian nationalism.

In "Construction," the third section of the book, there are offered a series of generative treatments of the relationship between Barth and core Reformed positions. The section opens with an essay from Beverly Roberts Gaventa, in which Gaventa addresses the understanding of *sola Scriptura* with which Barth operates in the Göttingen Dogmatics, downstream of his Romans commentaries. She highlights his emphasis both on the reliability of Scripture and on the authority and the freedom involved in its interpretation, but critiques the absence in Barth's theology of the role of the Spirit in illumination, particularly through the medium of other agents. Matthew Bruce takes as his subject Barth's controverted doctrine of election, and reframes this material against the backdrop of the medieval debate concerning free agency, the debate between nominalism and voluntarism. Along this path, Bruce contends that Barth's account of divine freedom has affinities with that of Thomas Aquinas, paving the way for future ecumenical rapprochement. Shifting focus to Christology, Rinse Reeling Brouwer offers a detailed analysis of the christological sections of Calvin's *Institutes*, and particularly of the three chapters devoted to the person of the Mediator. Reeling Brouwer clarifies the contextual debates underlying Calvin's work on these sections, and draws a distinction here between Calvin and Barth regarding the humility of the eternal Son. Alexandra Pârvan moves in her essay to consider the character of the literary movement of romanticism and the impact of this movement on the respective theologies of Barth and Bruce McCormack. She proposes ways in which attention to these romantic traits can both advance the interpretation of these authors and enhance the developing theology of McCormack, and she recommends that theologians develop their aesthetic capacities as they answer the need to pronounce new church creeds for the present. Bruce McCormack offers in his response to the work of Pârvan an affirmation and a further development of her claim that Barth's theology draws on romantic impulses, and engages in constructive vein with her proposed improvements to his own work.

PART ONE

Tradition

CHAPTER 1

Karl Barth and the Reformed Tradition
Katherine Sonderegger

Was Karl Barth a Reformed theologian? This is an odd question to ask, I know—and not just because I speak at a conference dedicated to Barth and the Reformed tradition! It is odd because in one sense it is hard to imagine anyone more Reformed than was Barth. He emerged out of a distinguished line of Reformed pastors and teachers on both sides of his family; he entered his theological studies as a Reformed candidate and, unlike so many of us in the West today, he never made pilgrimage through several denominations or churches. Not for Barth the trajectory from vague or anomalous spirituality to a distinctive Christian identity as we find in Evelyn Underhill or, in different idiom, C. S. Lewis. Nor did he seem to hover between allegiances, now drawn to Rome, now to Geneva or Wittenberg, or to points farther east, as did Avery later Cardinal Dulles, or the young Thomas Merton, or in more agonized keys, Edith Stein or Simone Weil or Ludwig Wittgenstein. Barth began, remained, and never repented of his sturdy Reformed identity. His whole life long Barth resolutely belonged to and represented the Reformed and Calvinist traditions, in his teaching posts, in his public presentation of the faith, in his churchmanship, and in his ecumenical engagement: he never wavered and he never moved. In this sense, Barth resembled more closely his seventeenth-century older divines, or nineteenth-century pillars such as Hodge or Bavinck, or even his United Church forebear Schleiermacher than he did the magisterial Reformers for whom a conversion—a turning of the bridle—constituted the entry into Protestant confession.

PART ONE | TRADITION

We might add here too a Reformed element unmistakable from *Church Dogmatics*: Barth dedicated much of his historical commentary and analysis to Reformed dogmaticians: to Calvin, certainly, but also to Ursinus and Beza and Zwingli, to Polanus and Cocceius and Wollebius, to Reformed exegetes in the modern style, to the Reformed modernists, Schleiermacher and Herrmann, and to the Reformed confessions and catechisms, among which the Heidelberg Catechism held pride of place. This volume unfolds the lifelong encounter Barth had with some of these major Reformed teachers; his dogmatic work is unrecognizable without this legacy. And yet.

And yet Barth is not a Reformed theologian in the expected fashion. Perhaps with an intellect as restless, capacious, and omnivorous as was Barth's, nothing ordinary could be expected here. Yet I would not want to assign Barth's idiosyncratic Reformed identity to simple biography or mentalité. Barth was strikingly, and studiously, reserved, almost reticent about his Reformed credentials. He was a sturdy Reformed theologian, yes; but I would say too, a reluctant partisan. Barth was never a Calvinist in the way some theologians are Thomists or Lutherans. He did not begin a theological discussion with the words "as a Calvinist, I hold the following," while it is entirely customary and apposite for a Dominican to begin a remark, "As a Thomist, I claim that." Now, this is not to suggest that Thomism is a monolith; far from it! As Fergus Kerr has amply demonstrated, Thomism is a complex, not a simple, especially in the modern era; to begin a doctrinal document with the declaration "As a Thomist, I" is simply to announce membership in a wide family. Perhaps this is only more true with Lutheranism. Some, but certainly not all Lutherans, consider themselves descended from the Protestant Luther, and hold themselves accountable for the dogmatic positions Luther advanced, whether for good or ill. Indeed, I would argue that Calvin considered himself a Lutheran in just this way: he understood his vocation to consist in the consolidation and expansion of the dogmatic revolution Luther began. He laid claim to *Luther redivivus*. Loyalty to the Lutheran or Thomist programmatic, for Calvin and for others, is signaled by citation—this is Thomas on nature and grace; or here is Luther on Law and Gospel—and by a willingness, even eagerness, to explicate the inner coherence of these views. I think we could say that many of us in this room are Barthians in just this sense. But Barth himself was neither Barthian nor Calvinist in this way. Thomists and Lutherans move within a tradition and under a particular Doctor of the Church whose doctrine is taken to be generative, authoritative, and foundational. Barth never recognized such a relation to Calvin, say, or to Zwingli. It may be that in his student days, Barth felt such an allegiance to Schleiermacher, or perhaps to Wilhelm Herrmann. He was more inclined in his early, liberal period to begin an essay with the proud words "We modern theologians hold such and such." But I think it is a striking and illuminating fact that Barth, once his break took hold, did not advert to a master, did not rely on a Reformed authority, and did not seek to remain loyal to a Magister's founding principles.

When we examine the long pages of *Church Dogmatics* we do not find in them the idiom of the school governing Barth's theological construction. He discusses Reformed theologians at length, yes. But so too does he devote long excurses to Thomas and to Anselm and to Augustine or John Damascene or Luther and Melanchthon. The *Church Dogmatics* reads as an ecumenical treatise, an extended reflection on the common heritage of the Christian church. Of course Barth was a great polemicist! His ecumenical Christian identity hardly stemmed from a melting irenicism. But it is characteristic of Barth's fierce debate with his contemporaries that his dogmatics rarely begins with a defense of Calvinist teaching, or a declaration that a vital Reformed principle lies under attack. All this we might say was too "religious" for Barth's palate. Indeed the very notion of "religion," so vital to an understanding of Barth's early dogmatic work, reflects this deep reticence about churchly belonging. Barth was famously self-critical and critical of his own kin. From this stems the "secular air" that Hans Frei detected in Barth, a decidedly "non-religious" and even more "non-churchly" atmosphere that characterizes Barth's milieu. Late in *Church Dogmatics* Barth insisted that proper theology is not a "worldview," a *Weltanschauung*; it does not inhabit a spiritual sphere, but is rather "worldly," a full citizen of the larger cultural and humane realm. All these elements lend Barth and his theology but an indirect purchase on Reformed identity.

But whence all this? Perhaps we spoke too hastily above in dismissing a biographical dimension to Barth's theological identity. After all, the lovely self-deprecating humor that makes Barth endearing to so many of us belongs hand in glove with his reserve about ecclesial identity. He was decidedly not a self-proclaimer. Such reserve extends to Barth's shorter and occasional works. Not surprisingly, his essays for ecumenical gatherings are less particular or denominational in scope and more attuned to large-scale ecclesial documents; but they do not stand alone. Barth simply begins his brief compositions with an exegetical or dogmatic topic—on preaching, or on ethics, or the state, or the sacraments—and holds in great reserve an identifying marker such as Calvinist or Reformed. The Reformed does not announce itself in Barth's mature theology. Like Barth's own pronounced reluctance to examine his inner life for the wider public, Barth's Reformed identity stood in the wings, so to say. It formed the deep background to his scholarly and religious life, not the entrance way. A comparison with Augustine might be instructive here.

Hardly any Christian thinker before Luther spoke in such introspective and personal tones as did St. Augustine. Even the sometimes querulous tone of Gregory Nazianzus—so miserable for him in the backwaters! yet more miserable in the big city of Constantinople!—cannot match the probing search for the inward way in Augustine's thought. There is nothing like the *Confessions* in Barth's expansive oeuvre; even his autobiographical sketches that head the Busch and Tietz biographies do not read as the pulsing inner skin of a life as does even a single page of the *Confessions*. But this is not simply a matter of individual style or literary power of self-disclosure; it is rather a sign of a particular form of identity. Barth simply does not announce himself. He does not explore himself, but he also does not declare himself or his badge. Identity for Augustine is a theology and a Church. Far more ready than Barth is Augustine to proclaim himself a defender of a school or movement. He is the stout champion of the Catholic Church, against Donatists, against Manichaeans, against heretics of many schools, against the pagans. Unlike Barth, Augustine is far more prone to declare the Catholic position on many subjects and in many venues. In the urgent, polemical, and seemingly never-ending crises of a long enduring Donatist schism, Augustine urges his congregation to recognize, acknowledge, and confess the true Church, its bishops and catechists, over against the vibrant, well-connected, and popular Church of the confessors, a Donatism that surged into the majority time and again, and caught the attention of Roman proconsuls. Certainly Barth knew how to defend and to attack; his place in the Confessing Church is well known. But once again we see Barth's characteristic hand in the Barmen Declaration, a document that takes its stand on exegetical grounds whose doctrine is an unfolding of the ethical demands of a God who lays claim to the whole of creaturely life. A school, a denomination, a particular and concrete Church or synod or judicatory is not to be seen. It too is not an explicit Reformed document, though claimed, to be sure, by the Reformed, worldwide. Unlike Barth, Augustine assimilated his urgent searching for the God of Truth to his identity as Catholic prelate, advocate, and teacher. Inward and outward, Augustine was a member and herald of the Great Church, the Catholic Church of the Roman *imperium*.

Barth was not a Calvinist in this sense. He was also not a Reformed theologian in the same sense as was Friedrich Schleiermacher. A comparison with the *Glaubenslehre* may be instructive as well. Essential to the structure of *Christian Faith* is the highlighting, in each dogmatic section, of Protestant confessions or creeds that spring from Reformed and Lutheran Churches of the sixteenth and seventeenth centuries. Because of the remarkable generativity and novelty of Schleiermacher's method, the student of his work may be forgiven for considering these citations a form of courtesy to ancient voices, a nod in the direction of honored forebears. Always conscious of history, and eager to find his place within a collective spiritual life, Schleiermacher did appeal to his ancestors in the faith for warrant for his own distinctive, sometimes radical, expression of a faith received from the past. But these citations do much more work in *Christian Faith* than mere courtesy or warranting suggest. Schleiermacher took his identity from the ecclesial documents of the Lutheran and Reformed Churches. He clearly read well beyond these confines; the appeal to Anselm's *Fides quaerens intellectum* graces the opening of the *Glaubenslehre* as well as Barth's celebrated investigation of the *Proslogion*. But Schleiermacher read Augustine or Thomas or Irenaeus as a Reformed theologian, a particular kind of pietist, descended from the Swiss Reform, and nurtured in Germany and Lutheran soil. He *begins* dogmatic work after the rupture with Rome. He cites the magisterial Reformers and knows them well. But what grounds Schleiermacher's mature work are the official teachings, the confessions and catechisms, of the Protestant world. The lengthy introduction to *Christian Faith* gives us Schleiermacher's method, his analysis of the religious development of humankind, and his delicate sense for the spiritual essence of monotheisms, as known by the cultured of early modern Europe. But the dogmatic content itself derives from the Church declarations of the seventeenth century, the established Lutheran and Reformed polities. Schleiermacher's theology has a *starting point*, a clear and distinct one, we might say, and that is in the groundwork of Protestant synodal and conciliar decrees.

Now, there is one document only in Barth's corpus—or only one that I know—that mirrors such a structure: Barth's early lectures at Göttingen on the Reformed confessions. Translated under the title *The Theology of the Reformed Confessions*, these lectures represent Barth's entry into professional theology as the incumbent of the newly created professor in Reformed Dogmatics at the University of Göttingen. Delivered during the summer semester in 1923, these lectures offer an unsurpassed initiation into Barth's theology in the dialectic period as it unfolded after the second edition of the Romans commentary. Poured into these lectures is the frantic work Barth took on as he moved from parish pastor into the university professoriate. Reading through the detailed and wide canvass of sixteenth- and seventeenth-century confessions, a lavish spread from Switzerland and the Low Countries, through Italy, France, and Germany into the United Kingdom and a side glance at the United States, one can well believe Barth's report that he flew between desk and bed, sleeping fitfully only to rise early to work some more. It is a remarkable portrait of a tireless researcher and a born historian. The central axioms of these lectures will detain us in a moment, but here it is worth pausing to reflect on the complexity and ambiguity of this work in Barth's writing.

Barth received the invitation to assume this chair while still holding the pastorate at Safenwil. The consortium that funded the post feared that the Reformed theology of Germany was fast disappearing and losing its cogency in the midst of the Luther and Lutheran revival of the inter-war years. For their part, the Lutherans on the Göttingen faculty were uneasy about this brash dialectician, and more uneasy still about a Reformed theologian teaching dogmatics on a Lutheran faculty. The major publications that issued from Barth's years in Göttingen reflected this simmering conflict: none were entitled *Dogmatics* or *Theology*, and each aimed to do both under indirect cover. More widely known, I believe, is Barth's first entry into systematic work, the *Göttingen Dogmatics*, as it is known in Anglophone circles, and originally titled—of necessity—*Instruction in the Christian Religion*, an obvious homage to Calvin. Significantly, this two-volume work followed the architectonic of all Barth's later work: a thesis statement, setting out the main lines of argument for the chapter, followed by a lengthy exposition and exegesis of key scriptural passages. No epigraphs from the Reformed confessions inaugurate the chapters. But the 1923 lectures on the theology of the Reformed confessions dare to do so. These are essays that purport to examine Reformed confessions as *starting point* and groundwork, the very substance of theological reflection. They do so in an intensely polemic atmosphere.

This is a species of *elenctic* theology, refining, clarifying, and distinguishing one's own position over against another; Francois Turretin is perhaps the best-known exemplar of this late Scholastic style. Barth has been forced by circumstances to step out into the public realm *as Reformed*. He stands before us in these lectures as an explicit member of the Reformed school in theology, and he cites the rich array of Reformed documents as warrant and foundation for doctrinal positions. The lectures repeat this dialectical self-definition in concentric circles: the nature of confession itself, Reformed and Lutheran; the Scripture principle, as he understood it in those years; Reformed over against Lutheran, followed by an extensive exposition of Reformed theology, divided into subdivisions along elenctic lines—debate with the Old Church (Barth's title for the medieval Church), the controversy with Lutheranism, the battle against modern Christianity (a fusillade of Barth's dogmatic firepower), and an illuminating section simply titled "The Positive Doctrine of Christianity." Here in extended form we see Schleiermacher's legacy at work. Barth presents himself as a Reformed theologian, a member of a school, deriving his dogmatic position from the official ecclesial documents of early modern Europe. This is rare, indeed I believe a *hapax legomonen* in all Barth's sweeping terrain. It differs *toto coelo* from Barth's later and repeated expositions on the Heidelberg Catechism, one of Barth's darlings, which simply treated the document as a Christian testimony worthy of our careful attention and theological gratitude.

This Göttingen lecture series differs too from another celebrated lecture cycle, the Gifford Lectures, delivered in the steamy years 1937 to 1938 under the title "The Knowledge of God and the Service of God." Underlying the whole is the Scots Confession of 1560, cited at the head of each lecture. Perhaps, one might think, this is the exception to my rule: Barth once again appears to place Reformed documents at the center of the theological task, to take his orientation from them, and to lay out for audience a dogmatics loyal to the sixteenth-century Reformers of the Kirk. Once again, too, Barth confesses himself a Reformed theologian, and time and again he describes himself as a member of the Reformed branch of the Church of Christ, a stubborn partisan of the school. Perhaps the Gifford Lectures are the black swan, and I must revise my austere account of Barth's Reformed identity. But I have not yet been persuaded of this fate because I believe something distinct and distinctive is underway in these lectures on the Scots Confession. I might best point to this distinctive by turning to James Barr's celebrated Gifford Lectures, delivered some half-century later, on the topic "Biblical Faith and Natural Theology." Barr has many targets in his sights, but Karl Barth is *primus inter pares*. It is tribute to the unique character of Barth's Gifford Lectures that

Barr finds himself still outraged by the arguments Barth advanced—and refused to advance—about revelation, about Scripture, and in indirect fashion, about natural theology. My own view is that Barr is not a successful interpreter of Barth, but that verdict does not touch on the force of Barr's assessment of those early lectures, nor on the marvelous plain-speaking of the whole series. Barr is a splendid lecturer, and his series is a bracing tour of his own preoccupations with the biblical theology movement. But Barr remains uneasy over Barth's stubborn example, irritating after all these years. Barr considers Barth to have a conceptual or philosophical position on natural theology and general revelation, and, Barr charges, Barth forces his biblical texts to fit into this ill-sized and ill-considered frame. Barr has not won the day on his analysis of Barth's exegesis, I would say, but he has put his finger on a defining character of Barth's Gifford Lectures.

Like the informal lectures given in Bonn some years later, Barth's Giffords are a précis of evangelical theology, or perhaps better, his own dogmatic program. Barth considered the theological task to be laid upon one: the theologian is accountable for the history of doctrine and must answer for his or her reception and assessment of the whole. As in Bonn, so in Aberdeen: Barth took upon himself the presentation of Christian dogmatics as he understood it, and as Scripture had to that moment instructed him. These lectures are a *verdict*, that is, and Barth confesses publicly to a Christian faith that echoes the Scots Confession but does not stem from it. He agrees, in the main, with its findings; but that only because they run consistent with the larger witness of Scripture. Once again, then, in this seeming counterexample, we find Barth offering only an indirect Reformed identity, one in which the Reformed position concurs with Barth's own testimony to Holy Scripture's record of Immanuel, God with us. Barr is right, then, in this one, narrow sense about Barth's Gifford Lectures: Barth brings to his task a mature dogmatic theology—by 1937 his *Church Dogmatics* are now well underway—and he does not need the Scots Confession or any Reformation document to ground or warrant his theology. Indeed, just this is Barth's insistence upon revelation, a Reformed position as he sees it, and upon a correlate, and indirect, opposition to natural theology, of Brunner's sort but of every sort, including Lord Gifford's. The *Glaubenslehre* is still not in view.

So we may well ask, Just how does Barth understand the Reformed tradition? In what sense may we vindicate the claim that Barth is a Reformed theologian, and stands as member of that proud tradition?

Here the *Theology of the Reformed Confessions* does the heavy lifting. On the basis of those lectures I want to suggest that Barth identified the Reformed tradition in a particular fashion that he never abandoned: he held that Reformed theology is a *mode* of Christian dogmatics, and not a series of doctrinal positions. We might, with some hesitation, characterize Barth's notion as a formal distinction over a material one. But as I hope to specify a bit further on, Barth's handling of the Reformed identity does not fit easily into that handy distinction, for Barth too finds the Reformed tradition rich in material, dogmatic content. It may be better to say that a particular doctrine of God gives rise to a particular mode of doctrine: content, in this sense, governs and gives rise to form, a position Barth enunciated early in his career and never yielded. The God who encountered the young Safenwil pastor was both *hidden* and *sovereign*. The fundamental claim of Barth's Göttingen lectures, indeed I would hazard of his entire majestic *Church Dogmatics*, is that Almighty God is Lord. This conviction never leaves him, even in the famed *Lichtelehre* of *Church Dogmatics* IV/3. That Barr considered that beloved excursus on the lights of the world to be a form of natural theology tells me that this fundamental orientation of Barth's Reformed theology has not been registered by Barr, or I think by the many admirers of that splendid section of the doctrine of reconciliation. God is hidden, transcendent, lofty, the Lord. I do not know if this is an episode in Barth's spiritual biography, but I believe that it is consonant with Barth's conviction, throughout his career, that the name of God is properly uttered by the word "Lord." It seems to be a decision of unknown antiquity, but certainly codified by the Tannaim, that the Tetragrammaton would be vocalized by the Hebrew plural, Adonai. For Barth such a decision could not be an act of simple courtesy or court protocol. Rather the rabbinic tradents are setting forth an *identity*: the true God of Israel, the High and Lofty One, cannot be addressed by his given name, but is rather identical to the spoken name, Lord. Thus is uncovered an analytic judgment, as Kant would have it, the predicate, Lord, "contained in"—that ambiguous and much studied relation!—the Subject, the unsaid Tetragrammaton. The shadow of the possessive, Adoni, is salient here too, I believe. To speak of this transcendent God is to speak of one's own Lord: Adoni, *my* Lord. Thus is laid out in Exod 3 the entire architectonic of Barth's doctrine of God: Israel's God is both hidden, unsaid and unutterable, and Lord, the direct and irresistible Sovereign of the people who know him. The dialectic of hiddenness and Lordship is embedded in the metaphysics of

God himself, and gives rise to the conceptual dialectic of transcendence and revelation, of veiling and unveiling, the dominant themes of the first volumes of *Church Dogmatics*. The mode that recognizes this austere and graceful truth is Reformed theology. I think Barth's Reformed identity is that simple and that demanding.

Let me express this in less methodological and more explicitly doctrinal idiom. I believe that in these early lectures, Barth clarifies, confesses, and articulates the conviction that Lordship is the essential predicate of Israel's God. By essential predicate I mean that any deity that would be conceived or that would appear without Lordship would not be God, in this world, or in any possible world. In the idiom of *Church Dogmatics* II/1, we would say that the true and hidden God is the One who loves in freedom. Now, notice here that I am speaking directly and simply of the doctrine of God, introducing a kind of "speculative" note, if you will, into this discussion and a sojourn into the land of divine attributes. This I believe to be the very heart of the matter.

We might begin by speaking of sovereignty as the *content* of the doctrine of God. This is not foreign, I believe, to Barth's entire enterprise. Indeed, in the Göttingen lectures, Barth considers Lutheran confessions, and most especially the Augustana, to teach this very material. In this way, Barth considers the Reformed and Lutheran confessions to be united: the material content of the doctrine of God is identical. And in just this way, we may think of Calvin as a Lutheran: he holds to the same material positions as does Luther and he defends them as the proper exegesis of Holy Scripture. Because Barth can speak in just this speculative or metaphysical fashion, it is easy and I think in some ways justified to range Barth's positions against other Scholastics, medieval and early modern, and to press his doctrine of God to clarify just how the transcendent or theological perfections of God relate to the economic and revealed attributes of this lordly God. Indeed in much of *Church Dogmatics* II/1, Barth defends a form of counterfactual reasoning to handle the relation between the transcendent and immanent attributes of the One God. The Lord need not reveal himself, Barth will write time and again; or the Lord is free in his condescension to his creatures; or more directly, the One Lord is sufficient Love in himself, and has no need of the world as site of his gracious loving-kindness. Rather, the perfections of God "overspill," "flow down," cascade upon the dry earth; but the Lord God himself is eternally rich, eternally free, in a word, sovereign over his very perfections. Israel's God is Lord.

Of course such straightforward metaphysical analysis of Barth's doctrine of God leads to many conceptual puzzles, ones that preoccupy much Barth scholarship. Should "grace" be considered a perfection of God's transcendent nature? Or more strikingly, "obedience"? Does this not undermine divine aseity or, in more stark terms, render the cosmos necessary to the sovereign God? How do these metaphysical worries relate to Christology? This last question seems to me vital in our larger reflections on Barth's relation to the Reformed tradition. Familiar to all of us is the notion of "christological concentration," the exclusive and unyielding insistence upon Jesus Christ as the proper and sole revelation of the true God. Such christological focus has been widely seen as the hallmark of Barth's theology, derided by his critics as "Christomonism," applauded by his followers as the mature expression of a Reformed doctrine of revelation. I would not want to set aside Barth's intense preoccupation with Christology—better with the person of Jesus Christ—and it is the maxim of Barth's early volumes in *Church Dogmatics* that "Jesus Christ is Lord," a consummation of the doctrine of divine sovereignty. But I think it is worth our consideration here, as we reflect upon Barth's theological identity, that his early and most direct expression of his Reformed allegiance is not christological in nature. The *Theology of the Reformed Confessions* is devoted to the doctrine of God exclusively, as were many of Barth's lectures from the dialectical era. They are not *contrary* to Christology; indeed if I am right, the Christology of the mature period is rather the full expression of this agonized encounter with the God who is Lord. (I take this to be the force of Bruce McCormack's periodization of Barth's development in those years as a "Dialectical Theology in the shadow of a consistent eschatology."[1]) Critical to our theme, however, is the recognition that for Barth, throughout his life, the essential Lordship of God governs all, including who Jesus Christ is and what he means, the Lord who became servant, the servant exalted as Lord.

To claim Lordship as absolute or essential is to bring the doctrine of God into the realm of relational attributes; it is to speak of God in relation to creature. God is Lord of the creation. Thomas Aquinas groups Lordship with Creator and Redeemer as relational attributes; they are disclosed in relation to the cosmos. Thomas to be sure has a complex arsenal to free such a classification from the suspicion that God is now prisoner to his own creation. But Barth does not avail himself of these

---

1. See McCormack, *Karl Barth's Critically Realistic Dialectical Theology*.

Scholastic weapons—and it is vital to his Reformed identity that he does not. For Barth here swings perilously close to the liberal relationalism, typified in Schleiermacher, that Barth opposed in bitter earnest throughout the 1920s and 1930s. "Lordship" will be the elixir that cures him, as he sees it, from the disease of liberal coinherence. In this way, Barth aims to relate metaphysics and epistemology in a different manner, one elemental to his Reformed identity. To be Reformed is to affirm that an essential predicate of God is in itself a mode: Lordship is a mode of Divine Being. Thus is the doctrine of God both a species of transcendence and immanence, of Being and knowing, freedom and love. And thus, much Reformed theology, while ever so faithful to the doctrine of the Reformation, cannot in truth be considered Reformed.

The modal construal of divine predicates transforms Barth's notion of epistemology. He does not think of the doctrine of knowledge as an ineluctable offshoot of our own self-involvement in any act of encountering reality. He is not simply making the observation, keenly set forth by Kierkegaard in his ridicule of Hegelianism, that the human subject cannot be erased from the description of the real. Of course the knower is implicated in the known! Barth is often thought to teach that faith is conformed to its Object in this sense: no one knows God in a neutral fashion, as if Almighty God were a piece of furniture in the cosmos. Certainly, this is true, and Barth affirms this. But Barth's fundamental conviction runs deeper, I believe. The proper knowledge of God, the One who is Lord, is acknowledgment of being mastered. That is why Christian life and Christian faith are forms, modes, of obedience. The Christian has a Lord. Just this *relatio* is revelation. Once again, the radicality of Barth's position is sometimes lost in the welter of conceptual reflection on the category, revelation. It is certainly true that Barth writes in many places, not least in the celebrated *Lichtelehre*, that God could have spoken wherever he wished, in the cosmos, in the famous "dead dog," but he elected to speak in Holy Scripture, and we should listen to him there.[2] All true. But Barth's claim here cuts far deeper, more incisively, than this summary suggests. Israel's God does not simply disclose that he is Lord. He does this. But revelation is the *event* of God's Lordship: God parts the heavens and comes down as the Lord of the creature. We are seized by that Power, and we are claimed for him. When this event has taken place, the creature is now freed for obedience, as Barth characteristically puts

---

2. *CD* IV/3, §69.2.

the advent of faith. Our intellect now is put in service of this Lordship, tracing its outlines, exploring its election and act, following the contours of its incursion into the land of unlikeness, the world of disobedience and folly. We do not master this Object, we do not enter into his infinite reserve, nor trace out the qualia of such a Being, as though the initiators of this search. God's hiddenness is the implicature of God's Lordship. Epistemology is ingredient in metaphysics because the ontology of the servant is analytically contained in the majesty of the Free Lord. There is no neutral knowledge of God just because speculative attributes that do not rest on Lordship cannot, by definition, belong to the true God. Christology tells this event: the disclosure of the Lordship of God and the true obedience of his creature, all in one history, One Life.

Now, all this is a mode of writing theology. It stems from a conviction that Israel's God is essentially Lord. The traditional attributes of God, sketched out in many Reformed confessions, and headlined in the Scots Confession, do not express a moment of natural theology or rational faith in the cardinal documents of the Reformation. Rather, *contra mundo*, Barth arraigns them as expressions and exemplars of the One Lord's hidden majesty: God cannot be contained or comprehended by our intellect, but is rather sovereign. To confess this, to halt before the irreducible Glory who is God, to place our hands over our mouths, to acknowledge our uncleanness before him, to wait upon him, like a servant: this is to speak and act as a Reformed theologian. Barth throughout his dogmatic career will disagree with many, many Reformed theologians; perhaps with them all. He was, as Christiane Tietz observes in her splendid biography, a "theologian in conflict."[3] Even James Barr cannot resist noting how many Reformed theologians oppose Barth's prohibition on natural theology and gladly pursue this ancient art with little regard for Barth's strictures. I think, once again, Barr has right on his side, yet not Barth on his side. For Reformed theology is not material content, not doctrine alone; it is rather that content, that doctrine under a *mode*, the mode of obedience to a Living Lord. Whoever speaks this way confesses that he or she has a Lord, and in just this way, confesses with the Reformed Doctors of the Church that Israel's God is Lord of all the earth. Just so, as Barth emphasizes in his early lectures, time and again, a Reformed theologian must have both doctrine and ethics as main ingredients: the Third Use of the Law, so common in Calvinist circles, simply expresses for Barth the knowledge of God which is

---

3. Tietz, *Karl Barth*.

obedience to one's Lord. This is a narrow way, a strait gate, and I think one against which many questions can be raised, but it is a splendid confinement, one that imprisons all, that the Lord may have mercy upon all. This is the way, Barth would say: walk in it!

CHAPTER 2

Karl Barth and Huldrych Zwingli
Paul T. Nimmo

INTRODUCTION

At the outset of a volume on Karl Barth and the Reformed tradition, an exploration of the relationship between Barth and Huldrych Zwingli may seem like an obvious thing to do. Zwingli, after all, is considered to be the first truly Reformed theologian—a pastor and scholar whose particular instincts around a series of key doctrines launched a fresh trajectory within the earliest days of the Protestant movement and whose work impacted not only the ecclesiastical city of Zürich and surrounding cantons, but also the political and economic future of the Swiss Confederation. It is no surprise that Barth himself took the work of his Swiss Reformed compatriot Zwingli to be the subject of one of his first lecture series as a professor in Göttingen. There would seem, on the surface, to be much to illuminate by way of exploring their relationship.

Yet scholarly attention to this historical and theological relationship has not been abundant—there are a smattering of articles available in diverse languages, but no monograph yet exists, with only one scholar seeming to have devoted significant attention to the theme.[4] In 2005,

---

4. The honorable exception to the trend of neglect is Matthias Freudenberg, who has illuminated the relationship between Zwingli and Barth over several publications: *Karl Barth und die reformierte Theologie*, particularly ch. 3, dealing with the reception of Zwingli in Karl Barth's lectures on Zwingli, 161–216; "Nach Gottes Wort Reformiert"; "Das reformierte Erbe," in *Reformierter Protestantismus in der Herausforderung*, 296–313; "[. . .] und Zwingli vor mir," in *Reformierter Protestantismus in der Herausforderung*, 314–32. Among the other most relevant texts are: Busch, "Vater Luther als Widerhaken gesetzt"; Courvoisier, "Zwingli et Karl Barth"; Demura, "Zwingli in the

John Webster described it as "one of the *lacunae* of Barth scholarship,"[5] and little has changed since. Indeed, Barth's own, regularly negative utterances about Zwingli across his own career—which utterances will be profiled and evaluated in the course of this essay—serve to caution against any assumption that there is significant gain to be realized through such focused study.

This essay hopes to suggest otherwise, and—in particular—to uncover a point of theological connection between their work that has hitherto been overlooked. It seeks, therefore, to build on the existing corpus of work on the theme, but to reject some of the routes it has followed and to forge new paths in their place. In the first section, by way of orientation, it will examine the historical course of Barth's interactions with Zwingli. In the second section, it will turn to consider and critique the theological resonances between their respective theologies that have been identified in the literature thus far. In a concluding section, it will indicate a final and crucial resonance, thus far insufficiently profiled, between their theological positions.

BARTH AND ZWINGLI: HISTORICAL INVESTIGATIONS

As a youngster growing up in the church in Switzerland, and with a father who not only lectured in theology at the University in Bern but also lectured on Zwingli among other topics, Barth doubtless became familiar with the name of Zwingli at a relatively early stage. Hence it is no surprise that one of his early essays as a student at Bern, for a course taught by his father in the winter semester of 1905–6, was on Zwingli—specifically, on Zwingli's Sixty-Seven Theses for the First Disputation in Zürich in 1523.[6]

Barth's impression of the Sixty-Seven Theses in his essay is broadly positive. As "a summary of [Zwingli's] teaching and his reformation program," he deems it "worthy of close inspection, since it gives to us a picture, in the most desirable brevity and conciseness, of the entire

---

Writings of Karl Barth"; Jehle, "Karl Barths Zwinglivorlesung 1922/23"; Myers, "Karl Barth as Historian"; J. Webster, *Barth's Earlier Theology*, especially ch. 2, "Theology of Zwingli," 15–39; and Winzeler, "Zwingli und Karl Barth."

5. J. Webster, *Barth's Earlier Theology*, 15.

6. The essay is "Zwingli's Sixty-Seven Articles," in Barth, *Early Barth*, 72–83. The quotations from this essay in the next paragraph are all taken sequentially from this translation, specifically from pp. 74–83.

theological and ecclesial position of the Zurich reformer." Barth divides the theses into two groups—the theoretical-dogmatic and the practical-ecclesial—and offers a clear summary of the main lines of each. Among the stand-out expository points that might be noted are the claim that "it is worthwhile to listen to Christ and his Spirit; the salvation of humans stands on faith in him, not on human doctrine," and the view that "in contrast to a churchdom that has usurped the mediation between God and humans . . . Zwingli wants to lead the community of Christ back to a simple, joyous message of their founder, 'who has made known to us the will of his heavenly Father and with his innocence has redeemed us from death.'" It is in view of "their powerful definition and demarcation of what the gospel is," Barth claims, that "[these theses] have enduring significance, also for the present and the future, even if we perhaps drew the boundaries with this and that point a little differently or even were content with a question mark." And Barth proceeds to make connections between the Sixty-Seven Theses and his views on the theology and the church of his own day. He cites at this point "Zwingli's basic principle . . . [that] the eternal truths of the gospel are not to be grasped in external forms, but are always to be understood spiritually. If we nevertheless retain such forms, they are nothing more than symbols of a spiritual reality." And he correspondingly observes that in the sacramental theology of the present, "something of Zwingli's sobriety may be in order." He concludes that "Zwingli must become dear especially to modern humanity. . . . In light of the current struggles about theology and church, we will do well, at any rate, to listen to his voice." There is evidence here of a broad material approval of Zwingli's instincts, and a clear recommendation to engage more with his work in attending to present issues.[7]

In the years that followed, however, Zwingli as an object of study largely recedes from Barth's view. A number of obvious reasons might be identified. The first is his relocation to Germany in the summer of 1906 to continue his studies, returning to Bern to study for only one further semester, in which he was heavily occupied with being president of the student body Zofingia. Zwingli was thus absent from his later educational curriculum. The second is that on his return to Switzerland in 1909, he

---

7. Freudenberg observes that for all his dependence on the work of Rudolf Staehelin in this essay, Barth nevertheless reaches his own judgment on Zwingli's theology, and manifests his interest in "establishing the ongoing significance of the theological legacy for the present." See "Reformierte Erbe," in Freudenberg, *Reformierter Protestantismus in der Herausforderung*, 298.

moved to Geneva, a city connected with a rather different Reformer. In precisely that year, the churches and city of Geneva celebrated the four-hundredth anniversary of the birth of Calvin, giving rise to a series of events and a plethora of publications. Barth was never in favor of celebrating the past for the past's sake, and may have viewed such attention with some skepticism. But it was not without impact upon his own study and writing. As Matthias Freudenberg has observed, Barth at this time followed Calvin's practice of sequential preaching, often drawing on Calvin's commentaries, and took time to read the *Institutes*.[8] In a series of talks and articles during his ministry in Geneva, he engaged with Calvin, albeit also with various other Reformational figures. Certainly, Barth was far from being a classical Reformed theologian in a restorationist sense: for one, he was still broadly in the stream of liberal Protestantism with its complex of idealist and romantic instincts, still busily reading Schleiermacher and other moderns as well; and for another, his primary interest was in the meaning of the Reformation *for the present*. Nevertheless certain important seeds were sown during this time in Geneva, and the variety for the most part was Calvin and not Zwingli.[9]

Barth's move to become minister of Safenwil in 1911 led to a new array of duties and challenges, but it is noticeable that it did not bring an end to Barth's engagement with Calvin. He noted in several letters to Thurneysen that he was drawing on Calvin's commentaries for his preaching, and his Reformation Day sermons continually invoked the need to make the insights of the Reformers one's own—that is, to live in and by the power of God's Spirit and to hear the Word of God in the present day.[10] Beyond preaching, Barth offered occasional papers on the Reformers and related themes, and there are scattered references in sermons, such as in 1913, where Zwingli is described as a "Swiss citizen of the grace of God."[11] But in truth such reference and attention to any Reformation figures is rare at this time. Increasingly, it was workers' issues and religious socialism as one vehicle of responding to those issues

---

8. "Reformierte Erbe," in Freudenberg, *Reformierter Protestantismus in der Herausforderung*, 300.

9. Freudenberg here details the "numerous reversions" to the theology of Calvin in particular that are evident in Barth's writing at this time. "Reformierte Erbe," in *Reformierter Protestantismus in der Herausforderung*, 305.

10. "Reformierte Erbe," in Freudenberg, *Reformierter Protestantismus in der Herausforderung*, 306–7.

11. "Reformierte Erbe," in Freudenberg, *Reformierter Protestantismus in der Herausforderung*, 309, citing a sermon on Jer 29:7 from September 21, 1913.

that dominated his ministry and his study. As early as the famous lecture on Jesus Christ and the social movement in 1911, Barth had linked socialism and democracy to Christianity, and had referred specifically to Calvin and Zwingli in doing so, observing that their ethical and pneumatological impulses had contributed to Barth's own development.[12] And he later reflected that it was the *practical* example of Zwingli and his reputation as a faithful shepherd of the community that led him and others to Swiss social democracy in 1915.[13] But in truth study of the Reformers was simply not a priority at this time.

Amid the theological and existential crisis of the First World War, however, Barth returned to a new and intense reading of Scripture, famously focusing upon Romans. In the preparing of his commentary on Romans, he described himself as being aided especially by Calvin's commentary, assigning it first place and describing it as "particularly valuable"—even as the first edition of his own commentary draws more on Luther; meantime, Barth described Zwingli's commentary as "less helpful."[14] And if the second edition quotes Calvin and Luther less frequently, nevertheless it explicitly purports to follows Calvin's method of *interpretation*—with the purpose that Paul *speaks* and the contemporary person *hears*.[15] Around 1919, then, it is monographs on and letters from *Calvin* that Barth is busy reading. There is one moment in 1918 when Barth does offer specific and detailed comment on Zwingli once again. Writing to Thurneysen in connection with a paper he had heard on Zwingli, he gave a rather distanced verdict. Barth pointed to what he now considered "sinister parallels" between Zwingli on the one side and liberalism and/or religious socialism—specifically, Ragaz—on the other side, and suggested that the Holy Spirit for Zwingli was basically piety.[16]

---

12. "Jesus Christus und die soziale Bewegung, 1911," in Barth, *Vorträge und kleinere Arbeiten, 1909–1914*, 405.

13. Barth, *Theologie Zwinglis*, 188.

14. "Reformierte Erbe," in Freudenberg, *Reformierter Protestantismus in der Herausforderung*, 311. According to the first edition of the commentary, "Zwingli and liberalism" are deemed to be correct on the sacraments, but only "*under the judgement of God.*" Barth, *Römerbrief (Erste Fassung) 1919*, 62–63. The same comment appears also in the second edition, lightly revised, where Zwingli and liberalism "have it right [but only] under the wrath of God!" (*Römerbrief [Zweite Fassung] 1922*, 108). The existing English translation of the second edition of Barth's commentary on Romans is not here cited on the grounds that it is not sufficiently reliable.

15. Barth, *Römerbrief (Zweite Fassung) 1922*, 12–13.

16. Barth, "Letter to Eduard Thurneysen of 25 March 1918," in Barth and Thurneysen, *Briefwechsel*, 1:270. That the latter claim especially is a travesty of interpretation

PART ONE | TRADITION

When Zwingli was held up as a model pastor, Barth now noted that such a prototype of a "liberal pastor" was "actually very far from me."[17] His view was evidently changing.

Thus Zwingli appears in the Safenwil period as a marginal figure in Barth's work. He is occasionally referenced positively, especially in the early years, but by the end Barth has become somewhat skeptical about his theological work and its enduring value.

It is therefore all the more noteworthy that, following his move to an honorary professorship at the University of Göttingen, Barth devoted one of his early series of lectures to the theology of Zwingli. Following series of lectures on the Heidelberg Catechism and on Calvin himself, Barth turned in the winter semester of 1922–23 to his fellow Swiss theologian. His context in Göttingen was particularly significant at this point: in an environment dominated by Lutheran faculty and students to a point that was oppressive and almost abusive, the name of Zwingli was bound to draw particular ire, following a long and dishonorable tradition among Lutherans of polemic abuse of Zwingli. It might simply be recalled that Luther himself described Zwingli as "of the devil" and rejoiced at the news of his death; four centuries later, little had changed: Barth described the reception of Zwingli in the new Lutheranism as a *Vernichtungsfeuer* (annihilating fire)[18]—and noted that the Lutherans simply could not stand (*vertragen*) Zwingli.[19] As Freudenberg summarizes, Barth found existing Lutheran presentations to charge "that Zwingli began from humanistic and patriotic ideas of reform instead of from religious experience, that he had a moral-political understanding of Christianity, and that his theology was oriented rational-philosophically."[20] Small wonder that Barth would want to confront the predominantly Lutheran students

---

should not be overlooked. This passage is not included in the selections of the correspondence translated into English.

17. Barth, "Letter to Eduard Thurneysen of 25 March 1918," in Barth and Thurneysen, *Briefwechsel*, 1:270.

18. Karl Barth, "Letter to Friedrich Gogarten of 31 October 1922," cited in Matthias Freudenberg, foreword to Barth, *Theologie Zwinglis*, xi.

19. Barth, *Theologie Zwinglis*, 5.

20. "[. . .] und Zwingli vor mir," in Freudenberg, *Reformierter Protestantismus in der Herausforderung*, 322. At the outset of his lectures, Barth notes the prevailing opinion that study of Zwingli is "necessary and useful for the Swiss," "relatively dispensable for other Reformed," and "an unimportant matter" for theological research in general (*Theologie Zwinglis*, 3).

of Göttingen with a closer look at the Swiss Reformer,[21] seeking precisely to reject the charge that Zwingli research was a "siding ... leading off from the main track of the Lutheran Reformation into the historically meaningless."[22] But Barth was also looking for fuel for his own theological fires. In his preparations for his series of lectures on the Epistle of James in the same semester, Barth wanted to explore the possibility of launching a "religious-socialist" broadside against German Lutherocentrism with its Pauline focus.[23] And it might be surmised that Barth at one point hoped that his work on Zwingli would serve the same purpose. Indeed, in a lecture a year earlier, Barth had (once again) praised Zwingli as "the prototype and ideal of a Swiss pastor ... a figure of the people, both pious and open to the world."[24]

Barth was thus full of high hopes, especially after his earlier lectures on John Calvin had noted some promising features of Zwingli's theology. In these lectures, while Barth ultimately preferred the "superior system" of Calvin, he nonetheless recognized much of value in Zwingli as the "so-to-speak classical representative of the Reformed possibility."[25] Zwingli and Calvin are identified as "the prophets of the new Christian ethos," both proclaiming a moral reformation grounded in the divine majesty, a sober approach to divine providence and ethical obedience, and a holding together of Law and Gospel.[26] Zwingli may have been a humanist, but he was "a converted Humanist" with a "zeal for monotheism," even if his style was "secular and worldly."[27] Similarly, Barth observes, the "rationalism" of Zwingli was "paradoxically the same as the exclusive belief in revelation," a "Christian rationalism."[28] Barth ultimately finds Zwingli's weakness—and greatness!—to lie in his naïve overconfidence in the power of the Reformation: he was, Barth avers, "reckless," knowing "no restraint," and in this Zwingli was the very opposite of the hesitant

---

21. Barth looks back on the need "to confront these Göttingen students at that time ... with a close look at the Swiss and the Reformed Zwingli" (*Barth in Conversation*, 328).

22. Barth, *Theologie Zwinglis*, 3.

23. Barth, "Letter to Eduard Thurneysen of 28 February 1923," in Barth and Thurneysen, *Briefwechsel*, 2:151; and in Barth and Thurneysen, *Revolutionary Theology*, 138.

24. "Die kirchlichen Zustände in der Schweiz, 1922," in Barth, *Vorträge und kleinere Arbeiten, 1922-1925*, 29.

25. Barth, *Theology of John Calvin*, 91.

26. Barth, *Theology of John Calvin*, 92-93.

27. Barth, *Theology of John Calvin*, 98-99.

28. Barth, *Theology of John Calvin*, 99-100.

Luther.²⁹ As John Webster notes, it was the combination of the zeal for God and the focus on ethics in the theology of Zwingli that particularly attracted Barth's interest at this time,³⁰ for all he was not uncritically positive, and for all he rejected Zwingli's memorialist approach to the sacraments.³¹

The lectures took place four times a week through this winter semester in front of a class of about twenty students.³² As Webster notes, the lectures were "written on the run," with Barth often feeling "inadequately prepared," and at points quoting his father's 1903 lecture series on Zwingli verbatim.³³ The course was divided into five sections. In the first, Barth offered an attentive survey of the broadly critical reception of Zwingli in modern Lutheranism. Much of this criticism was focused on his purported separatism, his supposed this-worldliness, and his allegedly rationalist understanding of Christian faith, and Barth treated such concerns seriously. However, it is worth noting in passing that at no point did he engage in depth any of the more recent research on Zwingli himself.³⁴ The second section sketched both the problematic of the Reformation, identifying in particular the relationship between theology and ethics, and the contours of Zwingli's own interests, notably in human ethics and in the divine transcendence over the creature.³⁵ The third section offered a biographical account of Zwingli's life and work. The fourth section, which was originally (and ambitiously) purposed to treat the writings of Zwingli, his conflict with the Anabaptists, *and* the conflict with Luther over the Lord's Supper, ultimately managed to

---

29. Barth, *Theology of John Calvin*, 96–97. Even here, however, Barth notes the need to move beyond the "caricature that associates Zwingli with the Anabaptist enthusiasts as a former Humanist who could not properly differentiate religion and culture, Christianity and politics" (97).

30. J. Webster, *Barth's Earlier Theology*, 17.

31. Barth offers a careful outline of Calvin's 1536 presentation of the doctrine of the sacraments (*Theology of John Calvin*, 172–77) and laments that "[his] farsighted and superior intelligence did not succeed in calling the confused minds on both sides [i.e., the sides of Luther and Zwingli] to order!" (177).

32. Matthias Freudenberg, foreword to Barth, *Theologie Zwinglis*, viii.

33. J. Webster, *Barth's Earlier Theology*, 18–19.

34. Freudenberg notes that Zwingli had been the subject of much attention on the occasion of the four-hundredth anniversary of the Zürich Reformation in 1919 ("[...] und Zwingli vor mir," in *Reformierter Protestantismus in der Herausforderung*, 318). However, as will be noted later, little of the attention at this point was in any meaningful way *theological* in orientation.

35. J. Webster provides a more detailed outline (*Barth's Earlier Theology*, 22–28).

cover only the last of these, albeit in extraordinary detail. In his extensive treatment of the conflict, Barth sought to present its history, uncover its motives, and consider its significance, drawing en route on voluminous quotations from the original sources. The fifth section was a one-lecture historical summary of Zwingli's fall at the Second War of Kappel in 1531.

In the autumn, Barth began the series with what he described as an *Ur-Disposition* toward Zwingli, and stressed the need to do justice to him.[36] Moreover, quite early in the lectures, he described Zwingli—in the midst of a lengthy encomium—as "a critical humanist, a warm patriot and friend of the people, but at the same time a pious man, . . . devout, . . . clever."[37] And at various points in the lectures he offered a vigorous defence of Zwingli over against the charges and caricatures of Lutheranism old and new.[38]

Yet by Christmas, halfway through the syllabus and in the midst of an onerous schedule, Barth's enthusiasm for the task had rather waned, and he observed, "I will be happy when the semester is finished."[39] Barth writes of arriving midsemester at a "fundamentally different, less favourable picture of the man,"[40] and correspondingly stated, "I have really lost my pleasure in Zwingli somewhat."[41] The Lutherans, Barth now avers, were right to rank Zwingli in a second row of the Reformers, at the head of the radical wing of the Reformation.[42] Indeed, Zwingli was nothing other than "a gigantic, unsentimental, unhysterical, non-anti-intellectualizing Ragaz."[43] Zwingli was "no great spirit" but only a "religious personality," offering "an insipid pathetic spiritualism, an unconcealed reconciliation

---

36. Karl Barth, "Letter to Friedrich Gogarten of 31 October 1922," cited in Matthias Freudenberg, foreword to Barth, *Theologie Zwinglis*, xi.

37. Barth, *Theologie Zwinglis*, 121.

38. Winzeler outlines the key points: Zwingli's Renaissance hope for emancipation; his soteriological hope even for pagans; his core conception of human beings as active ("Zwingli und Karl Barth," 306).

39. Barth, "Circular Letter on 23 January 1923," in Barth and Thurneysen, *Revolutionary Theology*, 127.

40. Karl Barth, "Letter to Martin Rade on 1 March 1923," cited in Matthias Freudenberg, foreword to Barth, *Theologie Zwinglis*, xii.

41. Barth, "Letter to Eduard Thurneysen of 16 February 1923," in Barth and Thurneysen, *Revolutionary Theology*, 132. It might be noted that Barth wrote this following health issues and extreme exhaustion.

42. Barth, "Letter on 23 January 1923," in Barth and Thurneysen, *Revolutionary Theology*, 127.

43. Barth, "Circular Letter on 18 December 1922," in Barth and Thurneysen, *Revolutionary Theology*, 120.

of faith and knowledge, religion as experience, basic elimination of miracle, complete confusion between knowledge and enlightenment."[44] As Freudenberg recounts, for Barth Zwingli "stood—on the one hand—in the line from Aquinas to Schleiermacher with his Aristotelian-influenced theology and—on the other hand—at the summit of the spiritualist branch of the Reformation."[45] After the end of the semester, Barth described his lectures as a "catastrophe . . . with Zwingli,"[46] and even in his retirement he reflected that in the midst of his lecture series, "Zwingli suddenly became repulsive to me . . . I experienced a sudden negative conversion."[47] As Akira Demura comments, "Deep and grave was Barth's disappointment."[48] How the initial hopes of Barth for the series had been dashed amid the stress of the semester.

At the center of this "decisive caesura"[49] is the doctrine of the Lord's Supper. It was in the middle of expositing the debate between Luther and Zwingli that the shift of mood happened. On the one hand, Barth agrees with Zwingli's view that the significance of the Lord's Supper lies in the eucharistic *action*; but on the other hand, he worries that Zwingli grounds his theology on *reason*—and specifically here on the fact that the real presence contradicts reason.[50] Along these lines, as Freudenberg observes, Barth considered that "Zwingli already carries in himself and prepares the way for the theology of Enlightenment and theological liberalism."[51] While Zwingli had raised the necessary objections against

---

44. Barth, "Letter on 23 January 1922," in Barth and Thurneysen, *Revolutionary Theology*, 125–26.

45. Matthias Freudenberg, foreword to Barth, *Theologie Zwinglis*, xiii.

46. Matthias Freudenberg, foreword to Barth, *Theologie Zwinglis*, xii.

47. Barth, *Barth in Conversation*, 328.

48. Demura, "Zwingli in the Writings of Karl Barth," 214.

49. Freudenberg uses this striking phrase ("[. . .] und Zwingli vor mir," in *Reformierter Protestantismus in der Herausforderung*, 324), yet Winzeler observes that "in all *privately* expressed displeasure Barth did not drop this 'impossible Zwingli'—neither dogmatically, nor ethically" ("Zwingli und Karl Barth," 307, quoting Barth, "Circular Letter on 28 February 1923," in Barth and Thurneysen, *Revolutionary Theology*, 137). Indeed, in the same circular letter, Barth lauded Zwingli's *De Providentia*, even while registering disagreement with it (136); in the lectures, Barth described this text of Zwingli as "simply brilliant," albeit with the qualification, "however one may view its content" (*Theologie Zwinglis*, 486).

50. See, for example, Barth, *Theologie Zwinglis*, 357–58 and 351–52, respectively.

51. "[. . .] und Zwingli vor mir," in Freudenberg, *Reformierter Protestantismus in der Herausforderung*, 324.

the position of Luther,[52] he had remained too focused on negation and had too little to say positively: in short, he was too undialectical.[53] Luther and Zwingli were trapped at opposite poles in their eucharistic debate, both being at the same time right and wrong. But in this case, this was a debate which, as Frank Jehle notes, Barth already considered not to be church dividing, either in the present or in the past.[54] In his own theology, Barth had simply moved beyond the whole controversy.

In truth, however, the position of Zwingli on the Lord's Supper was not a sudden revelation to Barth at this time. He had already significantly distanced himself from the eucharistic theology of Zwingli in the course of his earlier lectures on Calvin, as noted above. Indeed, not only in respect of the Lord's Supper, but also more generally, the theological die had already been cast: Calvin, for Barth, "stands *alone* as the one who, understanding what it was all about (Z[wingli] did not understand 'it') did justice to the humanist concern and to the necessary protest against Luther."[55] Yet for all the overpowering negativity, Barth's final word on Zwingli at this time was a little more concessive: he noted that "it is finally clear to me that one really cannot and ought not to 'judge' a man," and indicated that "I will surely lecture again on this impossible Zwingli, for there is certainly much more to be noted concerning him."[56]

However, despite his stated intention to revisit Zwingli in his later teaching, Barth only once engaged with Zwingli's work afresh—in the winter semester of 1943–44 he ran a seminar on the text *On True and False Religion*. And in his writing, he never again engaged with Zwingli in such depth. Indeed, Webster comments, "After 1923, the paucity of reference is quite striking."[57] There are an array of scattered references, certainly, but most of these followed in the established negative trajectory. Most immediately, his treatment of Zwingli in his Göttingen lectures on the theology of the Reformed confessions and on dogmatic theology

---

52. Barth, "Letter on 23 January 1922," in Barth and Thurneysen, *Revolutionary Theology*, 125.

53. Barth expresses this sentiment clearly (*Theologie Zwinglis*, 394).

54. Jehle, "Karl Barths Zwinglivorlesung 1922/23," 504.

55. Barth, "Letter on 23 January 1922," in Barth and Thurneysen, *Revolutionary Theology*, 125. Small wonder that Freudenberg observes that "it is undisputable that, besides Luther, Calvin was the Reformer from whom Barth learned the most for his own theology" ("Nach Gottes Wort Reformiert," 38).

56. Barth, "Circular Letter on 28 February 1923," in Barth and Thurneysen, *Revolutionary Theology*, 137.

57. J. Webster, *Barth's Earlier Theology*, 33.

(the *Göttingen Dogmatics*), as well as in a later essay on the sacraments from 1929, continue to reflect a fairly negative view of Zwingli, demonstrating material continuity with the earlier critiques.[58] Moreover, in his ethics lectures in 1928–29, Zwingli is ranged alongside—among others—Müntzer and Ragaz, as a "horrifying example" of Christian activism.[59] In a public miniseries of lectures on baptism in 1943, Barth noted that while Zwingli was right to speak of baptism as "a symbol of the faith of the Church" and its members and as "an act of confession," he was wrong to limit "the potency of baptism ... to the power of a faith that strengthens itself by the use of the symbol."[60] Barth further criticized Zwingli's teaching on baptism for being "strangely flat and cold ... and unsatisfactory in relation to the New Testament references."[61] In *Church Dogmatics* too, the negative sentiment occasionally re-emerges: there are several points at which Barth simply demurs in passing from the theology of Zwingli,[62] and there is evident relief that the Reformed churches followed Calvin and not Zwingli.[63] But in truth there is little sustained interaction with Zwingli, and his name has no prominence in the text.[64]

In later conversation, when asked about his relation to Zwingli in 1968, months before his death, Barth maintained his usual diffidence about Zwingli.[65] When asked about the work of Gottfried Locher and Jacques Courvoisier, both of whom had related the theology of Zwingli

---

58. A brief sketch is provided in J. Webster that confirms this reading (*Barth's Earlier Theology*, 33–34).

59. Barth, *Ethics*, 491. The negative force of the term "horrifying" (*abschreckend*) seems to counter Winzeler's reading of Barth as here "defending" Zwingli regarding the prophetic dimension of the third article of the creed, which "had gone missing in Lutheranism" (Winzeler, "Zwingli und Karl Barth," 307).

60. Barth, *Teaching of the Church Regarding Baptism*, 20.

61. Barth, *Teaching of the Church Regarding Baptism*, 28.

62. For example, Barth disagrees with Zwingli's rejection of Revelation from the canon (*CD* I/2, 476); locates Zwingli as being "not so far from Erasmus" (*CD* I/2, 540); contends Zwingli to be linked to "Renaissance pantheism" (*CD* I/2, 728); rejects Zwingli's doctrine of double predestination (*CD* II/2, 17); departs from various aspects of Zwingli's doctrine of providence (*CD* III/3, 4, 98, 115); rejects Zwingli's determinism (*CD* IV/2, 494); and draws attention to Zwingli's oversight of the importance of mission (*CD* IV/3, 23). Of course, it is not always Zwingli alone who is in the firing line at these points; nonetheless, his name is explicit on each occasion.

63. *CD* I/2, 836.

64. The prominent exception is *CD* IV/4, on baptism, which will be discussed in the next section.

65. The quotations from this conversation in the next paragraph are all taken sequentially from Barth, *Barth in Conversation*, 327–29.

closely to Barth's own theology,⁶⁶ Barth is skeptical. He makes reference to his unhappy experience of lecturing on Zwingli, then states, "I'm not convinced by what I heard from Courvoisier—I don't know what Locher is doing—that I'm now basically a neo-Zwinglian." Specifically with regard to his study of Zwingli in preparation for his work on baptism, he observes, "I did not want to go with Zwingli; I do not believe that." On being presented with the idea that Zwingli was genuinely Reformed and not a rationalist, that he defended a version of the *analogia fidei* against the *analogia entis*, Barth states, "I want to leave this question open . . . [but] I am not yet convinced of the matter." Indeed, he confesses that he was "astonished" when the thesis of the closeness of his theology to that of Zwingli emerged, maintaining that he had a far closer connection to Calvin—and even in respect of Calvin he had effected "around seven or eight fundamental departures!" To the end, then, Barth remained reluctant to acknowledge any indebtedness to Zwingli.

This historical sketch of the interaction of Barth with the work of Zwingli is not, however, quite complete. In the next section, which will consider possible material resonances, there will be space to consider some of the scattered positive references to Zwingli's theology in *Church Dogmatics*. But before moving in that direction, it is important to take a moment to consider critically the broad shape of Barth's critique of Zwingli further. It has been noted that Barth worried about Zwingli's humanism, his rationalism, his spiritualism, and his enthusiasm. But the question must be posed as to whether he was right in his worries, or whether he misread and misconceived Zwingli.

Time and space do not allow a full answer here. But it might be noted that in Barth's formative early years, the contemporary readings of Zwingli broadly available to him were those which portrayed Zwingli either as a humanist hero or as a religious socialist.⁶⁷ These, of course,

---

66. See, for example, Locher, *Theologie Huldrych Zwinglis*; and Courvoisier, "Zwingli et Karl Barth."

67. Freudenberg describes the two prevailing interpretations of Zwingli at that time: the (theologically) liberal Zwingli and the religious socialist Zwingli ("[. . .] und Zwingli vor mir," in *Reformierter Protestantismus in der Herausforderung*, 319). The former view saw Zwingli as a "hero of freedom" over against institutional religion and a promoter of ethics, focusing upon his social engagement, his connecting of antiquity and Christianity, and his humanism. Freudenberg notes that the latter picture highlighted Zwingli's public political intervening for social justice, and this image of pastor-activist had a powerful impact on Barth during his time in Safenwil (Matthias Freudenberg, foreword to Barth, *Theologie Zwinglis*, ix–x). Again, in neither interpretation does the theology of Zwingli feature prominently.

become major features of Barth's own critical reception of Zwingli, and this may not simply be coincidence. But in the wider literature at this time there was little by way of a *theological* account or corrective on offer. Moreover, it might be noted that when such resources did become available—in the context of the important new trajectories of Zwingli research that took place in Barth's own lifetime, Barth was neither particularly interested nor broadly persuaded.[68] Thus the richly theological accounts of Zwingli that arose in the twentieth century—let alone the excellent work published since—simply passed him by. All this would lead one to question whether Barth was fair to Zwingli in his early lectures and in his subsequent failure to revise his opinion . . . or whether Barth has fallen foul, just as he did with Schleiermacher, of failing sufficiently to read against the grain of his theological context to reach new and deeper theological insights. As noted above, even Barth was prepared to state, "I want to leave this question [of my relation to Zwingli] open," and encouraged others to consider investigating further.[69] The following section accepts that invitation, and proceeds to offer a concise investigation by way of orientation.

BARTH AND ZWINGLI: THEOLOGICAL RESONANCES

This section turns to the possible theological resonances between the work of Barth and the work of Zwingli. It might be feared—in light of the above historical account—that the findings would be rather scant. Yet the traces of Barth's engagement with Zwingli in his later works may also suggest something rather different. Hence Courvoisier, for example, writes of and then outlines "a certain connection of kinship" that goes beyond "the same ecclesiastical tradition,"[70] while Freudenberg claims that "Barth occasionally and in part unconsciously pursues Zwinglian lines."[71] In such

---

68. Busch, "Vater Luther als Widerhaken gesetzt," 245.
69. Barth, *Barth in Conversation*, 329.
70. Courvoisier, "Zwingli et Karl Barth," 369.
71. Freudenberg, "Nach Gottes Wort Reformiert," 47. Winzeler contends that Barth "1) was already in his early years moulded in a Zwinglian fashion [*zwinglisch geprägt*], 2) was helped to his breakthrough dogmatically by Zwingli and 3) poses to us precisely in this way the basic ecumenical decision of the *present*" ("Zwingli und Karl Barth," 303). J. Webster observes that "though Zwingli only rarely appears in Barth's writings after 1923, his theology is 'latent' in much of what Barth later thought" (*Barth's Earlier Theology*, 35, citing Winzeler, "Zwingli und Karl Barth," 307).

Zwingli scholarship from the mid-twentieth century to the present, a variety of such connections and lines have been explored, particularly by those not content to identify Zwingli by the poles of humanism, rationalism, and spiritualism, but who conceive him instead as—in Wayne Pipkin's words—"a biblically oriented, spiritually concerned pastor."[72] In what follows, five possible areas of connection between Zwingli and Barth are accorded in turn a preliminary investigation and evaluation, namely, providence, election, theological knowledge, church-state relations, and the sacraments.[73]

Just before turning to these traces, however, there arises one methodological consideration that demands attention. On the one hand, there are a large number of trivial resonances that emerge simply out of the fact that both are Christians and both are Protestants. It will hardly surprise, for example, that both Zwingli and Barth subscribe both to the doctrine of the Trinity and the full divinity and full humanity of Jesus Christ, and to the doctrine of justification by faith alone and the Scripture principle.[74] On the other hand, there are no points at which Barth acknowledges material dependence upon or registers unqualified approval of a doctrine of Zwingli, such as to be able to speak of a genetic or direct connection between their views. At best, then, it seems possible to speak of an indirect relationship at stake, of discerning a strong parallel between their positions—hence the language of resonance, to register material similarity yet not (at least not here) to claim genetic dependence.[75]

---

72. Pipkin, "Resonating with Zwingli," 101.

73. Other possibilities would include "the Protestant understanding of the Law," noted by Freudenberg ("Nach Gottes Wort Reformiert," 47); and "a profound love of their country," noted by Courvoisier ("Zwingli et Karl Barth," 370); as well as the doctrine of original sin, noted by Busch ("Vater Luther als Widerhaken gesetzt," 246).

74. This is not to claim that they frame or detail these doctrines the same way; but merely to state that there are shared patterns of belief that come to expression in their work. On the Scripture principle, for example, Barth explicitly notes Zwingli's affirmation of the same (*CD* I/2, 459–60).

75. These two may on occasion become slightly confused in the literature, where there is a constant temptation to propose a genetic connection. Winzeler, for example, offers a maximal case for the relationship between the two, arguing that over the years Barth "had not only engaged [*gerungen*] with Luther or Calvin, but—implicitly or explicitly, also *with Zwingli*, and had ultimately preferred [*bevorzugte*] him [Zwingli] almost all along the line," and stating that "Barth's *Church Dogmatics* is contained *in nuce* in Zwingli's 67 Theses, even if in rich, congenial interpretation" ("Zwingli und Karl Barth," 301, 304). Such claims are not borne out explicitly in Barth's work, and would require detailed demonstration.

First, then, there is a purported resonance in the doctrine of providence.[76] It has been noted already that in his Göttingen lectures, Barth's reading of Zwingli's *De Providentia* seemed a bright light that bucked the trend of his diminishing regard for Zwingli, with Barth describing it there as "simply brilliant."[77] But even at that point, Barth departed from Zwingli in profoundly critical fashion, finding his account to be devoid of mystery, built on principles rather than on revelation.[78] Barth's own later doctrine of providence affirms with Zwingli that God is sovereign and living Lord of his creature, but also repeatedly departs explicitly from Zwingli: rejecting his view that predestination is ordered to providence, rejecting his denial of secondary potencies beside God, rejecting his supposedly equivocal statements suggesting a mechanical understanding of causality, and rejecting his allegedly purely formal concepts of God and the divine will and work.[79] Of the Christocentric ontic and noetic ground of providence central to Barth's constructive account,[80] there is no trace in Zwingli's major treatise.[81]

Second, there is a possible resemblance in the doctrine of election.[82] On the one hand, in his references in *Church Dogmatics* II/2 to Zwingli's account of election, Barth twice references Zwingli's structural instincts: positively insofar as Zwingli positions his Christology directly after the doctrine of God (in *Fidei Ratio* [1530]),[83] and without critique where election arises again in the same text's ecclesiology.[84] And, doubtless correspondingly, Zwingli's account speaks of a universal covenant in its

---

76. Freudenberg, "Nach Gottes Wort Reformiert," 47; Winzeler, "Zwingli und Karl Barth," 308–11.

77. Barth, *Theologie Zwinglis*, 486. The English translation of Zwingli's work remains "On Providence," in Zwingli, *"On Providence" and Other Essays*, 128–234.

78. Barth, *Theologie Zwinglis*, 486–97.

79. *CD* III/3, 11; see also *CD* III/3, 4, 96, 101, 115.

80. *CD* III/3, 141–46.

81. Winzeler's view that Barth's reference to the overcoming of fear in respect of the doctrine of providence comes from Zwingli *may* be right ("Zwingli und Karl Barth," 308–9), but this observation cannot fully overcome the relative christological deficit between the two presentations.

82. Courvoisier mentions Zwingli's "christological universalism" ("Zwingli et Karl Barth," 376), while Winzeler observes that both thinkers deny universal salvation ("Zwingli und Karl Barth," 310).

83. *CD* II/2, 80. Courvoisier makes more of this in Zwingli than the text justifies ("Zwingli et Karl Barth," 384).

84. *CD* II/2, 81.

own way, as Barth explicitly notes.[85] However, for all there may be such structural and material echoes, Zwingli's account of election is only ever instrumentally and not ontologically Christocentric, such that it seems difficult to find here any true parallel between his account and that of Barth.[86] On the other hand, it has been argued that Barth approved of the way in which Zwingli's doctrine of election included virtuous pagans.[87] In *Church Dogmatics*, Barth refers to this particular teaching of Zwingli in connection with his reflections upon the existence of true words outside the church, though he indicates that he himself will not offer any examples of such true words.[88] Earlier, however, he was rather more critical of Zwingli at just this point, indicating that including virtuous pagans in heaven was good, but Zwingli's inclusion of *virtuous* pagans alone rather than "the lost, the poor, the truly godless pagans" was a problem.[89] Once again, the true material resonances between the theologians seems underwhelming.

Third, there is the question of a resonance in respect of theological knowledge, which raises two lines of inquiry. On the one hand is the way in which for Zwingli, as for Barth, God can be known only by God. In his *Commentary on True and False Religion*, Zwingli observes that "we can in no way attain of our own effort to a knowledge of what God is. . . . it must be admitted that only by God himself can we be taught what he is."[90] And hence, Zwingli observes, "Knowledge of God which we credit to some natural agency is really from God. 'For God,' Paul says 'manifested it.'"[91] This concurs with a basic premise of Barth's theology in *Church Dogmatics*, leading to his outright rejection of natural theology.[92] And Zwingli seems to be not far removed from this position, at least in the *Commentary*. On the other hand is the way in which, for Zwingli, humanity can only gain true knowledge of itself through God. Again in the *Commentary*, he writes, "To know human being is as toilsome as to catch a cuttlefish . . . [for] as soon as they see one is after them, they stir up such thick clouds of hypocrisy that no Lynceus, no Argus, can

85. *CD* IV/1, 57.
86. *CD* II/2, 94–127.
87. "On Providence," in Zwingli, *"On Providence" and Other Essays*, 201.
88. *CD* IV/3, 135.
89. Barth, *Theologie Zwinglis*, 496.
90. Zwingli, *Commentary on True and False Religion*, 61.
91. Zwingli, *Commentary on True and False Religion*, 59.
92. *CD* II/1, 85–128.

discover them."⁹³ Stated differently, human beings cannot know themselves because of their sin. And thus, Zwingli continues, "Under no other teacher or guide than God alone, the builder of human being, will it ever be granted to see the secrets of the human heart."⁹⁴ For Barth, meanwhile, the impossibility of human beings reaching true theological knowledge of themselves necessitates a theological anthropology grounded in revelation, in the "real human being," Jesus Christ.⁹⁵ Certainly, the parallels in this case are more striking, and more compelling, than in the first two cases.⁹⁶ However, it should also be insisted that in neither case does Zwingli offer the kind of christological specification of knowledge that Barth provides.⁹⁷

In each of the cases so far, however, and even in the case of the third, strongest link, the alleged parallels all seem to struggle under Barth's more basically Christocentric approach to the loci under review. This would seem to counter the core claim of Locher that Zwingli is a *Christocentric* theologian, or at least to temper the extent to which the Christocentricity one finds in Zwingli is truly comparable to that of Barth.⁹⁸ It is not clear that there exists in these three purported connections a genuine theological parallel, despite the presence of some promising signs. At each point, Barth simply goes beyond anywhere that Zwingli could have conceived. Yet things are a little different in respect of the final two parallels to be surveyed in this section.

---

93. Zwingli, *Commentary on True and False Religion*, 75. Barth cites this analogy positively at *CD* III/2, 28–29; IV/3, 372.

94. Zwingli, *Commentary on True and False Religion*, 76.

95. *CD* III/2, 132–202.

96. It is worth noting here that the phrase "the voice of a stranger," a (pejorative) reference to the phenomenon of natural theology found in the 1528 Bern Theses, is attributed by Barth to Zwingli (*CD* I/2, 459) and recurs throughout *Church Dogmatics*—at *CD* I/1, 151; I/2, 141, 459; III/4, 231; IV/1, 346; IV/2, 667; IV/3, 66, 133, 741—as well as in the Barmen Declaration §1. However, Busch cautions that the phrase is not quite Zwingli's own but derives from Johannes Comander (Busch, "Vater Luther als Widerhaken gesetzt," 245). Meantime, Barth himself traces the sentiment back to a (Zwingli-inspired?) text issued by the City Council of Zürich before the First Disputation of 1523 (*CD* I/2, 459).

97. Courvoisier fails to convince on this point ("Zwingli et Karl Barth," 376–77).

98. Locher, *Theologie Huldrych Zwinglis*, cited appreciatively by Courvoisier, ("Zwingli et Karl Barth," 373), who nonetheless concedes that "Zwingli evidently does not expose his Christology like a theologian of the 20th century" (374). Both theologians risk finding too many resonances between the theologians.

A fourth, and more promising, connection relates to the relation between church and state.[99] As his career in Zürich evidences, for Zwingli there was a clear connection between the church or the Christian and the state that was founded on Christ.[100] Faith in the righteousness of God gives rise to a distinct political option and duty; alternatively expressed, the proclamation of divine righteousness necessitates a response of human righteousness.[101] In this connection, Freudenberg has suggested that Barth's view—as expressed in his writings "Rechtfertigung und Recht" and "Christengemeinde und Bürgergemeinde"—is materially indebted to the work of Zwingli, and particularly to his early text on "Divine and Human Righteousness" and to his Sixty-Seven Theses of 1523: not only does Barth affirm the same christological foundation of the state as Zwingli, but he also similarly affirms that a particular political option and duty corresponds to the divine righteousness.[102] Certainly, Barth explicitly recognizes the ethical and political implications of faith, citing with approval Zwingli's plea to the Council of Zürich after the First War of Kappel in 1529—"For God's sake, do something brave!"[103] Moreover, Winzeler has argued that the Barmen Theses themselves are indebted to Zwingli: one need only impartially consider the most important of Zwingli's Sixty-Seven Theses alongside the text of Barmen "to recognize immediately the directing Spirit [*den spiritus rector*] of these theses."[104] There are possible overlaps too in respect of political neutrality and international politics in general, to which Courvoisier draws attention.[105] Here, then, there seems to exist a strong material connection between the two theologians, one that is worthy of far more detailed investigation than has hitherto been undertaken.

---

99. Freudenberg, "Nach Gottes Wort Reformiert," 47–48; Courvoisier, "Zwingli et Karl Barth," 382–86.

100. Courvoisier writes of "an analogy of relation between church and state, magistrate and minister" in the work of Zwingli ("Zwingli et Karl Barth," 383) yet "an analogy of faith and not an analogy of being" (384).

101. Freudenberg, "Nach Gottes Wort Reformiert," 48; Winzeler, "Zwingli und Karl Barth," 305–6.

102. Freudenberg, "Nach Gottes Wort Reformiert," 47–48.

103. *CD* IV/2, 540.

104. Winzeler, "Zwingli und Karl Barth," 304. Freudenberg lists some of the various parallels between Zwingli's Sixty-Seven Theses and the text of the Barmen Declaration ("Nach Gottes Wort Reformiert," 46).

105. Courvoisier, "Zwingli et Karl Barth," 384–85.

A fifth resonance seems even stronger, perhaps incontrovertible—the understanding of the sacraments.[106] This connection deserves more detailed investigation. Here, one might profitably begin with Barth. As is well known, in *Church Dogmatics* volume IV/4, Barth includes his doctrine of the sacraments in the ethics of reconciliation, rejecting the traditional notion of a sacrament.[107] And as is also well known, Barth distinguishes in this matter clearly between, on the one hand, the divine act of baptism with the Spirit, and on the other hand, the human act of baptism with water in the Christian community: the former is a divine act of grace, and a divine miracle in and of itself; the latter is a human response of obedience, a human work attesting that divine miracle.[108]

However, precisely these positions of Barth had already been staked out over four hundred years before, in Zürich.[109] And, fascinatingly, all these positions go against the position on the sacraments that Barth had articulated back in Göttingen, in fierce and explicit opposition to Zwingli. It is thus all the more interesting to see how Barth reflects explicitly upon this resonance in *Church Dogmatics* IV/4.[110] Barth clearly acknowledges that Zwingli was right insofar as he both "very definitely dissociates himself from the sacramental view of baptism," and affirms in contrast that "only the direct work of God, Christ and the Holy Spirit" can cleanse or save, give assurance or confirm faith. And Barth concedes that "in this delimitation we have undoubtedly followed Zwingli." However, Barth also claims that "both materially and exegetically we have laid the foundation more carefully," and repeats at this point his long-standing objection that "in Zwingli everything finally stands or falls with the principle, . . . more philosophical than theological, that an external thing cannot do an internal work, that a material thing cannot accomplish or reveal what is spiritual."[111] At the same time, Barth does affirm that, in "a certain kinship with Zwingli," a "positive aspect" of baptism with water has been sought. Shared by both theologians are the ideas that baptism is an act

---

106. Freudenberg, "Nach Gottes Wort Reformiert," 48–50; Courvoisier, "Zwingli et Karl Barth," 380–82.

107. *CD* IV/4, a structure intimated for the first time in *CD* IV/2, xi–xii.

108. *CD* IV/4, 41.

109. "A Short and Clear Exposition of the Christian Faith" gives the mature position of the Reformer (Zwingli, *"On Providence" and Other Essays*, 248–60, 276–93). For a detailed account, see Voigtländer, *Fest der Befreiung*.

110. The quotations from Barth in this and the next two paragraphs are all taken from *CD* IV/4, 128–30.

111. This objection will be critically analyzed in the conclusion.

of ecclesial proclamation, of confession of faith,[112] and that its historical grounding is in the event of the baptism of Jesus by John the Baptist.[113]

There are material differences too, of course. For Zwingli, Barth remarks, baptism is closely related to the covenant of circumcision, which precedent sanctions the baptism of infants, and Barth raises some complaints precisely here. He wonders whether here, with infant baptism, Zwingli has reinstated an *ex opere operato* understanding of the event, or done justice to the original sense of *sacramentum* which Zwingli himself had set forth. He observes that Zwingli correspondingly lacks an explanation of what takes place *in* baptism as a free human action. And this means that "the spiritual quality of the action . . . remains obscure" and that Zwingli's baptismal teaching remains "sterile." Clearly, Barth seeks to address these problems in his own presentation.

In the conclusion of his reflection, however, and despite these differences, Barth is forced to conclude that "both negatively and positively Zwingli was basically right." He concedes that his own doctrine might be described as "neo-Zwinglian," yet sharply insists that "its development does not in fact owe anything to Zwingli's influence."[114]

It is certainly true that Barth offered a radical account of the sacraments that went beyond even the position of Zwingli: his insistence that Jesus Christ is the one sacrament was a *novum* in theology, and his distinction from Zwingli in his rejection of infant baptism on the basis that such lacked the required exercise of human freedom is striking. At the same time, and without denying these differences, some of Barth's critical remarks about Zwingli in this connection do not stand up to closer scrutiny. Specifically, the idea that Zwingli based his position on a philosophical principle—that the material cannot accomplish or reveal the spiritual—is utterly flawed. In truth Zwingli not only rejects any such principle in practice, as will be seen below, but also reaches his position just as Barth does—on exegetical grounds, with John 6:63 prominent.

---

112. Albeit, as Demura rightly observes, the agent of cognition—at least in Zwingli's account of infant baptism—would be the Christian community ("Zwingli in the Writings of Karl Barth," 205).

113. However, as Demura again rightly observes, Barth distinguishes here between these two baptisms much more sharply than does Zwingli ("Zwingli in the Writings of Karl Barth," 206–9).

114. Barth concludes, "No one should label it thus, however, unless he is prepared to concede that an attempt is here made, in the well-known phrase, to understand Zwingli better than he understood himself or could make himself understood" (*CD* IV/4, 130).

His distinction between material and spiritual in fact serves a broadly parallel function to Barth's own distinction between divine action and human action.[115] Webster thus rightly notes that both theologians share "a deep-seated aversion for some ways of coordinating God and creatures, and an acute awareness of the potential losses entailed by a theology of mediation."[116] There remains a remarkable material parallel here between Zwingli and Barth—not to mention with Barth's first essay on Zwingli in 1906 and its view that external reality can only be a sign of spiritual, divine reality. There is scope for much further work to be undertaken on this particular connection.

CONCLUSION

This essay has explored the historical and theological connections between Barth and Zwingli. It has noted how Barth's initially positive disposition toward Zwingli gave way to an increasingly negative sentiment, particularly around the time of his lectures in Göttingen. And it has evaluated some of the purported points of resonance between their theologies, finding some to be rather underwhelming, but recognizing the strength of two in particular—those of church-state relations and the sacraments.

It has also been queried whether Barth ever gave Zwingli a truly fair hearing. Despite such strong resonances as exist, particularly in the case of these last two loci explored, the fact remains that, to the end, Barth was rather unwilling to recognize or concede much on this score: it seems not simply that Zwingli was the third man of the Reformation, but that he was the unwelcome guest at the party, one not worthy of great honor. Barth's recourse to the pejorative language of "sterility" in respect of Zwingli's theology illustrates once again Barth's prejudiced reception of Zwingli, one involving "tired parodies"[117] that he never overcame—even as Zwingli scholarship moved far beyond him with vigor and insight. Hence though Barth was ultimately prepared to ditch his own sacramental theology of thirty-five years standing, he seems never to have been quite ready to ditch his similarly long-standing prejudices against Zwingli.

---

115. Freudenberg, "Nach Gottes Wort Reformiert," 49.
116. J. Webster, *Barth's Earlier Theology*, 37.
117. Winzeler, "Zwingli und Karl Barth," 310.

By way of conclusion, there remains one further possible resonance which does not seem to feature in the existing literature, and which deserves illumination. The connection to be drawn regards pneumatology, and in particular the core insistence of both theologians on the freedom of the Spirit. The case to be outlined here is that this fundamental insight is crucial to the theology of both Zwingli and Barth, and that it may be more compelling and more significant even than those connections identified above.

At heart, it is the shared view that the Spirit of God is not bound but free—free from human control and human disposition. Of course, at one level all Christian theologians affirm this. But at another level, the way in which Zwingli and Barth pursue this insight with unerring focus has significant implications for several loci in their theology.

The Spirit is absolutely central to Zwingli's theology.[118] In this connection, however, two loci will suffice to demonstrate this case: knowledge of God, and the sacraments.

First, the Spirit is fundamental for Zwingli to all knowledge of God. Zwingli posits that "God reveals himself by his own Spirit, and we cannot learn of him without his Spirit," so that "once God has taught us with this anointing, that is, his Spirit, we do not need any other teacher."[119] For this reason, Zwingli observes that "before I say anything or listen to [human] teaching, I will first consult the mind of the Spirit of God."[120] Zwingli states, correspondingly, that the Spirit is essential to the right understanding of Scripture: "God's Word can be understood by a human being without any human direction: not that this is due to their own understanding, but to the light and Spirit of God, illuminating and inspiring the words in such a way that the light of the divine content is

---

118. As Stephens notes, "The emphasis on the Spirit [in Zwingli's theology] corresponds in part to the emphasis on the centrality and sovereign freedom of God in his theology and the contrast between God and [humanity]" (*Theology of Huldrych Zwingli*, 129). He further observes that "although Spirit and word are combined in Zwingli at all periods, yet his characteristic emphasis is on the Spirit, even where there is no strong contrast between the two" (136). Pipkin similarly observes that "the Spirit plays an important role throughout the whole of Zwingli's theology" ("Positive Religious Values of Zwingli's Eucharistic Writings," 129). Indeed, he claims, "The prominent place of the Spirit in the Eucharist in Zwingli is in some ways tantamount to the rediscovery of the Spirit in western eucharistic thinking."

119. Zwingli, "Clarity and Certainty of the Word of God," in Zwingli and Bullinger, *Zwingli and Bullinger*, 82.

120. Zwingli, "Clarity and Certainty of the Word of God," in Zwingli and Bullinger, *Zwingli and Bullinger*, 88.

seen in his own light."[121] It has been suggested by Locher, indeed, that one of the contrasts between Luther and Zwingli is that in Luther the Spirit is bound to the Word, whereas in Zwingli the Word is bound to the Spirit and the Spirit, by contrast, remains unbound.[122] And in respect of knowledge of God at least, Zwingli seems to endorse that view, writing, for example, that "we should hold the Word of God in the highest possible esteem—meaning by the Word of God only that which comes from the Spirit of God—and we should give to it a trust which we cannot give to any other word."[123] The ontic reason behind this epistemic insistence is that "the Spirit of God is that true life in which all things live and from which they derive their life."[124]

Second, there is—of course—the doctrine of the sacraments. A key passage for understanding Zwingli's mature view of the sacraments comes in his "Account of the Faith" of July 3, 1530—effectively Zwingli's own "Augsburg Confession," submitted to the same Diet of Augsburg and the same Emperor Charles V as that of Luther. In the section on the sacraments, Zwingli writes that "all the sacraments are so far from conferring grace that they do not even convey or dispense it."[125] The underlying logic is immediately rendered explicit: "grace comes from or is given by the Divine Spirit . . . so this gift pertains to the Spirit alone," and "a channel or vehicle is not necessary." And more than this, Zwingli writes, one does not read in Scripture that "visible things, as are the sacraments, carry certainly with them the Spirit." By contrast, he continues, "if visible things have ever been borne with the Spirit, it has been the Spirit, not the visible things, that have done the bearing." This statement gives the lie to Barth's earlier claim that—for Zwingli—the material cannot reveal the spiritual,

---

121. Zwingli, "Clarity and Certainty of the Word of God," in Zwingli and Bullinger, *Zwingli and Bullinger*, 78.

122. Locher writes, "To the end of his days Martin Luther marvelled that the Spirit should bind himself to the Word. In much the same way, Zwingli guarded most passionately the truth that the Word is bound to the Spirit. Thus our service of God is continually cast back . . . upon free grace" (*Zwingli's Thought*, 13).

123. Zwingli, "Clarity and Certainty of the Word of God," in Zwingli and Bullinger, *Zwingli and Bullinger*, 93. Zwingli is relentless here, venturing even to write that "even if you hear the gospel of Jesus Christ from an apostle, you cannot act upon it unless the heavenly Father teach and draw you by the Spirit" (79).

124. Zwingli, "Clarity and Certainty of the Word of God," in Zwingli and Bullinger, *Zwingli and Bullinger*, 64.

125. "An Account of the Faith," in Zwingli, *Latin Works of Huldreich Zwingli*, 46. The quotations in the remainder of this paragraph are taken from the same page of the same text.

and indeed, Zwingli proceeds to cite several occasions in Scripture where the wind, that is, the Spirit, performs miracles involving creaturely visible things. This, however, is not Zwingli's concern here. What Zwingli wants to emphasize is that there can be no *certainty* that any particular material will convey the Spirit or grace. And the reason is given in John 3:8: "The Spirit breathes wherever it wishes, i.e., just as the wind bloweth where it listeth, and thou hearest the sound thereof, and canst not tell whence it cometh and whither it goeth, so is everyone that is born of the Spirit." The corollary, for Zwingli, is that the sacraments are not able to guarantee grace: "The Spirit of grace is not conveyed by this immersion, not by this drinking, not by that anointing. For if it were thus, it would be known how, where, whence, and whither the Spirit is borne."

The Spirit thus remains sovereignly free above these ecclesial—indeed, above all creaturely—activities. Thus on baptism, Zwingli writes that "Peter and Paul and James did not administer any baptism but that of water and external teaching. They could not baptize with the Spirit, for God alone baptizes with the Spirit, and he himself chooses how and when and to whom that baptism will be administered."[126] Meanwhile, on the Lord's Supper, Zwingli posits that "it is the Spirit which gives life. I speak of the life of the Spirit, the life of the soul. There can be no doubt that only the Spirit can give life to the soul. For how could the physical flesh either nourish or give life to the soul?"[127] In neither case is the position due to philosophical principles—this is just exegesis of Scripture. One may—of course—disagree with this exegesis; but if one shares Zwingli's starting position on the authority of Scripture, one will have to do so on a similarly exegetical basis, not by way of misrepresentation.

For Barth, meanwhile, this theme of the absolute sovereignty of the Spirit is basic to the exposition of several loci in *Church Dogmatics*, from start to finish, from the dynamic account of the doctrines of Scripture (the written Word becoming the revealed Word in the power of the Spirit) and to the actualistic account of the church (the Spirit as the third dimension of the church).[128] Barth is always deeply concerned that the Spirit "not be quenched," and emphasizes—indeed, echoing Zwingli—that the Spirit

---

126. Zwingli, "Of Baptism," in Zwingli and Bullinger, *Zwingli and Bullinger*, 133. Of course, for Zwingli, the external operations of the Trinity remain undivided: "What the Father does, the Son and the Holy Spirit do also (John 5)" (164).

127. Zwingli, "On the Lord's Supper," in Zwingli and Bullinger, *Zwingli and Bullinger*, 206.

128. *CD* I/2, 457; IV/1, 650–51, respectively.

cannot be bound, that the Spirit is not "in our pocket."[129] A text from his late work *Evangelical Theology* makes the point: "The wind of the Spirit blows where it wills" because "the presence and action of the Spirit are the grace of God who is always free, always superior, undeservedly and without reservation." Hence it is a mistake for theology to think of the Spirit as one "whom it knows and over whom it disposes"—such a spirit is not the Holy Spirit.[130] The work of the Spirit cannot be tamed.

However, for Barth, as for Zwingli, the related course of action is also close to hand—the act of prayer. Barth writes, "Clearly, *I* also do not have the Holy Spirit. However, I have to *ask* again and again that he would be given to me, to my thoughts, to my 'critical' interpretation."[131] The reason is, Barth explains, that "grace like the Holy Spirit is not simply something that is 'present,' but rather is something that comes and that we must ask for and that we must receive."[132] Barth concludes, "Of course, absolutely nothing happens without the Spirit. But it has to be prayed for."[133]

Barth, of course, was famous for being a theologian of the Word. Indeed, the scope and depth of his pneumatology has at times been called into question. But it might just be that behind every good theology of the Word, there may lie an even better theology of the Spirit. And Barth himself noted in his later years, and despite his acknowledged historical hesitations, the possibility that one might write "a theology of the third article."[134] In that light, it might be suggested that what Barth earlier construed as the "spiritualism" of Zwingli may in truth be ascribed to "pneumatology" of an entirely justified and healthy variety rather than any dangerous "enthusiasm."[135] Spirituality, Christian religiosity of the kind that Barth feared in Zwingli is—in Pipkin's own words—"concerned with the ways in which faith is acted out, that is, lived out in society."[136] And such concerns were always central to Barth's own theological path.

---

129. For examples of the former concern, see Barth, *Barth in Conversation*, 287, 348; for the latter references, *Barth in Conversation*, 38, 45.

130. Barth, *Evangelical Theology*, 57–58.

131. Barth, *Barth in Conversation*, 265.

132. Barth, *Barth in Conversation*, 349.

133. Barth, *Barth in Conversation*, 53.

134. "Concluding Unscientific Postscript on Schleiermacher," in Barth, *Theology of Schleiermacher*, 278.

135. Busch, "Vater Luther als Widerhaken gesetzt," 246.

136. Pipkin, "Resonating with Zwingli," 102.

In this way, there may yet lie a deep pneumatological resonance between Barth and Zwingli that has not yet been sufficiently noted. This deep resonance is an evangelical willingness to take in all seriousness the theological claim that the Spirit of God is free, beyond human control or disposition. Indeed, it may be this resonance that underlies many of the other major and minor harmonies that make Zwingli Barth's "ancestor [*ancêtre*]," to use Courvoisier's term.[137] Certainly, it is this willingness that leads Zwingli, at the close of his work on Scripture, to offer the prayer: "May God grant us that Spirit."[138] With this, and with the underlying instinct, Barth might only agree.

---

137. Courvoisier, "Zwingli et Karl Barth," 387.

138. Zwingli, "Clarity and Certainty of the Word of God," in Zwingli and Bullinger, *Zwingli and Bullinger*, 95: "Den welle uns got geben."

CHAPTER 3

Revisiting Calvin and Barth on Natural Theology and Soteriology
Michelle C. Sanchez

Natural theology can refer to many things. Within traditions including and beyond Christianity, appeals to natural theology have underwritten the possibility of arguments for God's existence. For many others who work within and beyond the discipline of religion, some working assumption of natural theology has grounded the possibility for interfaith dialogue; for legible scientific processes; and even the ability to conjecture over the meaning of scientific facts. Generally, the assertion that there is a given order to nature supplies some common ground between peoples and different ways of knowing. Within Christian traditions, natural theology often refers to the claim that there is in fact genuine knowledge of God available to human beings in their natural, unregenerate state. Natural theology is commonly opposed to revealed theology, sometimes rebranded as general revelation and distinguished from special or biblical revelation. Many Protestants especially will insist on subsuming the desiderata of natural theology to a fundamental dependence on divine revelation, insisting that revelation constitutes a reality to which there is no proper "outside." In view of the historical and traditional diversity of natural theology, it is possible—perhaps probable—that two people will begin a discussion only to discover the need to pause and state clearly what specifically is at stake and what is being assumed.[1]

---

1. For accounts of these and more approaches to natural theology, see Re Manning, *Oxford Handbook of Natural Theology*, especially Re Manning's introduction.

Yet if there is one feature of natural theology on which everyone seems to agree, it is that Karl Barth opposed it. Barth's actual position is challenging to pinpoint. That it is deeply polemical is evident from the title of his most-associated 1933 essay: "Nein!," an essay in which he appears (intentionally?) to misrepresent his interlocutor Emil Brunner's position, or at least reads it in an uncharitable light, in order to make his own specific point.[2] It seems clear in this text that for Barth, something was at stake beyond a neutral analysis of theological and anthropological epistemology. Barth himself would later walk back some of his own claims.[3] Others, such as his own friend and ally Dietrich Bonhoeffer, registered concerns over Barth's implication of a rigid bifurcation between the content of revelation and everything else. In one of his prison letters, Bonhoeffer writes that Barth replaced the natural category of religion with "a positivist doctrine of revelation which says, in effect, 'Like it or lump it!': virgin birth, Trinity, or anything else; each is an equally significant and necessary part of the whole, which must simply be swallowed as a whole or not at all."[4] For Bonhoeffer, such a position is "not biblical" because it fundamentally separates human beings from the world in which they were created to dwell, erecting a lawlike barrier between the church and the world.

Similarly, later readers of Barth are generally inclined to view his position on the knowledge of God as an outlier in both the Reformed and the overall Chalcedonian tradition, with Calvin serving as a case in point.[5] Calvin posits a "knowledge of God the Creator" that remains available to human beings generally despite their postlapsarian condition.[6] This knowledge is distorted, yet sufficient to bar claims of ignorance and to fend off concerns over fundamental incommensurability between believers and unbelievers on matters of general experience and natural operations.[7] Calvin holds that all people are endowed with a

2. Barth, "No! A Reply to Emil Brunner."

3. See *CD* II/1, 78–81; III/1, 181–91. For broader context, see Johnson, "Reconsidering Barth's Rejection of Przywara's *Analogia Entis*."

4. Bonhoeffer, *Letters and Papers from Prison*, 286.

5. For a more detailed comparison of Calvin and Barth, see Van Der Kooi, *As in a Mirror*. See also the famous position taken by T. F. Torrance in defense of Barth and Richard Muller's reply (Torrance, "Problem of Natural Theology in the Thought of Karl Barth"; Muller, "Barth Legacy"). For a more public-facing critique of Barth on natural theology, see Rose, "Karl Barth's Failure."

6. Calvin, *Institutes*, 1.1.1–1.1.5.

7. Calvin, *Institutes*, 1.5.2; 1.14.21–1.14.22.

sensus divinitatis, a kind of inner sense that receives the marks of divine glory and refers them to the imagination that presents them to the understanding.[8] This sense, along with every other faculty of the human, is damaged and distorted by sin, but never entirely effaced.[9] In response to the question of whether there is a natural "point of contact" between God and human beings to enable a basis for natural knowledge, Barth replies, "Nein!"; Calvin, it would seem, would have said, "Yes, in minimal postlapsarian form and always given by grace."

In this article, I argue that Calvin and Barth are actually closer than they may seem on the question of natural theology, provided they are analyzed with a very specific sense of "natural theology" in mind—one that does not frequently appear under discussions of natural theology, but that I argue was fundamentally at stake for Barth in 1933: not natural revelation accessible to the unregenerate, but rather the question of whether *Christians* should understand themselves to possess special epistemic privileges, such as access to some divinely prescribed architecture of the natural world and the power to advance it. As is widely known, Barth wrote "Nein!" in the context of rising National Socialism and particularly the embrace of Hitler by German Christians, many of whom seemed ready and willing to index the Christian God to the quasi-biological, geographic, historical, and mythic identity of the nation as a source of revelation. In the years leading up to this—as evidenced in his Göttingen lectures—Barth had located an ally in Calvin for reasons that diverge from the specific question of the general knowledge of God. Instead, Barth observes that Calvin refuses to associate salvation itself with new, immediate, or hermetic-mystical access to natural knowledge. In order to grasp this similarity, one must consider both the respective scientific imagination available to Calvin and Barth across centuries of distance and the way each imagination, in turn, lends significance to the way each theologian gives an account of what salvation actually grants to a specifically constructed kind of human. This is what I will explore here.

Here is my claim: Barth and Calvin converge on their rejection of a specific kind of natural theology that has gained less attention in the overall discourse on natural theology.[10] That is, both deny that salvation

---

8. Calvin, *Institutes*, 1.3; 1.9.

9. Calvin, *Institutes*, 1.3–1.4.

10. This approach has been discussed to some degree and without consensus in Niesel, *Theology of Calvin*, 39–40; and Dowey, *Knowledge of God in Calvin's Theology*, 64–65.

bestows special access to natural knowledge or special insight into the world order on the part of the believer. One clear intervention I make is to highlight the extent to which Barth's critique of the German Christians is a critique of soteriological epistemology. However, I focus less on the political circumstances of the "Nein!" essay and instead look at the larger intellectual context in which Christian salvation could be associated with a specific kind of transformative-civilizational knowledge and power. It can be easy to miss the Calvin-Barth convergence on this point because their respective historical contexts upheld different scientific-anthropological-historical paradigms. Barth was thoroughly shaped by a post-Kantian milieu while Calvin was shaped by Christian humanism, including many humanists' engagements with the hermetic tradition, magic, and alchemy. To understand the way Calvin and Barth similarly conceive the post-salvific faculties of the human means taking seriously the way they are thinking theologically with and against the broader scientific imagination of their times. Thus, my goal here is to present these differing imaginative contexts and then to ascertain how Calvin and Barth, respectively, articulate the formation of the Christian life against their backdrop.

CALVIN'S CONTEXT AND RESISTANCE TO SPIRITUAL ALCHEMY

In Calvin's sixteenth-century humanist intellectual context, the imagination of matter was preoccupied with just that: the faculty of the imagination and its vulnerability to illusion and disease. There was an increasing rejection of the Aristotelian model of perception and a shift, among different groups, toward rhetorical practice and natural magic as methods for combating the challenge of skepticism. The Aristotelian paradigm, which had for many centuries dominated the basic model of perception adopted by European philosophers, framed the senses largely as unproblematic receptors.[11] To be sure, the senses could be deceived or suffer distortions, but on the whole, they operated with integrity in presenting external objects to the mind. According to Aristotle, the process obtains through a secure causal connection between objects and senses. Objects give off species—images—that are received through sense faculties and imprint in the imagination like a seal in wax. This allows sensory data

---

11. Clark, *Vanities of the Eye*, ch. 1.

to be sorted by the inner senses, a range of perceptive faculties that are sometimes consolidated as the imagination, a faculty that constructs an image and presents it to the faculty of judgment to be considered alongside other impressions stored in memory. Ultimately, the faculty of judgment uses reason to draw inferences from present and past perceptual experience in order to attain increasing certainty.[12]

From the fifteenth century and into the sixteenth, the Aristotelian model met increasing challenges on a number of fronts. Stuart Clark points to several developments, including increased attention to demonology and particularly the power of demons to disrupt the perceptual chain and generate illusion; Renaissance art's emphasis on perspectivalism; and especially Reformed critiques of the visual illusion of miracles, especially the Mass.[13] The reasons for the return of skepticism may be framed in relation to the Aristotelian model. If the imagination constructs an image and presents it to judgment, then that image is always already subject to the specificities of memory, precognitive judgments that undergird focalization, and the relative weakness or distortion of the senses themselves. Historically, these anxieties tracked with the gradually increasing popularity of ancient skepticism among humanist readers, beginning perhaps with the recovery of Ciceronian academic skepticism and reaching a high-water mark with the 1561 translation of the Pyrrhonian skeptic Sextus Empiricus.[14] Against this backdrop, there is a through line of shifting perceptual language that links intellectuals as distinct as Calvin, Michel de Montaigne, and Thomas Hobbes, all of whom move away from the vocabulary of "species" and instead explain perception in terms of visible "marks" that reach the senses with varying levels of clarity.[15]

The language of marks may have been grounded in the material emergence of printing, widespread by the early sixteenth century. For these authors similarly treat perceptual marks as imprinted figures encased by spaces. Marks provide a compelling example of something that can be seen without being meaningfully perceived, or that can be meaningfully perceived in multiple ways, contingent on how the individual perceiver focalizes the image. One might glance at a tree and

---

12. Pasnau, *Theories of Cognition in the Later Middle Ages*, 1–18. See especially 12–18 and Pasnau's discussion of Thomas Aquinas.

13. Clark, *Vanities of the Eye*, ch. 5.

14. See Lyons, *Before Imagination*, 22; Skinner, *From Humanism to Hobbes*.

15. Wandel, "Calvin and Montaigne on the Eye."

notice nothing at all (if one's mind is preoccupied on something else). Or one might notice a single leaf, or the color of the trunk, or a bird feeder hanging down. On the basis of these varying modes of "noticing," the perceiver may well draw radically different inferences on the significance or meaning of the tree. The Latin word for "mark" is, indeed, *nota*; and *noticia* is one of the two terms, alongside *cognitio*, that Calvin uses whenever the common English translations refer to "knowledge." Yet both terms may be more precisely translated as "perception," given that they refer to the work of the mind as it sorts and refers images rather than to that of rational judgment, which draws inferences about images.[16] A modern English cognate would be "to notice" or "to render as familiar."

For Calvin, like Montaigne and Hobbes after him, the imagination is vulnerable to "noticing" the wrong marks and then connecting them—signifying them—in pathological ways.[17] All of these thinkers view the imagination as a faculty that needs support, and support comes through tactical uses of language.[18] As a case in point, Calvin will consistently use the term *nota* to refer to what is common across both creation and revelation: *both* are rendered meaningful through the interaction of visible marks.[19] In the case of creation, God has engraved marks that, if properly read, reveal divine power and care. In the case of Scripture, the very arrangement and spacing of letters and words acts as a more vivid and powerful mark, capable of disrupting the fallen imagination while also conjuring and recombining images in the imagination.[20] Broadly speaking, this account accords with the technique generally proposed by the rhetorical tradition with which Calvin was deeply familiar. Following Seneca and Quintillian, a humanist who distrusts the imagination might look for pedagogical structures drawn from ancient wisdom that are useful for providing counter images, calming the emotions, remembering truths, and pursuing the common good.[21] This is the position that Calvin takes, even as he reframes rhetoric as a divine mode of teaching given by

---

16. Bridges, "Blindness, Imagination, Perception."

17. See "On the Power of the Imagination," in Montaigne, *Complete Essays*, especially 1.1–1.5.

18. While Hobbes holds an ambivalent position with respect to the rhetorical tradition, he would end up preferring a geometric algorithmic model of relating marks and signs (*Leviathan*, 3.23–3.24). See also Grant, "Geometry and Politics."

19. Wandel, "Calvin and Montaigne on the Eye," 139.

20. Calvin, *Institutes*, 1.5.1; 1.6.1.

21. Lyons, *Before Imagination*, 22, 28.

God, the consummate Orator. Additionally, following Augustine, Calvin makes prolonged use of a robust theory of signs in order to fill out the account of how it is possible to use the signs of Scripture to progress along the path of *cognitio Dei et nostri*, or the knowledge of God and ourselves—the goal he had set out in the opening lines of the *Institutes*. God the Creator has created the marks of divinity in the frame of the universe, once perceptible to unfallen eyes. God the Redeemer has provided a more vivid mark in Scripture by which humans may be led by the hand to perceive the signs of divine benevolence in creation once more and thus live a Christian life of fruition oriented by the pious practices of the church.[22]

Calvin's adaptation of Augustine's theory of signs hews closely to the logic of the latter's *De Doctrina Christiana* where that theory is most clearly laid out, even as Calvin also liberally adopts the aforementioned sixteenth-century vocabulary "marks" and "signs." In his reliance on semiotics, however, Calvin also evidences his awareness of another approach to the imagination of matter thriving in early modernity: that of natural magic, following a broadly Neoplatonic logic of signification intertwined, to a degree, with the Augustinian legacy. In *De Doctrina Christiana* and *De Magistro*, Augustine adapts a Neoplatonic account of knowledge through illumination. In Augustine's case, the illumination of the mind is a gift of God that enables one to know the relation of signs to things at first hand. He presents the incarnation as supplying a truer account of a broadly Platonic theory of recollection by which the believer is enabled to perceive the significance of things and render true judgments. If for Plato this happens through exercises of recollection of early, true impressions, for Augustine this happens through the inward illumination by the Holy Spirit of the reality of the incarnate Christ that enables the believer to perceive the order of signs created, and pointing to, God the Creator.[23] It is significant that this basic structure supplies the familiar scaffolding for parallel traditions of natural magic that accrued simultaneous popularity from the fifteenth to seventeenth centuries, notably through the translations of Marcilio Ficino (1433–99) and the

---

22. I have written about Calvin's reoccupation of Augustinian signification at length in Sanchez, *Calvin and the Resignification of the World*. See especially chs. 5–7.

23. For fuller accounts of Augustine's theory of signs, see Williams, "Language, Reality, and Desire in Augustine's *De Doctrina*"; "Faith and Reason in Augustine's *De Magistro*," in Mackey, *Peregrinations of the Word*, 57–78.

widespread influence of Paracelsus (1493–1541), perhaps peaking theologically in the work of Lutheran mystic Jakob Boehme (1575–1624).

Traditions of natural magic drew both on Christian and pagan Neoplatonisms as well as the traditionally Egyptian *Corpus Hermeticum* in order to construct an account of how the human being can know and ultimately transform or transmutate worldly elements for various purposes—spiritual, medicinal, and alchemical, among others.[24] While Augustine explicitly denounced certain persistent objects and texts associated with magic, such as the use of talismans and Hermes's *Asclepius*, he nevertheless lived in a cosmos structured by powerful resonances between signs and things, one to which his theory of the Eucharist was addressed.[25] That theory relies on the corporeality of the incarnate Christ to essentially replace pagan theurgy, or works designed to exert certain effects from the gods, while retaining the power of the sign to bring about an effect of grace.[26] Christ, as the Word made Flesh, engenders the power of both the spoken word and the physical effect that follows from the sacramental ritual. What this suggests, however, is that from Augustine's anti-pagan polemics through the resurgence of magic occurring in Calvin's time, both magical traditions and Christian sacramental traditions shared certain assumptions about the nature of the world as a creation

---

24. See Copenhaver, *Magic in Western Culture*; Waddell, *Magic, Science, and Religion in Early Modern Europe*.

25. Copenhaver, *Magic in Western Culture*, 36. See also the lengthy discussion of Marcilio Ficino's relation to Augustine, especially in ch. 8 (157–85).

26. Augustine was a vocal critic of theurgy, setting the tone for Christian orthodoxies to follow (see *City of God*, bk. 10). Yet his project often reoccupied the pagan and Platonic infrastructure, effectively showing how Christianity provided what were in his view superior practices to achieve similar goals. For example, *De Doctrina Christiana* reoccupies the problematic of teaching posed classically by Plato in the form of the eristic paradox (see, for example, the *Meno*). In the case of theurgy—rites and rituals designed to manipulate the gods—Augustine's doctrine of *ex opere operato* (from what is done) effectively retains the legibility of the sacramental rite while ascribing its power entirely to the divine. It is clear that, for example, Pseudo-Dionysius deliberately reoccupied theurgy with his explicit account of divine *theourgia*. Yet given the fact that Latin translators of Pseudo-Dionysius avoided a direct translation, thus obscuring the reference to theurgy, the question remains to contemporary scholars of how to trace the difference between reoccupation and categorical rejection. For the Dionysian context, see Shaw, "Neoplatonic Theurgy and Dionysius the Areopagite"; Stang, "From the Chaldean Oracles to the Corpus Dionysiacum." For a discussion that involves Iamblichus, Neoplatonism, Ficino, and Augustine, see Copenhaver, *Magic in Western Culture*, ch. 4.

structured by resonances and sympathies, mediated by the knowing and strategic use of signs as powerful symbols with transformative powers.[27]

This was true also for early modern intellectual work. Trajectories of Christian humanism differed on the kinds of magic they were willing to admit, but all shared the basic view that magic is effective. Tara Nummedal observes that "whatever we think of alchemy today, it is essential to remember that many people accepted the basic principles of alchemy in early modern Europe, even the transmutation of metals, and could point to religious and natural philosophical justification for their belief."[28] Ficino exemplified this tension insofar as he framed his interest in natural magic as thoroughly Christian while also widening the bounds of what Augustine would have recognized as the legitimate, divinely sanctioned use of magic.[29] Mike Zuber notes Martin Luther's long-standing affirmation of and interest in alchemy alongside Luther's unyielding commitment to the power of God's will over all things. This was precisely the paradoxical commitment that some later Lutherans like Boehme would blur, framing the regenerated human person as accruing active power over matter through the practice of spiritual alchemy, which is essentially a soteriology that emphasizes participation in the hidden divine work of transformative magic.

Two different sensibilities cast the way in which alchemy was either more or less indexed to varieties of Christian soteriology, particularly during the Reformation: first, whether one held the universe to be rational or primal beyond the domain of knowing; and then whether salvation confers greater powers of participation (in a basically rational universe) or of transmutation (of a primal, elemental universe). Both of these have to do with one's position on the nature of the incarnation and its effectual relation to the justification and sanctification of the believer. In particular, Zuber observes that some alchemists noticed a similarity between the rhetoric of death and rebirth (Latin *regeneratio* or, in German, literally *Wiedergeburt* or "born again") and the process of putrefaction and fermentation in nature generally.[30] Where Luther willingly adopted the alchemical metaphor and applied it to the eschatological realization of salvation, later Lutherans Valentin Weigel (1533–88) and Boehme

---

27. For example, see Waswo, *Language and Meaning in the Renaissance*, 250–80; Sluhovsky, "Calvinist Miracles."

28. Nummedal, *Alchemy and Authority in the Holy Roman Empire*, 16.

29. Copenhaver, *Magic in Western Culture*, 82–83.

30. Zuber, *Spiritual Alchemy*, 27.

himself drew from forebears like Meister Eckhart and Paracelsus to take a more literal reading of Christ's body incarnate as prime matter. They drew an analogy between the incarnation and the philosopher's stone, the mythical base element capable of effecting transmutations of all kinds and thus conferring power on the one who knows how to use it.[31] For Boehme, the incarnation anchors an alchemical process that yields the spiritual rebirth of the believer, granting the believer powers of knowledge that effect further transmutation.[32]

The doctrine of justification displays the tensions at play between an alchemical scientific imaginary and (post-)Reformation theology. Boehme's evaluation of the incarnation as a kind of matter with which the believer identifies in their own rebirth placed him outside the bounds of the forensic understanding of justification promoted by the major reformers including Luther and Calvin.[33] Interestingly, Andreas Osiander—who is subject to extensive polemics in Calvin's 1559 *Institutes*—similarly taught that salvation is made possible through the power instilled in Christ's humanity.[34] In his own time, Osiander was openly associated with both spiritual alchemy and the denial of forensic justification.[35] Of course, it is significant that forensic justification, while enabling a powerful critique of the existing sacramental system, also opened new questions over social legibility. If salvific grace is given apart from any legible logic of merit or desert, then it becomes unclear how practical judgments can be executed, communities organized, and authority recognized.[36] In the wake of the Protestant rejection of the existing socio-sacramental system, it would be expected for theologians to reconsider their own convictions over whether the universe is presumed as primal or rational, given a kind of raw material awaiting God-effected transmutation or structured with God-endowed significance. If it is primal, then one can see why alchemy would emerge as a privileged analogy for, or even a material component of, salvation itself. If rational, and suffused with God-given significance, then the question for Reformers

---

31. Zuber, *Spiritual Alchemy*, 27–28.
32. Zuber, *Spiritual Alchemy*, 49.
33. Zuber, *Spiritual Alchemy*, 56.
34. Calvin, *Institutes*, 1.15.3–1.15.4; 2.7.5–2.7.7; 3.11.5–3.11.12.
35. Zuber, *Spiritual Alchemy*, 17.
36. This, of course, is the question underwriting Max Weber's argument over the Protestant ethic and its affinity with capitalism in Weber, *Protestant Ethic and the Spirit of Capitalism*.

becomes how that significance is mediated to the believer through grace and what role the believer plays in realizing this significance.

Unlike Osiander, Calvin takes the latter path, coupling frequent strictures on speculation with Augustinian claims over creation's divinely endowed significance.[37] While he emphasizes God's self-disclosure to a striking extent, he also insists that human minds are not to venture beyond or behind the visibility of divine works to their secrets or inner mechanisms.[38] This characteristic accords with Calvin's heightened criticisms of Platonism, which—in keeping with the mood of his time—depart gently from Augustine. Though Calvin and his contemporaries in many ways defaulted to some mode of Platonism, he also refers to Augustine as an "extreme Platonist."[39] In the 1559 *Institutes*, he also calls Plato "the most religious of all the philosophers," a backhanded compliment.[40] For Calvin, *religio* fundamentally has to do with a practice of piety that foregrounds the difference between the Creator and the creation and that in practice proceeds against the backdrop of a non-Platonic ontology of creation, one in which divine being maintains a qualitative difference from that which the divine being creates. Calvin resolutely opposed any mixing of heaven and earth, for example, viewing the immortality of the human soul as an artifact of its creation and different in kind from the immortality possessed by God.[41] This is why signs were so important for Calvin, even as he rethought signification through the early modern vocabulary of marks. Signs offer a way for God to interface with creation without holding that divine being is somehow continuous with creation, precisely because the engraving of a mark mediates the absence of the engraver.[42] The relationship between God and humanity is thus repositioned away from questions of ontology toward questions of perception.

Calvin's emphasis on the position of the perceiver thus positions him in early modern debates by maintaining a skeptical distance between (a) the human who perceives the marks in creation and Scripture and (b) the way those marks structure the divinely prescribed order for creation.

---

37. Calvin, *Institutes*, 1.3–1.5.

38. Calvin, *Institutes*, 1.5.9.

39. See Calvin, *Commentary on the Gospel According to John*, on John 1:3. See also Partee, "Soul in Plato, Platonism, and Calvin," 294.

40. Calvin, *Institutes*, 1.5.11.

41. Partee, "Soul in Plato, Platonism, and Calvin," 291.

42. For an analysis of how signatures mediate the signatories' presence while marking their absence, see "Signature Event Context," in Derrida, *Margins of Philosophy*, 307–30.

For example, Calvin's doctrine of providence asks the reader to perceive the marks of divine care in creation, but the result is not knowledge concerning or empowerment to realize the world's purpose. Instead, the perception of the marks enables the believer to affirm God's goodness despite the continued competing perception of evil and chaos. Believers do not know the hidden purpose, rather they ascribe to God a purpose in faith that remains, for now, unknown. Although the eyes of believers are illumined to perceive divine marks, this illumination never sheds its forensic quality *from the believer's perspective*.[43] That is, the believer always stands at a distance from being able to "know" apart from their reliance on the accommodations and rhetorical aids that God has graciously provided. Divine aids are prosthetic, not transmutative. Calvin holds a reading of the mediating function of the incarnation that similarly avoids an alchemical analogy. For Calvin, Christ's human body is significant from a perceptual-pedagogical point of view. Human beings, he argues, cannot perceive, and thus cannot become familiar with, things that are purely incorporeal.[44] In other words, Christ's humanity functions as the central accommodation to human needs, retaining a clear mediatory function akin to the marks of the Word itself. It does not present itself as an object of material identification or a primal source of transmutation.

Effectively, Calvin is charting out a distinctively mid-sixteenth-century position that reconceives an Augustinian signification inflected by the resurgence of Stoic skepticism and the Stoic rhetorical tradition, veering away from the competing path leading to spiritual alchemy. Like a skeptic, Calvin consistently underscores the unreliability of the senses and frames knowledge as linked to practical use and benefit, even for believers who continue to rely on scriptural spectacles and other accommodations to retrain their interpretive impulses and direct their hearts.[45] He also argues that God, like a rhetorician, offers images that create signs out of constellations of marks in order to offer alternate interpretations that stun, address, and reframe the spectator's perceptive faculties.[46]

---

43. Calvin, *Institutes*, 1.16.2–3.

44. Calvin, *Institutes*, 2.12.2.

45. The language of training the heart and knowledge being authenticated by its use and benefit to the believer is language that is repeated across the *Institutes*. For some examples, see Calvin, *Institutes*, 1.2.1; 1.5.9; 1.16.3; 2.2.21; 2.3.8; 2.15.3–2.15.4; 2.16.13; 3.20.1–3.20.3; 3.21.5; 4.1.1; 4.1.6; 4.14.3.

46. Calvin frames God as the orator, opening God's most hallowed lips (*Institutes*, 1.6.1). Calvin likens divine teaching to lisping, the way an adult accommodates speech to an infant (*Institutes*, 1.13.1).

This technique offers a praxis-oriented model for regeneration and the life of sanctification, one in which the believer understands themselves as named forensically by God as the beneficiary of salvific grace and subsequently equipped with the necessary tools to aid their perception through the resignifying marks of the church: namely, scriptural preaching and sacramental observance.[47]

Calvin's theory of the sacraments may render this position most clearly. For Calvin, it is important to make clear that in the Holy Supper, the heavenly and earthly substances remain distinct from each other.[48] Moreover, he wants to maintain the locality of Christ's resurrected human body: in a Zwinglian gesture, Jesus is located at the right hand of God, neither in the eucharistic host nor ubiquitously present.[49] Yet Calvin still wants to claim that Christ "truly presents" the bread and wine.[50] The 1559 *Institutes* resolves these apparent tensions by offering an argument that draws on complex semiotics in order to emphasize the effectual way the sacraments enable a peculiar kind of knowing that Calvin indexes more to experience than to understanding, one that again relies on ontological difference.[51] Christ's real presence is a spiritual presence, addressed *to* matter by the work of the Holy Spirit who enables the perception of relationships of significance that obtain between the natural way bread nourishes the body and the spiritual way that Christ nourishes the soul. By taking and eating bread, human beings perceive and experience the effects of nourishment, the way the substance of another thing can work to strengthen one's own organs, muscles, and bones. The communal ritual of the Supper refers Christ's words and works to that very process. Just as Christ's human body teaches us through our ordinary abilities of perception what God is *like*, the bread teaches us in more particular detail *how* spiritual growth takes place in the context of church life.

Brian Copenhaver writes that the Eucharist should be considered within the broader logic of magic spanning centuries prior to the Reformation:

---

47. Calvin, *Institutes*, 4.1.7.

48. In a striking passage where he considers the usefulness of the saying "nature is God," Calvin emphasizes the intimacy between them while ultimately preserving the ontological difference between heaven and earth by writing that properly speaking nature is the order prescribed by God (*Institutes*, 1.5.5).

49. Calvin, *Institutes*, 4.17.12; 4.17.26.

50. Calvin, *Institutes*, 4.17.10; 4.17.32.

51. Calvin, *Institutes*, 4.17.32.

> The doctrine of the eucharist required believers to accept that objects on the altar which look, feel, smell, and taste like bread and wine are actually—because of words said and things done by a priest—the body and blood of Christ. But flesh and blood manifestly retain the qualities of bread and wine in a sacramental miracle of which transubstantiation is as good a philosophical account as could be had. The notions of substance and quality needed for this theory are the same ones that make philosophical sense—as much as could be made—of magical transformations, treating them as effects of special qualities called "occult."[52]

Despite his emphasis on signification, at no point in his discussion of the sacraments does Calvin suggest that they transform the senses to enable broader or superior perception more generally, nor do they unlock a different or better interpretation of nature or use of its powers. In other words, in keeping with Calvin's general pattern of teaching, the sacraments play an accommodating role in enabling a communal practice that effects the spiritual work of grace to the end of sanctification. They are framed as more of a lifelong exercise training perception than as a portal to transformation or a tool of transmutation. This distinction accrues meaning only after one considers the sixteenth-century scientific and perceptual imagination as well as the long history of associating the eucharistic miracle with a magical economy in ways that were neither pejorative nor controversial. I suspect that Calvin's resistance here has much to do with why Barth perceives Calvin as an ally in his peculiar struggle against the political and scientific tendencies he associates with "natural theology" 450 years later.

BARTH'S INTELLECTUAL CONTEXT AND ANTI-FASCIST SOTERIOLOGY

By the early decades of Barth's publishing career, magic and alchemy were no longer foregrounding paradigms of the scientific imagination. On the contrary, Barth operated in the aftermath of a nineteenth-century milieu that had programmatically forgotten and openly disavowed the significance of alchemy to the history of modern science, embracing positivism, evolutionary theory, and a continued commitment to Newtonian

---

52. Copenhaver, *Magic in Western Culture*, 36.

mechanics and modern chemistry.[53] Kant played an outsized role both at the beginning and at the end of the nineteenth century, first with his critical philosophy and then with the resurgence of neo-Kantianism. Kant's outsized impact on theology is well known and documented, compelling many theologians from across the spectrum to embrace distinctions between scientific knowledge and faith, value, or religious experience. By arguing that the human faculties constitute the objects of experience that comprise the phenomenal (knowable) world through a priori synthesis, and that beyond this no knowledge claims can be made, Kant secured confidence in the advancement of a scientific process rooted in analyzing and describing the phenomenal world. This came at the relative cost of drawing a hard distinction between things immanent and things transcendent, one that the subsequent speculative philosophy of the mid-nineteenth century would seek to overcome.

Barth embraced certain features of Kantianism and neo-Kantianism during the decade before he produced the Göttingen lectures and ultimately developed his critique of natural theology.[54] Neo-Kantianism emerged around 1870 as a rebuke to speculative philosophy. Neo-Kantians, in common with much of Anglo-American philosophy, emphasized Kant's first *Critique* where the phenomenal-noumenal boundary is most firm. It was the third *Critique*, however, that served as a key point of departure for the kind of speculative philosophy typified by Hegel earlier in the nineteenth century. In this *Critique of Judgment* (1791), Kant theorizes "reflective judgments" as judgments about the *relations* between things, relations that cannot themselves be empirically known but that comprise much of human life: interpretation, aesthetics, culture, and notions of purposiveness and sociopolitical order. In contrast to reflective judgments, "determinate judgments" are executed concerning objects of knowledge.[55] In shifting his focus to matters of judgment and interpretation, Kant perhaps felt compelled to give a more robust account of those features of life that are subject to historical, rather than strictly scientific,

---

53. There is ample literature on the importance of alchemy and natural magic to the formation of modern scientific disciplines and methodologies. For a few classic and more recent examples, C. Webster, *From Paracelsus to Newton*; Waddell, *Magic, Science, and Religion in Early Modern Europe*; Leong and Rankin, *Secrets and Knowledge in Medicine and Science, 1500–1800*; W. Newman, "From Alchemy to 'Chymistry'"; W. Newman and Grafton, *Secrets of Nature*.

54. Lyden, "Influence of Hermann Cohen."

55. Kant introduces this key distinction in the faculties of judgment in *Critique of the Power of Judgment*, 20.206–17.

progress. In order to make reflective judgments, the imagination has to be trained and cultivated by reflecting on ideas about magnitudes that exceed the bounds of phenomena.[56]

Here, Kant seems willing to probe the porosity of the boundary the first *Critique* erected between phenomena and noumena in order to give an account of social progress, a progress that hinges on the kind of pedagogical formation that makes scientific knowledge useful to civilizational ends. The transformation of society requires not just someone who has confidence in their knowledge of appearances and their causalities, but furthermore someone whose mind has been cultivated to know what to *do* with that knowledge. For speculative philosophers such as Hegel, who viewed the *Critique of Judgment* as a point of departure, subjective and objective knowledge are joined precisely in the expansion of human individual and collective self-consciousness which manifests externally in the structure of political, social, religious, and cultural life.[57] Where the earlier Kant framed the transcendental apperception as a mysterious power necessary to the a priori synthesis but unknowable in itself, speculative philosophy reframes self-consciousness as a genuinely transformative power, a power capable of transcending previously imposed limits by recognizing itself in the external world and bringing about a new, improved form of life. Bringing together the rational and the real bestows a kind of subjective command over the world, the privileged domain of a cultivated self-consciousness existing in a cultivated sociopolitical milieu.

Among other effects, this valorization of self-consciousness lent stronger philosophico-scientific backing to the kinds of racial and civilizational hierarchies common to anthropological theorizing in eighteenth- and nineteenth-century Western Europe. From Hume to Kant, many Enlightenment authors would argue that every human in principle possesses the ability to reason and attain objective knowledge. But eighteenth-century racial theory problematized who counts as a human for reasons biological, cultural, or both.[58] As German idealists increas-

56. For more on Kant, judgment, and the imagination, see Makkreel, "Role of Judgment and Orientation in Hermeneutics"; Matherne, "Kant and the Art of Schematism.:

57. Hegel, *Faith and Knowledge*, 80.

58. See Sylvia Wynter's volume of work on the relationship between the operative definition of the human and coloniality, for example, "Unsettling the Coloniality of Being/Power/Truth/Freedom." Vial's *Modern Religion, Modern Race* is immensely helpful in articulating the relationship between German idealism, theories of racial hierarchy and development, and the study of religion.

ingly prioritized self-consciousness at the frontier of nature and culture, an account of graduations of the human could be more easily linked to a society that inculcates putatively cultivated education. This furnishes an ideological account, amenable to colonial ambitions, of why some humans, produced in a certain civilizational milieu, possess knowledge and the capacity to master while others do not. It follows that only a specific set of humans will know best what to do with the knowledge they attain: those whose aesthetic and rational sensibilities have been trained to guide and establish conditions for the advancement of knowledge on a global scale.[59]

Here, the boundary between knowable phenomenal appearances and noumenal transcendent ideas that cannot be known—a boundary Kant even tries to preserve in the third *Critique* by distinguishing reflective from determinate judgments—becomes blurred. For Hegel, reflective judgments are mere precursors to determinate judgments. The expansion of self-consciousness accordingly expands the domain of knowledge itself, transforming the objective world in the process. A properly civilized consciousness capable of sophisticated reflection is therefore capable of effectively rendering "nature" into "civilization" and, ipso facto, taking charge of the self-appointed duty to transformatively "civilize" nature. There are structural echoes, here, of an alchemical imagination that views a certain material order as the prime matter uniquely capable of undergoing transmutation by a spiritually transformed consciousness—a consciousness that is imagined as existing in some relationship of identification with divine power.[60]

This is where I see the force of Barth's ire against natural theology, and particularly a kind of natural theology that indexes a kind of Christian-inflected chosenness with the particular powers of insight, possession, and world transformation that were associated with National Socialism. As someone remaining generally favorable to Kant and the neo-Kantian criticisms of speculative philosophy, Barth seemed to value the distinction between determinative judgments and reflective judgments, generally leaving Kant's account of empirical knowledge in

---

59. For an interesting argument on the role of the imagination as theorized by German idealists and shaped by popular literary culture, see Zantop, *Colonial Fantasies*.

60. For the broader conversation on the relationship between German idealism, aesthetics, alchemy, coloniality, and Blackness, see Armstrong, "Effects of Blackness"; Long, "Indigenous People, Materialities, and Religion"; Carter, "Anarchē."

place.[61] This commitment, however, enabled the early Barth's emphasis on the otherness of God and the event-like quality of the incarnation to carry a certain force precisely because these claims chasten and forbid the identification of divine revelation with human self-consciousness or progressive civilization. Against both liberal and conservative tendencies to link Christian salvation with a cultural mandate,[62] Barth consistently curtails the *Christian* ambition to penetrate further into anything like the hidden power of matter itself or to claim access to hidden natural laws or divine designs. The motif that emerges in many of Barth's early accounts of the post-salvific state—in the lectures of the 1920s as well as in the commentary on Romans—is that of salvation as "interruption," and in particular the interruption of the association of thinking with mastery.[63] Divine revelation, for Barth, drives a wedge in the process by which reflective judgments become naturalized in human self-consciousness, confronting the human with some "other" who refuses to be assimilated by or identified with the human mind.

This account, like Calvin's, raises its own soteriological challenges. For example, if salvation is conceived of in a largely negative sense as an interruption, then what does it look like positively to be saved? Does it look like being silenced, like quietude, or quiet-*ism*? What are ethical responses to an interruption, and what kind of relationship follows an interruption? Above, I argued that for Calvin, the signifying practices of church participation may supply a perceptive practice with legible and practical sociopolitical effects while still preserving Calvin's strictures on hidden speculation. Barth seems to share a similar overall confidence,

61. Woodard-Lehman, "Reason After Revelation."

62. Of course, Barth and others accused liberal theology of doing just this—of adopting a kind of natural theology that dangerously associated the achievements of modernity with the achievements of Christianity. Yet it is important to note that some conservative Reformed theologians were making a different move at the turn of the twentieth century, one that nevertheless yielded a suspiciously similar outcome in terms of its account of power. Neo-Calvinists like James Orr, Abraham Kuyper, and Herman Bavinck were happy to agree with Barth on the dangers and hubris of liberal theology and modernism. Yet they also viewed the regenerate human as endowed with certain cognitive powers yielding sovereign insights on natural law and civilizational order. Part of why Barth's criticisms of Brunner in "Nein!" can sometimes seem off point is that Barth is also concerned with denying various kinds of *Weltanschauung* theologies that he does not openly parse in any depth, one of which reinvests in a kind of post-salvific natural theology. For a helpful discussion of Barth and *Weltanschauung* theologies, see Anderson, "Jesus and the 'Christian Worldview.'"

63. See "Great Disturbance" and "Great Positive Possibility," in Barth, *Epistle to the Romans*, 426, 492.

exhibited for example in the Barmen Declaration project, that the church's engagement with the otherness of Christian revelation will effectively blunt human pride and curtail the kinds of judgments that fund fascist and colonial violence. In his later work, Barth sometimes offers a clearer argument for this phenomenology of interruption. In *Church Dogmatics* IV/1, he describes the judgment of the Redeemer as an interruption that creates the possibility for genuine freedom, freedom *from* the burden of judgment that has been lifted from the individual, the freedom to live in response to others, rather than domination over or identification with others.[64]

It makes sense, then, that Barth might show special appreciation for Calvin's view of the sacraments, not because that view rejects the relation of God to nature, but because it countenances that relation in a very specific way that avoids the dangers of the kind of Christian fascism Barth sees emerging between the world wars. In the 1922 Göttingen lectures, it is striking that Barth pinpoints his approval of the way Calvin frames the natural materiality of the sacrament as a "witness" to grace that we need because of the "imbecility of our faith."[65] One might be surprised to see Barth approving even of the language of "natural witness," yet he is willing to do so because in Calvin's view, the "naturalness" of the sacraments never supposes that special sites of materiality bear heavenly things in themselves. Here, there is a kind of inherent rationality endowed in material things simply by virtue of their creation that needs no further imposition, either through magical means or through human self-consciousness. There is nothing uniquely sacred about the natural qualities of those material things named by the two sacraments Calvin recognizes. Bread, wine, water, nourishment, washing are not transmuted matter nor are they dependent on the consciousness of the regenerated human mind. Instead, Scripture teaches believers to faithfully perceive them as marked by a forensic divine decision to point, by virtue of their ordinary qualities, to spiritual truths. The accommodating lens of faith is what makes the natural perception of bread as nourishing *refer* to the spiritual perception of the body of Christ as nourishing, a reference that maintains a distance even as it relies on the very practical ordinariness of the human relation to nature.

---

64. *CD* IV/1, §59, especially "Judge Judged in Our Place."
65. Barth, *Theology of John Calvin*, 281.

All of creation, for Calvin, is both ordinary and miraculous because it is upheld at every instant by divine providence. The key difference between Calvin's view of miracles and mysteries and other competing accounts lies not in whether such things are possible, but rather in Calvin's precise account of the *condition for the possibility* of properly recognizing something *as* a miracle or a mystery. For Calvin, to recognize a miracle properly as such requires a humble embrace of Christian teaching. To follow his own preferred metaphor, it requires the Spirit-granted humility to put on the spectacles given graciously by God rather than insisting that one's own natural vision is, or can ever be, suited to the task.[66] The spectacles are artificial lenses that yield a kind of double vision: a vision that continues to perceive the natural properties of things with general integrity while also perceiving divinely given marks pointing to divine care and power.[67] Thus, Calvin maintains that admissible knowledge must be hemmed around the work of God in Christ the Redeemer who—for Calvin—assumes an incarnate relationship to flesh in order to teach a way of life, not to empower transmutation.

Barth rightly observes that for Calvin revelation deeply involves corporeality. In his reading of Calvin, "the recollection of the distance between heaven and earth makes possible for Calvin the insight that corporeality is the end of the ways of God" and that this distance is precisely what vests Christian dogma with a genuinely vital power, intertwined but never collapsed with every ordinary decision.[68] The "end" is thus not a program of transforming corporeality into something putatively higher. It is to see corporeality as that which is addressed by God and which bears God's marks, existing in its ordinary state as a miracle. Barth calls this the "paradox of faith" that refuses the polarities of both Protestant naturalism and Protestant spiritualism, a faith that refuses to either finally separate or finally collapse divine things and material things. Faith instead maintains a mode of perception that holds them in mysterious and un-collapsible relation, enabling wisdom while refusing knowledge.

---

66. Calvin, *Institutes*, 1.6.

67. Calvin was fond of the Latin roots *specto* (to watch) and *specio* (to look at), roots that yield many terms of which Calvin is fond and that comprise the perceptual backdrop of his thinking: species, spectator, spectacle, spectacles. Creation is a spectacle that requires a "true spectator" (*Institutes*, 1.5.8), a postlapsarian figure who is precluded without scriptural spectacles. For a helpful discussion, see Bridges, "Blindness, Imagination, Perception."

68. Barth, *Theology of John Calvin*, 282–84.

PART ONE | TRADITION

CONCLUSION

When one takes "natural theology" to refer to the question of the cognitive effects of salvation and natural powers it may or may not bestow on the human, Calvin and Barth are closer than they may otherwise seem. The reason for their perceived difference has to do with the way Calvin frames the natural world as the site of divine glory and as suffused with divine significance, presenting himself at the very least as a strong proponent of natural or general revelation. Barth, especially in his writings preoccupied with the rising phenomenon of Hitlerian German Christians, seems to unequivocally deny any kind of natural basis for divine knowledge.

I have argued that is a less salient difference, especially in view of the way their historical and intellectual contexts similarly position Calvin and Barth as opponents of a transformational view of post-salvific power. In the mid-sixteenth century, Calvin was carving out a position that resisted the existing sacramental system alongside the pull of spiritual alchemy that was increasing in popularity during his time. Barth, on the other hand, wanted to undermine the civilizational temptations of Christians, and especially the German Christians who failed to perceive the distortions of fascism as an affront to Christian revelation. There is a through line, here, that connects the two, and it has to do with their soteriology: specifically, with the kind of perception and cognition that salvation bestows. Neither Calvin nor Barth conceives of salvation as an engine of special insight, substantial transformation, or world-historical progress. Instead, salvation interrupts the isolated and distorted cognitive processes of the fallen human by maintaining a relational distinction between what is God's and what is the world's. In so doing, the believer is equipped with accommodations that allow them to perceive the world as a theater for a reverent and responsive practice, in all of its materiality and mystery, designated as the end of the ways of God.

CHAPTER 4

Schleiermacher, Barth, and a Future for Reformed Theology
Kevin W. Hector

In this essay, I want to think about what it would mean to carry on the Reformed tradition today and, in particular, I want to think *with* the Reformed tradition about how we might do so. I want to argue, therefore, for three sorts of claim: first, a *methodological* claim, according to which Karl Barth and Friedrich Schleiermacher each exemplify an approach to theological construction wherein one offers a theological interpretation of one's context and then makes a theological intervention into it; second, a series of *interpretive* claims concerning the way Barth and Schleiermacher actually did this; and third, some lightly sketched *constructive* claims regarding the potential upshot of all this for people who want to do theology today. In keeping with the volume's theme, I will approach Schleiermacher and Barth dialogically rather than chronologically and then conclude with some thoughts about the lessons we can draw from this conversation.

We begin, then, with Schleiermacher, and, in particular, with his diagnosis of a pervasive trend in the then-prevailing intellectual culture.[1] To put it a bit simply, one of the fundamental problems animating philosophers, theologians, and other intellectuals during this period was the question of how freedom is possible in a mechanistic universe. That is to say, in light not only of advances in natural science but the

---

1. Here and throughout, I am repurposing a few arguments I have defended elsewhere; see Hector: "Karl Barth"; *Theological Project of Modernism*; "Barth on Theological Method"; "Theology as an Academic Discipline."

ever-harder-to-ignore worldview that these advances seemed to support—a worldview, in short, according to which everything in the world operates according to exceptionless natural laws, and, so, a world that operates more or less mechanistically—in light of this worldview, these thinkers faced an obvious, pressing question: Where is the place, in such a world, for freedom?

The list of thinkers who tied themselves in knots trying to answer this question is a veritable who's who of modern thought; we might think here, for instance, of Descartes's bizarre conjectures about the pineal gland, or Malebranche's occasionalism, or Spinoza's God-or-nature compatibilism, or Leibniz's preestablished harmony. Heroic attempts to solve it notwithstanding, this question was still very much a problem for Schleiermacher and his contemporaries, as we can gather from their uniform dissatisfaction with Immanuel Kant's would-be solution to it. Kant had claimed, recall, that the sensible realm of nature is governed by mechanistic laws, whereas the supersensible realm of freedom is governed by the moral law. This raised for him the familiar problem of explaining how these two realms could be related to each other and, in particular, how the moral law could even possibly be effective within the realm of nature. Kant recognized that this is a problem, going so far as to admit that there is an apparently unbridgeable chasm between the two realms, but he tried to address it by insisting that it must be reasonable to hope that the chasm would be bridged and, so, that we can simply postulate whatever is necessary to maintaining such a hope. Few of Schleiermacher's contemporaries found this solution compelling, and so they set off, once again, to come up with alternative ways of relating the two realms; this is what initially drove the projects of Fichte, Schelling, and Hegel, to name just a few prominent examples.

There is much more to say about all this, but the reason I am rehearsing this brief bit of intellectual history is that it helps us understand what is going on in Schleiermacher's theology. Indeed, I would go one step further, and suggest that we do not really understand what is going on in the *Glaubenslehre* unless we understand it as a constructive theological interpretation of, and response to, precisely this sort of problem.

In fact, we can see this from the very outset of the *Glaubenslehre*, when, in its very framing, Schleiermacher talks about the relative antithesis of freedom and dependence.[2] On his telling, the entire world, along

2. Schleiermacher, *Christliche Glaube*, §4. I borrow translations from Schleiermacher, *Christian Faith*, though I have occasionally revised these.

with our sensible consciousness of it, is composed of reciprocal relationships between freedom and dependence, but what we should experience as a *relative* antithesis between them comes to seem *absolute*, precisely insofar as we treat the *world* as if it were absolute. Schleiermacher thus characterizes this situation as a kind of "God-forgetfulness," for unless we acknowledge that freedom and dependence are both absolutely dependent upon God, we will be unable to see how they could be reconciled. Notice, then, that Schleiermacher is here offering a theological diagnosis of the besetting problem of modern thought: the reason modern thinkers cannot figure out how to connect freedom and nature, on this interpretation, is because they treat the world as if it were absolute; even if they eventually bring God into this picture, they do so only after this picture's main outlines have already been sketched, at which point it is too late. No wonder, then, that modern thinkers cannot find a satisfying solution to this problem.

Again, that is Schleiermacher's theological diagnosis of a long-standing problem in his intellectual context. He then offers us a theological response to that problem, in the form of a solution not to the freedom/nature problem per se, but to the problem that makes this seem like a problem in the first place. The solution proceeds through roughly the following steps. First, Schleiermacher claims that the Whence of absolute dependence must be pure, undivided activity vis-à-vis the world, for otherwise the Whence would be caught up in the antithesis of freedom and dependence.[3] On this account, then, God eternally subsists in a single activity, which means that the activity of creating and redeeming the world must likewise be an expression of that single activity. He then claims, second, that this activity becomes incarnate in Jesus. The argument here is fairly straightforward: if (a) the Whence of absolute dependence is pure activity, and (b) Jesus's perfect receptivity to this Whence governs his reception of and activity toward the world, then (c) the latter receptivity and activity are pure activity vis-à-vis the world, since they are governed not by the world but only by an absolute receptivity toward God, from which it follows (d) that Jesus's receptivity and activity reproduce, within the world, God's own activity.[4] This explains Schleiermacher's assertion

---

3. On this point, see Schleiermacher, *Christliche Glaube*, §§40.3, 94.2.

4. I lack the space to tackle Schleiermacher's doctrine of the Trinity, unfortunately, but the basic points are roughly as follows: (a) God is pure activity; (b) this pure activity is redeeming love; (c) this redeeming love is enacted in Jesus and the Spirit; and (d) God has eternally been in-the-act of begetting Jesus and pouring out the Spirit. See

that "every moment of his existence, so far as it can be isolated, presents just such a new incarnation and incarnatedness of God, because always and everywhere all that is human in him springs from the divine."[5] It likewise explains what Schleiermacher has in mind when he claims that "to ascribe to Christ an absolutely powerful God-consciousness, and to attribute to him an existence of God in him, are exactly the same thing," since his perfectly receptive God-consciousness ensures that every moment of Jesus's life reproduces, as his own, the pure activity in which God subsists.[6]

That brings us to Schleiermacher's third step: if Jesus incarnates the singular activity in which God eternally subsists, then it follows that the Whence of absolute dependence is *love*; and if the creation of the world is an expression of this same activity, then it follows that *all* freedom and dependence are ordered by and to that same love.[7] This explains, in turn, how absolute dependence would enable one to harmonize relative freedom and dependence, for the simple reason that one can now experience all such circumstances as an opportunity to receive and reproduce God's love. Schleiermacher is quick to insist, however, that we can so experience them only by sharing in Christ's own God-consciousness, and that this sharing depends upon the work of Christ's Spirit. On this account, then, the community founded by Jesus is the means by which Jesus's God-consciousness is communicated to others; their reception of his God-consciousness would obviously liberate them from their God-forgetfulness, which is why Schleiermacher terms this the *redemptive* activity of Jesus.[8] This is the basis, in turn, of Jesus's *reconciliatory* activity, since having a renewed God-consciousness enables one to reintegrate relative freedom and dependence, and, so, increasingly restores one's sense of harmony with the world.[9] Jesus's redemptive work thus plays a key role

---

Schleiermacher, *Christliche Glaube*, §§170–172. Schleiermacher's doctrine seems to imply (e) that God would not be triune apart from redeeming humanity, but this does not entail that God is only contingently triune, for, on Schleiermacher's necessitarian metaphysics, (f) God cannot be otherwise than God is, such that God is necessarily triune.

5. Schleiermacher, *Christliche Glaube*, §96.3.
6. Schleiermacher, *Christliche Glaube*, §94.2.
7. Schleiermacher, *Christliche Glaube*, cf. §§165–169.
8. Schleiermacher, *Christliche Glaube*, §100 thesis.
9. Schleiermacher, *Christliche Glaube*, §101 thesis. Schleiermacher thus claims that "the redeemed man, too, since he has been assumed into the vital fellowship of Christ, is never filled with the consciousness of any evil, for it cannot touch or hinder the life

in his reconciling work, since, by restoring persons' God-consciousness and, so, their receptivity to God's reconciling love, he enables them to experience worldly oppositions either as expressions of that love or as to-be-overcome by it. Those who are redeemed can therefore integrate all of their circumstances, and they themselves, into their God-consciousness, because they trust that these circumstances are one and all absolutely dependent upon a wise, loving God.

With these claims on board, we can now see that Schleiermacher offers a theological diagnosis of, and prescription for, characteristically modern anxieties about freedom and necessity. From his vantage point, the seeming antithesis between one's freedom and that upon which one is dependent—manifest in natural as well as social antagonisms—is due to "God-forgetfulness," for the relativity of such antitheses, along with their possible coincidence, can be recognized only when they are set in relation to one upon whom both are absolutely dependent. To overcome these antitheses, therefore, reconciliation is necessary, which is what Schleiermacher claims has been accomplished in Christ and mediated through his Spirit. As such, the redeemed can increasingly perceive all that is as absolutely dependent upon God, particularly God's loving wisdom, and since one's freedom will itself be shaped by one's devotion to God, it follows that one can see the world's relative oppositions as not finally opposed to that freedom.

Schleiermacher thus offers us a theological interpretation of his intellectual context, as well as a creative theological response to that context. We cannot stand around admiring these moves for too long, however, since this is supposed to be a dialogue with Barth, after all, and Barth has at least two significant concerns with Schleiermacher's theology and,

which he shares with Christ. All hindrances to life, natural and social, come to him even in this region only as indications. They are not taken away, as if he were to be, or could be, without pain and free from suffering, for Christ also knew pain and suffered in the same way. Only the pains and sufferings do not mean simple misery, for they do not as such penetrate into the inmost life. . . . The assumption into vital fellowship with Christ, therefore, dissolves the connection between sin and evil" (§101.2). Such reconciliation is brought about, as Schleiermacher has led us to expect, in our relationship to nature as well as in our community with others. Schleiermacher thus argues that, for Jesus, "the hindrances to his activity never determined any moment of his life until the perception of them had been taken up into his inmost self-consciousness, which was so completely one with his powerful God-consciousness that they could appear in it only as belonging to the temporal form of the perfect effectiveness of his being. . . . It was still less possible that hindrances arising out of his own natural or social life could be taken up in this innermost consciousness as hindrances; they could be no more than indications of the direction set for his activity" (§101.2).

in particular, with the proposal just sketched—and as it happens, these concerns are part of Barth's diagnosis of a larger problem implicit in his own intellectual circumstances. We will consider the less serious concern in this section and return to the more serious one below.

As is well known, Barth thought there was something deeply problematic about the then-prevailing intellectual culture—as evidenced in its support for capitalist bosses, World War I, and National Socialism, among many other things—and he came to think that this culture's central, and indeed fatal, flaw lay in the fact that it absolutized a human standpoint, whether by treating culturally prevailing criteria as if they were the ultimate norms by which all else should be judged—including the church's proclamation—or by thinking of God as the embodiment of our ideals or as a kind of metaphysical reinforcement of those ideals.[10] As Barth saw it, then, the crucial theological task of his day was simply to "acknowledge that God is God," and so recognize God's radical discontinuity from creatures and their frameworks.[11] Barth thus insisted that there is an "infinite qualitative difference" between God and humanity, and therefore that theology must be based not upon any presumed "point of contact" between the two, but solely upon God's self-revelation. Again, this is meant as a theological intervention into the theological pathologies of his time.

In the Romans commentary, accordingly, Barth argues that Jesus is, and so discloses, the highest achievement of human possibility, but that his achievement is simply to set aside all such possibilities and so rely upon that which utterly transcends them. Barth lays this out in a crucial passage: Jesus "takes his place," Barth writes,

---

10. Barth thus became convinced that liberalism could not hope to stand against the cultural tide, since, for it, "to think of God meant to think, in a scarcely veiled way, of man, more exactly of the religious, the Christian religious man. To speak of God likewise meant to speak, in an elevated tone, but once again and now more than ever, of this man" (*Menschlichkeit Gottes*, 5). He then applies this judgment to Schleiermacher: so Barth claims, for instance, that for Schleiermacher "the *object* of theology is a *phenomenon*—namely, so-called piety—and though it is, of course, a *spiritual* phenomenon, its psychical *givenness* is like any other" (*Theologie Schleiermachers*, 275). As such, he claims that "Schleiermacher thus makes the Christianly-pious person into the epistemic foundation and content of his theology" ("Nachwort," 303). This is what Barth terms "Schleiermacher's Copernican Revolution" (*Unterricht in der christlichen Religion*, 1:13), namely, his transformation of theology into a science focused on faith or piety itself; Barth thus hails Schleiermacher as a revolutionary of sorts, since he adopted for theology a "conscious and thoroughgoing and conspicuous anthropological approach in the center of its thinking and its statements ("Nachwort," 302).

11. Cited in Busch, *Karl Barth*, 102.

> where God can be present only as a question about God. He takes the form of a servant. He goes to the cross, to death. Hence his is, at best, as the goal of his journey, a purely negative greatness. . . . Yet precisely in that he *sacrifices* all intellectual, physical, heroic, aesthetic, and philosophical possibilities—in sum, every thinkable human possibility—precisely in that he sacrifices all such possibilities to something impossibly *more*, to an invisible *other*, just so he is their fulfillment. . . . *Therefore* God has exalted him; *therein* he is reckoned as the Christ; thus he is the light of the last things, who is over all and gives light to all. For in him, in the depths of hell, we see the real faithfulness of God.[12]

On this account, then, the life of Jesus is not revelation per se, but the condition of the possibility of revelation: because Jesus renounces all creaturely possibility, it becomes clear—it so much as *can* become clear—that his redemption depends wholly upon a possibility which utterly transcends the creaturely realm. Hence, by rejecting any road from creation to God, and so any possibility of absolutizing a human perspective, Barth thus takes up a position fundamentally opposed to the prevailing intellectual culture.

As he soon realized, however, and as critics would in any case soon point out, Barth had not yet done justice to the theological commitments by which he was animated, since he could not yet account for revelation's actual entrance into creaturely history; so Barth later remarked that his *Romans* was guided, to some extent, by "a picture of revelation remaining transcendent to time, merely delimiting time and determining it from without," and that, as a result, "in it John 1:14 does not have justice done to it."[13] Absent an account of such entrance—an account, that is, of how God could act within creaturely history—it was not clear how anyone could actually receive such revelation, nor how "God," so conceived, differed in kind from liberalism's idea of God as a "highest" or "limiting" idea; hence, looking back at his commentary on *Romans*, Barth comments,

> Of all things, the one-sided, supratemporal understanding of God that I had set out to combat remains the lone tangible result on this plane. Precisely here one can object, as some soon did

---

12. Barth, *Römerbrief (Zweite Fassung) 1922*, 136–37.
13. *KD* I/2, 55–56. I have borrowed from, but often extensively revised, the standard English translation, *CD*.

object (whether with friendly or hostile intent), that although the optimism of the neo-Protestant conception of time is here fundamentally disturbed, this conception is in fact newly confirmed in the radicalization that had befallen it.[14]

In order to do justice to his own theological commitments, therefore, Barth felt it necessary to press beyond their elaboration in his *Romans*.

The next steps in Barth's theological development can thus be seen as an attempt to think more consistently about how God reveals Godself—where one vital reason for doing so, recall, is to resist the sort of absolutization of human perspectives that Barth associated with the prevailing intellectual culture. On the one hand, then, Barth argues that if revelation is not something that falls within the range of human possibilities, then it follows that the possibility and actuality of revelation must be grounded wholly in Godself. This claim, in turn, leads Barth to understand God "in Godself" as the one by whom such a possibility could be supplied, and so as the one in whose being such possibilities are grounded: God must therefore be the one who determines to reveal Godself, the one in and by whom God is revealed, and the one who conveys this revelation to creatures or, in sum, Father, Son, and Holy Spirit.

So far, so good, but the mere fact that Barth can now say that *God is capable* of revealing Godself does not by itself entail that God *could* reveal Godself, for it might still appear—and did so appear to many of Barth's critics—that Barth's putatively "Manichaean" denial of creaturely goodness was so extreme that God could hardly be thought able to enter into the creaturely realm. That brings us to Barth's other key claim. If God truly reveals Godself in Christ and Spirit, and if the God who is revealed is likewise the God who creates, then it follows that "God can become the Creator and thus have a counterpart external to himself, without coming into conflict with his innermost essence; quite the contrary, he can do so in confirmation, in glorification of that essence."[15] This means, among other things, that creation is inherently oriented toward the covenant; as Barth claims, what God created was "not just any space, but that which had been determined for the founding and history of the covenant, nor just any subject, but the subject who in this history is supposed to be God's partner."[16] Hence, creation "has no attributes, no life-conditions, no substantial or accidental predicates of any kind, in virtue of which it

14. *KD* II/1, 635.
15. *KD* III/1, 205.
16. *KD* III/1, 262.

can, may, or must be alien to the founder of this covenant."[17] Barth thus arrives at an account according to which both God and creation are, as it were, "fit" for revelation, in the sense that God can enter into creaturely history as Godself, and creaturely history is suited for this entrance.

It seems fair to say that this is the strongest possible response to the problems that Barth identified in the prevailing culture, for if God can and does reveal Godself *as Godself*, and if there is no point in all creation that is not created precisely for this revelation, then it follows that there is absolutely no place left for us to build our towers of Babel. Importantly, though, it is also not far from what Schleiermacher had in mind when he talked about creation as an expression of God's loving wisdom, which means that if we take this step with Barth, it does not mean that we have to leave Schleiermacher behind. Perhaps we are getting somewhere, then.

Yet just here, it might appear that Barth's theology is liable to his own critique of absolutized human perspectives, for surely a human perspective must be involved in our interpretation and application of revelation, but if that is the case, then we need to be able to judge that perspective in light of revelation, yet we have no perspective-free grip on revelation that would enable us to do this. Hence, it would appear either that Barth's method must end up unwittingly canonizing his own interpretation of revelation, in which case he is measuring theological perspectives not against revelation but simply against his own absolutized perspective, or else that his method is quite literally impracticable.

Barth's response to this objection, developed especially in the 1931 book on Anselm, is thus important for our purposes. The crucial development here, simply stated, is Barth's realization that theological perspectives can be tested one at a time, in light of other theological perspectives not then being tested, such that the relevant testing can proceed piecemeal rather than all at once (as if one were starting from scratch). On this approach, then, the proper theological procedure is one in which

> now this, now that article [of faith] figures as the unknown x, for which the investigation solves by means of the articles of faith a, b, c, d, etc., which are presupposed as known (without presupposing knowledge of x and, in this respect, *sola ratione*).... These are the a, b, c, d, etc., on the basis of which the x... is thus shown to be "reasonable" or "necessary"![18]

---

17. *KD* III/1, 105.

18. Barth, *Fides Quaerens Intellectum*, 54–55; see a similar characterization of Anselm (situated within a discussion of theological method) in *KD* I/2, 9.

The idea, then, is that one can test, and so exhibit, the faithfulness of any theological perspective by suspending one's belief in it, as it were, in order to determine whether it is supported by other perspectives to which one remains committed—whether, that is, one can work one's way back to it on the basis of those other perspectives. By following this procedure, then, each of one's theological perspectives—even those involved in one's interpretation of revelation—can be tested, just not all at once.

This is a smart approach, and Barth certainly uses it to good effect. But contemporary readers may not be entirely convinced by it or, perhaps more precisely, they may worry that this approach may not allow us to be sufficiently critical of our own perspectives. After all, the mere fact that I subject each of my perspectives to critique in light of my other perspectives does not mean that I have gotten outside my own perspective. To be sure, this is not entirely fair, since Barth does subject his perspectives not only to his own perspective, but to those of a broader theological tradition. This is surely a step in the right direction, yet contemporary readers may still wonder whether it is enough, particularly since the figures with whom Barth converses may all take certain things for granted and, so, may end up absolutizing certain aspects of their shared perspective (wittingly or not). If so, then perhaps we need not so much to abandon Barth's approach as to broaden it.

Again, that is one of the pressing concerns that many contemporary readers bring to theology, and I will say more about how it might be addressed in a moment. Before doing so, though, I want to mention a related concern, which I might put this way: Can people see themselves in our theologies? Do our theologies speak to their experience, in other words, and provide them with resources with which to bespeak their experience? This concern is obviously connected to the previous one, though here the worry is more to the effect that if Barth's theology includes only a narrow range of perspectives, then persons outside that range may have a hard time identifying with it. If I read our cultural moment correctly, these are two of the biggest concerns that contemporary theology—and the church—need to address.

Perhaps surprisingly, Schleiermacher was animated by a version of just these concerns, and I think he sheds some interesting light on them. To understand what I have in mind here, we can return to one of the ideas with which we began, namely, the idea that the relative antithesis between freedom and dependence can be reconciled insofar as we relate both sides of the antithesis to the Whence of absolute dependence.

I focused earlier on the antithesis between freedom and natural necessity, but it is important to note that we see a similar antithesis between freedom and our dependence on communal life and, in particular, the antithesis between individuality and the norms implicit in communal life. By addressing this problem, Schleiermacher helps us address the two concerns I just mentioned—or so I will argue.

So how might this antithesis be reconciled? The key, for Schleiermacher, is that communal norms must be such that the individuals constrained by them can see these norms as self-legislated and, indeed, as self-legislated because they enable one's self-expression. Schleiermacher then offers us a social-practical model of normativity to explain how this might work. On this model, briefly stated, to engage in a social practice is to recognize others as so engaged and seek their recognition, and, so, to confer authority on their performances and seek such authority for oneself, as well as to demarcate an "us" and seek inclusion in it. One's recognition of certain practices and practitioners thus selects the precedents relevant to judging one's own practice, just as one seeks this same recognition for oneself; one thus engages in a practice, accordingly, by trying to go on in the same way as certain precedents, such that one's own engagement in the practice could then contribute to the series of precedents that others seek to carry on, and so on. So understood, social practices bear a resemblance to common law jurisprudence, wherein a judge decides a novel case by looking to prior cases which they take to set the relevant precedents; their recognition of these cases confers authority on them and establishes the normative trajectory in terms of which their own decision is to be judged, yet they intend for their decision to stand in line with, and so carry on, this trajectory, which would mean that it would serve as precedent for still other cases.[19]

---

19. Schleiermacher thus claims that "each particular formation [of that which has been given to one] must as such endeavor to bring it before others for recognition and recognize the sphere of their formation; and this in its unity completes the essence of sociality, which consists in the recognition of alien property in order to let it be opened up, and in the opening-up of one's own property in order to let it be recognized" (*Ethik*, 265). "My" norms can thus be "ours," and "our" norms can be "mine": an obvious allusion to Hegel's famous description of *Geist* as "I that is *We*, and We that is *I*" (*Phänomenologie des Geistes*, 108–27), though we find precisely the same thought in Schleiermacher, who insists that in a norm-circulating community, "the common will emerges from the individual, and the individual from the common" (*Ethik*, 314). Schleiermacher claims, accordingly, that a *free* community must be characterized by "a reciprocal action that is interwoven among all the participants, but one that is also fully determined and made complete by them," such that "the impetus to community . . . is

Schleiermacher's model thereby explains how our norms can and do change over time. Thus the practice of claiming certain rights, for instance, progressively came to include, as claimants, not only landowning white men, but all persons, and the rights claimed came to include not only a right to one's property, for example, but a right to safe working conditions, a right to free and appropriate public education, a right to use gender-appropriate bathrooms, and so on. Because the normative trajectory implicit in a series of precedents can change every time a new performance is recognized as carrying it on, and because the series itself does not exhaustively predetermine what would count as doing so, it follows that novel performances, in novel circumstances, by novel practitioners can take these trajectories in new directions, such that the norm implicit in them can change over time. This means, in turn, that novel performances can open up new possibilities for others to carry on those practices, which can open up new possibilities for still others, and so on. (Think here of a jazz trio in which each musician "does their thing" with a common melody: each contributes novel riffs and improvisations on that melody, and these riffs take that melody in new directions, thereby opening up new possibilities for the improvisations of others, and so on, such that each continually opens up new possibilities for the others, and vice versa.) Schleiermacher thus claims that novel expressions "preserve the mobility" of a norm and "make room for other ways of framing it": because the normative trajectory implicit in a series of precedents changes every time a new expression is recognized as carrying it on, and since such changes are the rule rather than the exception, it follows that novelty is continually opening up the possibility of still further novelty.[20] As a result of being constrained by precedent, accordingly, one can produce novel expressions, and as a result of such expressions, a whole range of further expressive possibilities is introduced. In this way, the texture of a community's normative patterns can constantly be enriched, thereby opening up more and more space for persons' expressions to be both recognized by their community and recognizable as *self*-expressive. These new possibilities mean that there is more and more room for persons to express themselves in ways that are recognizably their own—in language, music, social roles, occupations, and so on—and their so expressing

---

satisfied in each person through all and in all through each person" ("Versuch einer Theorie des geselligen Betragens," in *Schriften aus der Berliner Zeit, 1796–1799*, 169; and in *Kurze Darstellung*, §166).

20. Schleiermacher, *Kurze Darstellung* [1830], §203.

themselves makes room for others to do so, and so on. The net result of this, then, should be a set of communal norms that are constituted by mutual recognition, and that are broad and richly textured enough that persons can express themselves in and through them.[21]

Importantly for our purposes, Schleiermacher's approach to theology follows this same model. Schleiermacher understands theology as a gathering up and expression of the prevailing piety—that is, as an individual expression of that which has currency within the church and as itself a candidate for such currency.[22] For a theological claim to circulate as an expression of the community's piety, accordingly, it must be recognizable as going on in the same way as precedents which have circulated as such.[23] To recognize a candidate expression is thus to treat

---

21. This understanding of normativity, in turn, implies that in order to be free with respect to one's commitments, the communities of which one is a part must be characterized (a) by openness to novel, individual expressions, and (b) by mutuality—they must be characterized, that is, by patterns of recognition that are both capacious and reciprocal. With respect to the former, Schleiermacher claims that a community "forms only a mediating mass, out of which each receives his or her cognition of individuality, and in which he or she places his or her individuality for others to cognize"; this being the case, one can "find oneself in" a community just to the extent that it "provides one with increased leeway for individuality" (*Ethik*, 77, 175). A community supports self-expressive freedom, accordingly, only if its "highest tendency" is "the formation of an art treasury by which the attunement of each is formed and in which each deposits his or her distinct attunement and the free presentations of his or her way of being attuned" (122). Taken by itself, however, this condition is insufficient; it is also necessary that these patterns be the product of mutual recognition—rather than, say, only of an elite hierarchy's recognitive attitudes—for otherwise, the norms thus instituted would ultimately be legislated by "them" rather than "us" or "me." For this reason, Schleiermacher argues that in a community of free expression (in this case the church), there must be no fixed distinction between recognizer and recognized, authorizer and authorized, or priest and layperson, for "each is a priest in that he or she draws others to him- or herself in the field for which he or she has particular aptitude and in which he or she can present him- or herself as a virtuoso," and "each is a layperson, in that he or she follows the art and ways of another where he or she is an alien in religion." In such a community, accordingly, "each follows that power in others which he or she feels in him- or herself, and with which he or she also rules over them" ("Über die Religion: Reden an die Gebildeten unter ihren Verächtern," in *Schriften aus der Berliner Zeit, 1796–1799*, 270).

22. Schleiermacher thus characterizes theology as "the discipline which systematizes the doctrine prevalent [*geltenden Lehre*] in a Christian Church at a given time," and he understands such doctrines, in turn, as "accounts of the Christian pious disposition-states portrayed in speech"—as accounts, that is, of "that which, in the public proceedings of the Church ... [,] can be heard as a portrayal of its common piety" (*Christliche Glaube*, §19 thesis; §15 thesis; §19.3).

23. It is for this reason that Schleiermacher claims that "we could not at all grant the name of Dogmatics to a presentation composed of nothing but idiosyncratic doctrines,"

it as going on in the same way as such precedents, which means that subsequent expressions can then be recognized as such if they go on in the same way as a series of precedents which now includes the expression in question.[24] On this account, then, individual theological expressions are "a product of the past and a kernel of the future,"[25] since the norm by which a novel expression is assessed is provided by prior expressions which have been recognized as expressions of the community's piety, and if the novel expression is recognized as going on in the same way, it contributes to the norm according to which still other expressions might be recognized.[26] Here too, then, communal norms constrain and enable individual expression, and individual expression contributes to the norm that constrains and enables still other expressions.

That brings us, finally, to the vision of God underlying this whole approach. The crucial idea here, which we find already in Schleiermacher's earliest writings, is that God's infinite goodness can and should be expressed in infinitely many ways, and that every person's life is meant to be just such an expression: we are thus called to appreciate more and more of the goodness expressed in the lives of others and so allow that goodness to enrich and enable our own expressions, which should enrich and enable the expressions of others, and so on. In this

---

and that, indeed, "even the earliest presentations of the evangelical faith could bear that name only insofar as they linked up with what went before and had most of their system in common with what was ecclesially given" (*Christliche Glaube*, §25.1).

24. Hence, as Schleiermacher puts it, a doctrine counts as an expression of Christian piety only if a community "finds its norm" in that doctrine—only if, that is, it takes that expression as normative for future expressions of piety. As Schleiermacher comments, "An edifice [of doctrine], even if entirely coherent, of nothing but wholly peculiar opinions and views, which, even if really Christian, did not link themselves at all to the expressions used in the churchly communication of piety, would always be taken only as a private confession and not as a dogmatic presentation, until there came to be attached to it a like-minded society, and there thus emerged a public preaching and communication which found in that doctrine its norm" (*Christliche Glaube*, §19.3).

25. Schleiermacher, *Kurze Darstellung* [1811], §33.

26. Thus Schleiermacher: "Consider . . . how much there is which was originally decried as heterodox in our Church, which afterwards came to count as orthodox but always through an earlier orthodoxy becoming obsolete" (*Christliche Glaube*, §25 thesis). Or again, "if heterodox matter comes to be counted as being better attuned to the spirit of the Evangelical Church than is the letter of the Confessions, then the latter become antiquated and the former becomes orthodox" (§25 postscript). This prospective/retrospective distinction is crucial to understanding how "changes nevertheless do not compromise the unity of [the Church's] essence," since it explains how novel expressions can be seen as both carrying on and contributing to that essence (*Kurze Darstellung* [1830], §47).

way, Schleiermacher thinks, we can each become a microcosm of God's infinite goodness, and that infinite goodness can come to ever-fuller expression.[27] Schleiermacher thus maintains that his "highest intuition" is the idea that "each person is meant to represent humanity in their own way, combining its elements uniquely, so that it may reveal itself in every mode, and all that can issue from its womb be made actual in the fullness of unending space and time."[28] Nor, importantly, is this vision limited to humans, since Schleiermacher insists that God's infinite goodness comes to expression not only through humans, but through all that is, such that the truly religious person will be on the lookout for such expressions in all of their surroundings.[29] The picture that emerges, then, is one of ever-increasing abundance: every time God's infinite goodness finds expression, it creates new expressive possibilities, which beget further possibilities, and so on.

With that, we can return to the questions with which this section began, for if we were to follow the approach outlined here, it is obvious that more and more people would be able to see themselves in our theology—and, indeed, in our communities—just as our theologies would present us with a fuller, less partial, vision of God's goodness. We could thus address the concerns raised against Barth's theology, though we need not leave Barth behind in so doing, for Barth's own theology bears striking similarity, on this front, to Schleiermacher's. Barth thus claims, for instance, that

---

27. Schleiermacher elaborates this claim: "When we also perceive our fellow creatures in the intuition of the world and it is clear to us how each of them without distinction is his own representation of humanity just as we are, and how we would have to dispense with intuiting this humanity without the existence of each one, what is more natural than to embrace them all with heartfelt love and affection without any distinction of disposition and spiritual power?" ("Über die Religion: Reden an die Gebildeten unter ihren Verächtern," second speech, in *Schriften aus der Berliner Zeit, 1796–1799*).

28. Schleiermacher, *Monologen* (Kritische Gesamtausgabe), 31. Note that Schleiermacher contrasts this "intuition" with a Kantian approach to individuality: "For a long time," he writes, "I too was content with the discovery of a universal reason; I worshipped the one essential being as the highest, and so believed that there is but a single right way of acting in every situation, that the conduct of all men should be alike, each differing from the other only by reason of his place and station in the world. I thought humanity revealed itself only in the manifold diversity of outward acts, that man himself, the individual, was not a being uniquely fashioned, but of one substance and everywhere the same" (30); this is a point he reiterates in his second speech.

29. "Über die Religion: Reden an die Gebildeten unter ihren Verächtern," second speech, in Schleiermacher, *Schriften aus der Berliner Zeit, 1796–1799*.

> God's glory is the indwelling joy of his divine being which as such shines out from him, which overflows in its richness, which in its super-abundance is not satisfied with itself but communicates itself. All God's works must be understood also and decisively from this point of view. All together and without exception they take part in the movement of God's self-glorification and the communication of his joy. They are the coming into being of light outside him on the basis of the light inside him, which is himself. They are expressions of infinite exultation in the depth of his divine being. It is from this point of view that all his creatures are to be viewed both first and last. God wills them and loves them because, far from having their existence from themselves and their meaning in themselves, they have their being and existence in the movement of the divine self-glorification.[30]

Again, then, we need not leave Barth behind if we take up Schleiermacher's vision here, and this is good news, not least because Barth helps us see how this could simultaneously be a vision of *grace*.

So far, so good. But that brings us back to Barth's other, more serious objection to Schleiermacher's proposal. Happily, the objection can be briefly stated: Schleiermacher is right, Barth thinks, that we should not treat relative antitheses as if they were absolute. He likewise thinks, with Schleiermacher, that it represents a kind of God-forgetfulness insofar as we treat such relative antitheses as if they were absolute. This is all fine, as far as it goes, but it does not go nearly far enough: the trouble, in Barth's estimation, is that Schleiermacher fails to reckon with antitheses that are *not* relative, since it is crucial that that which stands in opposition to God as well as to creation—in a word, *evil*—not be regarded as if it were a relative antithesis to which we must be reconciled. As Barth sees it, then, Schleiermacher is right to insist that we must not absolutize relative antitheses, but he makes the mistake of handling all antitheses as if they fell under this rubric. And while it is true that we must not absolutize relative antitheses, it is even more important that we not relativize absolute ones. The fact that Schleiermacher does so represents, to Barth, one

---

30. *KD* II/1, 730. Barth continues with the claim that "it is in this light that they are to be seen and heard. This is their secret that will one day come out and be revealed. And it is to this that we are always required and will always find it worth our while to attend and look. It is for this revelation that we should always wait. The creature . . . echoes and reflects the glory of the Lord. . . . The angels do it . . . but even the smallest creatures do it too. They do it along with us or without us. They do it also against us to shame us and instruct us. They do it because they cannot help doing it" (*KD* II/1, 731).

of the chief failures of Schleiermacher's system; indeed, he characterizes it as "a theological catastrophe of the first magnitude."[31]

In support of this claim, Barth points, unsurprisingly, to Christ: "In him there is revealed not only the goodness of God's creation in its twofold form," he argues,

> but also the true nothingness which is utterly distinct from both Creator and creation, the adversary with whom no compromise is possible, the negative which is more than the mere complement of an antithetical positive, the left which is not counterpoised by any right, the antithesis which is not merely within creation and therefore dialectical but which is primarily and supremely to God himself and therefore to the totality of the created world.[32]

The argument here, then, is that in Christ, we see that God does indeed reconcile to Godself that which can be reconciled, but God also vanquishes that which cannot and must not be reconciled—God does not come to terms with evil or the destroyer, in other words, but instead destroys them. Such oppositions must be opposed rather than harmonized, and if we get this wrong—if we think of them as relative rather than absolute oppositions—we end up giving aid and comfort to the adversary, one of whose principal weapons, after all, is deception.

To illustrate Barth's argument here, it might be helpful consider two kinds of problem that might arise within a friendship. On the one hand, someone may find it frustrating that their interests, style, temperament, and the like differ from those of a friend, but in the face of such frustrations, they may remind herself of that friend's—and the friendship's—value, and they may thus try to see the ways that these differences and their consequent friction are actually a good part of their relationship. On the other hand, someone might come to realize that their friend is constantly ridiculing them, bullying them, and seeming to delight in their distress; in that case, the appropriate response is not to try to see their friend's behavior as a good part of their relationship, but to insist, in no uncertain terms, that such behavior is unacceptable and, if necessary, to terminate the friendship. Needless to say, it would be a mistake if friends were to treat every difference as if it were abusive. But it is also a mistake, and a far more dangerous one, to treat abuse within a friendship as if it were

---

31. *KD* III/3, 377.
32. *KD* III/3, 345.

akin to a difference in style or temperament. This, very roughly, is Barth's point regarding Schleiermacher: while Schleiermacher is right to maintain that we should not treat relative oppositions as if they were absolute, he is wrong—gravely so—to treat all oppositions as if they were relative.

So where does this leave us? With each of the previous steps in this dialogue, I have suggested that Barth and Schleiermacher could take the other's insights in stride: Schleiermacher could gladly accept Barth's Christocentric account of creation's fitness for the covenant, just as Barth could accept Schleiermacher's insistence that God's infinite goodness should be expressed in infinitely many ways and that we should be on the lookout for these and let them enrich our theologies. At this point, though, we have reached a bit of an impasse, since it seems clear that Schleiermacher could not simply take this objection in stride. That does not mean, however, that here we must simply choose between the two; rather, it seems to me that the best way to honor the insights of Schleiermacher as well as Barth is to see them as operating within concentric circles: Schleiermacher's proposal applies brilliantly within the domain of the smaller (!) circle of creation, whereas Barth's objection helps us see that there is something beyond this circle, something by which it is circumscribed and which must be approached very differently from that which lies within the first circle.

CONCLUSION

We began this paper by considering Schleiermacher's theological diagnosis of some intellectual ills by which his era was beset, along with his proposed remedy for those ills. The problem, as he saw it, was that the then-prevailing intellectual culture treated relative antitheses as if they were absolute; their so doing, he maintained, was due to a kind of God-forgetfulness, such that the solution would be to recall the absolute dependence of everything that is upon a God who is wholly loving and perfectly wise. We then turned to the first of Barth's objections to this proposal, to the effect that Schleiermacher's theology, in keeping with the spirit of his age, is finally and fundamentally anthropocentric: he tries to build a bridge from human religiousness to God, and thus ends up trying to speak about God by speaking loudly about humanity. Against this approach, Barth insists upon God's infinite qualitative difference from everything that is not God, yet this insistence eventually leads him to hold that the one who created all that is is the God of Jesus Christ and, so, that all that is exists for the sake of God's determination to be God with us. On this point, at least, Barth's mature theology thus comes very near to Schleiermacher's own, yet just here we ran into a worry about Barth: How can he address the charge that he, too, is finally speaking about God by speaking loudly about his own perspective? To deal with this concern, we turned to Schleiermacher's contention that God's infinite goodness must be expressed in infinitely many ways, from which it follows that our theologies should try to incorporate, and thus be open to, more and more of these expressions. Here again, we found a potential convergence between the two theologians, but that left us with Barth's other, more serious objection to Schleiermacher's proposal: Schleiermacher is right, on this objection, that we should not treat relative antitheses as if they were absolute, yet he fails to recognize that some antitheses—particularly the antithesis between God and creation, on the one hand, and evil, on the other—are in fact absolute. Far from reconciling ourselves to the latter antithesis, Barth insists, we must simply put our faith in the decisive No that God has pronounced upon it in Christ and thus do our best to echo this No. Here we reach a point where Barth and Schleiermacher are not finally on the same page, and where the best path forward is probably to accept the import of Barth's criticism and, so, to recognize the limited scope of Schleiermacher's otherwise brilliant proposal.

With a few grains of salt, then, we might draw from this conversation two implications for contemporary Reformed theology: on the one hand, that we need a theology that helps us come to terms with relative antitheses but that says No to absolute ones; and on the other, that we need a theology that not only sees God in light of Christ, but also, precisely because it does so, draws from a wide array of perspectives and opens up space for them. Such a theology might thereby speak to some of today's most pressing concerns, namely, whether we can overcome our sense of alienation from the world, ourselves, and one another; whether we can stand uncompromisingly against abuse, oppression, cruelty, and other forms of wickedness; and whether people can see themselves in our theologies and whether our theologies are sufficiently attentive to and reflective of a suitably wide range of voices. In its own way, each of these concerns represents a yearning for the grace of God, and one of Reformed theology's most important callings, it seem to me, is to bear clear witness to precisely that grace. Barth and Schleiermacher offer us some important clues about how we might do that, or so I hope.

PART TWO

Dialogue

CHAPTER 5

On *Sacra Doctrina* and the *Analogia Entis*
Karl Barth and Roman Catholicism[1]

Thomas Joseph White

If the truth revealed by God is one, why are there diverse theological understandings of it, even within the Catholic Church which claims to hold authoritative understanding of the apostolic teaching of the Old and New Testaments? Do these diverse theological interpretations of the faith follow only from the limitation, partiality, and diversity of viewpoints of human beings, and if so, how is the unity of the confession of the Catholic faith maintained across time? Or is the truth of the faith itself somehow so ineluctably transcendent that it can hardly be uttered or understood across time and place in any unified way? If pluralism in Catholic theology poses important problems, so does the existence of schools of thought, such as that of Thomism, as distinct from, say, Scotism, or the modern "Communio" school that takes inspiration from authors like Henri de Lubac, Joseph Ratzinger, and Hans Urs von Balthasar. But perhaps it is even an artifice and a superficial notion when one speaks of such schools that apply obliquely to diverse figures in history not subject to easy categorization. And what is the role of philosophy in this mix of questions, since there are a number of diverse philosophical theses in Christian intellectual history that affect the stances authors take in their diverse theological regards, as they speak not only about philosophy but

---

1. An earlier version of this essay was originally published in *Nova et Vetera*. See White, "On the Ecumenical Work of Reforming Christology."

about the mystery of God, making use of philosophy? Last, what is the relation of this kind of problem of pluralism *within* Catholic theology when one compares it with non-Catholic Christian theology, such as that of Protestant theologians, especially those such as Karl Barth, or in his own way, G. W. F. Hegel, who have greatly influenced conversations in modern Catholic theology? My aim below is not to treat such questions comprehensively, which would not be possible for many reasons, but rather to underscore some signal points of reference for a sound understanding of the practice of Catholic theology as *sacra doctrina*, the study of the revealed mystery of God, as it relates to philosophy and ecumenism. I will relate my comments in particular to the contrasting figure of Karl Barth at points, since Barth's view of theology as a form of thought distinct from and outside of philosophical metaphysics (including metaphysical reflection on God) stands in vivid contrast to the tradition of Aquinas, and to mainstream Catholic theology more generally, but there are also important points of contact between Aquinas and Barth that are worthy of mention, and that help one consider in greater detail the possibility of ecumenical exchange between Catholic and Protestant theologians seeking in diverse ways to speak of the mystery of God and of Christ, as well as of other key themes in dogmatic theology.

SACRA DOCTRINA

At the start of our reflections on the topic of Catholic unity of the truth, and legitimate theological pluralism, it is important to make a few comments about Thomistic self-understanding regarding the practice of theology as a normative discipline and how it relates to Scripture, tradition, dogma, and philosophy, as well as normative claims about orthodoxy and heresy. As anyone recognizes, Aquinas is only one theologian among many in the Catholic tradition. Evidently, no one who is a member of the Catholic Church is required intellectually to be committed to Thomistic interpretations of commonly held doctrine, let alone to Aquinas's own distinctive philosophy. What then do Catholic Thomists make, methodologically, of the inherent theological pluralism within their own Church, and how does it relate to argumentative claims Thomists sometimes propose regarding the supposed insufficiencies of alternative theological viewpoints, or the conceptual advantages of Thomistic positions in Christology?

First let us simply note some levels of authority that Aquinas himself recognizes in question 1 of *Summa Theologiae* (*ST*) I, and questions 1–2 of *ST* I–II. My list below is affected by an interpretation of Aquinas made in light of the Second Vatican Council Dogmatic Constitution on Divine Revelation, *Dei Verbum*, but it is not for that reason, I think, artificial or extrinsically imposed.

1. God reveals himself in free self-disclosure and self-communication by way of grace, teaching us through the medium of the prophets and apostles, and this teaching is found in Scripture and early apostolic tradition. It is received, transmitted, and understood within the living tradition of the Church. The whole Church is assisted by the Holy Spirit in this process to understand and receive the teaching of God revealed in Christ faithfully down through the ages, not without the assistance of the apostolic college, the episcopal authorities of the Church acting in communion with the See of Rome.

2. This teaching is itself codified at times in dogmatic universal pronouncements, which are not identical with primal revelation as such but which seek to promote and protect right understandings of integral elements of it. The dogmatic teaching of Chalcedon, for example, is not identical with scriptural revelation but is taken to indicate something perennially true about the ontology of Christ that is revealed implicitly in the New Testament. Most Catholic theologians agree that the Church understands this kind of dogmatic teaching as infallibly expressive of divine revelation, and irreformable. This does not mean that the teachings given in these locales are comprehensive or fully adequate, but they do indicate core confessional truths, manifest implicitly or explicitly in Scripture, that must be preserved through the ages, even if such conciliar teachings also can be reinterpreted in various ways in subsequent ages, *in new theological and philosophical formats*. The latter formats, novel though they may be in each age, need to preserve sufficiently the acquisitions of the Church's previous claims. This includes whatever is essential in the ontological content of the classical dogmatic tradition.[2] Of course theologians working with the magisterium of the

---

2. One may think here of John Henry Newman's explorations on the topic of the continuity that takes place in the development of doctrine in *An Essay on Development of Christian Doctrine* and of Yves Congar's understanding of actualizing tradition in *Tradition and Traditions*.

Church try to work out over time what is essential in the ontological signification of the past teachings as they are interpreted within the horizon of new contexts.

3. There are different schools of theology within the Catholic Church, for example, Augustinian, Syriac, Byzantine Eastern Catholic, Bonaventurian, Thomist, Scotist, Suarezian, Rahnerian, Balthasarian, and so on. This is not a comprehensive list. *These distinct schools of thought all have a common commitment to the two levels indicated above: divine revelation and its doctrinal formulations.* They are united within the Church by this common confession of faith, and come to distinct interpretations of that revelation. It is true that sometimes members of one of these schools argue that the position of another school leads implicitly toward a heretical position inadvertently. Aquinas seems to have thought this about Alexander of Hales's theology, as leading inadvertently toward a problematic form of Nestorianism, for example. And I think this about Rahner's Christology, as I have argued elsewhere.[3] More often, however, they accuse them of being wrong theologically, which is not an identical charge. Neither of these forms of argumentation entails the accusation of heresy of course. Heresy amounts to a willful defense of a teaching condemned by the Catholic Church or the willful denial of a proposition taught by the Church. By contrast, theological error is something most theologians traffic in at some time, perhaps even daily, despite their best intentions, and has to do with the struggle to understand the truth of revelation within diverse traditions, some of which may promote less perfect, erroneous, or deficient understandings. Of course some also think that the various positions of major schools each have it partly right, or are compatible or convergent tending to a mutual consideration of mystery, or are equally inadequate. A Catholic Thomist, then, who claims that a Scotist Trinitarian theologian who refuses to think of the persons in the Trinity as subsistent relations is doctrinally outside the Catholic Church is not speaking reasonably. The Thomist can argue, however, that the Scotistic view of the Trinitarian persons is problematically univocalist, that is, erroneous, or the Scotist can argue that the Thomist holds a view of divine persons that is incoherent. Both are arguing about the actual content of what they already agree on (the

---

3. See White, *Incarnate Lord*, ch. 1.

dogmatic confession of Trinitarian faith) but have distinct and partially incompatible accounts of that content. I take it that Barthians and Thomists are often doing something analogous, if not precisely identical (since Barthians are not Catholic, typically, and believe in reformable dogmatic ecclesial claims).

4. How do distinct philosophies relate to the distinct schools? It is true that distinct philosophical views emerge among various theologians and their followers. Aquinas famously believes in the real distinction and composition of essence and existence in all creatures and in its non-distinction in God, a view Scotus and Suarez each reject in distinct ways. Aquinas's view on this point has many implications for his theology of creation, the Trinity, and the hypostatic union. Henry of Ghent and Scotus, meanwhile, have irreconcilable anthropological notions of the way human beings formulate concepts, and make use of these distinct ideas in their reflections on the eternal Son as the *Verbum* of God. Balthasar and Rahner differ deeply on the nature of anthropology, natural knowledge of God, and the possibility of metaphysics in a post-Kantian setting. What should we make of all this diversity that is so deeply interrelated to the diverse "philosophies" used within theology?

First, differences among the schools do not arise only or even primarily from their respective philosophies. *They arise from different conceptions of the truth about the mystery of revelation itself.* That is to say, differences of opinion in various schools arise *principally* from diverse conceptions of the *formal objects* of faith as such (i.e., from diverse conceptions of the Trinity or incarnation) rather than the *philosophical instruments* of *sacra doctrina*.

That being said, differences among the schools do arise *in part* due to distinct philosophical commitments. Scotus and Ockham come to very distinct views of the Trinity and the psychological analogy in part because of the ways they understand divine simplicity, which are related in turn to their metaphysical views about composition in creatures and the truths we can infer about God from those compositions.[4]

On this view, there is no point in Catholic theological history at which non-Christian philosophical ideas were taken up into the practice of theology uncritically, without being discussed, vetted, reformulated,

---

4. See the study of Friedman, *Medieval Trinitarian Theology from Aquinas to Ockham*.

and reconsidered in light of Christ and the New Testament revelation. The use of *ousia* metaphysics in the fourth century, for example, already entails a reformation of ambient philosophical concepts in view of the exposition of a distinctively Christian, Trinitarian confession of faith at Nicaea.[5] The medieval project of trying to understand philosophical notions in Aristotle or Avicenna within a Christian context (substance, relation, and so forth) took place overtly by critique of these philosophical concepts, conducted in light of Christ and the apostolic tradition. This was the main point of the dispute of how to critically receive and evaluate the Aristotelian heritage in the high Middle Ages.[6] The modern Catholic use of the classical terms like "essence," "person," "relation," and "nature" in creedal formulations retains a decidedly ontological signification, but distinct schools of thought interpret in varied ways how we might best preserve their use. Many modern Catholic theologians seek to preserve classical ontological significations while transposing them into modern philosophical idioms. Walter Kasper, for example, has quite impressively sought to make use of ideas from both F. W. J. Schelling and the Frankfurt school to articulate a commitment to classical Nicene Chalcedonian dogma in modern ontological idioms.[7] Rahner seeks to do something analogous in developing his own Thomistic version of transcendental anthropology.[8]

We should note three sub-presuppositions latent in what has been argued up to this point:

First, Catholics can agree with Protestants at least in some ways when the latter claim that "there is never any nature that does not presuppose grace": philosophical reflection in the Catholic theological tradition presupposes always already an ongoing reformation of all prior philosophical notions in light of Christ. This is not a novel view, as any historian of patristic or medieval theology should rightly attest.

Second and simultaneously, grace does presuppose nature: there are no philosophically innocent theologians. Every theologian makes some use of philosophical and indeed metaphysical notions, whether modern or classical, even if they also seek to baptize them within a theological

---

5. See, for example, the helpful analysis of Anatolios, *Retrieving Nicaea*; and Daley, *God Visible*.

6. See on this point the analysis of Friedman in *Intellectual Traditions at the Medieval University*.

7. See Kasper, *God of Jesus Christ*.

8. Rahner, *Foundations of Christian Faith*.

format, as presumably Barth has tried to do (however successful one thinks he is) with Kant and Hegel, or Schleiermacher with his modern metaphysics of consciousness, or Eberhard Jüngel with Heidegger. I take it that none of these thinkers operates without at least an implicit commitment to philosophical and metaphysical positions, and none can rightly be understood without some philosophical analysis as such. I am not convinced therefore of the epistemological possibility of a post-metaphysical theology, but only of options among alternative metaphysical influences.

Third, all this need not lead to the conclusion that medieval ontology in general or Thomism in particular must represent the apex of faith. The idea that "older is better" or "newer is better" is misleading. What is best is what is true, not what earlier or later appears in time.

Where does this leave us? Based on the account I am offering, there is no tradition free from the philosophically influenced reading of the New Testament or the patristic tradition. New Testament exegetes and Protestant theologians who interpret Paul's ontology in relational terms may well be influenced by the Barthian tradition, and by that very measure, I think one can perceive in such interpretations some effect antecedently of Hegel's *Logic*, in the rendering of relation in Paul. That does not mean Barth's relational analysis of covenant in Paul, inspired as it is partly by Hegelian ontology and in reaction to it, is erroneous. But it does mean that, if I am correct, we should treat skeptically any claim of Protestant theologians to provide us with chemically pure interpretations of Scripture that are free from the taint of or dependence on frameworks of reception through the medium of a theological tradition that has itself assimilated philosophy (however critically or uncritically).

Neither Schleiermacher's nor Barth's use of post-Kantian ontological categories indicates a theological problem per se, based on what I have mentioned above. As I have argued elsewhere, a Catholic theologian can think of Barth in particular as a helpful resource for thinking about how to express many biblical and traditional Christian claims in a distinctively modern context and idiom.[9] If one interprets him as successfully "modern and orthodox" on various points of theology, this does not make him better or worse than Athanasius or Aquinas, but it means we have a right and responsibility to compare them among themselves and with others to think about what we take to be the best formulations

---

9. See White, "Crucified Lord."

ontologically, in light of tradition, and in accord with Scripture and common doctrine (like Chalcedon), as well as sound philosophical practices.

This being said, we should, I believe, treat the acquisitions of the great tradition as having a greater weight than lone innovations, if only because the popularity of the "common doctors" suggests, by their widespread acceptance and use, the possibility of a greater accord with the *sensus fidei* of all the baptized. Augustine is a reference in part because he helps us get to the Church's common thinking regarding the truth of divine revelation, and he does so by making constructive use of the ambient pre-Christian philosophical heritage. The same could be said of many notable theological "doctors" of the past. This means that newer ideas should, as John Henry Newman said, be subject to assessment by association with the various references of the tradition in those instances where the latter displays "chronic vigor."[10]

There is admittedly an outstanding difference between Barth and the Catholic tradition at least on this point: whether the Christian critique and reformation of all non-Christian forms of ontology may give rise to a "philosophy on Christian soil," or a Christian philosophy, that is fully assimilated to and compatible with the scriptural deposit of faith and the dogmatic tradition but susceptible in principle to extraction for the purposes of teaching philosophy (or metaphysics) as a distinct field of reflection.[11] *After Christ and in his light* is it possible for there to be a philosophical ontology as such? Concretely speaking, can one teach a class of philosophy in a seminary that offers metaphysical analysis of what a living thing is, or a human person, or philosophical arguments for the existence of God, and so on? Here Catholic theologians most typically hold that such philosophical instances of thought are possible and even salutary, especially given the effects of sin (original, personal, collective) on human intellectual endeavors outside of grace. Due to the effects of sin and the need for grace, non-Christians may be unlikely to interest themselves in or accept such a Christian philosophy, but if grace presupposes and must heal and rehabilitate nature in the light of Christ, then some re-formation in philosophy is necessary even on—and

---

10. J. Newman, *Essay on Development of Christian Doctrine*, where chronic vigor is the seventh of the famous seven notes of authentic development.

11. I take it as a matter of historical fact, on this point, that Aquinas, for example, does think that there are philosophical demonstrations of the existence of God. See Dewan, "Existence of God."

especially on—Christian soil.[12] Relatedly, the Catholic Church teaches that there are *praeambula fidei*, philosophical and moral truths accessible to reason in principle but difficult to attain in our fallen state, which the Church teaches for that reason but which are philosophical as such.[13] It also teaches that there are "reasons of credibility," derived from signs of the truth of revelation, in things like ongoing miracles or the moral witness of the saints, that designate obliquely the truth of the Christian faith to human reason in *extrinsic* ways that do not provide the grace of faith as such but do show its rationality or non-irrationality.

This last point does remain an outstanding topic of division, but how important is it? Regarding this question, I will now turn to the question of philosophical theology as it affects ecumenical theology, specifically in exchanges between Catholic and Protestant theologians.

THE *ANALOGIA ENTIS* AND ECUMENICAL THEOLOGY

Clearly the engagement between Erich Przywara and Karl Barth in the early 1930s was an occasion of elevated ecumenical encounter and gave rise to subsequent conversations of great importance, not least in virtue of Balthasar's famous book *The Theology of Karl Barth*, as well as in many other instances. Nevertheless, we should ask ourselves whether either Przywara or Barth rightly identified the theologically essential differences between Protestantism and Catholicism. Is Barth correct to say, for example, in *Church Dogmatics* I/1 (*Doctrine of the Word of God*, part 1), that the use of the *analogia entis* presents the only reason not to be Catholic?[14]

I would like to suggest two errors that were made in this debate, and refer to one intervention that acts as a remedy. The first error as I see it, and perhaps the most consequential, stems from Przywara, who famously claimed that the *analogia entis* is the "fundamental form of

---

12. There are famous twentieth-century disputes on the nature of Christian philosophy, a concept that appears in the papal encyclical of John Paul II *Fides et Ratio*. I propose ways of thinking about this theme that take some inspiration from Jacques Maritain in an appendix of my book *Wisdom in the Face of Modernity*.

13. Vatican Council I, *Dei Filius*, §2.

14. "I regard the *analogia entis* as the invention of Antichrist, and I believe that because of it it is impossible ever to become a Catholic" (*CD* I/1, xiii).

Catholic theology."¹⁵ When most Catholics speak, admittedly somewhat vaguely, of an *analogia entis*, they mean to refer to the human ability to know something of God by way of natural philosophical reflection. (Incidentally, this is how I almost always use the term as well.) Przywara does not mean this alone, however, as John Betz has repeatedly and rightly pointed out.¹⁶ Importantly, Przywara's definition includes philosophical knowledge of God by way of metaphysical reflection and analogical discourse. However, this form of knowledge is itself, for Przywara, taken up into a larger Catholic thought form that includes properly theological reflection on the mystery of the Trinity and Christ, as well as the Virgin Mary, the Church, and the sacraments. In fact he is referring by this term to ontological similitudes between the Trinity and creatures that emerge in a variety of instances, in the rhythm of creation (characterized in part by the metaphysics of the real distinction), by the history of human beings under grace, by the incarnation in the two natures of Christ, by the fiat in grace of the Virgin Mary, by the life of the Church in the Holy Spirit.¹⁷

What is significant for our purposes is that Przywara claimed that the study of this structure of ontological similitude that is evinced both in the orders of nature and grace and that is known philosophically and theologically is the essence of Catholic theology. If I understand him rightly this means that the essence or formal object of Catholic thought is the study of the similitudes between the Trinity and creatures, making use of a sound metaphysics. He contrasts this, in turn, with what he takes to be "essential" to Protestantism, a distrust of human mediations, behind which Przywara posits a latent oppositional mode of thinking between God as sovereign agent and the human agency of persons, their natural powers even under grace, their cooperation in the order of sanctification, and so forth.¹⁸ One suspects he is suggesting that there is an implicit meta-ontology that lies behind the doctrine of justification in Luther's early theology, which is reflected in the subsequent Lutheran and Reformed refusal of various facets of the Catholic tradition, such as

---

15. See Przywara's expression of this idea following his debate with Barth (Przywara, *Analogia Entis*, 348–99, 2.2: "The Scope of Analogy as a Fundamental Catholic Form").
16. See Betz, "Erich Przywara and Karl Barth."
17. See Przywara, *Analogia Entis*, 185–91, 234–37, 493, for example.
18. Przywara, *Analogia Entis*, 348–53.

instances of authoritative doctrinal clarification, Mariology, theories of instrumental sacramental theology, and so forth.

Przywara's ideas are interesting and perfectly appropriate to explore within the context of a robust ecumenical conversation. But I think he in fact misled Barth by his characterization of the "fundamental form" or essence of Catholic theology. Let us return to our consideration of *sacra doctrina* from the first part of this essay. What is the formal object of Catholic theology? Medieval theologians expended great effort arguing about this topic, presenting diverse theories, some saying Christ the Word made human, others saying the Church's life and sacraments.[19] Aquinas's view is that the proper object of theology is God the Holy Trinity.[20] The fundamental form or essence of theology then is the study of God, revealed in Christ. Aquinas then stipulates that one must understand all things in light of the Trinity, which is why the Niceno-Constantinopolitan Creed functions as a reference for core principles, as it allows us to read Scripture correctly in a Trinitarian light, and interpret the scriptural revelation in a Trinitarian perspective.[21]

What none of the medievals—or any one else before or since Przywara—has ever claimed is that the formal object of theology is the study of the ontological similitudes between the Trinity and the creation. That is not a ridiculous suggestion, and indeed it has some potential connections to Aquinas, as I have just intimated. But note the difference. In Aquinas it is clear that theology "looks" first and foremost at the Trinity and interprets the world in light of the ultimate truth revealed in Scripture, making some measured use of philosophical ontology within theology. Przywara seems to invert the order of procession; the philosophical study of the analogy of being, which has roots in Greek philosophy, anticipates a rhythm of being we will discover again at a higher level, in the domain of revealed truths about Trinitarian ontology. It may be possible to defend his claim, from a Thomistic point of view, but what Przywara does is give us the impression that if we begin with the right metaphysics we will reach the right theology.[22] The study of philosophical ontology inaugurates the engagement with revelation itself.

19. See Leinsle, *Introduction to Scholastic Theology*, 120–81.
20. Aquinas, *ST* I, q. 1; II–II, q. 1, a. 1.
21. Aquinas, *ST* I, q. 1, a. 7.
22. Perhaps his idea could be restated in a more measured way: "Without a realistic sense of philosophical ontology one will not be able to cooperate well with the articulation of the theological mystery." But his view seems to go further than this.

Barth's reaction is equally nebulous or disputable, to my mind. It seems clear enough that the classical disputes stemming from the Reformation era are about mediation: Is there an episcopal structure stemming from apostolic times that is an essential part of the constitution of the Church? Are there seven sacraments, or only two, and what is a sacrament? In what sense is it a sign and instrument of grace or is it? Can Church councils be said to formulate irreformable, infallible doctrines that are free from error, and in what sense is it true to say that the Church preserves infallible teaching? Are the Virgin Mary and the "saints" exemplars of the life of grace, whose actions under cooperative grace manifest the saving power of Christ's action in the world, or is this Catholic superstructure an extrinsic scaffolding obscuring the true face of Christ? The Reformation "solas" regarding Scripture, justification by faith alone, and grace alone (meaning God acting prior to and above human cooperation) work to assure a more restricted view of mediation, presumably in view of the greater manifestation of the glory of God alone and the centrality of Christ as the unique Mediator of salvation.

Many classical Lutheran, Reformed, and Anglican theologians reserve a place for the measured use of philosophy within dogmatics, including philosophical arguments as such for the existence of God and the determination of what we might say or not say about his attributes. Barth presented the rather novel claim in *CD* I/1, however, that the *core differences* between Catholic and Protestant theology stem from the *analogia entis*, initially interpreted largely as "natural theology," which then creeps into every facet of Catholic theology.[23]

This is, historically speaking, a very novel claim. It may be defensible, especially if one thinks that Przywara's account of *sacra doctrina* as "the fundamental form of theology" in the Catholic tradition is correct. However, Przywara's claim amounts to nothing more than a very brilliant and eccentric thought experiment, one held by virtually no one before him or

---

23. See Barth on the *analogia entis*: "E. Przywara purports to give us final clarity in the matter when he writes that there are contained 'in the Catholic doctrine of the *analogia entis* the possibilities of a true incarnational cosmos, including body and soul, community and individual, because in their totality . . . they are 'open' to God. From the standpoint of the Catholic doctrine of the *analogia entis* creation in its totality is the vision, mounting from likeness to likeness, of the God who is beyond every likeness. It is, therefore, a receptive readiness for Him. In its final essence it is, as it were, already Mary's 'Behold, the handmaid of the Lord. Be it unto me according to Thy word' (*Religionsphil. Kath. Theol.* 1926, p. 53)" (*CD* I/2, 144-45).

since. But Barth takes it as insightful and constructs a counterreaction, which is somewhat similar in content, but distinct in method.

It is distinct in method because the fundamental core of Reformed theology, according to Barth, is determined by knowledge of God procured only by revelation and only by the consistent activity of the Holy Spirit, without *any* contribution from philosophy. We should note the dialectical reaction here: if Przywara suggested that philosophical metaphysics set the tone for Catholic theology as a kind of initiation, Barth reacts by denying any role to specifically philosophical or metaphysical knowledge of God as such even *within sacra doctrina*. Neither of these positions seems to reflect that of Aquinas, who thinks that theology studies God the Holy Trinity, and can make use of philosophy as a subordinate science, in the service of theology.[24] Many Reformed theologians, especially in the Protestant Scholastic traditions, have a similar view, and arguably there is a good bit of harmony here between Aquinas and Calvin himself.

However, this now all seems to be obscured. What the Reformation is about, we are told after the Barth–Przywara debate, is a new Barthian idea of unilateral divine activity without human agency, allied with an idea about the absence of any natural knowledge of God in the human community. Now we can gain access to the classical Reformation "solas" only if we also acknowledge these new Barthian truths. Is this correct, however, simply as a reading of the Protestant tradition? It is powerful and intriguing, surely, but I think it falls into the same category within the Protestant community that Przywara's thought falls into within the Catholic community. That is to say, it is an eccentric and deeply original proposition, with the difference that it has been far more influential among Protestants than Przywara's idea has been among Catholics. And there is one more very important difference: the methodological extensiveness of Barth's proposal. Effectively, what Barth proposed in *CD* I/1 is related methodologically to the christological ontology of election,

---

24. "This science can in a sense depend upon the philosophical sciences, not as though it stood in need of them, but only in order to make its teaching clearer. *For it accepts its principles not from other sciences, but immediately from God, by revelation.* Therefore it does not depend upon other sciences as upon the higher, but makes use of them as of the lesser, and as handmaidens: even so the master sciences make use of the sciences that supply their materials, as political of military science. That it thus uses them is not due to its own defect or insufficiency, but to the defect of our intelligence, which is more easily led by what is known through natural reason (from which proceed the other sciences) to that which is above reason, such as are the teachings of this science" (Aquinas, *ST* I, q. 1, a. 5, ad. 2; emphasis added).

covenant, and creation that he develops later in *CD* II/2 (*Doctrine of the Word of God*, pt. 2), III/1-2 (*Doctrine of Creation*, pts. 1-2), and IV/1-2 (*Doctrine of Reconciliation*, pts. 1-2). Here he does assimilate and reformulate all kinds of philosophical notions from modernity in a creative and innovative way, ideas from Hegel, Kant, Sartre, and others. So one could believe that those constructive proposals are all somehow logically dependent upon or conceptually intimately related to the ideas of the start, regarding "natural theology" and the conditions of theology. This means that if one is committed to ideas from Barth's later Christology one is also likely to see this as somehow connected to his earlier ideas of revelation.

Perhaps within the logic of Barth's overall oeuvre such connections are indeed essential and must be maintained to make use of any of his later ideas, but personally I doubt it. In fact it is fairly simple to articulate an argument to the contrary. Take Barth's theology of the relation of the divine essence and the human essence of Christ in *CD* IV/2, which posits a relational account of the divinity and humanity of Jesus within a dynamic view of the unfolding of the covenant in time as a place where God's Trinitarian prehistory, or eternal identity, is manifest to us precisely in God's filial human life. It would be possible to develop a more ontologically rich account of these very ideas in conversation with the classical Chalcedonian tradition (Barth in conversation with Maximus and Aquinas, for instance), and to make use of concepts developed on "Christian philosophical soil" to do so. This could be done in conversation with Hegelian notions of relation and divine-event ontology, and Kantian ideas about the limitations of human knowledge, as a moment of explication of the "novelty" of revelation in Christ. But the articulation of all these ideas could include a more overt set of reflections about the philosophical warrant of the ideas of Maximus, Aquinas, Kant, Hegel, and so forth, and this "moment of philosophical reflection" is lacking in Barth, by design. I do not think this helps his case, in the end, but rather weakens it considerably, because his notions of topics like "relation" and "event" in God seem slightly incoherent and under examined. Whether or not I am right about this, I do not think my judgment should be considered "Church dividing," and I think it is a very serious error within Protestant theology to think that it is. There are many Lutheran, Reformed, and Anglican theologians who would agree with me and other Catholics on philosophy, as they themselves accept that there is a place for overt philosophical reflection within *sacra doctrina*.

The person who saw things similarly and who sought to put the debate in the right framework was Gottlieb Söhngen.[25] Söhngen's essays on the controversy famously influenced Barth, who indicated in a somewhat nebulous way that, if Söhngen's view of the *analogia entis* was correct, he had no difficulty with the doctrine.[26]

Some take Söhngen's view to be a kind of Catholic reformulation of the idea of natural knowledge of God made in concession to Barth's theology, one that anticipates the later theories of Vatican I offered by Balthasar in his book on Barth. However, Söhngen is well versed in modern Scholastic theology, and his analysis of the debate is based, as I see it, on the kinds of points I have been making above. Catholic theology studies the object of revelation, God himself, and in doing so, seeks to unfold the *analogia fidei* as understood in Catholic thought, which is the likeness or resemblance found between the mysteries, the *nexus mysteriorum*.[27] It can do so by making use of philosophical knowledge of God or creatures, now placed in subordinate service to theological reflection. The latter process presupposes that the philosophical ideas of human culture, including evolving Christian intellectual culture, be analyzed and reformulated in light of divine revelation and ultimately in view of a christological center of theological reflection on Scripture. The Church's tradition and way of reading Scripture provide normative points of reference for the understanding of Scripture as a unified text and as a text understood in a unified, coherent way down through time (in Church doctrine). Söhngen was critical of the Przywarian definition of theology, and rightly so. Balthasar in turn also followed Söhngen in his adjudication, as did of course the most famous doctoral student of Söhngen, Joseph Ratzinger.[28]

---

25. See Söhngen: "Analogy of Faith: Likeness to God from Faith Alone?"; "Analogy of Faith: Unity in the Science of Faith." The originals appeared in the German theology journal *Catholica* in 1934. However one interprets Barth's claims that he had buried the debate, I agree with Keith Johnson that Barth in fact held out against natural theology for the duration of his theological career; see Johnson, *Karl Barth and the* Analogia Entis.

26. See the analysis of Balthasar, *Theology of Karl Barth*, 328–34.

27. I have offered a sympathetic recent interpretation of this point in Söhngen in "*Analogia fidei* in Catholic Theology."

28. See Balthasar's criticism of Przywara on this point in *Theo-Logic*, 94n16; and the logically congruent remarks on 273n109. For Ratzinger, see *Introduction to Christianity*, 74–79, 137–61; and *In the Beginning*; Benedict XVI, encyclical *Deus Caritas Est*, §§10 and 13.

In the first section of this reflection I have argued that a Thomistic understanding of *sacra doctrina* rightly understood has a place for contributions from philosophical ontology, critically assimilated in light of divine revelation.

In this second part I have argued that this conception of the use of philosophy within *sacra doctrina* is not Church dividing. Przywara and Barth together have bequeathed us a legacy of thinking that it is or must be. However, I think that this legacy is something of a poisoned chalice, one that Protestants and Catholics together should refuse to drink from. The terms of agreement and disagreement should be reevaluated, including in christological conversation. *Ecclesia semper reformanda est.* Surely if Barthians hold that conciliar definitions such as those of Nicaea and Chalcedon are reformable in principle, they must consider Barth's own "dogmatics of the Church" as reformable in principle as well (unless Barth has become a paper pope, on the so-called *analogia entis*). Of course I am not suggesting that Catholics and Protestants have no significant theological divisions among them, but only that these need not and should not be framed in terms of the *analogia entis*. Catholics and Protestants can and should argue about the truth or falsehood of diverse christological ontologies, and about the value of various philosophical ontologies, whether classical or modern, but *those* arguments need not be Church dividing. Referring back to my hierarchical degrees from the first section of the essay: one can agree on Chalcedonian principles in Christology while belonging to distinct schools of thought that in turn harness concepts from diverse philosophical traditions. There are arguments worth having between the schools, but they are not arguments about the truth of the common creedal confession of faith per se.

CONSIDERATION OF A TEST CASE: CHRISTOLOGY AND KENOSIS

Having made these comments about revelation, dogma, schools of theology, philosophy within theology, and the necessary distinctions between them, I would like to consider an example. This is the idea central to the thought of many modern Catholic and Protestant theologians that the Holy Trinity is revealed especially in the abandonment of Jesus crucified, in dereliction and his suffering unto death. Such an idea is based essentially on the idea of God's solidarity with humanity in our "godforsakenness," wherein God has descended by self-emptying (kenosis) into our worst condition of suffering so as to reveal to us what is most ultimate and salvific in God (his life as the Holy Trinity, able to unite us to himself by grace and glory). Let me begin with a stipulation and then I will make three basic claims, all too succinctly, due to the constraints of our format.

The stipulation is the following: It is natural to think that the profound existential confusion and moral evil experienced by many in the twentieth century should be the occasion for the Church to meditate theologically upon the crucifixion of God so as to make progress in understanding the mystery of the Trinity revealed by the Cross. My own limited reflection on the cry of dereliction seeks in its own way to acknowledge this facet of modern theology, albeit in a Thomistic light,[29] and I take it that my own analysis bears some resemblance to (and takes inspiration from) that of Pope John Paul II, as offered in a well-known passage in *Novo Millennio Ineunte*.[30] This view seems close to that of other influential twentieth-century Thomists, such as Charles Journet.[31] These authors, while deeply influenced by Aquinas, were also deeply affected by and engaged with the terrific suffering of human beings evidenced in the mid-twentieth century.

This being said, history is not destiny in theology. Barth proved that in the face of Schleiermacher and Harnack. After their work seemed to have defined modern Protestant academic theology, his work and vision of Protestant theology, at least for a time, displaced theirs. Why then might we prefer modern theologians engaged with the problem

29. See White, *Incarnate Lord*, ch. 7.

30. "Jesus' cry on the Cross, dear Brothers and Sisters, is not the cry of anguish of a man without hope, but the prayer of the Son who offers his life to the Father in love, for the salvation of all. At the very moment when he identifies with our sin, 'abandoned' by the Father, he 'abandons' himself into the hands of the Father. His eyes remain fixed on the Father. Precisely because of the knowledge and experience of the Father which he alone has, even at this moment of darkness he sees clearly the gravity of sin and suffers because of it. He alone, who sees the Father and rejoices fully in him, can understand completely what it means to resist the Father's love by sin. More than an experience of physical pain, his Passion is an agonizing suffering of the soul. Theological tradition has not failed to ask how Jesus could possibly experience at one and the same time his profound unity with the Father, by its very nature a source of joy and happiness, and an agony that goes all the way to his final cry of abandonment. The simultaneous presence of these two seemingly irreconcilable aspects is rooted in the fathomless depths of the hypostatic union" (John Paul II, *Novo Millennio Ineunte*, §26). This passage bears remarkable similarities to Aquinas's analysis in *ST* III, q. 46, aa. 6–8.

31. See, for example, Journet, *Septs paroles du Christ au croix*, 88–90.

of suffering to those who came before? After all, the reflections on the dereliction of Christ crucified found in Catherine of Siena, Thomas Aquinas, Francis of Assisi, Bonaventure, Julian of Norwich, John of the Cross, and Theresa of Avila should matter to us as much as those found in Balthasar or Adrienne von Speyr, and the views of these former thinkers differ notably from the latter (and sometimes from one another). If Barth, Balthasar, and/or Speyr are set up as a unique guiding canon to the whole tradition, one may wonder rightly about the method and criteria at work. I do not think this criterion in Balthasar comes primarily either from mystical experience or from an insight related to Barth's rejection of natural theology. I think it comes from another source. I am referring here to the important influence of Hegel's Christology upon Barth and Balthasar, both of whom engaged for and against his positions in diverse ways.

Hegel's Christology and the Ontology of Freedom

Why focus on Hegel in this context? Surely Hegel is one of the most underrated theologians in modern theological studies, even among those who are most influenced by him. This influence is indirect, mediated through the post-Hegelian Trinitarian theologies of the twentieth century.[32] This is true above all when one thinks of his proposals regarding kenosis in God that stem in great part from his theological innovation with regard to the communication of idioms. Hegel knew of the seventeenth-century debate between the Giessen and Tübingen schools of thought regarding the communication of idioms, the predication of the attributes of the divine and human natures to the person of Christ. Both schools presuppose some version of the *genus majestaticum*: the idea that certain properties of the divine nature may be attributed to the human nature of Christ.[33] In the *Lectures on the Philosophy of Religion*, Hegel

---

32. See the pertinent analysis of Marshall, "Absolute and the Trinity."

33. The former school held that the Son of God incarnate simply concealed his divine prerogatives during the course of his earthly life, while the other held that he in some sense suspended their use by way of a kenotic abandonment of the divine properties. Like Aquinas and Calvin, I take it that the very idea of an attribution of the divine attributes (such as omnipresence) to the human nature is itself problematic and contrary to the mainstream use of the communication of idioms in patristic representatives such as Gregory of Nazianzus, Cyril of Alexandria, Leo the Great, and John Damascene. They attribute natural properties of each nature not to the alternative nature but only to the person of the Son, who genuinely subsists in each nature, such that the natures are united but not confused.

inverts the perspective of the Tübingen school regarding the *genus majestaticum*. Whereas they speculated on how or in what way the attributes of the deity might be communicated to the humanity, Hegel speculates on how the attributes of the humanity might be communicated to the divinity, a view later referred to as the *genus tapeinoticum*. In virtue of the incarnation, God is able to take attributes of human finitude, such as temporality, suffering, and death, into his own divine life and being. The foundation for this capacity of the deity is located in God's freedom, his capacity to identify even with his ontological contrary by way of self-exploratory diremption.[34]

Barth rightly identified problems with this view in *CD* IV/1, §59, but sought to reformulate the idea in what he acknowledged in turn to be a very novel way.[35] The condition of possibility in God for his taking on human properties into his own life and essence as God is not due to a developmental history of God in the economy, but due to an eternal precondition in the life of the Trinity, in which the eternal kenotic life of the Son from the Father anticipates (by analogy we could say) the temporal historical life of the Son as human.[36] Balthasar in turn basically adopts this view from Barth, with additional ideas from Bulgakov (who was himself also deeply dependent upon Hegel's conception through the mediation of Thomasius).[37]

---

34. A characteristic example: "'God himself is dead,' it says in a Lutheran hymn, expressing an awareness that the human, the finite, the fragile, the weak, the negative are themselves a moment of the divine, that they are within God himself, that finitude, negativity, otherness are not outside of God and do not, as otherness, hinder unity with God. Otherness, the negative, is known to be a moment of the divine nature itself. This involves the highest idea of spirit. . . . This is the explication of reconciliation: that God is reconciled with the world, that even the human is not something alien to him, but rather that this otherness, this self-distinguishing [of the divine nature through diremption], finitude as it is expressed, is a moment in God himself" ("The Consummate Religion" in Hegel, *Lectures on the Philosophy of Religion*, 468–69). On historical aspects of the communication of idioms in the Tübingen school, see also Kasper, *Absolute in History*, 459–65.

35. See *CD* IV/1, 157–357.

36. See, for example, *CD* IV/1, 129, 177, 179.

37. See, in this regard, the important notion of a Trinitarian inversion in Balthasar, *Theo-Drama*, 183–91, 521–23. The processions of the Son and the Spirit are supposedly inverted in the economy: due to this kenosis of the Son, during the time of his incarnation and prior to the resurrection, the Son proceeds from the Spirit and is utterly relative to him not merely in his human instincts of mind and heart (i.e., in virtue of Christ's capital grace), but rather in his very person and being as Son. Likewise consider the thematic argument of Bulgakov, who interprets the Third Council of Constantinople in a kenotic way, so that the human consciousness of Christ in his historical life,

Balthasar rightly saw that, if this account is to be defended, it requires an exploration of the "similitude" or analogy between the Son as God and the Son in his human dereliction in ways that are not previously anticipated in the classical Christian tradition. This is especially the case since, in light of the move Hegel and Barth make, we now seek to identify the eternal mutual relations of persons in the Trinity based on the kenotic human actions and sufferings of Jesus. The Son's obedient self-offering to the Father in the abandonment is the outward economic face of an inward immanent Trinitarian love of mutual freedom, characteristic of the eternal differentiation of the Father and the Son. Freedom of mutually self-giving *wills* (in the plural) seems now to become the condition for an understanding of all divine and human ontology.

Thus we are faced with the obligation to undertake a rejection or radically dialectical reassessment of key elements of the patristic and medieval tradition. Most notably, Balthasar realizes that the psychological analogy for the processions of the Son and Spirit according to a likeness of Word and Love from the Father will have to be abandoned (though it is arguably biblical in origin).[38] Consequently the central theological motive in all of Western Trinitarian theology is in fact displaced in modern Catholic theology, in light of the novel insights of Hegel and Barth. Traditional theology of the unity of God, based on the study of the shared divine attributes, and in particular the unity of will in the three persons, is also now rethought in light of an ontology of primal reciprocal freedom.[39]

---

suffering, and dereliction is *commensurate* with his divine self-emptying love (*Lamb of God*, 247–63). The distinction of natures is reinterpreted as a diremption of the divine nature into a human form.

38. See the very clear remarks where Balthasar distances himself from the psychological analogy (*Theo-Logic*, 128–34) and then proposes an alternative conception of divine self-emptying love (134–37).

39. See Balthasar, *Theo-Logic*, 94–95, 173–218, 273n109. Likewise: "How can Jesus say of himself, 'I am the Truth'? This is possible only because all that is true in the world 'hold[s] together' in him (Col. 1.17), which in turn presupposes that the *analogia entis* is personified in him, that he is the adequate sign, surrender, and expression of God within finite being. To approach this mystery we must try to think: In God himself the total epiphany, self-surrender, and self-expression of God the Father *is* the Son, identical with him as God, in whom everything—even everything that is possible for God—is expressed. Only if God freely decides in the Son to bring forth a fullness of non-divine beings can the Son's essentially 'relative' and thus 'kenotic' act in God be seen as a personal act (*esse completum subsistens*) within the act of creation that gives to everything its real identity (*esse completum sed non subsistens*)" (*Epilogue*, 89–90).

Of course one can argue that all this represents the right way to go. However, my suspicion is that we should return to Hegel and ask whether he interpreted the communication of idioms correctly, and whether Barth and Balthasar made the right decision to try to develop this new "school" of analogy. Hegel departs in problematic ways from the classical tradition in this domain, and in turn there are problems with the decision to assimilate, reformulate, and "correct" his thought christologically, in the way these later theologians undertake to do. In the final part of my argument I will explain briefly what I take the better option to consist in.

Dyothelitism and the Christological Analogia Entis

There is of course a likeness between the human nature and activity of Christ as human and his divine nature and activity as Lord and God. The former is reflective in some way of the latter, even when the Son voluntarily suffers, is crucified, and dies. The dyothelitist principle established by the Third Council of Constantinople, following Maximus the Confessor, notes that there is a distinction of two natures in Christ and thus also a distinction of two activities (or natural operations) and wills. However, it is also the case that each "set" of operations is attributed only to one subject and person, the eternal person of the Son, who is truly divine and acts as Lord and truly human and acts and suffers as human.[40] The human actions and sufferings are therefore also (a) subordinate to the divine actions and (b) expressive of the Son's personal identity and nature as God. In short, all that Jesus does and suffers in his human nature, life, and operations is indicative of his divine Sonship and at least obliquely indicative of the divine work he is accomplishing with the Father and the Holy Spirit.

It follows from this that the mode in which Jesus is human (his distinctive way of subsisting uniquely in human nature) is utterly personal and filial, due to the hypostatic union. His nature, grace, actions, and sufferings *as human* are always *revelatory* of his personal being as Son, who exists in personal filial relation to the Father and to the Spirit (in distinct ways) in all he is and does. So, to respond to one significant question: Is Jesus's beatific or immediate vision as human (by which he knows the Father immediately and intuitively in the heights of his human

---

40. I have tried to give greater articulation to this idea in White, "*Dyotheletism* and the Consciousness of Christ."

intellect by grace) specifically the same as ours or is it filial? We should say theologically that it is distinctly human in species or kind, but filial in mode. If Jesus's beatific vision is not specifically of the same kind as ours then God has not truly identified with us in our condition as human and realized our salvation as one of us from within our human condition. Here the famous claim of Gregory of Nazianzus to Apollinarius applies: what God has not assumed he has not saved. However, if Jesus has this immediate vision as a human being, he also has it in a filial way, much as he is humanly free but also acts freely as the Son of God, always from and in relation to his Father and in conformity with his own divine willing. When the Son is humanly conscious of God, he is humanly conscious of the Father being his Father, and of being the Son of the Father, and of being the co-principle of the Father's Spirit, whom he wishes to send upon the world.[41]

If we recognize that the human nature of God as human can and does reveal his divine identity and the relations of the Father, Son, and Holy Spirit truly, in Jesus's human life, suffering, death, and exaltation, it is because we recognize that these human actions take on this distinctive filial mode of expression proper to the Son incarnate.

To recognize this, however, is to acknowledge also the difference of the human nature qua nature from the divine, as it is truly human that God has become, and indeed God has become human precisely to express his inner mystery of Sonship in flesh and blood, within our human sphere. This presupposes difference and analogical dissimilitude of the two natures, not only likeness. There is no strict identity between the humanity of God and his divinity, nor can there be.

However, I think it is just this that is compromised by Hegel's innovative use of the communication of idioms, since he transmits the human attributes into God and evacuates the divine attributes, or at least makes them disposable at the discretion of God's evolving freedom in history. Barth does something very different but arguably more radical, since he renders the human attributes "always, already" present in God as the condition of possibility for the personal differentiation of the Father and the Son.[42] In various ways, Pannenberg, Balthasar, Jüngel, and Moltmann are all downstream from this decision, and commonly adopt this

---

41. "But when the Counselor comes, whom I shall send to you from the Father, even the Spirit of truth, who proceeds from the Father, he will bear witness to me" (John 15:26).

42. I argue this at further length in White, "Crucified Lord."

way of proceeding, albeit in various ways and with significant interesting differences between them.

What emerges in all these thinkers, due to this primal conceptual decision, is what may be termed a form of "inverted monophysitism," in which the divine nature of the Son is conceived of not in terms of analogical similitude, but in fact by way of univocity. Simply put, the properties and characteristics of the human nature of Jesus, particularly in his voluntary acts of freedom, obedience, suffering, dereliction, experience of abandonment as separation, and death, are transposed onto the divine nature, as indicative of a polarity in God that exists between the Father and the Son eternally. I do not think this inverted monophysitism comes from a close reading of Paul, but from the Christology of Hegel, and I take it that this is a matter of historical fact, not speculation, and one that can be verified readily not by an attentive historical study of the New Testament, but by a close historical-critical study of Barth and Balthasar in their proximate intellectual context.[43]

I am in no way denying that these thinkers aspire to read Scripture in harmony with the Chalcedonian tradition, and I am not claiming that they are necessarily less orthodox or more philosophical than Aquinas. They take up other options as theologians, making proximate use of philosophical ideas critically, and therefore simply present us with a distinctive school of thought, or perhaps two schools of thought. What I am claiming, however, is that what their schools argue on this point is in fact disadvantageous to a better understanding of Scripture regarding the kenotic suffering of Christ as indicative of the inner reality of the Trinity (which it is in some way).

This argument allows one to return to the question of a need for analogical reflection in both Chalcedonian Christology and metaphysics as distinct but interrelated modes of reflection. Balthasar certainly does

---

43. In passing I should note that my concern is that modern kenotic theology in practice if not always in theory risks collapsing the distinction of natures, characterizing the divine nature of the Son by reference to his human mode of being, thus projecting irreducibly and uniquely human traits onto the transcendent divine nature. It is worth noting that this theological tendency can have very detrimental effects on the Church's theological conversation with adherents of modern Judaism and Islam, who would tend to see in this kind of inverted monophysitism the danger of a human projection in Christianity that obscures one's rightful acknowledgment of the transcendence of the divinity of God. This is not to say that I advocate for any form of Nestorianism, classical or revised. John Damascene's Chalcedonianism is a model in this respect, both for dialogue of Western and Eastern Christians, and for conversation with Muslims regarding the transcendence of God.

aspire, with sophistication, to distinct and related forms of reflection on such topics, and he wanted as well to speak about the *analogia entis Christi*.[44] However, when he speaks of the eternal Son under the auspices of human actions and sufferings, I take it that he is in fact speaking univocally of the divine nature in human terms. This kind of discourse could be metaphorical at best, but of course followers of Balthasar do not interpret him this way, nor should they, if they wish to defend Balthasar's own (to my mind implausible, problematic) claims. If God is incomprehensibly but truly one in being and one in will, as the Church basing herself on Scripture teaches is the case, then there is no eternal obedience, surrender, infinite distance, separation, self-emptying, or suffering in God. To the extent that we use these notions to describe the inner life of the Trinity, I think we step out of the world of the Bible and into a new form of univocity theory, in which all-too-human attributes are hypostatized. Instead we should return to the use of the psychological analogy, and the theology of divine attributes, as a way to understand the eternal processions of the Word and Spirit, who each possess in themselves eternally from the Father the indiminishable plenitude of divine life. The tradition provides us already with this distinctive theological analogy of what is proper to the inner life of the Trinity. However, in *sacra doctrina* as I understand it, we can press forward with this analogy of the immanent eternal life of the Trinity to ask more overtly the question that the post-Hegelian theologians ask. How does the mystery of the cross reveal God, the Holy Trinity? Might we offer new answers to this question, other than those presented by Balthasar, even if we also remain in dialogue with his great work?

What then would be the way forward in a deeper dialogue between Thomists and Balthasarians? We would need to think about christological principles and how we each hold to them, especially the interpretation of the communication of idioms and the teaching of the Third Council of Constantinople regarding dyothelitism, and we would *also* need to talk about analogical terms for the divine nature and what should and can, or should not and cannot be prescribed of the eternal nature and life of God.

I take it that many ideas of Barth in *CD* II/1 regarding the attributes of the one God could be of help in this conversation. Many modern

---

44. It is interesting to notice how with this term from Balthasar we are somehow back to Przywara's nonphilosophical usage of the notion of the *analogia entis*, but now from the top down, as it were, knowing all being in light of the mystery of Christ.

post-Hegelian theologians, Catholic as well as Protestant, fail to engage in any sustained way with the tradition of the divine attributes of the one God received from the classical theological tradition, both patristic and medieval. What ought we to make today of the divine simplicity, goodness, unity, omnipotence, infinity, and so on? In that volume Barth engages in profound conversation with figures like Augustine, Boethius, and Aquinas in considering the Church's confession *de Deo uno*: on the oneness of God, in his freedom, eternity, sovereignty, universal presence, and other attributes. This reflection has a grounding in the classical tradition even as it engages with modern questions in a creative way. As such it can contribute to an ongoing discussion of the Church's common confession of the *unity* of the triune God, and the *real distinction* of the divine and human natures of the incarnate Lord. In pursuing such topics together, Protestant and Catholic theologians alike can contribute together in fraternal collaboration to the responsibilities and work of Christology. This example is interesting because it suggests that sometimes Catholics can also allow themselves to be inspired or provoked by Protestant theologians so as to recover profound elements of their own tradition, and in doing so, rethink their content and expression in a contemporary setting. This kind of ecumenical practice can also invite non-Catholic Christians to consider anew the depths and specific doctrinal and philosophical content of the Catholic tradition, as well as to think with and for Catholics about how the classical truths of conciliar theology may be exclaimed today with renewed understanding and vigor.

CHAPTER 6

"His claim upon our whole life"

The Revelational-Exegetical Politics of the Barmen Declaration and the Declaration on the Russian World Teaching

Brandon Gallaher

INTRODUCTION

There has been growing interest in the last decade in the links between modern Eastern Orthodox theology and the work and legacy of Karl Barth. Much of this work has, up until now, focused almost entirely on the historical engagement of Barth with leading Russian theologians and philosophers (such as Sergii Bulgakov, Georges Florovsky, and Nikolai Berdyaev) and the conceptual points of contact between Barth's theology and the broader Russian and Orthodox traditions.[1] Furthermore, much of this work has been profoundly influenced by the historical-theological style of Bruce L. McCormack as well as his major theological concerns (e.g., election and the Trinity, Christology, and theological epistemology and methodology). What has been less well documented is the profound influence of Barth and Barthian theology on Eastern Orthodox political theology. This is especially evident in the legacy of the Barmen Declaration (1934). Its model of a revelational and exegetical confessional politics has echoed far beyond the synod of the German Evangelical Church in late May 1934 as it stood up to National Socialism. This essay will

---

1. See Baker, "Offenbarung, Philosophie, und Theologie"; Moyse et al., *Correlating Sobornost*; Gallaher, *Freedom and Necessity in Modern Trinitarian Theology*; Valliere, "Influence of Russian Religious Thought on Western Theology in the Twentieth Century"; Zwahlen, "Da ili Net"; Zwahlen, "Over a Beer with Barth and Bulgakov."

argue that it has gone on to change the face of the Orthodox churches in Ukraine and beyond.

In this essay, I will first outline the March 2022 "Declaration on the Russian World (*Russkii Mir*) Teaching," drafted in reaction to the Russian Orthodox Church's ideological underwriting of both the regime of Vladimir Putin and the Russian invasion of Ukraine. I will then explore the Barmen Declaration by giving a sketch of its historical context and contents and highlighting some of its major theological points, before making a comparative study of both.

THE DECLARATION ON THE RUSSIAN WORLD TEACHING

On March 13, 2022, the Sunday of Orthodoxy, the beginning of Orthodox Lent, seventy-five Orthodox theologians and scholars from around the world issued a theological declaration that draws on many sources, including the Barmen Declaration, entitled "A Declaration on the Russian World (*Russkii Mir*) Teaching." The declaration is structured, following Barmen, in terms of six theses headed by citations from Scripture, followed by affirmations of Orthodox teaching and negations or anathemas of heterodox or heretical teaching. It was published simultaneously on the websites of the Orthodox Christian Studies Center at Fordham University and the Volos Academy for Theological Studies in Greece, and has garnered over fifteen hundred signatories from every Christian tradition and nation and been translated into twenty-one languages.[2] The text has obtained media attention globally, unprecedented for a theological text, and inspired multiple international initiatives responding to the Russian Church's involvement in the war in Ukraine. It was directed against the ethnophyletist and nationalist "Russian world" ideology that, the text argues, serves as the religious underpinning for Vladimir Putin's invasion of Ukraine on February 24, 2022. This ideology, as the text also contends, is fundamentalist in character and was developed by Patriarch Kirill (Gundiaev) of Moscow and All Rus' (the head or primate of the Russian Orthodox Church, Moscow Patriarchate); both Putin and Patriarch Kirill repeatedly reference it in their active support of the Russian invasion. Having briefly outlined this Russian world ideology, the declaration identifies the ideology's main propositions, which are declared

2. Gallaher and Kalaitzidis, "Declaration on the 'Russian World'" (*Mission World*).

"heretical" from an Orthodox theological perspective. By contrast, the Orthodox scholars systematically outline affirmations drawn primarily from Scripture as witnessing to Orthodox Christianity. Finally, the declaration calls all to be mindful of the theological principles outlined in their reflections on and decisions in church politics.[3]

Within days of its publication, scholars, particularly from Protestant backgrounds in the USA and the UK, and especially throughout the German-speaking world, declared the declaration on the Russian World teaching to be an "Orthodox Barmen." Certainly, this declaration is not the first text that has been inspired by Barmen. Here one also thinks of the Hong Kong Pastors Network's Hong Kong 2020 Gospel Declaration in response to the actions of the government of China during the Umbrella Movement. But why would the Orthodox, not known for their sympathy with Barth or Reformed theology, draw on Barmen in responding to the war in Ukraine? To answer this we first need an overview of Barmen, which may give us some sense why it has been drawn on in the contemporary period.

BARMEN DECLARATION: A HISTORICAL OVERVIEW

The Theological Declaration of Barmen was written by the Confessing Christians who met at the synod of Barmen (Wuppertal) in May 1934 in reaction to the German Christian Movement which had brought Nazi ideology into German Protestantism. The Confessing Christians were a group of Lutheran, Reformed, and United churches that began to coalesce in the period following Hitler's appointment as chancellor on January 30, 1933, to lead a Nazi-Conservative coalition government. Barth and his circle, including Fritz Lieb (who was, incidentally, Barth's key link to the world of Russian Orthodox theologians),[4] were horrified as they listened to the proceedings on the radio, with the Nazis marching through Berlin in a torchlit parade. Barth was ill at that time but said in retrospect that he immediately knew where he stood and what he had to do, because "I saw my dear German people beginning to worship a false

---

3. In full disclosure, I was one of seven core drafters of the text and, with Pantelis Kalaitzidis, a coordinator of the drafting committee.

4. See Iantsen, "Pisma Russkikh Myslitelei v Bazel'skom Archive Fritsa Liba."

God."⁵ What was clear from Hitler's speech the next day was that he saw Christianity and the Christian church as simply a vehicle for the spirit of the German people as led by himself. Hitler says:

> We are filled with unbounded confidence for we believe in our people and their imperishable virtues. Every class and individual must help us to found the new Reich. The National Government will regard it as its first and foremost duty to revive in the nation the spirit of unity and co-operation. It will preserve and defend those basic principles on which our nation has been built. It regards Christianity as the foundation of our national morality, and the family as the basis of national life.⁶

Barth feared, and his fear only increased after he read Hitler's work *Mein Kampf* (1925), that the path of National Socialism would lead to the gradual assimilation of the church, its message, and its life into the Nazi state.⁷ Later during the Second World War, he would reflect on Nazism as a "heathenish religion of blood, despotism [*Autorität*] and war,"⁸ with the church offered a "'German Faith' based on old German paganism. In this cult the mystical personage 'Germany' took the place of the Godhead, Führer Adolf Hitler became the prophet, and the church services were replaced by rites exalting the German national character."⁹

In these early months, Barth began to develop his position against this feared apostasy and the assimilation of the church to the state, a position in which there was an absolute opposition to all forms of natural theology, and to any attempt to found theology and the proclamation of the church on anything other than the one Word of God, Jesus Christ. Indeed, in June 1933 he arranged a working group on the Fourteen Düsseldorf Theses, which was a theological declaration on the form of the church. The first thesis would later be rearticulated at Barmen: "The holy Christian Church, whose sole head is Christ, is born of the Word of God, keeps to it and does not hearken to the voice of the stranger."¹⁰ Again, a few months earlier in March 1933, in a lecture on "The First Commandment as a Theological Axiom" he warned Christians not to hanker after other gods than the one true God revealed in Jesus Christ and so to

---

5. Busch, *Karl Barth*, 223.
6. Hitler, "Proclamation to the German Nation, February 1, 1933," 144.
7. Busch, *Karl Barth*, 223.
8. Barth, *Letter to Great Britain from Switzerland*, 6.
9. Barth, *Church and the War*, 7.
10. Busch, *Karl Barth*, 225.

connect the concept of revelation with other authorities which are then elevated—such as human existence, order, the state, the people, and, one might add, the word of any preeminent leader. One must instead say farewell "to any and every kind of natural theology, and . . . dare to trust only in the God who has revealed himself in Jesus Christ."[11] Later in April 1941, writing from Switzerland (having resigned from Bonn in 1935 after refusing to swear an oath to Hitler), he pleaded with those in Great Britain experiencing the Blitz, using Barmen as an example, not to attempt to refute Nazism on the basis of natural law but only on the confession of Christ from the "Ecumenical Creed" since the only "really sure foundation" to build resistance to Hitler was to "resist him unequivocally in the name of [a] peculiarly Christian truth, unequivocally in the name of Jesus Christ." Barth observed that all arguments based on natural law were "Janus-headed. They do not lead to the light of clear decisions, but to the misty twilight in which all cats become grey. They lead to—Munich [Agreement, 1938: i.e., Appeasement]."[12]

The warnings of March 1933 were needed as in these same days the German Christian Movement was gathering its strength. In April 1933 there were calls by the church leaders of this new movement for the assimilation of the church to the Nazi state, and Hitler chose Ludwig Müller (1883–1945), a nonentity of a naval chaplain, to have full powers in church affairs. The churches were being pressured to "aryanize," to expel Jewish Christians from ordained ministry and to adopt the "Führer Principle" in church government. The Führer Principle argued that Hitler's word was above all written law and that all government policies, decisions, and offices should enact his sacred word. Every organization in society needed to have one leader heeding Hitler as the Führer. There was a demand for a Reich bishop, but when the Nazis did not have their desired candidate appointed as bishop, they abolished constitutional freedom of religion and overrode the various religious organizations, claiming that the election of the non-Nazi-friendly candidate Friedrich von Bodelschwingh (1877–1946) had contravened the constitutions of the various Protestant churches and directly appointing the magistrate August Jäger (1887–1949) as the new state commissar for the Prussian Church on June 24, 1933.[13] Barth noted at the time that this move to "assimilation" (*Gleichschaltung*) of the church to the German state directly

---

11. Busch, *Karl Barth*, 224.
12. Barth, *Letter to Great Britain from Switzerland*, 17.
13. Busch, *Karl Barth*, 226.

contradicted Hitler's promises the previous March that "the rights of the Churches will not be diminished, nor their position as regards the State be altered."[14] With the church's reform and its pronouncements being always preceded by "political Preambles" Barth had to conclude that she "had listened to the voice of a stranger, i.e., not to the voice of the Word of God, but to the voice of human judgement."[15]

Barth, in response to these events, wrote in *Theological Existence Today* on the eve of June 25, 1933, that the teachings of the German Christians were "heresy," including the determination of church membership by race and blood, for the "Church has not to be at the service of mankind, and so, not of the German people."[16] The church is compelled to proclaim the Gospel in all the kingdoms of this world, not just Germany, and to preach it "also *in* the Third Reich, but not *under* it, nor in *its* spirit." The fellowship of the church "is not determined by blood, therefore, not by race, but by the Holy Spirit and Baptism."[17] Barth emphasized that we could "have no other gods than God, that holy scripture was enough to guide the Church into all truth, that the grace of Jesus Christ was enough to forgive ours sins and to order our life."[18] Gradually, especially toward the end of 1933, an organized opposition to the German Christians started to gather, first with the Pastors' Emergency League of Martin Niemöller (1892–1984) and then with the Confessing Church.

By late May 1934 there was sufficient unity across the multiple churches comprising the Confessing Church to call a synod of all the churches from across Germany to confront the new heresies being promoted by the German Christian Movement. What they agreed on was that Hitler was no revelation of God; that God's Law was not to be accounted equivalent to the "hour of the Germans"; that the church of Jesus Christ was not to be subject to the Führer Principle; that the state was not the single totalitarian order of human life; and that the church must not place itself in the service of external and arbitrarily chosen desires and plans.[19]

14. Barth, *Theological Existence To-Day*, 24.
15. Barth, *Theological Existence To-Day*, 27–28.
16. Barth, *Theological Existence To-Day*, 51.
17. Barth, *Theological Existence To-Day*, 52.
18. Busch, *Karl Barth*, 227.
19. Wolf Krötke, "Historical Overview of the Barmen Theological Declaration of 1934," in Dallmayr, *Legacy of the Barmen Declaration*, 41–42.

In preparation of a document for the synod, Barth, representing the Reformed Church, famously met with the Lutherans Thomas Breit and Hans Asmussen at a hotel in Frankfurt. The Lutherans had a three-hour nap, and Barth claims that instead of napping he drafted the Barmen Declaration. Research over the last four decades has confirmed Barth's claim for primary authorship,[20] though has somewhat nuanced his rather pleased account: "The Lutheran Church slept and the Reformed Church kept awake.... I revised the text of the six statements fortified by strong coffee and one or two Brazilian cigars.... The result was that by that evening there was a text. I don't want to boast, but it was really my text."[21] He claims that the Lutherans, who later also pushed on both the issue of Christ being proclaimed in Word and sacrament and the issue of church and state, refused to call the text a confession: it had real anathemas incorporated into the six theses or articles like a confession, accepting and rejecting doctrine as heretical, but they said it was to be a mere "theological declaration."[22] The synod proper was held from May 29–31, 1934, and accepted the text on May 30. It was discussed deep into the night, resulting in the nuancing of various clauses, especially the third thesis on Christ acting in Word and Sacrament through the Holy Spirit. The final text was passed unanimously on May 31 at 11:30 a.m., with the synod members rising spontaneously and singing the third verse of the great seventeenth-century Lutheran hymn by Martin Rinkart (1586–1649) ("Nun danket alle Gott"): "All praise and thanks to God / the Father now be given, / the Son, and Him who reigns / with them in highest heaven, / the one, eternal God, / whom earth and heaven adore; / for thus it was, is now, and shall be evermore. Amen."[23]

BARMEN DECLARATION: AN INTERPRETATION

At the core of the drafters' concern, as just mentioned, was to emphasize that Hitler and the state more broadly were in no way a revelation of God, that his word was not the Word of God, and that the state itself, besides its appointed task of providing justice and peace in an unredeemed world,

---

20. Derek Woodard-Lehman, "Democratic Faith: Barth, Barmen, and the Politics of Reformed Confession," in Dallmayr, *Legacy of the Barmen Declaration*, 56 (for a summary of the scholarship).

21. Busch, *Karl Barth*, 245.

22. Busch, *Karl Barth*, 245.

23. Busch, *Karl Barth*, 246.

was not "the single and totalitarian order of human life, thus fulfilling the Church's vocation as well."[24] Only the one Word of God, Jesus Christ, attested in Scripture, had a total claim upon the whole of human lives with his Reich or Kingdom of God, commandment and justice. In short, in contemporary terms, Barmen was a Christian theological statement against totalitarianism and the attempt of a political order and ruler to subsume the total claim of the Gospel upon human life.

It is for this reason that the first thesis is key for it asserts that only Jesus Christ is the way, the truth, and the life by whom we know the Father, the door of salvation, citing John 14 and 10: only *this Jesus* "is the one Word of God" whom we must hear and which we must trust and obey in life and death.[25] Barth, in his subsequent reflection on Barmen,[26] is very clear that we are dealing with a confession of the church, despite the aforementioned Lutheran reservations about this term. Barth understood the church as the "community of hearing and receiving" the Word of God, divine revelation, as it is given to us through Scripture, and by confessing the church makes known the faith which it has received by and from the Word of God.[27] This Word is both jealous and absolutely dynamic and living and it will not brook any other foundation for the faith it gifts to the church. Hence the negation or anathema is equally clear in its rejecting the "false doctrine" that the church might have and might "acknowledge as a source of its proclamation" apart from the Word "still other events and powers, figures and truths, as God's revelation,"[28] such as the word of Hitler or the voice of the German people. There is no other foundation . . .

Barth saw all confession as involving the church: on the basis of a "definite exegesis of Scripture,"[29] it represented a setting up of limits to teaching and thereby a making of doctrinal decisions in articulating dogma. This was particularly crucial when a new false dogma arose—as

---

24. Evangelical Synod 1934, "Theological Declaration of Barmen," in Dallmayr, *Legacy of the Barmen Declaration*, 8.23, 18.

25. Evangelical Synod 1934, "Theological Declaration of Barmen," in Dallmayr, *Legacy of the Barmen Declaration*, 8.11, 17.

26. *CD* I/2 (original text published 1938), with Barmen references found throughout §20 on "Holy Scripture" in its discussion of "Authority in the Church," for example, at 628, 630.

27. *CD* I/2, 588.

28. Evangelical Synod 1934, "Theological Declaration of Barmen," in Dallmayr, *Legacy of the Barmen Declaration*, 8.12, 17.

29. *CD* I/2, 628.

Barth explicitly says is the case with the German Christians turning to other events and powers, figures and truths, as God's revelation.[30] Bluntly: Barth regarded the assimilation of Nazism in the church as involving a new heretical dogma. The church gathers, as it gathered in synod at Barmen, whenever the existing confession of the common faith and with it the standard exegesis of Scripture are thrown into question, because with this throwing into question, the unity of the faith and the unity of the church are simultaneously attacked. Therefore the unity of faith must be rediscovered through an exegetical process involving "definite antithesis and conflict,"[31] a Yes or theological affirmation and a No or anathema, both of which are equally important. A Yes is issued which involves scriptural exegesis and doctrine positively stated, and a definite No "is said to the counter doctrine."[32] Upon Barmen's first confession in Christ as the wholly sufficient revelational foundation given to us in the witness of Scripture in thesis 1 there follow the subsequent theses, and here the declaration gradually enters the political realm. In the second thesis, Barmen asserts that in the revelation of Christ we know God's will for us, which is our salvation and liberation in him who claims "our whole life" that frees us for grateful service. In turn, this negates the false teaching that there can be other "areas of our life" which do not belong to Christ but to other lords such as Hitler and the state or German culture and that these other areas could somehow stand apart from justification and sanctification in Christ.

Instead, and here we see in the next two theses (3 and 4) the political inching in yet further, the revelation of Christ shapes the church as the congregation in which he dwells as Lord through his Spirit in Word and sacrament. The church is solely his property and is called to testify to his Gospel in message and order in the midst of this sinful world, so that it is impossible that it might have another message or order and that its offices could somehow stand apart from service and witness to someone lording over others a power from an external source, when any dominion they have is given to them by the congregation that listens to God's Word. Thus, Barmen rejects the false teachings that the church can abandon the form of its message and order based on the prevailing ideological and political convictions of the day (Nazism) and that it can invest "special leaders" such as Hitler and his representative in the Reich bishop with

---

30. *CD* I/2, 628.
31. *CD* I/2, 629.
32. *CD* I/2, 630.

"HIS CLAIM UPON OUR WHOLE LIFE"

ruling powers apart from the ministry of Christ's church. This means that the Christian message cannot be simply adapted according to the needs of Nazi ideology and that neither Hitler nor his minions can be regarded as somehow standing over the church.

The final two theses are the most explicit politically and were contested by some who felt that the church had to leave the realm of civil society to be ruled by civil actors in a form of the Lutheran "two kingdoms" theology. It sadly leaves out any explicit or implicit critique of Nazi anti-Semitism or its cult of violence and war. Wolf Krötke noted that Barmen is "not a document of Christian resistance against a murderous ideology" and regarded this as a "limitation in the confession that we cannot be content with"; he posits that "if we take seriously the fundamental meaning of the theses of Barmen regarding the life of the church of Jesus Christ *in the world*, we shall have to go 'with Barmen and beyond Barmen.'"[33] Barth's silence on the murder of the Jews and the sacralization of violence in the service of the glorification of Germany was practically necessary because no text mentioning these matters would have been able to be passed at Barmen given the makeup of the synod: many were of two minds about Christian ties to the state and wishing to be quiet about politics in the face of the lawful rulers who wielded the sword of authority. The Lutheran pastor Hans Asmussen, who was one of the three primary drafters with Barth, and who snoozed for three hours while Barth worked, had insisted at the synod in the name of all the Confessing Church that the theological declaration "was not a protest against 'the recent history of the people'" or "against the new state" but simply aimed at the "preservation of the church," presumably from assimilation.[34] Barth, reflecting in May 1967 on this failure to stand up against the Holocaust (Dachau opened in March 1933), regarded the lack of tackling the "Jewish question" and of making it decisive in the "church conflict"—which he said Bonhoeffer was the first to do "so centrally and energetically"—as "a fault on my part."[35] He observed that even if the "confessors of that time" would have objected, it did not excuse the fact

---

33. Krötke, "Historical Overview," in Dallmayr, *Legacy of the Barmen Declaration*, 42–43.

34. Krötke, "Historical Overview," in Dallmayr, *Legacy of the Barmen Declaration*, 42–43.

35. "Letter to Rector Eberhard Bethge, May 22, 1967," in Barth, *Letters 1961–1968*, 250.

that he had not "formally put up a fight on the matter" because his "interests were elsewhere."[36]

The last theses also introduce an eschatological element that would be taken up by subsequent inheritors of Barmen. Thus, in the fifth thesis, on the basis of 1 Pet 2:17 ("Fear God. Honor the Emperor"), we are told that in the unredeemed world the state is called solely to provide "justice and peace," which it does by wielding the sword or force. The church certainly acknowledges this divinely appointed role and acknowledges the relationship of ruler and ruled with gratitude. It is a sort of shadow, a foretaste, of the Kingdom ("It calls to mind the Kingdom of God, God's commandment and righteousness")[37] but only of the true Kingdom which is to come and which is properly imaged by the church itself. Here Barmen rejects the false doctrine that the state can break out of its heavily delimited commission of allowing for "peace, order and good government" (to echo the Constitution of Canada) to "become the single and totalitarian order of human life, thus fulfilling the Church's vocation as well." The church cannot appropriate the characteristics, the tasks, and the dignity of the state without becoming an organ of the state, which is exactly what happened with the German Christians and their Nazi Church, and which is exactly the position that Barmen rejects.[38]

In a 1946 essay which reflects on Barmen, Barth says that it is above all the church which reminds humanity of God's Kingdom, which means that it does not expect the state to become that Kingdom. The Kingdom, on the contrary, is the redeemed world to come where there is no legislature, executive, and legal administration. It is the "world dominion of Jesus Christ in honour of the Father, revealed in the clear light of day." The state knows nothing of this reality and would be negating its purpose if it acted as if its role was to become the Kingdom of God. It is the vocation of the church to remind humanity of "Jesus Christ who came and is to come again," but it can never do this if it seeks, proposes, and attempts to enforce the state into the likeness of the Kingdom of God.[39]

---

36. "Letter to Rector Eberhard Bethge, May 22, 1967," in Barth, *Letters 1961-1968*, 250.

37. Evangelical Synod 1934, "Theological Declaration of Barmen," in Dallmayr, *Legacy of the Barmen Declaration*, 8.22, 18.

38. Evangelical Synod 1934, "Theological Declaration of Barmen," in Dallmayr, *Legacy of the Barmen Declaration*, 8.23, 18.

39. Barth, "Christian Community," 167-68.

And here we reach the sixth and final thesis, where the church is commissioned to deliver the message of the free grace of God in Jesus Christ to all people "in the ministry of [Christ's] own Word and work through sermon and sacrament."[40] In the political sphere, Barth tells us many years later, the Christian community can draw attention to the Gospel only indirectly, by witnessing to Christian truths[41] and above all by the "prophetically political" message that it preaches of the "King and the Kingdom that is now hidden but one day will be revealed."[42]

So we see in Barmen a form of political theology that is based on a definite exegesis of Scripture, founded on the sole basis of revelation in Jesus Christ attested in that Scripture and with a decrying of any attempt by the state and by the church to collapse the church into the state so that the Kingdom of God somehow becomes immanentized in culture and political order. What Barth called for was an eschatological form of politics in which, through exegesis, the revelation of God was witnessed to and the affirmation was made of the Kingdom as a coming reality of Christ, in which we would reign with the Father through the Spirit.

THE DECLARATION ON THE RUSSIAN WORLD: THE IDEOLOGY

But how was this taken up later by 2022's Orthodox Christian Declaration on the Russian World? I want to argue, as indeed is also contended by the declaration itself, that both the Russian Church and state now have a common ideology called *Russkii mir* or the "Russian world teaching" which is the ideological rationalization for the Russian invasion of Ukraine.[43] In order to understand how Barmen was utilized by the declaration, we need to first have a grasp of the main lines of the Russian world ideology.

Russkii mir teaches that there is a transnational Russian sphere or Russian world that includes Russia, Ukraine, and Belarus (and sometimes Moldova and Kazakhstan are added along with the Baltic countries) but

---

40. Evangelical Synod 1934, "Theological Declaration of Barmen," in Dallmayr, *Legacy of the Barmen Declaration*, 8.26, 19.

41. Barth, "Christian Community," 183.

42. Barth, "Christian Community," 184–85.

43. For further discussion on the Russian world ideology (with references), see Gallaher: "Road from Rome to Moscow"; "Tale of Two Speeches," 2:819–24; "Pure Signifier of Power."

also ethnic Russians and Russian-speaking peoples in Western Europe, North and South America, and Japan. It holds that the Russian world has a common political center (Moscow), a common language (viz. Russian—I have often encountered the view among some Russians that Ukrainian is not a "real language" but just a dialect of Russian), a common spiritual center (Kiev—the "mother of all Rus"), a common church with a common patriarch (the Moscow Patriarchate with its primate Patriarch Kirill of Moscow *and All Rus'*) who works in "symphony" with a common tsar/president/great leader (Putin), and common moral values, art, spiritual vision, and even financial system. The different nations and peoples of the unified Russian world—from Russia, Ukraine, and Belarus to Kazakhstan, Moldova, and even Latvia—Patriarch Kirill says "belong to a single, unique civilizational space within which values, knowledge, and experience have accumulated that have always helped our peoples occupy a worthy place in the human family."[44] The Russian world, it is alleged, stands against the corrupt "Collective West" which is bedeviled by "radical secularism," being characterized by "alternative lifestyles" and pervasive "gay parades," and which, it is asserted repeatedly, has lost its spiritual center and is a plaything of the corrupt and lying Americans and the equally perverse European Union.[45]

With *Russkii mir* a vague Christian teaching on the sacred nature of the nation has been collapsed into a far-right political, ethnic, and religious ideology with a mythological renarration of history that fits a vision of an eternal holy Russian Empire. This ideology is a form of ethno-national religious fundamentalism, in contemporary Western terms, "Christian nationalism," with an appeal to blood, soil, faith, nation, people, a great tsar/leader, and especially the Russian language. Unlike some other ethno- and Christian nationalisms, which appeal to a very specific race or ethnos and one tightly defined nation state, the Russian world ideology is a form of civilizational nationalism where the "Russian land" and its all-embracing traditional Christian culture, language, and vision embrace many diverse peoples beyond the Russian Federation as "Russian." The Russian world ideology might, as Paul Gavrilyuk has argued, be seen as a new Nazi ideology for the twenty-first century,[46] and much of the behavior of the Russian state—from its mass "Z" cult

---

44. Gundiaev, "Address at the Grand Opening of the Third Assembly of the Russian World (November 3, 2009)," 59.

45. See Gallaher, "Tale of Two Speeches."

46. Gavrilyuk: "Hitler and Putin"; "Moral Defeat of the Russian World."

seen in rallies and schools to the advocating of something like Ukrainian genocide⁴⁷—increasingly seems totalitarian in character and is reminiscent of the Nazis.

The ideology of *Russkii mir* proper was developed first in the early 1990s by liberal Russian intellectuals looking for an ideology to bring together a fragmented post-Soviet landscape, drawing on the work of multiple figures—from the nineteenth-century Slavophiles and early twentieth-century Eurasians to political philosophers like Ivan Ilyin (1883–1954) and Aleksandr Dugin (b. 1962).⁴⁸ It was then taken up by Russian government figures in the early 2000s, assisted by the Church. The Russkii Mir Foundation, started in 2007 by the Russian government, has been the main soft-power vehicle of the ideology (with centers funded at the Universities of Edinburgh and Durham). It encourages worldwide Russian language, culture, and heritage as a "global project" with "interaction with the Russian Orthodox Church and other faiths in promoting the Russian language and the culture of Russia."⁴⁹ The English part of the site notes that the Russian diaspora is made up of the "largest diaspora population the world has ever known."⁵⁰ The Russian site is even more expansive in describing the *Russkii mir*:

> The Russian world is not only ethnic Russians, not only Russian citizens, not only our fellow compatriots in countries near and far abroad, emigrants, immigrants from Russia and their descendants. These are also foreign citizens who speak Russian, study or teach it, all those who are sincerely interested in Russia, who are concerned about its future.... The Russian world is the world of Russia. The calling of every person is to help his fatherland and take care of his neighbor. Very often you hear what a country could do for its people. But just as important is what each of us can do for our Motherland. We should turn from the spirit of parasitic dependency to the idea of serving Russia.⁵¹

The ideology was taken up in earnest, collaborating with the state, by ideologues in the Russian Church from the early 2000s, especially

---

47. Sergeitsev, "RIA NOVOSTI Has Clarified Russia's Plans Vis-à-Vis Ukraine and the Rest of the Free World in a Program Like Article."

48. See Aleinikova, *"Russkii Mir": Belorusskii Vzgliad* [Russian world: A Belarussian perspective].

49. Russkii Mir.

50. Russkii Mir.

51. Russkii Mir.

Patriarch Kirill, who hoped that the Russian Church might provide the common ideological foundation for the nation. This latter ecclesification of the concept of the Russian world tracked with the political rise of Putin and his instrumentalization of Orthodoxy, and there is now a growing literature studying this "ideology" or "initiative" as part of the nationalist drive in post-Soviet Russian history.[52] However, a minority of scholars, in some cases Western Slavists and often having strong personal and professional ties to the Moscow Patriarchate, have declared the ideology of the Russian world not a "heresy" (as the declaration does) but a "political doctrine" which is a collocation of quite common nostalgic nationalist ideas that have been weaponized in the Russian invasion;[53] a "myth" having no real coherence to even count as a "teaching/doctrine" or an "ideology" (let alone a "heresy") so having no contemporary relevance in Russia and not helping to explain the war in Ukraine;[54] and, finally, with considerably more sophistication, not a "heresy" or a distinct "ideology" but a collection of ideas forming one prop of a much larger "ideology of holy war" which forms part of post-Soviet Russian identity.[55]

Orthodoxy has long struggled with the danger of ethno-phyletism, that is, the theological tendency to confuse the church with a particular race, tribe, and (recently) nation by divinizing a particular nation, culture, and political order into a sacred order that swallows up the Christian Gospel. Ethno-phyletism is anti-eschatological in character as it collapses the Kingdom of Jesus Christ which is to come with the kingdoms and worldly divisions of this fallen world. In order to appeal to Orthodox tradition and to show canonically that in the case of the

52. Denysenko, "Fractured Orthodoxy in Ukraine and Politics"; Chapnin, "Church of Empire"; Pieper, "Russkiy Mir"; Suslov, "Russian Orthodox Church and the Crisis in Ukraine"; Hovorun, "Interpreting the 'Russian World'"; Denysenko, *Church's Unholy War*.

53. Shishkov, "Some Reflections on the Declaration on the 'Russian World.'" The writer goes further and claims the "Declaration on the 'Russian World'" is no Barmen Declaration but a paternalist and colonialist ploy by Western theologians further silencing repressed Russians. This sort of critique, dependent on notions of authenticity and the cultural and theological preeminence of Orthodox nation churches and having little understanding of "pan-Orthodoxy," has also been recycled by non-Orthodox scholars connected to the University of Münster.

54. Bremer, "Mythos 'Russische Welt'"; and see his earlier article, "Diffuses Konzept." Bremer is an opponent of the war but has received vocal criticisms from multiple Ukrainian scholars, for both his claim that the "Russian world ideology" does not exist and his support of the religious rights of the Ukrainian Orthodox Church (UOC-MP) with its critique of the Orthodox Church of Ukraine (OCU).

55. Griffin, "Russian World or Holy World War?"

Russian world teaching we were dealing with not only a tendency but a positive heresy, the declaration appeals to the Council of Constantinople of September 1872, which condemned as a heresy the ethnic organization of the church.[56] For centuries the Bulgarian Orthodox living in the Ottoman Empire were under the jurisdiction of the Ecumenical Patriarchate, which sadly forced on the unhappy Bulgarians the Greek language and practices. In early 1870, the Ottoman Sultan created a new Bulgarian Exarchate that was ethnically ordered and constituted and was transnational in reach, extending beyond traditional Bulgarian territory. Most dangerously, if a diocese had two-thirds of its inhabitants who were ethnic Bulgarians, then it could be transferred to the new exarchate. The Bulgarians saw their new church as the reestablishment of their ancient patriarchate that had been suppressed centuries before, while Constantinople and the other churches (Alexandria, Antioch, and Cyprus–Jerusalem refused to sign and left the council) saw it as a schism and a heresy. The Council of 1872 condemned the introduction into the church of "the idea of phyletism, or the national Church . . . an unauthorized and unprecedented Church assembly, based upon the principle of the difference of races." In its first article, it goes beyond the mere condemnation of an ethnically based polity and more generally condemns the false teaching of phyletism: "We censure, condemn, and declare contrary to the teachings of the Gospel and the sacred canons of the holy Fathers the doctrine of phyletism, or the difference of races and national diversity in the bosom of the Church of Christ."[57]

Russkii Mir—Vladimir Putin

But let us give concrete examples in both Putin and Patriarch Kirill of the Russian world ideology we have just sketched. Putin, it is arguable, is essentially enforcing membership in his mythical Holy Rus' or Russian world on Ukraine by the sword. Mythical geography with a mythically unified Russian people has become a weapon for Putin against real nations with real borders, cultures, and peoples. In Putin's speech

---

56. See Namee, "'Bulgarian Question' and the 1872 Council of Constantinople," pts. 1 and 4; Stamatopoulos, "Orthodox Ecumenicity and the Bulgarian Schism"; Todorov, "Historiographical Rethinking of the Bulgarian Schism (1872) Through the Postsecular Perspective."

57. See Namee, "'Bulgarian Question' and the 1872 Council of Constantinople," pt. 4.

on February 21, 2022, just days before Russia invaded Ukraine, Putin argued that Ukraine is a "fake" country created by Lenin. This is because Ukraine is really part of the same common Russian world, and so should legitimately be part of the Russian Federation, as can be seen in the common Russian religious and cultural nexus shared by Ukraine with Russia:

> I would like to emphasise again that Ukraine is not just a neighbouring country for us. It is an inalienable part of our own history, culture and spiritual space. These are our comrades, those dearest to us . . . relatives, people bound by blood, by family ties. Since time immemorial, the people living in the south-west of what has historically been Russian land have called themselves Russians and Orthodox Christians.[58]

This appeal to the Russian world teaching is not an isolated statement from Putin. In his July 2021 essay "On the Historical Unity of Russians and Ukrainians," which arguably might be seen as his most important ideological rationale for the invasion of February 2022, Putin argues that a common sacred ethnic-spiritual bond unites all those who are descendants of Rus'. More disturbingly, and here we see that *Russkii mir* is far from a harmless romantic or ordinary national doctrine according to which the church is the soul of the nation, Putin argues that the alleged forced assimilation of Russians to Ukrainian culture and the "ethnically pure Ukrainian state, aggressive towards Russia, is comparable in its consequences to the use of weapons of mass destruction against us."[59] He sees, in particular, an expression of this use of weapons of mass destruction in Russian assimilation to an ethnically pure Ukrainian state to lie in the founding by the Ecumenical Patriarchate in January 2019 of the Orthodox Church of Ukraine (thus undermining the centuries-long hold of the Russian Orthodox Church, Moscow Patriarchate, over religious life in Ukraine).[60]

For Putin, alien or foreign or hostile cultures and peoples and an independent church apart from Russia in Ukraine are identical to the exploding of a missile or weapon of mass destruction. They are simply different versions of weapons to be used against Holy Rus'. It is clear how Russia's military aggression follows from this Russian world doctrine since, for Putin, ideas and cultures are weapons, and the existence of a

---

58. Putin, "Address by the President of the Russian Federation."
59. Putin, "On the Historical Unity of Russians and Ukrainians."
60. For commentary, see Gallaher, "Pure Signifier of Power," 183–87.

separate Ukrainian state, people, language, and culture that contradicts Russian hegemony is for him the enactment of violence which can only be met with violence in turn. Here there is a clear link between the ideology of Putin and his bombardment of Mariupol or the horrors of Bucha.

Russkii Mir—Patriarch Kirill

As I have argued above, you see this ideology also throughout the statements of major leaders of the Moscow Patriarchate, who *actively* helped to create the ideology acting as a soft-power instrument of the Kremlin. Indeed, Patriarch Kirill (Gundiaev) of Moscow even published a separate book of his multiple talks from 2012–15 on the subject—with the general theme of the borderless cultural and spiritual identity and unity of the Russian world roughly mapping on to the former Soviet Union. The work is called *Seven Speeches on the Russian World* and includes talks "On Russian Unity," "On the Boundaries of Russian Statehood," and "On Russians in the Caucasus."[61] In a 2009 speech at the Third Assembly of the Russkiy Mir Foundation, Patriarch Kirill (whose title is of Moscow and All Rus') gives one of the clearest articulations of the Russian world teaching:

> It is necessary in this context to understand clearly what we mean by the Russian world today. It seems to me that if we regard the Russian Federation within its current borders as the sole center of the Russian world, then we sin against historical truth and artificially cut ourselves off from many millions of people who are aware of their responsibility for the fate of the Russian world and consider its construction the chief cause of their life. The core of the Russian world today is Russia, Ukraine, and Belorussia. The Holy Reverend Lavrentii Chernigovskii expressed this idea in the well-known sentence: "Rus, Ukraine, and Belarus—that is Holy Rus."[62]

For Patriarch Kirill, certain common values characterize Holy Rus', including "religious faith and interreligious peace, freedom and the moral transformation of the personality, self-sacrifice for others, a strong family, respect for elders, *sobornal* decision-making and decision-taking, creativity, hard work, justice, love for the Fatherland, care for creation."

61. Gundiaev, *Sem' Slov' o Russkom Mire*.
62. Gundiaev, "Address at the Grand Opening of the Third Assembly of the Russian World (November 3, 2009)," 58.

Russian culture is characterized by "the principles and forms of social life, and also the unique features of lifestyle" that are "formed under the influence of the Russian system of values." The peoples making up Holy Rus' are united and holy, insofar as they have a common spiritual task, by this common system of values and their collective task of effecting their "incarnation in history."[63]

The spiritual unity of Holy Rus' has come about through what has been widely asserted in Russia to be a second Christianization of Rus' following the collapse of communism after 1991. This has been deemed just as "providential" as the baptism the nation underwent with the conversion of St. Prince Vladimir of Kiev (ca. 960–1015). Kiev, as the mother of all Russian cities and indeed Russian civilization, serves as a sort of spiritual focus in *Russkii mir*, as it is held that Saint Vladimir established his ideal society there after his legendary baptism at Korsun or Chersonesus (in the Crimea) and with him came the baptism of All Rus'. We see some of this sacralizing of Rus' and of this mapping it on to Ukrainian geography in 2019 when Patriarch Kirill explained to multiple international Orthodox hierarchs who had gathered in Moscow that

> Ukraine is not a periphery of our Church. We call Kiev "the mother of all Russian cities"; for us Kiev is exactly what Jerusalem is for many people. From there Russian Orthodoxy began, and under no circumstances can we renounce this historical and spiritual bond. The unity of our whole Local Church is founded on this spiritual bond.[64]

This appeal to various parts of Ukraine as being a sort of Russian Holy Land for Rus' is far from an exception. President Putin in an address to the Federal Assembly in late 2014, explaining the significance of Crimea, which had been seized early 2014, said that "Crimea, the ancient Korsun or Chersonesus, and Sevastopol have invaluable civilisational and even sacral importance for Russia, like the Temple Mount in Jerusalem for the followers of Islam and Judaism. And this is how we will always consider it."[65] Returning to more recent times, just days after the Russian invasion

---

63. Gundiaev, "Vystuplenie Sviateishego Patriarkha Kirilla na otkryitii IV Assamblei Russkogo mira [Address of His Holiness Patriarch Kirill at the Opening of the Fourth Assembly of the Russian World]."

64. Gundiaev, "Sviateshii Patriarkh Kirill rasskazal delegatsiiam Pomestnykh Pravoslavnykh Tserkvei o situatsii na Ukraine [His Holiness Patriarch Kirill Told the Delegates of the Local Orthodox Churches Concerning the Situation in Ukraine]."

65. Putin, "Presidential Address to the Federal Assembly."

of Ukraine, on February 27, 2022, Patriarch Kirill in his initial homiletic response to the war (which term he did not use in this sermon) is even more explicit on the link between the "limited military operation" and his belief in Holy Rus'. What is notable here also is the citation (which we see frequently in Putin as well) of the twelfth-century legendarium, the Russian *Primary Chronicle* (or *Tale of Bygone Years*) that serves as a sort of alternative Holy Scripture for the Russian world teaching:

> God forbid that the present political situation in fraternal Ukraine so close to us should be aimed at making the evil forces that have always strived against the unity of Rus' and the Russian Church, gain the upper hand. . . . May the Lord protect from fratricidal battle the peoples comprising the one space of the Russian Orthodox Church. . . . May the Lord preserve the Russian land. When I say "Russian," I use the ancient expression from "A Tale of Bygone Years"—"Wherefrom has the Russian land come," the land' which now includes Russia and Ukraine and Belarus and other tribes and peoples.[66]

It was entirely natural that the Russian world teaching would eventually be expressed with changes to the liturgy in order to fully sacralize the teaching and incarnate it in the Russian people. On March 4, 2022, Patriarch Kirill ordered all his clergy worldwide to add an extra prayer to the liturgy, whose totality is entitled "Prayer for the Restoration of Peace," which includes this line: "Rebuke the foreign nations who want and take up arms against Holy Rus'! Prohibit and overthrow their plans!"[67] He then updated the prayer in September 2022 focusing on the "victory" of Rus' over its enemies in the "Prayer for Holy Rus." Multiple clergyman have been suspended or defrocked by the Moscow Patriarchate for refusing to say this prayer or replacing "victory" with "peace":

> O Lord God of might, God of our salvation, look with mercy upon Your humble servants, hear and have mercy upon us: behold, those wishing to fight turned against Holy Rus, wishing to divide and destroy its one nation. Rise, O God, to the aid of Thy people, and grant us Thy mighty victory. Assist your faithful children who are zealous for the unity of the Russian Church, and strengthen them in the spirit of brotherly love, and deliver them from their troubles. . . . Strengthen the soldiers and all

---

66. Gundiaev, "His Holiness Patriarch Kirill Calls on the Faithful to Pray for Peace and Unity of the Church."

67. Gundiaev, "Molitva o vosstanovlenii mira [Prayer for the restoration of peace]."

defenders of our homeland in Your commandments, give them the strength of spirit, and keep them from death, wounds, and captivity. . . . Give forgiveness of sins and blessed repose to all who were killed in these days, and of wounds and diseases. Fill us with the faith, hope, and love that we have in Thee; and raise up once more in all the countries of Holy Rus' peace and harmony.[68]

In this vein, and perhaps most infamously, as it attracted wide media attention worldwide, on Forgiveness Sunday (March 6, 2022) Patriarch Kirill preached that the present war had "metaphysical significance." The collective West, he claimed, was attempting to force on the locals in Donbass a "test of loyalty." This "test" was the demand that they hold gay pride parades. What was happening in Ukraine, therefore, was a matter of salvation, for Russia was having to defend itself as a holy nation.[69] In the months that followed Patriarch Kirill has doubled down on his Russian world rhetoric. He has routinely performed liturgies to support the military in the Armed Forces Cathedral, which has become infamous for its iconography celebrating war and the glory of Russia. On the Sunday of the Triumph of Orthodoxy on March 13, 2022, the patriarch gave a large wonder-working icon of the Mother of God, Our Lady of Augustow (fabled to have protected Russian soldiers in the First World War), to the head of the National Guard of Russia so that the forces might be victorious over the "Nazis" in Ukraine.[70] In a homily of September 2022, shortly after the "limited mobilization" of reservists by the Russian government, Patriarch Kirill claimed (reminiscent of Pope Urban II's plenary indulgence in 1095 before the First Crusade) that if a soldier dies fighting for Russia in Ukraine "we believe that this sacrifice washes away all the sins that a person has committed."[71] This statement is part of a larger theology of holy war and victory. Patriarch Kirill sees WWII ("the Great Patriotic War") as a sort of national crucifixion or Soviet Golgotha and wholesale Russian state and national redemption. He holds that those Soviets who

68. Russian Orthodox Church, "Molitva o Sviatoi Rusi"; translation in Paert, "How Do Orthodox Christians Pray in the Year 2022?"

69. Gundiaev, "'Patriarshaia propoved' v Nedeliu syropustnuiu posle Liturgii v Khrame Khrista Spasitelia [Patriarchal sermon on Cheesefare Week after the liturgy at the Cathedral of Christ the Savior]."

70. Denysenko, *Church's Unholy War*, 114.

71. Gundiaev, "'Patriarshaia propoved' v Nedeliu 15-iu po Piatidesiatnitse posle Liturgii v Aleksandro-Nevskom skitu [Patriarchal sermon on the 15th Sunday after Pentecost following the liturgy at the Alexander Nevsky Skete]."

perished in WWII were part of a providential plan in that they were sacrificed by God on the "altar of victory" so that the sins of the October Revolution and Stalinism could be forgiven. He thus identifies the sacrifice of the cross with the twenty-seven million deaths in WWII from the Soviet nation. The Main Cathedral of the Russian Armed Forces is the center and concretization of this new "cult" of Russian Orthodox Holy War.[72] On September 27, 2022, he claimed that "our spiritual mobilization, to which I now call everyone, will also help the mobilization of all the forces of our Fatherland. And it will undoubtedly help in the end the complete reconciliation of Russia and Ukraine, which constitute a single space of the Russian Orthodox Church."[73] On March 27, 2024, at the twenty-fifth World Russian People's Council in the Cathedral of Christ the Saviour in Moscow, the Russian Church formalized the *Russkii mir* doctrine in the text "The Present and Future of the Russian World." The Council was attended by sixty priests of the Moscow Patriarchate, twenty of its bishops (six of whom were permanent members of its synod, that is, half of that synod), having in attendance the then Defence Minister Shoigu and the philosopher Dugin and being chaired by Patriarch Kirill. The text, among other things, declared that Russia is the creator and supporter of the Russian world and that the special military operation is a Holy War, in which Russia and its people, defending the unified spiritual space of Russia, fulfill the mission of the "restraining force [*uderzhivaiushchii*]," protecting the world from the onslaught of globalism and the victory of the West that has fallen into Satanism.[74]

The patriarch, and many leading politicians in Russia today, see the present Ukraine conflict in apocalyptic terms and are using an obscure apocalyptic idea popular among the Orthodox far right (for example, Konstantin Malofeev and Aleksandr Dugin)[75] to argue that Russia is the defender of Christianity from hostile demonic forces. Russia is today attempting to return Europe to family values as it is caught by the forces of Satan (liberalism, secularism, pluralism, and so on) and fighting daily for

72. See Griffin, "Putin's Holy War of the Fatherland."

73. Gundiaev, "'Patriarshaia propoved' v prazdnik Vozdvizheniia Kresta Gospodnia posle Liturgii v Khrame Khrista Spasitelia [Patriarchal sermon on the Feast of the Exaltation of the Holy Cross following the liturgy at the Cathedral of the Christ the Saviour]."

74. World Russian People's Council 2024, "Nakaz XXV Vsemirnogo russkogo narodnogo sobora [Order of the XXV World Russian People's Council]"; commentary at Shumylo, "Ordinary Fascism."

75. See the website of their think tank, https://katehon.com/.

truth and virtue in Ukraine, just as Russia once "saved Europe" from the "Satanic forces of Nazism" in the Second World War (hence Ukrainians are portrayed as Nazis in the present conflict).[76] In late November 2022 at a reception for Patriarch Kirill's birthday in the Cathedral of Christ the Saviour, the patriarch called on the Church to play an active role in "the struggle of our Fatherland against Global evil" and in opposition to "this movement of the Antichrist, which is capable of destroying both the entire world and Russia." All of the forces of the antichrist, he claimed, would be directed at Russia, because Russia was the "restraining force [*uderzhivuaiushchii*]," as the apostle Paul (2 Thess 2:6: *to katechon*) had foretold, which was blocking the revelation and rise of the antichrist, "the man of lawlessness" (2 Thess 2:3). This Pauline power that restrains or hinders the appearance of the antichrist is traditionally interpreted by exegetes to mean the Roman emperor and the empire but, the patriarch noted in a sermon of April 2022, it had been extended by Russian philosophers to the Second and Third Romes (Byzantium and Moscow, respectively).[77] Here he is referencing the ideology of Russia as "Third Rome" of Filofei of Pskov (ca. 1465–1542).[78] In the April 2022 sermon, Patriarch Kirill claimed that the restraining force was also "the entire pious people of all times and all countries, it is the Orthodox faith which lives and acts in the Orthodox Church." And this, he opined, was why the enemies of the Church were attacking ecclesial unity. By the end of the year the Russian Church as the *katechon* seems to have been collapsed by Patriarch Kirill into the holy nation of Russia as the restraining force.[79]

This bellicose rhetoric, elaborate apocalyptic theology, and support of the Russian world teaching by Patriarch Kirill has led to a crisis in the Russian Orthodox Church.[80] The large and most faithful Ukrainian branch of some fifty-three dioceses and millions of faithful (Ukrainian Orthodox Church–Moscow Patriarchate) broke from Moscow on May 27, 2022, by declaring its independence, changing its name (removing reference to the Moscow Patriarchate), and stating that it disagreed with Patriarch Kirill, its ultimate head, on the war. There have also been

---

76. See Denysenko, *Church's Unholy War*, 70–71; Perrie, "Apocalypse Delayed." Compare Persh, "War and Eschatology."

77. Perrie, "Apocalypse Delayed."

78. See Poe, "Moscow, the Third Rome."

79. Perrie, "Apocalypse Delayed."

80. For the most detailed analysis and sources, see Denysenko, *Church's Unholy War*, 111–49.

protests by some Moscow Patriarchate priests against the war. The boldest initiative so far was undertaken in mid-April 2022 and was directly inspired by the Declaration on the Russian World that it cites, that is, an open letter penned by Fr. Andrey Pinchuk of Moscow Patriarchate Ukrainian Orthodox Church signed by 438 priests asking the Council of the Primates of the Ancient Eastern churches to try canonically Patriarch Kirill for both upholding heresy with the Russian world teaching and committing moral crimes in blessing the war. The bishops being appealed to are the leaders of the most ancient Orthodox churches: the Ecumenical Patriarchate based in Istanbul/Constantinople, Jerusalem, Alexandria, Antioch, and Cyprus. The letter of these Ukrainian priests references the 1666 canonical trial in Russia of Patriarch Nikon of Moscow and All Rus' (Patriarch Kirill's predecessor) at which the patriarchs of Antioch and Alexandria tried Nikon and deposed him at a council of bishops, making him into a simple monk. These Moscow patriarchal priests wish their own leader to be defrocked for his support of the war.[81] On July 27, 2022, Metropolitan Epiphanius of Kyiv and All Ukraine of the Orthodox Church of Ukraine, the rival to the Moscow patriarchal church newly established by the Ecumenical Patriarchate in 2019 (causing a schism between Moscow and multiple Orthodox churches who recognize the new church), wrote a synodal letter to Ecumenical Patriarch Bartholomew of Constantinople (with copies sent to all autocephalous churches). He asked him to initiate pan-Orthodox consideration and condemnation of Patriarch Kirill's schismatic and immoral activities and especially of his promotion of the ethno-phyletist and heretical and racist teaching of the Russian world teaching.[82] In 2023, the synod of the Patriarchate of Alexandria and Ecumenical Patriarch Bartholomew (in a speech) declared *Russkii mir* to be a "heresy." It does not seem so far a stretch to predict that soon world Orthodoxy will enter its most profound schism in many centuries over the issue of the Russian world teaching and ethno-phyletism more broadly. There will perhaps in the years to come be two Orthodox churches,[83] one established around the idea of the Russian world, ethno-phyletism, and Christian traditionalism led by the Moscow Patriarchate, and the other led by Constantinople

81. Pinchuk, "Open Appeal of the Priests of the UOC-MP to the Primates of Local Orthodox Churches."
82. Orthodox, "Head of the OCU."
83. Leustean, "Russia's Invasion of Ukraine."

rejecting this teaching and the general anti-Western and anti-modern stance of the Russian Church.

In my opinion, the Russian world ideology is a new form of religious fundamentalism which in practice has become a new form of twenty-first-century fascism. This ideology is being taken up and popularized by fundamentalist ideologues in Italy (the disgraced Catholic Archbishop Vigano) and in America (Rod Dreher, who advocates a culture war in the West). It is also found in multiple traditionally Orthodox countries in different forms where Russia is seen as a traditional family-friendly savior of Orthodoxy that can stand up to the tyranny and corruption of the West and its military expression in NATO. But let us now turn in detail to the declaration to see how it adapts Barmen in confronting a new Nazism with the Russian world teaching.

BARMEN MEETS ORTHODOXY: THE THEOLOGY OF THE DECLARATION ON THE RUSSIAN WORLD TEACHING

The Declaration on the Russian World Teaching—like Barmen, upon which it was consciously modeled—has the character of a quasi-confession of faith both affirming the essentials of Orthodox Christianity and negating those aspects which depart and contradict the essentials. As is the case with Barmen, it begins by affirming the centrality of Jesus Christ for the faith. After citing John 18, in which Jesus says that his Kingdom is not of this world, it affirms that Jesus Christ is the sole foundation of revelation and that one cannot turn to other sources to ground our affirmation of the Gospel. Here it identifies Jesus Christ with the Kingdom as witnessed in Scripture but, with an Orthodox twist, it asserts that this must be authoritatively interpreted by the Church fathers or in "Holy Tradition." Yet, differing from Barmen, though still in its spirit, it says that this Kingdom of Christ is given as a foretaste at the Divine Liturgy which announces the Kingdom of the Father, the Son, and the Holy Spirit (as every Orthodox liturgy begins). This is a clear reinterpretation of the first thesis of Barmen in Orthodox terms and bringing out the eschatological element in Barmen's final theses. It also is a negation of the idolatrous eschatology of Russia as the *katechon* of 2 Thessalonians that has been put forward in the Russian world teaching and a countering of it with a true Christ-centered apocalypticism:

> We affirm that the divinely appointed purpose and accomplishment of history, its *telos*, is the coming of the Kingdom of our Lord Jesus Christ, a Kingdom of righteousness, peace and joy in the Holy Spirit, a Kingdom attested by Holy Scripture as authoritatively interpreted by the Fathers. This is the Kingdom we participate in through a foretaste at every Holy Liturgy: "Blessed is the kingdom of the Father, the Son and the Holy Spirit, now and ever and unto ages of ages!" (Divine Liturgy). This Kingdom is the sole foundation and authority for Orthodox, indeed for all Christians. There is no separate source of revelation, no basis for community, society, state, law, personal identity and teaching, for Orthodoxy as the Body of the Living Christ than that which is revealed in, by, and through our Lord Jesus Christ and the Spirit of God.[84]

But like Barmen again, the declaration follows this affirmation with an anathema ("we condemn as Orthodox and reject"; earlier drafts used the word "anathematize"), rejecting the idea—and here it is also following Barth—that one can replace the church as a foretaste of the Kingdom which is to come with any earthly kingdom. The term "heresy" is used only once in the declaration ("Therefore, we reject the 'Russian world' heresy") to avoid unnecessarily inflaming matters and detracting from the focus on the content of the declaration. This has proved perhaps the most controversial inclusion with many liberal Orthodox critics of the Russian Church and Putin's regime rejecting the declaration as they argue that non-conciliar teachings on matters such as morality or politics (cf. conciliar teachings on topics such as Christology and Trinity) cannot by definition be "heresy." In response, the declaration's defenders have argued that the category of heresy is far broader and that the Russian world teaching looks for a revelational foundation other than Christ and his body the church. Furthermore, they have argued that the condemnation of *Russkii mir* includes all forms of Orthodox ethno-phyletism and is not just "de-platforming" and attacking Russia. The sacralization of earthly kingdoms is a perennial temptation for Orthodoxy. This is emphasized by the declaration's cover letter: "Nor can we fool ourselves that this ideology is an exception in the history of Orthodoxy: we must condemn all Orthodox ethno-phyletist ideologies akin to the false teaching of the 'Russian world' in every age, nation and culture."[85] Like Barmen,

---

84. Gallaher and Kalaitzidis, "Declaration on the 'Russian World'" (*Mission Studies*), §1, 273.

85. Gallaher and Kalaitzidis, "Declaration on the 'Russian World'" (*Mission Studies*),

the declaration holds that the church reminds humanity of "Jesus Christ who came and is to come again," but observes that it can never do this if it projects, proposes, and attempts to enforce the state into the likeness of the Kingdom of God and that it negates its calling if it obscures the fact that Christians are migrants and refugees in this world and have no continuing city but a city that is on high:

> We therefore condemn as non-Orthodox and reject any teaching that seeks to replace the Kingdom of God seen by the prophets, proclaimed and inaugurated by Christ, taught by the apostles, received as wisdom by the Church, set forth as dogma by the Fathers, and experienced in every Holy Liturgy, with a kingdom of this world, be that Holy Rus', Sacred Byzantium, or any other earthly kingdom, thereby usurping Christ's own authority to deliver the Kingdom to God the Father (1 Corinthians 15:24), and denying God's power to wipe away every tear from every eye (Revelation 21:4). We firmly condemn every form of theology that denies that Christians are migrants and refugees in this world (Hebrews 13:14), that is, the fact that "our citizenship is in heaven, and it is from there that we are expecting a Savior, the Lord Jesus Christ," (Philippians 3:20) and that Christians "reside in their respective countries, but only as sojourners. They take part in everything as citizens and put up with everything as foreigners. Every foreign land is their home, and every home a foreign land." (*The Epistle to Diognetus*, 5).[86]

In its second thesis, the declaration once more affirms, as does Barmen, that in anticipation of the King and his Kingdom, we affirm the "sole and ultimate authority of our Lord Jesus Christ."[87] Echoing Barmen's fifth thesis, it says that "earthly rulers provide peace, so that God's people might live 'calm and ordered lives, in all godliness and sanctity' (Divine Liturgy)."[88] But now echoing Barmen's fourth thesis on the independence of churchly offices and the self-integrity of the church it asserts that

---

270–71. See also Gallaher and Kalaitzidis, "Declaration on the 'Russian World'" (cover letter).

86. Gallaher and Kalaitzidis, "Declaration on the 'Russian World'" (*Mission Studies*), §1, 273.

87. Gallaher and Kalaitzidis, "Declaration on the 'Russian World'" (*Mission Studies*), §2, 273.

88. Gallaher and Kalaitzidis, "Declaration on the 'Russian World'" (*Mission Studies*), §2, 273–74.

"there is no nation, state or order of human life that can make a higher claim on us than Jesus Christ," and it anathematizes any teaching that

> would subordinate the Kingdom of God, manifested in the One Holy Church of God, to any kingdom of this world seeking other churchly or secular lords who can justify and redeem us. . . . We firmly reject all forms of government that deify the state (theocracy) and absorb the Church, depriving the Church of its freedom to stand prophetically against all injustice. We also rebuke all those who affirm caesaropapism, replacing their ultimate obedience to the crucified and resurrected Lord with that of any leader vested with ruling powers and claiming to be God's anointed.[89]

In its subsequent theses, unlike Barmen, which is considerably less political and which sadly did not negate anti-Semitism, the declaration asserts that all divisions of the flesh whether of "race, religion, language, ethnicity or any other secondary feature of human existence," are secondary, and to assert superiority based on such divisions—negating minorities—is contrary to the Gospel.[90] Some of the drafters used the language "secondary feature of human existence" to reference the attacks of the Russian Orthodox Church on LGBTQ+ individuals. Here the text is also attacking the elevation of Russians as innately superior to other peoples:

> We therefore condemn as non-Orthodox and reject any teaching that attributes divine establishment or authority, special sacredness or purity to any single local, national, or ethnic identity, or characterizes any particular culture as special or divinely ordained, whether Greek, Romanian, Russian, Ukrainian, or any other.[91]

Following on from this critique of attacking minorities and elevating one people above others, the declaration then attacks the Russian world teaching, which often glorifies war. This is also something sadly missing in Barmen, which in no way criticizes the Nazi glorification of violence. The declaration says that war is a failure of love. This in no way is a negation of war as self-defense or war as a protection of the motherland when

---

89. Gallaher and Kalaitzidis, "Declaration on the 'Russian World'" (*Mission Studies*), §2, 274.

90. Gallaher and Kalaitzidis, "Declaration on the 'Russian World'" (*Mission Studies*), §3, 274.

91. Gallaher and Kalaitzidis, "Declaration on the 'Russian World'" (*Mission Studies*), §3, 274.

invaded by a hostile power. The declaration is not simply a pacifist text, as some have interpreted it. It condemns rather any teaching that "encourages division, mistrust, hatred, and violence among peoples, religions, confessions, nations, or states,"[92] including the sacralization of war, the attacking of minorities and foreigners, and the demonization of the West. It especially critiques Patriarch Kirill's insertions of condemnations of those he says are attacking Holy Rus' into liturgical prayers.

The last two theses are as much directed at those in the Moscow Patriarchate that uphold the Russian world teaching as those other Christians who are guilty of spiritual quietism. It affirms that Christians are called to help the needy, thus those in Ukraine who are being bombed daily by drones by the Russian state and those who are migrants across Europe and are fleeing the violence being waged against Ukraine. This, it is asserted, is peacemaking by protecting those who are vulnerable as Christ himself was vulnerable on the cross: "We rebuke those who pray for peace while failing to actively make peace, whether out of fear or lack of faith."[93] Last, the declaration once more goes beyond Barmen—with Barmen but beyond Barmen, as it were—by calling for an end to the lies that characterize the totalitarianism of both the present Russian state and the Moscow Patriarchate, who call an invasion and a war "a special military operation." It also takes aim at the narrative so popular among the Moscow Patriarchate of a fraternal people with the older brother being Russia and the little brother being Ukraine. This whole narrative simply binds Ukraine and prevents its liberation; it shackles it spiritually, and allows violence and paternalism even when it is used in a well-meaning way by certain Moscow Patriarchate hierarchs in Ukraine who speak of "repetition of the sin of Cain, who killed his own brother out of envy."[94]

CONCLUSION

There were many reasons the drafters of the Declaration on the Russian World drew on Barmen as an inspiration. The major pragmatic reason for drawing on it was that the drafters believed that the Russian world

---

92. Gallaher and Kalaitzidis, "Declaration on the 'Russian World'" (*Mission Studies*), §4, 275.

93. Gallaher and Kalaitzidis, "Declaration on the 'Russian World'" (*Mission Studies*), §5, 275.

94. Gallaher and Kalaitzidis, "Declaration on the 'Russian World'" (*Mission Studies*), §6, 275–76.

teaching was a contemporary form of ethno-phyletist and ethno-nationalist fascism, as deadly as the Nazi ideology that Barmen once confronted, and that this heresy was being falsely identified with the Orthodox faith and the Orthodox Church. It was felt that this false teaching endangers the true unity of Orthodoxy, which is found in its pan-Orthodox, trans-national, and trans-ethnic common faith in Christ crucified and resurrected according to the Scriptures, as interpreted through tradition. The Russian world heresy, as heresy it is, endangers the faith confessed by the Orthodox Church by its inclusion in the official church teaching of the largest Orthodox Church of the world—insofar as it has been systematically preached and proclaimed by Patriarch Kirill and various senior hierarchs of the Russian Church—and is a violent teaching that is being used to harm the innocent in Ukraine. More theologically, the drafters wished to emphasize, as did Barmen and Barth's theology more broadly, that the sole foundation and authority for Orthodox Christianity is not any of the kingdoms of this world but the Kingdom of the Father and the Son and the Holy Spirit which is coextensive with the person and Kingdom of Jesus Christ crucified and resurrected according to the Scriptures which is to come. Barmen provided the drafters of the declaration the necessary tools to respond to a contemporary analogue to Nazism through its revelationally driven, exegetically framed, and eschatologically characterized political theology. The Russian world declaration certainly is no simple reiteration of Barmen either as a Barthian text or as a confession that has grown out of the tradition of the churches of the Reformation. The declaration is part of something new, an additional gift, which is Barmen's unexpected and multifarious ecumenical legacy. This Barmen legacy is an ever ancient and ever new Barthian theo-political gift to all the churches and the nations in both East and West.

CHAPTER 7

Karl Barth's "Farewell" and the Challenge of Christian Nationalism in America
Keith L. Johnson

THE CHALLENGE

In a slate of recent studies, sociologists and historians have shown that Christian nationalism is among the forces most responsible for the present polarization in American life. Christian nationalism is "a cultural framework . . . that idealizes and advocates for a fusion of Christianity with American civic life."[1] It appeals to many Americans because it offers a "deep story" reflecting the traditions, symbols, narratives, and values central to their cultural and religious identity.[2] This story goes something like this: America is a Christian nation because it was founded by men who shaped the nation's documents in light of Christian principles. The most important of these principles is *freedom*, understood in the libertarian sense of being free from regulation. The founders recognized that every person has inalienable, God-given rights, and any restriction on these rights, especially by the government, runs contrary to God's order for creation. Because the United States has upheld this order, God has blessed it with power and prosperity and given it a unique role in world history. But now the American way of life is threatened by people inside and outside American borders who seek to undermine American values. So faithful Americans need to take their country back by electing leaders who will recover America's Christian heritage, restore law and order, and protect America from outside threats. If these political means fail, then

1. Whitehead and Perry, *Taking America Back for God*, 10.
2. Gorski and Perry, *Flag and the Cross*, 4.

Americans might have to take up arms to defend their freedom and their country from those who seek to destroy it.

Millions of American Christians believe some version of this story. It reflects the history they were taught in their schools and the theology they receive in their churches. This story has been reinforced by a constellation of books, movies, politicians, church leaders, and media figures. It gives them a framework for understanding their citizenship and provides moral stability, giving them a sense of heroes and villains, right and wrong, justice and injustice. It also helps them make sense of the Bible, because it allows them to apply often-obscure biblical stories directly to their daily lives at work, home, and in society. It is the default political theology many of my students have when they enter my classroom, and the same is probably true in many American classrooms and churches.

The problem is that this story is neither true nor Christian. Historically, the story of America envisioned within Christian nationalism is mythological. It depends upon a misleading account of American history that overlooks well-established facts like the diverse religious views of the founders, the variety of philosophical influences behind the Declaration of Independence and Constitution, the reality that much of America's prosperity and power over the centuries is the result of stolen land and slave labor, the ongoing dehumanization of minorities, and the inconsistent application of human rights.[3] Theologically, Christian nationalism in America can be labeled "Christian" only because its adherents identify it as Christian.[4] But it is *not* Christian in any recognizably biblical or traditionally orthodox sense. It is a disfigured, hybrid version of Christianity, a theological distortion grounded upon an incoherent form of supersessionism and the co-opting of Christian language and imagery to justify the pursuit of political and economic power.[5]

We are pursuing our various vocations in a world shaped by this false story. How do we counteract it? What difference can we make through our teaching and writing and preaching? How can we address the challenge of Christian nationalism in America today? And how can we do so in a manner that is also *for* rather than merely against the people we meet in our classrooms and churches?

---

3. Gorski and Perry, *Flag and the Cross*, 5.
4. Gorski and Perry, *Flag and the Cross*, 5.
5. Whitehead and Perry, *Taking America Back for God*, 153, 161–62.

Karl Barth faced similar questions as he pursued his theological work at the University of Bonn in 1933. That year turned out to be among the most significant in Barth's life, in part because of lessons he learned while facing the challenge of Christian nationalism. Barth knew the dismay that comes with seeing Christian symbols co-opted by politicians; he knew the sting of betrayal and the pain of broken relationships; and he knew the anxiety of watching a church you love embrace idolatry. Ninety-one years later, Barth's decisions, statements, and actions have much to teach us as we consider the challenge of our moment. Let us tell his story.

DIALECTICAL TENSIONS

We begin on January 3, 1933, with a letter written that day to Barth's close friend, Eduard Thurneysen, by Charlotte von Kirschbaum. She writes: "Karl currently is experiencing difficult days as he thinks about his theological friends."[6] These friends were Emil Brunner and Friedrich Gogarten, both of whom were associated with the dialectical theology movement that Barth had helped start over a decade prior. Barth's relation to them had been growing increasingly strained, and matters were near a breaking point.

The first volume of Barth's *Church Dogmatics* had appeared in print just two months earlier, and Barth had used the preface to distance himself from the dialectical theology movement.[7] Brunner received his copy in late November, and on December 13, he wrote a letter to thank Barth. He said Barth's new book was a "cathedral of impressive proportions," but he also noted that he and Barth were moving in opposite directions methodologically. While Barth was looking backward to theological tradition, Brunner was moving toward a "dogmatics that sees its service as answering the questions that people today are asking."[8] This description aggravated Barth. In a letter to Thurneysen, he complained that Brunner gave him an "honorary salute, only then to come back all the more

---

6. Charlotte von Kirschbaum, letter to Thurneysen, January 3, 1933, in Barth and Thurneysen, *Barth–Thurneysen*, 3:337.

7. *CD* I/1, xiii.

8. Emil Brunner, letter to Barth, December 13, 1932, in Barth and Brunner, *Barth–Brunner Briefwechsel*, 210.

unteachably" with the same ideas Barth had been rejecting since his *Römerbrief*.[9]

Barth's relationship with Gogarten was even more strained. Their affiliation began in 1922, when Gogarten, Barth, and Thurneysen became the founding editors of *Zwischen den Zeiten*, the journal that served as the primary outlet for the dialectical theologians. But careful readers noticed a rift opening between Gogarten and Barth as the years progressed. Their differences came into full view with Gogarten's 1929 review of Barth's *Christliche Dogmatik*, his first published volume of dogmatics. In the review, Gogarten criticized Barth for downplaying the role of human natural capacities in the event of divine revelation. He insisted that Christ's incarnation means theologians can begin with the human recipient of divine revelation and then speak of God.[10] Barth responded to Gogarten in a five-page, small-print section of *Church Dogmatics* I/1, where he calls Gogarten's suggestions a "fresh betrayal" in the pattern of the older liberal theology.[11] He argues that any knowledge of God's relation with humanity available through God's act of creation was lost through the Fall, and this knowledge is "restored . . . only in the Gospel, in special revelation." A theologian who begins by reflecting on created human capacities thus can only mislead. Barth concludes that "there must not even be the appearance of an anthropology serving as the basis of the understanding of God's Word."[12] Although the work was published in 1932, Barth had sent the draft of his response to Gogarten in 1931 and asked for feedback.[13] Gogarten had never replied.

Barth had spent the opening days of 1933 preoccupied by the arguments in Gogarten's new book on political ethics.[14] He was particularly disturbed by Gogarten's use of the word "creation" as a cover to ground his dogmatic claims in philosophy and natural theology. Barth's anxieties reached a boiling point on the evening of January 2. Ernst Fuchs, who at that time was a young minister and aspiring professor, visited Barth at home and pleaded with him to publicly break ties with Brunner and

---

9. Barth, letter to Thurneysen, December 23, 1932, in Barth and Thurneysen, *Barth-Thurneysen*, 3:31.

10. Gogarten, "Karl Barths Dogmatik."

11. *CD* I/1, 130.

12. *CD* I/1, 131.

13. Barth, "Letter to Friedrich Gogarten, July 28, 1931"; cf. also Barth and Thurneysen, *Barth-Thurneysen*, 3:288n14.

14. Gogarten, *Politische Ethik*.

Gogarten because failing to do so would be "dangerous" given the current situation.[15] Events were, in fact, chaotic in both the church and the state. In the Prussian Church elections of mid-November, the Deutsche Christen had won a third of the seats. Shortly after the church election, German Reich Chancellor Franz von Papen resigned, in part due to his inability to restrain the growing street violence between Nazis and Communists. After two weeks of uncertainty, Minister of Defense General Kurt von Schleicher reluctantly accepted the position of Reich chancellor on December 3. But Schleicher struggled during his first weeks in office because he lacked the authority to restrain the parties in the conflict. Meanwhile, the Nazis were calling for a Hitler chancellorship, saying only Hitler could fix Germany's problems.

The morning after Fuchs's visit—the same day Kirschbaum wrote her letter to Thurneysen—Barth wrote to Gogarten to ask for a meeting on January 6 to talk through their disagreements.[16] Gogarten quickly responded with a postcard claiming that he did not have time to meet.[17] From this moment on, Barth spoke openly about ending *Zwischen den Zeiten*. On January 10, Barth wrote Brunner that their difference was not about method but substance. The prior year had been painful, Barth wrote, but many things were now clear between them. Clearest of all was the fact that the dialectical theology movement had always been a "fictitious alliance."[18]

Word of Barth's concerns traveled fast. On January 17, Georg Merz, who served as the managing editor of *Zwischen den Zeiten*, wrote to Barth in an attempt to mediate the situation and save the journal.[19] Barth replied that he wanted to be free from "this tiresome and unpleasant matter." He worried that anyone who saw his name next to Gogarten's on the journal would be misled, and he suggested that either Merz resign as editor or the journal end publication.[20] On January 24, Merz informed Barth that he had removed the editors' names from the title page of the

---

15. Charlotte von Kirschbaum, letter to Thurneysen, January 3, 1933, in Barth and Thurneysen, *Barth-Thurneysen*, 3:37.

16. Letter to Friedrich Gogarten, January 3, 1933, in Barth, *Briefe des Jahres 1933*, 25.

17. See Barth and Thurneysen, *Barth-Thurneysen*, 3:340.

18. Letter to Emil Brunner, January 10, 1933, in Barth, *Briefe des Jahres 1933*, 32.

19. Georg Merz, letter to Karl Barth, January 17, 1933, cited in Beintker, "Barths Abschied von *Zwischen den Zeiten*," 207.

20. Letter to Georg Merz, January 20, 1933, in Barth, *Briefe des Jahres 1933*, 40.

latest issue to avoid confusion. For the time being, Barth accepted this compromise.[21]

On January 28, Reich Chancellor Schleicher resigned. After two days of intense negotiations, Adolf Hitler was sworn in as new Reich chancellor of Germany. Barth was sick in bed that day, and he later recalled it was there that he realized the German people "were beginning to worship a false god."[22] The next day, Barth met with his publisher Albert Lempp and told him he wanted to end *Zwischen den Zeiten*. But for now, the journal continued.

CAPITULATION AND THE FIRST COMMANDMENT

On February 4, in the name of national security in advance of the March 5 German parliamentary elections, Reich Chancellor Hitler placed temporary constraints on the press and on political gatherings. In the weeks that followed, Hitler depicted the election as a decisive turning point in the battle against Marxism. On February 27, less than a week before election day, the German Reichstag building was burned down. Hitler blamed the Communists, and the next day he acquired emergency powers to imprison anyone suspected of undermining the government. On election day, partly due to these measures, the National Socialists won a coalition majority. With new power, Hitler immediately banned the Communist Party from operating in Germany. By March 20, the first concentration camp opened in Dachau for Communists and other political resisters. With the passage of the Enabling Act on March 23, Hitler effectively became dictator of Germany. Throughout these historic weeks, Hitler displayed keen awareness that his power in Germany would be limited without the support of the Catholic and Protestant churches. He regularly called both churches to assist the government in the "moral elevation" of the German people.[23]

As these events were unfolding, Barth traveled to Denmark to deliver a lecture entitled "The First Commandment as the Axiom of Theology." He used it to criticize those he believed were intentionally or accidentally laying the theological groundwork for the capitulation

21. Merz, "Letter to Karl Barth, January 24, 1933"; excerpts published in Lichtenfeld, "Georg Merz."

22. Busch, *Karl Barth*, 223.

23. *Verhandlungen des Reichstags, VIII. Wahlperiode 1933*, vol. 457 (Berlin, 1934), 28; quoted in Scholder, *Churches and the Third Reich*, 226.

of the German Church to Hitler. He explains that those who know the God of Sinai do not speak of "a timeless *relation* between humanity and God, but of a *history* which occurs in time."[24] This God who speaks at Sinai is none other than the God of the Gospel. "Revelation takes place in reconciliation," Barth says, "in the covenant between God and humanity which is established and kept by God. It takes place through forgiveness of sin, justification, and sanctification, even as revelation of the law! Jesus Christ is the meaning of the law of Sinai inasmuch as he is the revelation of God."[25] Barth argues that the Reformers operated with this Christ-centered method by measuring every external source of knowledge by the criterion of Christ as attested in Scripture. Even those Reformers who engaged in natural theology, Barth says, did not allow nature, history, or reason to judge divine revelation; instead, they judged these realities in light of Christ.[26]

The problem is that many Protestant theologians—and here Barth mentions Brunner and Gogarten by name—place God's revelation in Christ alongside reason, history, culture, creation, humanity, or the state. It is not surprising, Barth says, that these theologians always "speak the loudest, the most urgently, the most solemnly, whenever [they] speak of those things which have been brought into relation with revelation by means of that little word, 'and.'"[27] The inevitable result is Christ's subordination. Barth says: "Whenever theology has seriously operated with the arbitrary concept of a . . . revelation derived from creation by means of some more or less intelligent exegesis of our existence, the consequence has always been that the revelation of which the *first commandment* speaks has been reduced to something subordinate, a mere shadow."[28] The way forward is for Protestant theology to "take its leave of each and every natural theology and dare, in that narrow isolation, to cling solely to the God who has revealed himself in Jesus Christ."[29]

Barth drew firm lines in this lecture, but because his words were delivered in another country and not yet in print, they made little impact in Germany. On March 28, German Catholic bishops who had previously objected to National Socialism were forced by the Church to issue a

24. Barth, "First Commandment," 66.
25. Barth, "First Commandment," 69.
26. Barth, "First Commandment," 74.
27. Barth, "First Commandment," 73.
28. Barth, "First Commandment," 76.
29. Barth, "First Commandment," 77.

statement withdrawing their objections. A concordat between Rome and the Third Reich was on the way. Meanwhile, Hitler grew frustrated with the organizational complexity of the Protestant church, which was divided by region, confession, and governance. He wanted a unified Reich church under a single Reich bishop with whom he could work. Nazi officials began urging Protestant leaders to implement structural reforms in the church, and they found these leaders willing to listen. Since both Hitler and Joseph Goebbels were Roman Catholic, many Protestants were anxious about losing influence with the government.

In April, Barth traveled to his mountain retreat of Bergli near Lake Zurich. But he could not hide from the crisis. Georg Merz wrote to Barth that if he was going to get involved in the church situation, he needed to "confess the German fate" and "not stand against" the changes taking place. Barth replied brusquely that he would do the exact opposite. Meanwhile, events in Germany continued to develop. Hitler appointed Deutsche Christen partisan Ludwig Müller as his representative for church affairs and instructed him to work toward a unified Protestant Church. Church leaders created a new committee to work with Müller on a revised church constitution. In their initial statement, the committee said: "A powerful nationalist movement has seized and uplifted our German people. . . . To this turning point in history we say a grateful Yes. . . . We recognize in the events of our day a new commission given by our Lord to his church."[30]

Barth returned to Bonn determined to do something, but he spent the first weeks of May navigating a changing university. Every administrator who refused to publicly support the new government was removed from their position, which led to a reshuffling of responsibilities. Barth unexpectedly had to take on a heavy teaching load. When the summer semester began, student groups organized rallies for the Nazi regime and urged boycotts of the lectures of Barth and other suspect faculty.[31] A book burning took place in the Bonn *Marktplatz* on May 10, led by several university professors.[32] Barth did not restrain his speech in the classroom, but he chose his words carefully. Instead of confronting the German Christians directly, he focused on his subject matter and sought to undermine their theological presuppositions.

---

30. Statement quoted in Scholder, *Churches and the Third Reich*, 305.
31. See Barth, *Briefe des Jahres 1933*, 197n1.
32. See Hancock, *Karl Barth's Emergency Homiletic 1932–1933*, 262.

The church situation was complicated by the formation of a new mediating party, the Young Reformation Movement, consisting mostly of Lutheran pastors. They supported the Nazi Party and its proposed reforms, but they sought a clearer operational distinction between the church and the state than the Deutsche Christen were seeking. On May 18, Friedrich Gogarten publicly aligned himself with this mediating movement. He argued that the church could not stand idle in the midst of the great renewal God was bringing to Germany through the new government. While maintaining its independence, the church needed to link arms with the new political leadership and participate in this divine movement.[33] In his writings, Gogarten began to cite the arguments of German Christian theologian Wilhelm Stapel, who declared in his book *The Christian Statesman* that the Law of God should be seen as one and the same as the law of the German people.[34]

That same week, the newly formed church committee issued its initial proposal for a unified Reich Church consisting of different confessions overseen by a national synod and single Reich bishop. The Deutsche Christen, and Hitler himself, wanted Ludwig Müller to be the new bishop, but instead the committee recommended the Young Reformation Movement's preferred candidate, Pastor Friedrich von Bodelschwingh. The committee summoned the leaders of various *Landeskirchen* to a meeting on May 26 to adopt the proposed constitution and bishop. Despite vocal German Christian opposition at the meeting, the measure was approved.

However, the German Christians flatly refused to accept the legitimacy of this election or Bodelschwingh's appointment, creating a public rift in the church. As the controversy rose in the days that followed, Ludwig Müller appealed to Hitler for help. Hitler quickly announced that, due to the controversy, he would not receive the newly elected bishop. The governing bodies of the Lutheran and Reformed Churches were called to a meeting on June 23–24 to settle the matter. These days were full of high drama. In the end, the result was the resignation of Bodelschwingh as Reich bishop and the appointment of German Christian partisan August Jäger into a newly created office, the "state commissioner" of the Prussian Churches. This unanticipated result provoked intense controversy in the churches.

---

33. See Beintker, "Barths Abschied von *Zwischen den Zeiten*," 215; also see Gogarten, "Predigt über Joh. 15:26–27."

34. See Gogarten: "Selbständigkeit der Kirche," 448; *Einheit von Evangelium und Volkstum*. Also see Stapel, *Christliche Staatsmann*.

A PLEA FOR THEOLOGICAL FREEDOM

In the days before this pivotal church meeting, friends urged Barth to make a public statement. Barth worried that, because he was Swiss, his words would make little difference and perhaps even hurt the cause. But finally he decided to write an essay addressing the theological issues at stake. He composed it over the weekend of June 24 and 25, revising along the way as he heard the news of Bodelschwingh's resignation and Jäger's appointment. Since he had been criticized for focusing too much on the theology of the past, Barth gave it the title "Theological Existence Today!"

He begins by noting that Protestant leaders have been urged to consider national interests as part of their ministerial vocation. But this is a mistake. Their calling and vocation is to proclaim Jesus Christ, who is found "nowhere else in the whole world except each day afresh in the Holy Scriptures of the Old and New Testaments."[35] Any church leader seeking reform should begin from this particular starting point. But the German Christians have not followed this method. They have begun from the presupposition that the church should support the German government, and so their goal is to install a leader who has the trust of Adolf Hitler and operates in his image.[36] "What I have to say to this is simple," Barth writes: "I say, absolutely and unreservedly, No! to the spirit and letter of this teaching . . . I believe it would be the end of the Protestant church if, as is the will of the German Christians, this teaching were to reign in the church."[37] Even so, Barth says he will not waste time arguing with the German Christians. As he puts it, a movement that can sing "'A Mighty Fortress Is Our God' to the accompaniment of drums" is "so dangerous that it is certainly more prudent not to get involved in arguments with it, but rather to move beyond it, or at least its leaders, and speak to other audiences."[38]

He turns then to the Young Reformation Movement with which Gogarten associated. Barth argues that, while they present themselves as a viable alternative to the German Christians, in reality they agree with the German Christians about the church's role in society and are captive to the same politicized theology. "I believe," Barth says, "that the church will soon be able to deal with the openly wild heretics. But who will have

---

35. Barth, *Theologische Existenz heute!*, 28.
36. Barth, *Theologische Existenz heute!*, 56–57.
37. Barth, *Theologische Existenz heute!*, 57.
38. Barth, *Theologische Existenz heute!*, 61–62.

protected it from the sweet-talking voices of those who appear to be correct according to ecclesiastical, biblical, and Reformational standards, and who yet, in principle, do not think differently from the heretics?"[39] While the leaders of the Young Reformation Movement are right that the church needs to maintain its freedom, they misunderstand the nature of this freedom. "The freedom that must be preserved," Barth says, "is the freedom of the rule of the Word of God in preaching and theology."[40] Church leaders should not be worrying about the church's operational independence or the procedural tactics of the German Christians, but about the fact that "God is free to take the lampstand of the gospel away from the church in Germany."[41] The church will survive not because certain parties win or lose elections, but because its leaders remain obedient to the church's true calling. Barth writes: "What we need primarily today is a *spiritual* center of resistance that would give meaning and substance to a corresponding church-political resistance."[42] Yes, the German Church must be *for* the German people, but "we must be for them as who *we* are, and we must do for them what *we* have been called to do. And we are called to serve the Word of God in the midst of this people."[43]

Albert Lempp rushed Barth's manuscript into print so that it appeared just a week later, on July 1, as a special "supplement 2" of *Zwischen den Zeiten*. The pamphlet sold twelve thousand copies within two weeks. Emil Brunner wrote Barth an admiring letter thanking him for his prophetic stance: "It is a word on the situation that only you could have written."[44] Barth sent a copy to Hitler with a note saying that the Protestant Church in Germany should be free to focus on its own task. He did not hear back from Hitler, nor did he hear from Friedrich Gogarten. But through friends he heard that Gogarten was saying that Barth had committed "theological suicide" by publishing his essay.[45]

On the same day Barth's essay went into print, the draft of the concordat between the Roman Catholic Church and the Third Reich was finalized and sent to Hitler for ratification. Hitler wanted to approve it

---

39. Barth, *Theologische Existenz heute!*, 75.
40. Barth, *Theologische Existenz heute!*, 77.
41. Barth, *Theologische Existenz heute!*, 77.
42. Barth, *Theologische Existenz heute!*, 80.
43. Barth, *Theologische Existenz heute!*, 84.
44. Brunner, letter to Barth, July 14, 1933, in Barth and Brunner, *Barth–Brunner Briefwechsel*, 224.
45. See Barth and Thurneysen, *Briefwechsel*, 3:512–24.

together with the new Protestant agreement, and so he urged Ludwig Müller to complete the reform process. Over the next two weeks, Müller wrangled the final form of the new church constitution out of the original committee and called Protestant leaders to Berlin to vote on the proposal. He urged them to move quickly so that the Catholics, who already had their agreement with Hitler in hand, did not gain an advantage.[46] On July 11, church leaders approved the new constitution unanimously, and Hitler signed it on July 14 along with the Roman Catholic concordat.

Later that day, with the agreement now signed, Hitler surprised Protestant leaders by ordering a new round of church elections on July 23, just nine days later. He then ordered Nazi propaganda offices to help German Christian candidates secure a decisive victory. The fix was in. Given the inevitability of the results, most areas in Germany featured only German Christian nominees on the ballot. But the Young Reformation Movement was able to organize an alternative slate of candidates in several cities, including Bonn. There they were joined by a third slate of candidates from a newly launched group called the For the Freedom of the Gospel Party. Its list of candidates included the name Karl Barth. Since he believed that the other two parties presented no real choice at all, he felt obligated to offer one.

On election eve, Hitler commandeered every radio station in Germany to deliver a speech about the church's role in the Germany. He argued that, while the Protestant Church would always remain free, it should use its freedom by "standing up for the freedom of the nation."[47] That same evening, Barth delivered a speech to one thousand people in Bonn. He told the crowd that we cannot "discover that God is for us and with us in nature or in history or in the treasure of [our] life experiences." This Gospel becomes known only through the free act of God, the Word spoken to us in Jesus Christ, to whom the Scriptures bear witness.[48] On the basis of this criterion, Barth argued that there was little difference between the two other parties in the election, because the Young Reformation Movement merely says "secretly, mutedly, and restrainedly what the German Christians say openly, loudly, and consistently."[49]

---

46. Scholder, *Churches and the Third Reich*, 376–77.
47. Scholder, *Churches and the Third Reich*, 446.
48. Barth, *Für die Freiheit des Evangeliums*, 5; see also Barth, *Vorträge und kleinere Arbeiten, 1930–1933*, 385–414.
49. Barth, *Vorträge und kleinere Arbeiten, 1930–1933*, 409.

The next day, the German Christians candidates won three-quarters of the vote throughout Germany. In the Bonn precinct, the candidates from the For the Freedom of the Gospel Party garnered 10 percent.[50]

FAREWELL

The next issue of *Zwischen den Zeiten* appeared in August. It featured Barth's lecture on the first commandment, which was printed alongside a review by Hinrich Knittermeyer, who had recently joined the German Christians. It also contained an editorial by Georg Merz assessing Barth's "Theological Existence Today!" Merz had supported the Young Reformation Movement during the recent elections, and he maintained this mediating posture in his editorial. He writes that while he agrees with Barth's theological arguments, he sympathizes with many of the practical questions being raised by Barth's critics. He also thinks Barth's criticisms of the theologians associated with the Young Reformation Movement are unfair, because their motivations certainly are not what Barth suspects. Barth called this essay a "classic document of the decision for no-decision."[51]

But Friedrich Gogarten had no problem making a decision, as he demonstrated in mid-August when he joined the German Christian movement. He offered his rationale in a letter to Georg Merz a few weeks later. He explains that theologians must do more than simply offer negative judgments about the current situation; they also have to present a positive vision for the church's relationship to the state in its current form. "That is the reason for my declaration that I have joined the German Christians," he writes. "For that is the historical place where what is going to happen in our churches will be decided. The decisive theological debates will take place there."[52]

When Barth learned of Gogarten's conversion, he demanded a decisive conversation about the future of *Zwischen den Zeiten*. Publisher Albert Lempp arranged a meeting for the editors on September 30, but only Lempp, Barth, Thurneysen, and Merz attended. Gogarten sent a letter. He wrote that he was "extraordinarily shocked" about the possibility

---

50. Busch, *Karl Barth*, 228.
51. Barth, "Farewell," 88.
52. Friedrich Gogarten, letter to Georg Merz, September 20, 1933, cited in Merz, "Abschied," 552.

of ending the journal because the German church needed it more than ever. "We definitely cannot be silent now," he insisted. Barth disagreed, and he proposed that Gogarten be removed as editor and the journal adopt a new structure. But Merz rejected Barth's proposal, in part because he thought a compromise was still possible. At this point, Barth and Thurneysen decided to break ties with the journal. Their future writings would now be published in a new journal named *Theological Existence Today!* after Barth's essay. As a concession to Merz, they each agreed to write a final essay explaining their decision. Merz also asked them not to depict their new journal as a permanent alternative, because he hoped that Barth and Thurneysen could return to *Zwischen den Zeiten* after the controversy died down.[53]

Barth composed his essay two weeks later, titling it simply "Farewell." He writes that *Zwischen den Zeiten* was the result of a "productive misunderstanding" among those who identified with the dialectical theology movement. While they initially had thought they were allies, recent events had made it clear that they are not. He explains that Emil Brunner's recent publications mark a "grievous return . . . to the Neo-Protestant or Catholic schema of 'reason and revelation'" they once had rejected.[54] But at least Brunner opposes the heresy of the German Christians. Gogarten's recent writings and his endorsement of Wilhelm Stapel's political theology "filled me with a grief that could no longer be suppressed," Barth says.[55] "I regard Stapel's dictum about the law of God as the complete betrayal of the Gospel."[56] The trajectory of Gogarten's theology meant that Barth was not surprised by the news of Gogarten's decision to join the German Christians: "I acknowledge without further qualification that Gogarten's entire path has led him with the highest degree of consistency to condone everything."[57] The fact that Georg Merz cannot recognize the serious nature of their disagreement "proves that there is a misunderstanding," Barth says. He expresses astonishment that Merz and so many readers believe they can "leisurely listen to me with

---

53. See Beintker, "Barths Abschied von *Zwischen den Zeiten*," 218–19.

54. Barth, "Farewell," 84–85. For an example of what Barth has in mind here, see Brunner, "Andere Aufgabe der Theologie." Also see Barth's harsh critique of Brunner's position in his essay, "No! A Reply to Emil Brunner."

55. Barth, "Farewell," 84. In addition to Gogarten's *Politische Ethik*, see Gogarten, "Schöpfung und Volkstum."

56. Barth, "Farewell," 87.

57. Barth, "Farewell," 86.

one ear and Gogarten with the other." But doing so is impossible, Barth says. "Misunderstandings exist in order to be eliminated. *Zwischen den Zeiten* will no longer be a misunderstanding after I have withdrawn from it."[58]

Barth insists that his decision does not mean that his theology has changed: "I have always aimed straight at what we at that time, at the beginning of the twenties, appeared to fight together, which is now the agenda, in concentrated form, in the doctrine, in the mentality, and in the attitude of the German Christians."[59] Nor is his decision the result of a political disagreement or the fact that Barth is Swiss. "I could not better prove my love for Germany," Barth writes, "my belonging to it, than by the fact that I am in the thick of things in Germany, contrary to many Germans."[60] No, the reason for Barth's break is strictly theological: "I think our journal could have been a truly ecclesiastical force in modern times if only it had proven itself to be a humble but unbreakable dam against the German Christian flood."[61] In the absence of this commitment, Barth calls those who agree with him on theological matters to abandon their neutrality and to make a final decision.

Barth sent his draft to Merz on November 1, with Thurneysen's essay following close behind. After reading both pieces, Merz realized that there was no way forward for the journal. On November 9, he announced that the next issue of *Zwischen den Zeiten* would be its last.

THE REFORMATION DECISION

The intervening weeks had been busy for Barth. On October 27, professors in Bonn were instructed to begin and end each class with "Heil Hitler!" Barth refused, prompting several meetings with administrators.[62] He traveled to Berlin on October 30 to speak to Martin Niemöller's "Emergency Alliance of Pastors." Barth lectured on the topic of "Reformation as Decision," arguing that the Reformation stemmed from the Reformers' rejection of the conjunction of the Gospel with Catholic culture. German Protestants face a similar decision again, Barth says:

58. Barth, "Farewell," 89.
59. Barth, "Farewell," 86–87.
60. Barth, "Farewell," 92.
61. Barth, "Farewell," 89.
62. Tietz, *Karl Barth*, 225.

"[A] person must now say Yes or No, want this or that, stand here or there."[63] Barth spent Reformation Day with multiple groups of German pastors. He emphasized the importance of the first commandment and their need to make a decision about their true calling. When a pastor asked whether he should stay in the church or resign his pulpit, Barth said pastors should remain in their positions as long as they realize that "to collaborate now means to protest."[64]

On November 13, German Christian district leader Reinhold Krause delivered a widely publicized speech to an audience of twenty thousand people in the Sports Palace in Berlin. To sustained ovations, he called for "a second German Reformation" in the tradition of Luther.[65] The crescendo came with Krause's call to eliminate Jewish influence throughout the German church. "The Jews are certainly not God's people," he shouted. "If we National Socialists are ashamed to buy a necktie from a Jew, then we should really be ashamed to accept from a Jew anything that speaks to our soul . . . people of Jewish blood do not belong in the German people's church." This rejection of all things Jewish extends to the Old Testament itself, he argued, because pastors cannot appeal to the Old Testament and also proclaim a Christianity for the German people. "For all practical purposes," Krause argued, "the one excludes the other."[66] Krause's speech sparked intense controversy, prompting many German Christians to end their affiliation with the movement. This included Friedrich Gogarten, whose association had lasted a total of four months. In the wake of the ensuing scandal, Barth again traveled to Berlin to meet with disaffected pastors. He left the meeting disappointed that they were far more concerned with ecclesial politics than with the theological issues.[67]

On December 10, Barth had the opportunity to give a speech of his own, an Advent sermon for the university of Bonn. He selected Rom 15:5–13 as his text, and he focused on verse 7: "Welcome one another, therefore, just as Christ as welcomed you." Barth says that the central message of Christmas is that Jesus Christ has welcomed us into God's life.

---

63. Barth, *Reformation als Entscheidung*, 23; also see Barth, *Vorträge und kleinere Arbeiten, 1930–1933*, 515–57.

64. Originally quoted in Busch, *Karl Barth*, 231.

65. Reinhold Krause, "Speech at the Sports Palace in Berlin," in Solberg, *Church Undone*, 257.

66. Reinhold Krause, "Speech at the Sports Palace in Berlin," in Solberg, *Church Undone*, 258.

67. Busch, *Karl Barth*, 232–33.

In Christ, God adopts us, includes us, and takes us in. But the incarnation gives us something else "special to consider," Barth says: the fact that Jesus Christ was a Jew. "*That* people's blood was, in his veins, the blood of the Son of God. *That* people's character he accepted by taking on human being."[68] Barth says that Christ's Jewish flesh reminds us that those who are not Jews are by nature outsiders to the promises of God. But in God's mercy he allows gentiles to be included alongside Jews in the salvation Christ brings to Israel. "Salvation comes from the Jews," Barth says,[69] and through this salvation, Christ binds humans together "in a way that no friendship or common convictions or community or state can hold human beings together."[70] During Barth's sermon, several audience members walked out in protest.[71]

THEOLOGICAL EXISTENCE TODAY

The story of how Karl Barth faced the challenges of 1933 has several lessons to teach us as we consider how we might face the challenge posed by Christian nationalism in America today. I will mention four of these lessons, and then turn to the discussion.

First, Barth teaches us that opposition to Christian nationalism begins with a decision about the nature of our calling. Barth navigates the complexities of 1933 by repeatedly drawing lines and demanding a decision about them. He rejects every attempt at mediation. When Emil Brunner writes Barth kind letters and says that they are allies who simply disagree about method, Barth draws a line and says no. When the Young Reformation Movement justifies its cooperation with the government by insisting that the church can still remain distinct from the state, Barth draws a line and says no. When Merz and Gogarten want *Zwischen den Zeiten* to continue as a forum where their disagreements can be debated, Barth draws a line and says no. Barth was willing to break friendships, end his journal, lose his job, and damage his reputation to make his opposition to Christian nationalism clear. As he says in "Farewell," this rigidness does not stem from stubbornness but from his prior decision about the nature of his calling as a theologian. There is a reason the first

---

68. Barth, "Sermon on Romans 15:5–13," 313.
69. Barth, "Sermon on Romans 15:5–13," 315.
70. Barth, "Sermon on Romans 15:5–13," 317.
71. Busch, *Karl Barth*, 234.

article of the Barmen Declaration of 1934 comes first: "Jesus Christ, as he is attested to us in Holy Scripture, is the one Word of God which we have to hear, and which we have to trust and obey in life and in death."[72] Barth would say that this statement draws the line about which we must decide now, and then again every day, if we are to make the same decision about Christian nationalism when the crucial moment comes.

Second, Barth teaches us that the problem of Christian nationalism will not be solved through the acquisition of power. Throughout 1933, Barth expressed frustration with church leaders who focused on political maneuvering or church processes. By trying to beat the German Christians at their own game, these leaders simply reinforced the theological presuppositions that made the German Christians possible. Christian nationalism will not be overcome by trying to win elections; this merely masks, prolongs, and strengthens its existence. Barth would tell us that worrying about the news cycle, responding to the latest outrage, or arguing with the convinced is a distraction from our most important work. We must be focused on the deeper theological issues at stake.

This leads us to the third lesson: Barth teaches us that Christian nationalism stems from a possessive theological logic. Many in Barth's time were confused when Barth said that Brunner, Gogarten, and the German Christians were all committing the same error he had been rejecting ever since his break from liberalism. The key to understanding Barth's claim is to grasp the precise problem he is identifying. As he sees it, Protestant liberalism, natural theology, and Christian nationalism all depict knowledge of God in possessive terms, as something present and available to humans that can be discerned through a process of self-understanding, self-realization, and accumulation. Barth worried that this approach inevitably allows the knowledge of God to be connected directly to one's culture, people, and nation. The central insight of Barth's *Römerbrief* is that knowledge of God can never be a possession, something humans obtain, control, and deploy. No—God's otherness means that God can be known only through God in the midst of an ongoing relationship with God, one in which our self-knowledge is interrupted, broken, and re-formed by God again and again. Knowledge of God involves obedience rather than possession. In this light, Barth would tell us to look for possessive logics within American Christian nationalism. And one need look no further than the biblicism that runs through much of American

---

72. For the text of the Barmen Declaration, along with an analysis of it, see Johnson, *Essential Karl Barth*, 320–24.

Evangelicalism, where common-sense hermeneutics and democratic perspicuity means that anyone can know God and apply the truths of the Bible without consulting church tradition or pretty much anyone else at all.[73] Barth would urge us to help our students and congregations recognize that owning a Bible does not mean possessing God's Word; and that the Bible is not a handbook for life in this world but an invitation to enter a strange, new one.

Fourth, and finally, Barth teaches us by what he failed to do in 1933. Barth later regretted that he did not do more for the Jewish people during the crisis. While no one could have predicted everything, I think Barth's failure to do more reflects the unfinished nature of his theology during this period. Throughout 1933, Barth's solution to Christian nationalism was largely methodological: we should begin with Jesus Christ as attested in Scripture and be obedient to what we hear. This solution is partial and abstract, in part because it neglects to spell out a corresponding way of life in concrete terms. But as Barth's Advent sermon reveals, the biblical text was already showing Barth the way forward, even if he did not yet fully see it. The deep story of Christian nationalism will be overcome only as we learn to live together as a people whose communal life is shaped by the even-deeper story of Christ's divine welcome to humanity and the corresponding mutual welcome of Jew and gentile in Christ. While Barth began to work out the implications of this way of life in the later volumes of *Church Dogmatics*, it has been Barth's readers who have done so more directly.

Leading the way have been those readers of Barth working from within tradition of the Black Church, which has borne the brunt of centuries of white Christian nationalism. We find Barth's christological trajectory clarified in the early work of James Cone, who sees the particularity of the Jewish Jesus as a revelation of God's identification with the oppressed and the Christian calling to struggle for freedom.[74] We also see it more recently in the work of Willie James Jennings, who extends Barth's thought to show that cultural continuity should be measured by our desire to belong to others; and that the way of Christ involves a willingness to be transformed by the languages, landscapes, and logics of the people around us.[75] These later readings reveal to us that Barth's

---

73. For a trenchant analysis of evangelical biblicism, see Smith, *Bible Made Impossible*.

74. See Cone, *God of the Oppressed*, 99–126.

75. See Jennings: *Christian Imagination*; *Acts*, especially his exegesis of Acts 10.

core insights have yet to be fully worked out, just as the true nature of human being has yet to be fully worked out. They teach us that resistance against Christian nationalism begins with fighting on behalf of those most harmed by it; that life with God is more about surrendering than defending our freedom; and that we will become what we always have been destined to be only as we walk the way of Jesus and love across difference.

PART THREE

Construction

CHAPTER 8

"In your light, we see light"

The Scripture Principle in Karl Barth's *Göttingen Dogmatics*

Beverly Roberts Gaventa

> The Word ought to be exposed in the words. Intelligent comment means that I am driven on till I stand with nothing before me but the enigma of the matter; till the document seems hardly to exist as a document; till I have almost forgotten that I am not its author; till I know the author so well that I allow him to speak in my name and am even able to speak in his name myself.[1]

When Karl Barth wrote those lines in the preface to the second edition of his Romans commentary, he knew they would be inflammatory, as he says in the sentence that immediately follows: "What I have just said, I know, will be severely handled." Having read the prefaces many times with students, particularly with doctoral students in New Testament, I can attest that this statement has not lost its capacity to incite powerful responses. For some readers, they are—as I think Barth intends—an invitation to consider what it means to read and engage Scripture responsibly, to take it seriously. For others, the same lines are presumptuous in the extreme.

I am neither a Barth scholar nor a systematician. I am a New Testament scholar with a keen interest in Barth, most particularly in his commentary on Romans. And I am convinced that Barth's *Römerbrief* is in

---

1. Barth, *Epistle to the Romans*, 8.

fact a commentary, a book with much to teach us about Paul and Paul's letter; it is not only a work of dogmatics or theological reflection on the way to dogmatics.[2] Time and again, as I have worked through Barth's commentary alongside Paul's letter, I have learned something about Romans itself.

Invited to contribute and present on Barth and *sola Scriptura* for this volume, I turned to Barth's first dogmatic undertaking to see how he reflected on that exegetical endeavor, tacitly at least, in his earliest work of dogmatics. In the wake of his commentary, the *Göttingen Dogmatics* is well situated for a glimpse at Barth's own early reflection on what he had done.[3] He is beginning his work as a professor of dogmatics, making the transition from the parish into academic life.[4] Yet for all that the *Göttingen Dogmatics* stands as his initial foray into dogmatics, and reflects the intense labor that was involved in that shift, his treatment of Scripture, revelation, and interpretation bears the marks of being deeply connected with the actual interpretation of Scripture involved in that early commentary.

As a reader, moving from the commentary to the *Göttingen Dogmatics* has its challenges. The difference in context and genre needs to be respected, as well as the difference in topic. In one case Barth is commenting on a specific biblical text, although at times the path from Paul's text to that of Barth is obscure; in the other he is addressing the place of Scripture in Christian life and thought more theoretically. Yet we see in Barth's discussion of the Scripture principle some important afterthoughts about the commentary, as he continues to defend his work against his critics and grapple with issues raised by them.

THE WORD OF GOD AS HOLY SCRIPTURE

The discussion of Scripture in the *Göttingen Dogmatics* occupies some seventy pages, divided in three sections. The first section delineates what is meant by the Scripture principle, the second addresses Scripture in relationship to authority, and the third addresses Scripture in relationship

---

2. See, for example, the comments of Martinus de Boer in "Karl Barth, Theological Exegesis, and the Apocalyptic Interpretation of Paul." For a defense of Barth's *Romans* as commentary, see J. Webster, "Karl Barth."

3. Barth, *Göttingen Dogmatics* (trans. Bromiley throughout).

4. On this transition, see Tietz, *Karl Barth*, 100–120.

to human freedom.⁵ The topics are frequently interwoven, however; in the style of a good teacher who knows that repetition is of the essence of learning (or in the style of the apostle Paul), he refers back to what will be "recalled" from previous lectures and anticipates where he will go next. I will first review and reflect on Barth's remarks before introducing what I think is a curious silence in his treatment.

The Scripture Principle

Section 1 opens by repeating the goal of the project as a whole, which is to address dogmatics as preparation for proclamation: "Christian preachers dare to talk about God.... The church dares to talk about God on the basis of a historical fact in which it sees its marching orders and working instructions, that is, the biblical canon."⁶ Yet Scripture is not to be identified with revelation; rather, it bears witness to that revelation.

Unsurprisingly, Barth emphasizes the paradoxical character of the revelation in Scripture. Revelation comes about through human words of Scripture that participate in God's Word. "These human words are the words of the prophets and apostles as witnesses of Jesus Christ."⁷ To be sure, he admits, we may have "been placed before the reality of revelation much more impressively and clearly" by Luther, or by some unknown witness (including devout mothers) "than by Paul or John, not to speak of Jude or the Apocalyptist, or one of the in some ways very odd witnesses of the O[ld] T[estament]."⁸ But the question is not "where we learn most, but where we learn the one thing, the truth." By saying that Scripture is God's Word, Barth means that "we do not know Christ outside or alongside scripture but only in scripture. We also know nothing about the Holy Spirit apart from scripture. We know nothing about a church where there is no scripture."⁹

How is it, then, that Scripture *becomes* the Word of God for us? Barth's answer strongly recalls that of the early Reformers: "Only the

---

5. Barth, *Göttingen Dogmatics*, 199–262.

6. Barth, *Göttingen Dogmatics*, 201–2. See the helpful overview by Daniel Migliore, "Karl Barth's First Lectures in Dogmatics," in Barth, *Göttingen Dogmatics*, xv–lxii; as well as the discussion in McCormack, *Karl Barth's Critically Realistic Dialectical Theology*, 327–74.

7. Barth, *Göttingen Dogmatics*, 213.

8. Barth, *Göttingen Dogmatics*, 213.

9. Barth, *Göttingen Dogmatics*, 215.

Word of God himself can bear witness to the Word of God in scripture."[10] Scripture is *autopistos*, reliable in itself. It is not to be subjected to defense or proof or apologetic; the only witness is "the inner testimony of the Spirit."[11] Here Barth invokes Calvin's claim that "the same Spirit who has spoken through the mouths of the prophets must find entry into our hearts and persuade us that they rendered faithfully what they had been told to say by God."[12]

Underscoring the paradox that Scripture is God's Word does not exempt it from "purely historical consideration. Naturally, like any other literature, the Bible has its place in the history of literature, culture, and religion." This means that the entire Bible, in all its parts, may and should be studied with all the methods available.[13]

Barth concludes that the notion of verbal inspiration emerged because some people were threatened by such free investigation. Unable to abide the paradox of Scripture as God's Word, some people reduced revelation to "direct revelation," making Scripture into a "paper pope, from which we are to get oracles as we get shoes from a shoemaker."[14] The problem was a lack of conviction, a lack of confidence in the face of historical inquiry. And the result, writes Barth, was disaster: "Historicism would never have taken on the openly anti-Christian significance that it did had Christianity itself, and especially Christian theology, ventured to insist on its own truth and credibility, and to maintain the *indirect* identity of the Bible with revelation."[15]

Authority

From this beginning point in the paradox that Scripture is the Word of God but indirectly, Barth takes up two issues: authority and freedom. By these he means the authority of the church in interpretation and the freedom of the individual in interpretation. Yet neither authority nor freedom belongs properly to the human side. It is Scripture as God's Word that has "true and definitive authority," and Scripture as God's Word that

---

10. Barth, *Göttingen Dogmatics*, 222.
11. Barth, *Göttingen Dogmatics*, 223.
12. Barth, *Göttingen Dogmatics*, 225, citing Calvin, *Institutes*, 1.7.4.
13. Barth, *Göttingen Dogmatics*, 216–17.
14. Barth, *Göttingen Dogmatics*, 217.
15. Barth, *Göttingen Dogmatics*, 218.

has "true and definitive freedom."[16] The church's authority and the individual's freedom are both "historical, relative, and formal."[17]

By way of introducing the church's authority, Barth observes that when Scripture "comes to us," it does so not only in Hebrew and Greek words in the biblical texts but through a complex of other words. "No one reads the Bible directly. We all read it through spectacles."[18] We read from within a historical fellowship.[19]

Barth's first evidence of this situatedness of reading is the canon itself. Even the Hebrew and Greek words we read come to us through the church. Although individuals might wish to include the Didache or other profitable works, those personal judgments do not alter the canon; such judgments have no authority.[20] Establishing not only the canonical books but even establishing the text itself is properly the work of the church and is not a task to be handed off to historical scholarship. Barth offers Rom 5:1 as an example: whatever the historians may claim and "no matter what the manuscripts or textual research may say," a "Protestant church [that] really knew what it was doing" would insist that Paul "could not possibly have written" the subjunctive ("let us have peace") but must have written the indicative ("we have peace with God").[21]

Another way in which the church exercises authority is through its teachers and its confessions. Here Barth observes that Luther and Calvin do function as authorities, whether named as such or not, and Scripture is read through them. He wrestles with the notion that other such "fathers" might be recognized: Do Protestants possess the freedom to include Kierkegaard or Dostoevsky? Might that someday mean including St. Catherine of Siena or St. Theresa of Jesus as church mothers? His point is simply that such teachers as Luther and Calvin "do in fact speak very vigorously in the church," a reality that the "church must have the courage openly to confess."[22] Similarly, the historic confessions of the church play a role in the reading of Scripture, but the Protestant churches have failed to establish an appropriate teaching office (although Barth is silent on what such an office should be). As a result, "there *is* an authority

16. Barth, *Göttingen Dogmatics*, 229.
17. Barth, *Göttingen Dogmatics*, 227, 250.
18. Barth, *Göttingen Dogmatics*, 229.
19. Barth, *Göttingen Dogmatics*, 231.
20. Barth, *Göttingen Dogmatics*, 234.
21. Barth, *Göttingen Dogmatics*, 236.
22. Barth, *Göttingen Dogmatics*, 238–39.

of the church. The only question is whether the church itself knows and claims and uses it because it believes, because it really is grounded in scripture."[23]

Barth includes an important qualification to this discussion of the church's authority, one that is chilling in light of the church struggle in Germany that lies only a decade ahead of these lectures, to say nothing of contemporary struggles in the United States and elsewhere.[24] He writes:

> This office of the church as watchman and leader, which it should discharge every historical moment as an organ of the truth which is truth here and now today, and which has to be proclaimed as such, should naturally be absolutely free from all national, social, and cultural ties, and is an authority only in such freedom, like the Word to which the prophets of Israel listened; free also from regard for the church as an external institution, basically nondiplomatic, not opportunistic, not asking what respectable people want or say, not asking at all but knowing, knowing the word as it is to be received today. I refer to remote and apparently impossible things. But nothing is impossible to those who believe [Mark 9:23]. The church must believe again. Then it will have authority, real authority.[25]

By introducing "social and cultural ties" Barth runs the risk of being severely misunderstood, as if the church had no temporal location, no context whatever. What he is driving against, however, is the notion that the church is beholden to national mores, the notion that it should cater to the popular and the powerful instead of to the Gospel.

Freedom

As Barth turns to the third and final section, the one on freedom, he again insists that "direct, absolute, and material" freedom belongs to Scripture as God's Word.[26] Yet there is also freedom for the individual who encounters Scripture in her subjectivity. God's Word does not speak

---

23. Note the similar move here: "Since, however, neither the Church nor theology has the courage to be what it is, the pertinent question arises as to whether it would not be better if both were to be declared bankrupt" (Barth, *Epistle to the Romans*, 531).
24. On this point, see Keith Johnson's chapter in this volume.
25. Barth, *Göttingen Dogmatics*, 244.
26. Barth, *Göttingen Dogmatics*, 250.

automatically, like a ball necessarily rolls when set in motion. It "either takes place in freedom or not at all."[27]

To begin with, every reader operates with a historical picture of the prophets and apostles, one that she or he has constructed. This is the case whether the reader is Harnack or "an old peasant sitting down with a Luther Bible.... [N]o one can evade the act of historical inquiry ... [but] the historical picture that I form is never an authority that confronts me but always a work of my own freedom."[28] Importantly, the findings of historical work are to be respected, but they must not become an idol, "as though the speaking of God's Word in scripture took place in the mere contemplation of such a historical picture (e.g. to mention the most important, the historical Jesus)." Barth elaborates: the authority of Scripture should not reduce or impinge on historical inquiry. Historical inquiry is essential, "so long as it is radically aware of its relativity."[29]

In addition, every reader operates with a set of presuppositions, a philosophy. Barth observes that even the "supposedly pure historians" work with presuppositions, citing the work of Hans Lietzmann and Johannes Weiss. Even such scholars have "a specific epistemology, a specific logic and ethics, specific ideas about the relations of God and the world and humanity, specific ideals—in short, a specific philosophy." This is true of every reader: "Even the old peasant has some philosophy—and perhaps not the worst."[30] No one escapes this fact and no one should claim objectivity for her work, whether biblicist or historicist.[31]

Yet the capricious exercise of individual freedom in interpretation must be tempered, lest we think that "anything and everything is possible." What is needed is "free thinking," but free thinking oriented by the Nicene Creed or by Luther and Calvin.[32]

In addition to freedom in historical understanding and in philosophy, Barth posits the role of what he identifies as prophecy. He does not spell out what he means by prophecy but uses the term to introduce his own experience of working on the Romans commentary, returning to that provocative statement with which I began: "In the second edition of my *Romans* I caused some offense by saying that in exposition a point

27. Barth, *Göttingen Dogmatics*, 251.
28. Barth, *Göttingen Dogmatics*, 256.
29. Barth, *Göttingen Dogmatics*, 257.
30. Barth, *Göttingen Dogmatics*, 258.
31. Barth, *Göttingen Dogmatics*, 259.
32. Barth, *Göttingen Dogmatics*, 260.

is reached when I almost forget that I am not the author, since I almost understand him so well that I can have him speak in my name or can even speak in his."[33]

Barth explains that there must something like a sense of

> identification between me and the author, the author and me. ... With it the whole process of hearing finally moves out of the empirical sphere and the reflective sphere and into the existential sphere. I do not merely investigate and think. No, the witness to revelation now appears to me in this very special light. ... The witness becomes for me a Word, a Word for the hour.[34]

This sense of identification is not something for which one must be a theologian. It is a description "that applies wherever there is real hearing of the Word. The author here crosses my threshold, or I cross his. The *nyni de* [but now (Rom 3:21; 7:6; etc.)] comes into force here. Without our raising the ridiculous claim to be prophets, what we do comes under the concept of prophecy."[35]

Barth brings this discussion of freedom to a conclusion by returning to his earlier claim that direct, absolute, and material freedom are God's alone. Apart from God's freedom, "all our freedoms become irrelevant and meaningless liberalism, subjectivism, or spiritualism."[36]

REFLECTIONS FROM ANOTHER CENTURY OF BIBLICAL INTERPRETATION

It should be clear why I observed at the outset that in this discussion of the Scripture principle we see Barth continuing to reflect on his own work as commentator. That seems especially the case in his discussion of the role of history and in this final discourse on what he terms "prophecy," reading until the gap between author and interpreter disappears.

Reviewing this discussion a century later, from the vantage point of a dramatically altered landscape in biblical studies, certain observations press in. I shall comment only briefly on this familiar territory, in order to reserve space for what I noted above is a larger gap in this account.

---

33. Barth, *Göttingen Dogmatics*, 260–61.
34. Barth, *Göttingen Dogmatics*, 261.
35. Barth, *Göttingen Dogmatics*, 261.
36. Barth, *Göttingen Dogmatics*, 262.

First, in these remarks, Barth offers little or nothing by way of an actual account of or defense of *sola Scriptura*. Barth focuses more on the work of interpretation—authority, freedom—than on a theoretical defense of this principle. That also may reflect a lingering preoccupation with his commentary, but it may be that he has the luxury of presupposing that the principle is widely shared and does not need a defense. He does distinguish the Scripture principle as a feature of Protestantism from the ecclesial principle of Roman Catholicism, but he does not seem to feel the need to make a case for it. To the contrary, he warns against any sense of superiority on the part of Protestants. "To have the breath . . . to say something adequate against Roman Catholicism, we need a good conscience. But modern Protestantism does not have a good conscience."[37] Such a presumption about the rightness of *sola Scriptura* would scarcely be the case in contemporary theology.[38]

Second, Barth emphasizes the paradoxical relationship between the Word of God and the human words of Scripture, concerned about the dissolution of that crucial paradox into either historicism or biblicism. Only God can reveal God, and if God "gives himself to be known by scripture," then we "can hardly avoid seeing in this mediation God's own Word." Human words participate in God's Word.[39] They remain human, these words of prophets and apostles, but they are nonetheless revelatory of God's Word.

Reading that discussion a century forward, I can only observe the continuing impulse toward resolving that paradox. In particular, historicism or at least overconfidence in the results of historical reconstruction flourishes. That is true in much of the secularized study of the Bible in the context of university departments of religion. What is more disturbing to me is the role of historicism within the church that produces an increasingly anthropocentric view of Scripture, such that the human words of Scripture are understood to point only to a human world and not to the Word of God.

---

37. Barth, *Göttingen Dogmatics*, 211.

38. In a recent account of the viability of *sola Scriptura*, Philip G. Ziegler takes up three criticisms: that *sola Scriptura* takes insufficient account of the role of the church (i.e., the Bible is "the church's book"); that in view of the pluralism of interpretation, it has contributed to the demise of Western Christianity; and that it fails to account for the role of interpreters in their vast diversity ("On the Present Possibility of *Sola Scriptura*").

39. Barth, *Göttingen Dogmatics*, 212.

PART THREE | CONSTRUCTION

There is another and perhaps more vexing problem with the paradoxical relationship between the human words of Scripture and the Word of God, namely, the fact that some of those human words constitute a barrier to hearing. The relationship between the story of Jephthah's daughter and the Word of God provides a particularly egregious example. How long might one contemplate that story in Judg 11 before the gap between author and reader would dissolve, to use Barth's language, and what would one see? While it is important not to criticize Barth anachronistically, as if he were liable to account for the prominence of such questions of critical scholarship in recent decades, the story of Jephthah's daughter has challenged readers going back at least as far as Origen.[40] And that story offers but a single example of the many ways in which the very human words of Scripture serve as barrier.

Third, when Barth discusses such limited authority as belongs to the church in matters of scriptural interpretation, he does so largely in terms of the authorities who are being used, urging that Protestant Christians acknowledge that they do have authorities who guide their reading, particularly Calvin and Luther. There is real wisdom in this discussion, lifting up as it does those features of Christian tradition that serve as something like senior conversation partners in interpretation.

As we do that, however, those conversations will be enhanced if we attend more carefully to the large communion of saints who have labored in scriptural interpretation over the centuries. I have in mind especially the women who have been interpreters of Scripture from the beginning, as these figures are being recovered by scholars such as Joy Schroeder and Marion Taylor,[41] to say nothing of the rich vein of interpretation exposed by Lisa Bowens's recent work on African American interpreters of Paul.[42] To take only a single example, African American Zilpha Elaw, born with free status and working early in the nineteenth century, cast her own vocation in language drawn directly from Paul. That vocation propelled her to preach even in slave states, where she could legally have been arrested and even enslaved. Her persistence in the face of such great personal danger, a persistence she connected with passages such as 1 Cor

---

40. John L. Thompson observes that early commentators on Judges, however few there are, regularly discuss the story of Jephthah's daughter. See Thompson, *Reading the Bible with the Dead*, 33–47.

41. Schroeder and Taylor, *Voices Long Silenced*. In addition, see Marion Taylor's earlier edited volume, *Handbook of Women Biblical Interpreters*.

42. Bowens, *African American Readings of Paul*.

1:27; 16:9; and 2 Cor 4:7, might readily have become a resource for Barth as he took up Romans in the wake of World War I and as he approached the ecclesial crises of the 1930s.[43]

To return to what seems to have been a facetious question on Barth's part, yes, I could well imagine including St. Catherine among those authorities of interpretation, and Zilpha Elaw as well. Barth's discussion may have been adequate for the 1920s, but it is not for the 2020s. Again, my point is not to criticize Barth's limited understanding of authoritative voices in the church's tradition but to recognize the need to extend those boundaries. The compartmentalization of womanist, feminist, and queer readings—to take only examples—serves none of us well.

In fact, in a slightly later publication, Barth makes my point elegantly, if unintentionally. In the introduction to his history of nineteenth-century Protestant theology, Barth writes:

> The theology of any period must be strong and free enough to give calm, attentive and open hearing not only to the voices of the Church Fathers, not only to favourite voices, not only to the voices of the classical past, but to all the voices of the past.... We cannot anticipate which of our fellow-workers from the past are welcome in our own work and which are not. It may always be that we have an especial need of quite unsuspected (and among these, of quite unwelcome) voices in one sense or another.[44]

Fourth, a tiny point in Barth's discussion of presuppositions warrants attention. The claim that all readers have presuppositions has become a given, almost to the point of a truism in biblical scholarship in recent decades, sometimes touted as if no one knew it previously. In discussing Barth's treatment of the presuppositions that play a role in even the most "objective" work, I mentioned his reference to Hans Lietzmann's commentary and how even the commentary reflected Lietzmann's own views. In that case, Barth could not have realized how right he was. One of the presuppositions with which Lietzmann operated is that a woman could not be among the apostles. Confronted with the name of a woman—Junia—who is identified as an apostle in Rom 16:7, Lietzmann concluded that the name must be that of a male by the name

---

43. On Elaw, see Bowens, *African American Readings of Paul*, 83–91; Schroeder and Taylor, *Voices Long Silenced*, 154–57.

44. Barth, *Protestant Theology in the Nineteenth Century*, 3; cited in J. Webster, *Barth's Earlier Theology*, 112. I am indebted to Philip Ziegler for drawing my attention to this passage.

of Junias. His single observation, that the context means this must be a male, influenced secondary literature on that question—and remained unchallenged for decades.[45]

These several issues have consequences even at what will seem to be the mundane level of translation. For example, Paul opens his letter to the Romans with the words:

Paulos doulos Christou Iēsou, klētos apostolos aphōrismenos eis evangelion theou.

That second word, *doulos*—how should it be translated? It is among the terms routinely used for slaves. About that translation, there is no dispute: a *doulos* is a slave.

And yet that word is a barrier for many readers and hearers of this passage, particularly for those who hear the word "slave" and immediately associate it with the institution and industry of slavery as practiced in the all-too-recent past. Barth's understanding of the church's authority (limited, temporal authority) might prompt us, in the face of the barrier created by *doulos*, to employ the word "servant" instead, and indeed, many (perhaps most) English translations of the Bible do just that (including both the NRSV and the NIV). "Servant" removes the stench of slavery and may make it possible for people to hear this opening line, people for whom it would otherwise be objectionable. We have here a curious tension between being historically accurate (the precise translation of the word) and exercising ecclesial authority to make it possible for contemporary hearers or readers to stay with the text of Scripture.

Yet this is not simply a matter of translating a single word so that it no longer rankles. Once we decide for "Paul, a servant of Christ Jesus," we continue reading. Immediately following this initial identification Paul says that he is "called as an apostle, set apart for the gospel of God." Each of these additional phrases signals that Paul does not belong to himself. He is called. He has been set apart. God has compelled him, which is after all what he says in Phil 3 and Gal 1 and what Luke reinforces in his account of Paul's calling (see Acts 9:22, 26). Paul does not act as a volunteer

---

45. Lietzmann's commentary on Romans, *An die Römer*, is only 134 pages long, consisting of little more than text-critical and philological observations, cross-references to other ancient literature, and the occasional historical observation, which makes this particular observation of his even more unusual. His conclusion entered into the scholarly literature, where it was recycled for decades until Bernadette Brooten ("Junia . . . Outstanding Among the Apostles") and later Epp (*Junia*) revisited the question. Barth was certainly right: Lietzmann had presuppositions, and in this case his presupposition had a deleterious impact on the church's reception of Paul.

agent on behalf of Jesus Christ but as a slave. The stench of *doulos* actually takes us into the heart of the Gospel Paul preaches. In the face of a world full of presuppositions about individual independence, Paul writes to the Corinthians, "Do you not know that . . . you are not your own? For you were bought with a price" (1 Cor 6:19–20).[46]

Several of Barth's concerns come together at this point: historical inquiry necessitates one translation, the church's concern for the possibility of hearing a passage necessitates another, and presuppositions about the shape of Paul's Gospel may be argued on either side.

A PLACE FOR ILLUMINATION

All these points could be developed at more length, but I want to give my remaining space to a curious gap in this account of the Scripture principle and the work of scriptural interpretation, and that has to do with the illumination of Scripture. Barth's discussion involves the Word of God in human words in Scripture, the church's role as authority, and the individual's role in free reception. We are left for the most part with an account of the paradox of the Word of God in words of Scripture, the role of the church (largely in its historical rather than contemporary form), and individuals as readers. Barth does allude to the historical and cultural situatedness of readers, but he offers no account of the ways individuals come to read, to hear, to be confronted. Yet much of Christian encounter with Scripture is with or through a second human party— whether that second human party be a preacher, a teacher, even a written text other than Scripture.

Throughout these chapters, Barth does refer to the work of the Holy Spirit. His initial discussion of *autopistia* prompts several pages of reflection on the work of the Spirit. The Spirit acts "in both the biblical authors and ourselves," he affirms.[47] The Spirit is "neither a magical quality of some ancient text nor an inner sentiment. The Holy Spirit is God speaking to us, making us his children and servants, giving us mouths and ears

---

46. Raquel Lettsome opts for the translation "slave" for Mary in the case of Luke 1:38, 48, but she does so on different grounds. She identifies the translation as a "homeopathic practice," in that Mary is both slave and "beacon and resistance" ("Mary's Slave Song").

47. Barth, *Göttingen Dogmatics*, 225.

and eyes for God's revelation."[48] Presumably, the prophecy Barth invokes under the heading of freedom involves the work of the Spirit as well.

That statement is all well and good, but it still understands the work of the Spirit as taking place in Scripture and in the reader/hearer, who is apparently a solo performer. What I want to propose—and I think this proposal is not alien to Barth's own work—is that illumination also takes place (or may take place) through the agency of other humans. And those human agents are absent from this account. Just as Scripture as God's Word has "true and definitive authority" and "true and definitive freedom," so genuine illumination of Scripture comes through the Spirit. Nonetheless, there is a subsidiary, temporal, and limited role for humans—by means of the Spirit—to act as agents of illumination.[49]

This human agency is implicit even in some of Barth's asides. The "old peasant's" absorption in Scripture reading is not irrelevant, as his reading witnesses to the Spirit's activity in his own life. That "devout mother" to whom Barth refers may be the one who places Scripture before the child. In her memoir *Dakota*, Kathleen Norris recalls venturing into a church after years of absence, only to find that "doctrinal language slammed many a door in my face, and I became frustrated when I couldn't glimpse the Word behind the words." Yet, she was drawn to the "strong old women in the congregation. Their well-worn Bibles said to me, there is more here than you know."[50] There may well be individuals who have direct, unmediated prompting from the Holy Spirit "to take and read," but I suspect they are rather few in number.

Those human agents of the Spirit do more than simply point to Scripture, however. They may invite readers into the world of texts. Almost everyone I know in biblical studies has some origin story that involves not only an encounter with Scripture or with a work of biblical scholarship but with a teacher, with someone whose own absorption in the text of Scripture becomes itself a kind of witness, a compelling invitation.[51]

---

48. Barth, *Göttingen Dogmatics*, 224–25.

49. The title of this chapter, a quotation from Ps 36:9, acknowledges that this illumination is ultimately from God, but illumination that is "yours" can be received through human agency.

50. Norris, *Dakota*, 94.

51. A sampling of such origin stories appears in the collection edited by Byron and Lohr, *I (Still) Believe*.

"IN YOUR LIGHT, WE SEE LIGHT"

Illumination is not limited to an initial invitation (explicit or implicit) into readership, however. It extends to acts of interpretation. When a preacher opens up a particularly challenging text such that the human words become God's Word, or when a teacher exposes a word of grace in a passage previously heard only as judgment, the Spirit may well be at work in that new hearing of Scripture.[52] This is a highly unfashionable remark, since contemporary scholarship is preoccupied with exposing the toxic effects of many forms of scriptural interpretation, but toxicity is not the only possible outcome of preaching and teaching.

In addition, other texts may serve as agents of illumination. I think of Barth's reading or rereading of Kierkegaard—at the suggestion of Thurneysen—between the first and second editions of the *Römerbrief*.[53] While that reading may be cast as the influence of Kierkegaard on Barth or as Barth writing in his Kierkegaard phase, a different account might be given in which, for Barth, Kierkegaard's writings become an agent that illuminates Paul. The difference between formulations is slight, but it is also revealing. In the former, Kierkegaard remains extraneous to the act of interpretation; indeed, Barth is writing about God in conversation with Kierkegaard and also Paul. In the latter, Barth is engaged in an act of scriptural interpretation, and Kierkegaard has become an enlightening partner in that act.

Examples from experience could be multiplied, including those drawn from my own close work with Barth's Romans commentary over a period of years.[54] Instead of multiplying anecdotes, however, I will turn to a far better source, that of Scripture itself. Recall the encounter between Philip and the Ethiopian eunuch in Acts. Returning from Jerusalem in his chariot, the Ethiopian is reading Isaiah when Philip comes upon him. Philip asks, "Do you understand what you are reading?" To this the Ethiopian replies, "How can I, unless someone guides me?" (Acts 8:30–31). Philip does just that, prompting the Ethiopian to ask for baptism.

That way of narrating the encounter severely reduces Luke's account, however, since Luke casts the entire episode as a divine act. It is an "angel of the Lord" who commands Philip to go to the road from Jerusalem to

---

52. To be sure, there are also readings that corrupt and deform, as already acknowledged as early as 2 Pet 3:15–17.

53. Tietz, *Karl Barth*, 125–27.

54. See Gaventa: "Paradox of Power"; "That Grace Should Come Into Its Own." For a rich and suggestive reflection on the way texts live in contact with other texts, see Linebaugh, "Relational Hermeneutics."

Gaza (a deserted and thereby unlikely place for a missionary encounter). It is the Spirit who commands Philip to go and join up with the Ethiopian. And it is the Spirit who "snatches" Philip away following the baptism. If the Ethiopian reads Isaiah until the gap between Isaiah and the Gospel disappears, he has some powerful assistance along the way.

This observation ought not be perceived as conflicting with or even diminishing Barth's theme in the *Göttingen Dogmatics*: God is God. Yes, to be sure, God is God. And the Spirit is the Spirit, and the Spirit can and does use humans as agents of illumination. To be sure, qualification is needed here. Not every human agent in interpretation is from the Holy Spirit. There are human agents whose effect is simply pernicious. Paul's warning in 1 Thess 5 about "testing everything" certainly applies to our reading and hearing of Scripture.

To return to the conclusion of Barth's remarks in this discussion, he describes reading "after" Scripture and "thinking with" Scripture as preliminary to "this identification between me and the author, the author and me."[55] My desire is to amplify and specify the role of the Spirit here. If that sense of profound understanding, confrontation, hearing, takes place, it is not simply that Barth or anyone else acts alone. Illumination by the Holy Spirit is at work. And the Holy Spirit can and does make use of humans in that illumination.

CONCLUSION

Barth will have far more to say about the Scripture principle in *Church Dogmatics*, of course. What I appreciate in this early account is his articulation of the challenges that persist in the work of scriptural interpretation. And what I wish he had done is to reflect a bit more expansively and explicitly on the Spirit's work in that venture.

---

55. Barth, *Göttingen Dogmatics*, 261.

CHAPTER 9

Going Medieval with Karl Barth

Divine Agency in Karl Barth's Doctrine of Election
and His Dialogue with Medieval Scholasticism

Matthew J. Aragon Bruce

INTRODUCTION

Karl Barth's doctrine of election has generated rival interpretations and a significant degree of controversy and debate concerning divine freedom. In this essay, I aim to reframe the debate so as to move beyond the controversy or at least move it along. To do so, I introduce into the conversation another theological and philosophical debate about freedom, one that is deeply rooted in the Western intellectual tradition, viz., the debate between intellectualism and voluntarism, two rival theories concerning rational agency and the freedom of choice. This debate has origins as early as Plato's *Euthyphro*, but comes to a head in the moral psychology of late medieval Scholasticism and is carried on well into the Reformation and modern eras. I will define these two positions shortly. But a few qualifications are initially required.

First, it may seem odd to attempt a resolution of one debate by introducing another. My argument is that Barth develops his account of God's freedom and power in his doctrine of election in dialogue with the tradition, and in particular, with attention to Scholasticism. Barth was aware of the intellectualist-voluntarist debate and touched on it several times in *Church Dogmatics*, and moreover he took a side. Thus, by examining this historical debate, Barth's understanding of it, and the position he takes, we have a means of ascertaining Barth's own position—and then we can decide if we want to follow, repair, or reject Barth's view. As a preview: Barth explicitly rejects the voluntarist side, often referring to it as "nominalism" and connecting it to medieval thinkers such as Duns Scotus and William Ockham, and he has great sympathy with the intellectualist side, represented by Thomas Aquinas.

Second, why, if the goal is to understand Barth, should we investigate a medieval debate? Again, the answer is because Barth does. But it is also the case that the medieval origins of debates over freedom of choice, necessity, contingency—of both God and human agents—in early modern Reformed theology are presently the subject of debate by scholars of Reformed Scholasticism, with several recent books on the subject.[1] One major feature of this debate concerns whether the Reformed tradition is normatively Scotian (and thus voluntarist) or if it is more eclectic and draws equally upon both Scotian and Thomistic concepts and language. Drawing attention to Barth's view of these issues has the benefit of initiating a conversation between Barth scholarship and the present debates among scholars of Protestant orthodoxy. For, when it comes to the issue of God's freedom of choice, Barth, in his doctrine of God in *Church Dogmatics* II/1 and II/2,[2] surprisingly engages little with Protestant Scholasticism directly. Not only could Barth have drawn on the Reformed Scholastics; he could also have drawn on Kantian or idealist notions of freedom as they were used in nineteenth-century Protestant theology—Kant and Hegel, for example, are both anti-voluntarists, while Fichte and Schelling are both voluntarists. But Barth does not—he, strange as it seems, turns to the theology of later medieval Scholasticism to negatively elucidate his position on God's freedom of choice and power. Barth refers to this late medieval debate throughout both part-volumes of *Church Dogmatics* II—making frequent reference to late medieval voluntarism and nominalism—often showing that both Luther and Calvin share problematic features of later medieval voluntarist theology. He firmly rejects such views, and defends an intellectualist account, often by direct citation of Thomas Aquinas.

Third, a comment on Barth's relationship to medieval theology: Barth, of course, wrote a book on Anselm. He also taught seminars on the early questions of Thomas Aquinas's *Summa* and seems to have read

---

1. For an introduction to and summary of this debate see, for example, Muller, *Divine Will and Human Choice*, 19–45.

2. *CD* II/1, II/2. In what follows, references are also made to the original text, *KD*.

in the *Summa* broadly. But, apart from these texts, there is little evidence that Barth engaged in much careful and sustained reading of medieval texts at all.[3] Most of his knowledge and what he says about medieval figures and texts is mediated through secondary sources. So, while one often encounters quotations in Latin from hefty medieval tomes cited in quick succession in *Church Dogmatics*, especially the early volumes, it is almost always the case that these are not from direct reading; rather Barth has lifted them from secondary sources. Some of the more common sources are the multivolume dogmatics or histories of doctrine from nineteenth-century authors such as Bavinck, Dorner, Troeltsch, Loofs, and Seeberg. He also sometimes mines quotations from the medievals out of Protestant Scholastic texts. Hence Barth does actually draw on nineteenth-century theology in his doctrine of divine freedom, but historical theology more than systematic or philosophical theology.

One additional qualification: my focus is on Barth's use and understanding of medieval figures and his sources. Whether he gets them right, especially the figures he disagrees with, is a different question. These late medieval theologians are far more complex than Barth and his sources imply, and Barth uses them largely as a foil—in other words he is not primarily focused on nuanced and sensitive accounts of these figures.

INTELLECTUALISM AND VOLUNTARISM DEFINED

What are intellectualism and voluntarism? One of Barth's sources, the nineteenth-century mediating theologian Isaak Dorner, defines voluntarism and intellectualism succinctly in his long essay on the immutability of God—an essay which Barth read closely and with deep appreciation, and which he cites in *Church Dogmatics* II/1 when he treats divine simplicity and freedom.[4] Dorner asks, echoing Plato's question in the *Euthyphro*, "Does God will the good because it is good? Or, is the good good just because God so wills it?" Dorner classifies the former position as intellectualist, attributing it to Thomas Aquinas, and the latter as voluntarist, represented by Duns Scotus. Both positions recognize that the world is "accidental" to God—God did not have to create. The difference is "that for Thomas this position of the world is determined by the

---

3. For an excellent treatment of Barth's engagement with medieval thought, see Adam Eitel, "Barth and Medieval Theology," in Jones and Nimmo, *Oxford Handbook of Karl Barth*, 86–100.

4. See *CD* II/1, 493 (*KD* II/1, 554).

nature of the divine substance, while for Scotus it is determined by God's absolute freedom, i.e., an absolute power that proceeds groundlessly and arbitrarily."[5]

Voluntarism (Scotus's view, according to Dorner and Barth) gives primacy to the divine will. In short, God chooses with absolute freedom what is good: there is no determinative standard of goodness, and thus the identity of the good is contingent upon divine whim. The intellectualist (Thomas Aquinas) on the other hand contends that God is constrained by the intrinsic goodness of the good: there is a standard of goodness that even God must conform to, but that standard is not something external to or other than God, rather it is the essential goodness of the divine being itself. Thus, according to Dorner, intellectualism holds that God necessarily wills the good, that is, God acts in correspondence to the goodness that God eternally is. Divine action flows from and corresponds to what God knows as good and what God knows is God's own self. This means then that God is limited and constrained to act in the way that God does, for God's being is antecedent to and determinative of God's action. This might seem to call into question divine freedom, but the intellectualist does not claim that God necessarily must act—for example, that God has to create—but that when God does act to create, God is bound to act in a manner that corresponds to the divine essence.

On the other side, voluntarism seeks to uphold a robust notion of divine freedom at the cost of making divine freedom and action float free of the divine essence. The problem with this is that God's actions are thus arbitrary, and God is so wholly other that he is practically unknowable by human beings. Dorner puts it thus:

> The independence of the world [that is, its contingency] is achieved by Scotus at a high price. God is for him the absolute causality, but not self-communicating. God is a realm all by himself that has no similarity and nothing in common with our own being. God in himself is transcendent to the world. . . . God's absolute freedom, by which the knowledge of God is present for us, is the ground of the contingent world, and the latter does not have to be what it is, not even in respect to its ethical principles and determinations. For God has not willed the world because it is intrinsically good. Rather everything is good simply because God wills it. The good is understood as

---

5. Dorner, "Ueber die richtige Fassung des dogmatischen Begriffs der Unveränderlichkeit Gottes," 261. This passage is underlined in Barth's personal copy found in the Barth-Archiv in Basel.

whatever corresponds to the will of God, that is, the arbitrary will that Scotus identifies with freedom. The moral law that God ordains for the world could have been otherwise and has no internal connection with God's nature.[6]

Intellectualism rejects the voluntarist concept of the arbitrariness and inscrutability of the divine will and defends the constancy of divine goodness at the price of limiting divine freedom: God is bound by the divine nature and cannot act in a way that does not conform to the divine essence. God cannot act in a way that is discordant with his own being, his attributes of love, justice, and so on. Instead, God's knowledge of his own essence determines and limits the range of God's choices and subsequent actions.[7]

To provide a more analytic description: Both theories assume that there are two faculties of an agent's mind, whether God or a creature: the intellect and the will. The intellect is the faculty of knowledge and the will the faculty of desire. The most basic distinction between the two positions is evident in the names given to them: intellectualism gives priority to the intellect and voluntarism to the will (*voluntas*). Both views take it for granted that rational agents act freely to pursue some end they recognize as good. The difference between the two theories lies in their respective conceptions of how an agent determines what is good *and* how the agent subsequently chooses to pursue this good. This leads to disputes over which faculty is ultimately responsible for the agent's free choice. The question in other words is: In which faculty is freedom most properly located?

Broadly defined, intellectualism holds that the good an agent pursues is determined by a judgment of the intellect. The intellect makes a judgment about the best good to pursue *in light of an antecedent inclination or desire*, and once this judgment is made the agent pursues this good necessarily. The key here is there is that there is an ultimate antecedent that is not the result of a choice. Intellectualism can be illustrated by Aristotle's theory that all human beings basically desire to be happy or to flourish. Human beings seek happiness by nature, not by choice; choice concerns the particular means used to achieve happiness. Now, we human beings are finite: we can fail to recognize that we are happiness-seeking creatures; we can make bad choices out of ignorance; and of

---

6. Dorner, *Divine Immutability*, 98.

7. Whether Dorner rightly understands Duns Scotus and Thomas (especially the latter) is a very different question, which there is not space to address here.

course sin corrupts. But the choices we make are all ultimately connected to a fixed feature of our being we did not choose—we desire happiness and act in pursuit of it. This is true even when we sin: we choose to sin in part because we think it will provide something that will serve our quest for happiness. To kill a rival lover, to steal the work of another: these are acts performed because the sinner thinks, errantly, that such acts will contribute to their flourishing.

It is also the case that to choose other than what the intellect judges best is to act in an irrational or arbitrary way. Of course, some rational agents, created ones, who have competing and/or disordered desires and less than perfect knowledge of themselves and the world can make wrong judgments about the good. God, at least in classical Christian theology, cannot, and thus always necessarily acts in accord with what is best. God is bound to choose the best option for achieving God's end. But, God, who is omniscient, has perfect self-knowledge; God knows his own nature, being, and always knows the best means to achieve what he wants to do, and thus God's range of choice is limited by his knowledge of himself and of the best means available.

For voluntarism, on the other hand, willing can float free of the judgments of the intellect. While the will requires knowledge in order to make a choice, and the source of this knowledge is the intellect, the will can overrule the intellect's judgment. There is thus something indifferent and arbitrary about the will and its choices. For a voluntarist, the will is free because it is not bound by the judgments of the intellect about the highest good but can pursue a good even though it knows, on the basis of the intellect's judgment, that it is not the best. Even more significantly, at least in radical versions of voluntarism, a rational agent is not bound by natural inclinations but can "free" themselves from them. They can, in a sense, attempt to be their own Lord, i.e., to self-determine the kind of (natural) ends they seek and thus the sort of creature they are.

The extreme version of this view can be seen in William Ockham. Ockham held, for example, that while theft and adultery are presently evil, on account of God's command, this is not necessarily the case. Tomorrow such acts could be obligatory and meritorious because God could issue different commands. Ockham even states that "if someone should love God and should perform all the deeds acceptable to God, God could annihilate this person without any injustice; so that after such works, God is able to refuse eternal life to this person, and give eternal punishment, without injustice."[8] For Ockham, God can seemingly do whatever he wants on a whim without any connection to antecedent divine decisions or, moreover, to the divine essence, God's attributes of love and justice. Herman Bavinck, another of Barth's mediating sources, writes the following in critique of Ockham, commenting on this very quotation: "From this point of view, the will in God is completely detached from his nature [*wezen*] and all his virtues; it consists in nothing but formal arbitrariness. Creation, incarnation, atonement, good and evil, truth and falsehood, reward and punishment, everything could just as well have been different from what it actually is. There is nothing natural anymore; everything is positive."[9] God in sum is free to act justly or unjustly, free to be inconsistent. God is not bound by any standard, not even by God's own nature.

The original basis for the disagreement between intellectualists and voluntarists concerned human moral agency. But as the debate soon came to include argument over the relationship between human beings as moral agents and God as the giver of the Law, the two categories were also soon applied to divine agency. Late medieval voluntarism placed a radical emphasis on divine freedom and on God's *potentia absoluta*.[10] In fact, voluntarism arose forcefully in the medieval period as a response and alternative to prior intellectualist theories of agency (particularly those developed in light of the reintroduction of Aristotle, such as those of the radical Aristotelians or Averroïsts and the more moderate Aristotelian accounts developed by Albert the Great and Thomas Aquinas), which were understood to undermine divine freedom.

What is at stake here is God's *ad extra* agency: Is there any necessity to God's extra-Trinitarian action? Pithily stated: For the voluntarist, if God is to be God, then God must be sovereign and free in regard to any and all constraints. God can choose to be just and loving in one instance and not so in another. Whereas for the intellectualist, if God is to be God, then God is eternally, because essentially, loving and just (among other divine attributes) and God's being is determinative of God's action. God is essentially limited and bound to act externally in correspondence to

---

8. *Reportatio* IV, q. 5, in William of Ockham, *Opera philosophica et theologica*, 7:55.11–55.13.

9. Bavinck, *Reformed Dogmatics*, 237; translation revised. See Bavinck, *Gereformeerde Dogmatiek*, 238. Barth rejects a "nominalist" understanding of divine simplicity for quite similar reasons and likewise stresses the reality of the divine perfections.

10. Kent, *Virtues of the Will*, 94–95.

God's own being. God's freedom of choice is constrained on all sides by God's own essence. The shorthand way for putting this, by both Thomas and Barth, is to say that "God's essence is God's existence."

BARTH'S ANTI-VOLUNTARIST ACCOUNT OF DIVINE FREEDOM

God's Being Is a "Decision"

I now turn to Barth. I will first explain Barth's language that God's being is a "decision." The concept "decision" has a technical meaning for Barth. A decision is an act of self-determination. A decision requires knowledge: it requires knowledge of what we seek to do and how to do it. As a human being, you of course have to acquire this knowledge. But God always already has it.

Nonetheless, a decision, even for God, involves self-recognition: because God knows who God is, because God has perfect knowledge of himself, of all that God is and can do, God can self-determine. But a decision is not merely recognition, not merely self-knowledge—in other words, not merely an act of the intellect. This knowledge is put to use. God chooses what he will do on the basis of this knowledge. A decision is an act of self-determination accomplished by means of knowledge and will working together. So, in God's self-recognition of who God is, that is, by knowing the divine essence, God thereby determines the mode of God's existence. Put more simply, God chooses what to do to achieve his goal. It is precisely in this manner that Barth understands a decision as an act of self-determination.

What Barth means by all this is that God has an essential determination to exist in the way that God does. Yet, because God is God, God does not merely have this determination but *is* this determination. God, eternally, recognizes who God is essentially and wills to actualize this essence, that is, to exist, to act, such that the divine being is the perfect actualization of, and in perfect correspondence to, the divine essence. This is perhaps best explained with reference to sin. When we as human beings sin, we are acting in a manner that is out of line with and does not correspond to our essence—our God-given nature is to be creatures who love and obey God, who recognize that God is our Lord. When we sin, we act contrary to our given nature.

In sum, when Barth says God's being is a decision he means that if God were to exist and act in any other way than in correspondence with the divine essence, God would not be (in his concrete existence) what God is (essentially). In Barth's own words:

> That God's being is an event, that it is the event of God's act, this must mean (if we, when we speak of him, do not will to look somewhere else than to his revelation): that it is his own, conscious, willed and executed decision. It is his own decision and thus independent of the decisions in which we actualize our existence. It is his conscious decision and thus not the mechanical outcome of a process, whose rationality, to the degree that such a thing is spoken of, would have to be sought outside of himself. It is his willed decision and thus not something that takes place as a result of an alien impulse or also only in an alien conditioning operating outside of himself. It his executed decision: executed once and for all in eternity and anew in every second of our time and thus not in a way that it stands vis-à-vis that which is not divine being as a mere possibility but also in a way that it stands before that [which is not divine being] as self-contained, complete-in-itself actuality. Certainly God's being is also spirit in this self-movement of his, but just so divine spirit, certainly also nature, but just so divine nature, certainly both in the unity and the ordered-togetherness of a person, but just so the divine person whom we must comprehend first of all to be distinguished thereby from other persons by the fact that it is a self-moving person. No other being is absolutely in its act. No other being is absolutely its own, conscious, willed and executed decision. Only in the illusion of sin can human beings ascribe to themselves, or in an embodiment of the world as the projection of themselves, such a being.[11]

Moreover, without God's knowledge and subsequently determined will, God would not have any reason to act. God's decisions and choices would thus be arbitrary because there would be no antecedent reason upon which a choice might be based. It is only because God recognizes who God is as God that God is capable of acting in such a way that God's action is authentically divine (that is, in accord with the essence of divinity). Barth's language of self-determination might therefore be better understood in terms of self-affirmation: God knows who God is, God

---

11. *CD* II/1, 271 (*KD* II/1, 304).

has perfect knowledge of all of his attributes, and God acts in accord with this knowledge. Once again, God's essence is God's existence.

The Divine Knowledge and Will

I now turn to Barth's treatment of God's knowledge and will in §31, which considers the perfections of divine freedom, in particular the constancy (Barth's term for immutability) and omnipotence of God.

Barth's treatment of the divine perfections follows upon his defense of divine simplicity in §29. In his treatment of simplicity and the perfections, Barth seeks to uphold a rather traditional version of divine simplicity that God does not merely have divine attributes, but rather really *is* all of the divine attributes and moreover that none of these attributes is more basic to God's being than any other. Moreover, Barth was deeply resistant to any hint of nominalism as concerns the divine perfections, that is, the idea that there is no real distinction between the various perfections.

> Now God's knowledge is God himself and in turn God's will is God himself, so we cannot avoid the further proposition that God's *knowledge is his will* and *God's will his knowledge*. However, this further equation needs to be completed with caution. It cannot mean that God might lack the characteristic of either knowledge or will, as if it were possible that his knowledge and will as such were understood as merely figurative, as anthropomorphisms to be stricken from the divine essence in favor of a higher third, which would than as such be neither knowledge nor will. The equation can also not mean, that—<u>according to the intellectualist or the voluntarist taste of the respective thinker</u>—God's will might arise from God's knowledge or God's knowledge from his will, such that a so-called "primacy" would thus be ascribed to one and the other understood as a merely figurative description of God's essence. Rather, we have to take both with utmost seriousness: "God knows" and "God wills," his knowledge as knowledge and his will as will and in the unity, but also in the *particularity* of both, [and so he knows and wills] himself as *Spirit*, as a divine person. He would not be a *person*, if he were not actually and ultimately in himself something other than knowledge and will or if he were only knowledge or only will. He is a person in that he is both and in fact he is both in his particularity. He is the *divine* person in that in both he is one, fully knower and fully willer, neither conditioned or limited

in his knowledge through his will, nor in his will through his knowledge, but—because he himself just is both—he is conditioned and limited in both only by himself, in both he is freely and fully himself.¹²

In his treatment of God's knowledge and will, Barth rails against nominalism. He states that God has an intellect—which he calls knowledge—and a will and is thus analogically comparable to that of human beings. For Barth, such language cannot be metaphorical. Because, if it was, all talk of God deciding and choosing would be merely figurative. Barth is worried about giving "primacy" to one faculty over the other because he seems to think that by granting primacy to one over the other, the result is the effective elimination of the other faculty such that our speech about God would be merely figurative (only nominal). Now, there is no form of historical intellectualism or voluntarism of which I am aware that effectively eliminates one of the faculties. I suspect that Barth, wrongly, thinks that later medieval nominalist figures, such as Ockham or Gabriel Biel, do this. Indeed, one of the chief tasks of §29 on divine simplicity is to reject a nominalist account of our linguistic attribution to God and to defend the reality of the knowledge given us in God's self-revelation. This particular paragraph contains the only instance in *Church Dogmatics* where Barth explicitly cites Ockham, writing:

> The extreme antipode [to Barth's own position] is the strict *nominalistic* thesis, as it is represented by Eunomius in antiquity and by William of Ockham and Gabriel Biel in the Middle Ages, according to which all individual and distinctive statements about the being of God as such have no other value than that of pure subjective representations and designations (*conceptus, nomina*), to which in God, who is absolute simplicity, there is no corresponding reality.¹³

We see then that the real enemy is nominalism/voluntarism. Barth's doctrine of revelation essentially teaches that God reveals to us the knowledge that he has of himself—it is a self-revelation after all. Indeed, one of the features of voluntarism and nominalism that Barth seeks to repudiate is that God is unknowable in himself and his will entirely inscrutable to human beings. By contrast, Barth thinks that God reveals the

---

12. *CD* II/1, 551 (*KD* II/1, 620); italics original, underlining my emphasis.
13. *CD* II/1, 327 (*KD* II/1, 368); emphasis original.

knowledge that God has of his being and will to us, albeit we are limited in our ability to fully understand.

Barth thus affirms that knowing and willing are distinct operations in God, each with its own distinct task; the intellect knows, the will desires. Moreover, these are precisely the distinct operations that are required to be a "person," a rational agent who knows, desires, and makes decisions and choices based on knowledge and desire. If God does not have these operations or faculties, then God is not personal: God would be a mechanism that does not decide or choose but just acts as programmed.

Later, Barth takes up the theme of God's knowledge and will in relation to God's omnipotence. According to Barth, God knows what is possible and "what is from him and through him impossible."[14] Now, what is impossible for God? Barth explains that what is impossible for God is for God to act in any way that does not correspond to the divine essence. Moreover, for Barth the shorthand definition of the divine essence is that "God is the one who loves." What is impossible for God, according to Barth, is for God to not be in act as the one who loves.

What God knows to be impossible is therefore that which God did not, and cannot, will because it would be contradictory to the divine essence. All of this flows logically from Barth's assertion that God's essence is God's existence. Barth's affirmation of this traditional notion is often missed because Barth not only uses the traditional language of substance ontology, concepts like essence and existence, but also "actualistic" language, concepts like act and decision. In fact, he combines them: "What makes God to be God, the divine selfhood and authenticity, the *essentia* or the 'essence' of God—we will either encounter where God acts towards us as Lord and Saviour or we will not encounter it at all."[15] Or as Barth states elsewhere, "The essence of God is: to be the one who loves in freedom."[16]

---

14. Barth writes: "[God] knows the *reality* outside of himself as that which through him is raised to reality and just so he wills it too. He knows the *possible* as that which is possible from him and through him, be it that which he raises to reality in its own time, be it that which in eternity is from him and through him in any case a possibility, but also is and remains only a possibility. And he also wills even this possibility as such: be it as future, be it as a never to be actualized possibility. But he also knows the *impossible*, namely that which from him and through him is impossible" (*CD* II/1, 551–52 [*KD* II/1, 621]; emphasis original).

15. *CD* II/1, 261 (*KD* II/1, 293).

16. *CD* II/1, 322 (*KD* II/1, 362).

Barth on Divine Power

Later in *Church Dogmatics* II/1, Barth turns to the distinction between *potentia ordinata* and *potentia absoluta* and explicitly rejects the voluntarist account of divine freedom in late medieval nominalism and "endorses" the doctrine of Thomas Aquinas.[17] Barth defines the terms *potentia ordinata* and *potentia absoluta* by reference to Thomas's definition in *Summa Theologiae*: "*Potentia absoluta* should be understood as the power of God to do what he is able to will and do in himself, and, vice versa, what he does not have to will or do and in reality neither wills nor does; by *potentia ordinata*, on the other hand, is understood God's power as used and exercised in reality and therefore in a definite *ordination*."[18] Barth further states that this distinction is "nothing other than a paraphrase of the freedom of divine omnipotence" and is intended to provide an answer to the question of "whether God is able to do that which he has not done?"[19] Barth states that the question must be answered in the affirmative: of course God could have done things other than what God has done.[20] The reason for this is that God is not a mechanism but a personal agent.

---

17. *CD* II/1, 539–43 (*KD* II/1, 606–10).

18. Aquinas, *Summa Theologiae* (*ST*) Ia, q. 25, a. 5, ad. 1, cited in *CD* II/1, 539 (*KD* II/1, 606). However, it should be emphasized that the standard English translation of the *Church Dogmatics* is both inconsistent and incredibly misleading at this point. Above all, the problem is that frequently in this short passage, and indeed throughout §31, forms of the verb *wollen* are translated as "to choose" instead of "to will" or "to want." The word for "to choose" or "to elect" is of course *wählen*, and is also used by Barth in this section. The translator more often than not conflates the meanings of *wollen* and *wählen* as "to choose" even when the verbs occur in the same sentence! Grasping the distinction between "to will/want" and "to choose/elect" is essential, for choosing concerns a means of acquiring what is wanted; choosing is dependent upon, logically posterior to, desire. The two actions cannot be elided without fundamentally distorting Barth's argument.

19. *CD* II/1, 539 (*KD* II/1, 606).

20. Barth writes: "God would not be powerful, his power would not be in his hands, it would not be the power of a Lord, not actual power over everything, if it amounted to his omnicausality . . . in which what he actually wants and does, if his actually willing and doing was not a decision, did not happen in freedom, if the ability of which he in fact does makes use, was not set apart from another ability of which he does not actually make use. . . . Insofar as the distinction between *potentia absoluta* and *ordinata* reminds us that God's omnipotence is also his free power, it is to be approved" (*CD* II/1, 539 [*KD* II/1, 606]).

Barth thus affirms the Thomistic distinction between *absolute divine power* and *ordered divine power*.[21] At this point, it is essential to note that neither Thomas nor Barth means that God can do *absolutely anything*. For God's being and act are constrained or determined by the divine essence. God cannot, therefore, not be gracious, merciful, loving, and so on in all the ways that God exists and acts.[22]

But Barth sees in late medieval theology a transformation—this is his language—of *potentia ordinata* into a *potentia ordinaria* and the *potentia absoluta* into a *potentia extraordinaria*. The latter is taken to be God's capacity to interrupt the former, the ordinary use of God's power in the world. This supposed capacity to interrupt the regular workings of God's *potentia* is basically how divine freedom is understood in voluntarism. Barth rejects such a distinction as "entirely unbearable."[23] Why? Because:

> The *potentia divina absoluta* was understood, in particular by the nominalists of the later Middle Ages, such that *potentia extraordinaria* was looped back again into the essence of God: indeed, in virtue of his *potentia ordinata* God was actually able to do everything he wanted to do and did do, but in virtue of his *potentia absoluta* he would also be able to act in an entirely different way than he actually did, and he still can; thus originally and for all intents and purposes God's power is [understood by the nominalists] such that in its use he would have been just as free, and still is, to create and preserve a world ruled either according to his wisdom and justice or equally by their opposites. Virtually by chance, i.e., on the basis of an absolutely inscrutable decision, God willed and did and thus was able to do what now stands before us as his will, action, and ability; but after and before there stands behind and above his work, and in the will, ability, and action revealed in it, also a quite wholly other ability and thus possibility of God, which manifests and reveals itself in a quite wholly other work as a "Wholly Other." It cannot be denied that Luther sometimes spoke of his *Deus absconditus* as if he had understood by this a *potentia absoluta* or in fact an *inordinata*. From the power to *work wonders* alongside or behind the power active in the sphere of certain regularity, there

---

21. See Aquinas, *ST* Ia, q. 19, and esp. a. 3 co.

22. See Aquinas, *ST* Ia, q. 45, a. 2. Thomas posits that God can create *aliquid* (anything), and that every *aliquid* is created by God. He does not say that God can create absolutely anything but rather affirms that God can create something *ex nihilo*.

23. *CD* II/1, 541 (*KD* II/1, 609).

> now enters in alongside or behind the actualized power of order an *arbitrary power* [*Willkürmacht*] which only accidentally corresponds to the actual work of God.[24]

Barth thus rejects, in *Church Dogmatics*, the understanding of divine omnipotence and freedom found in the late medievals and Luther (on occasion), and even perhaps some of the unguarded turns of phrase by the author of the famous *Römerbrief* and its "wholly other" God.

What Barth rejects is the idea that God works in the world in a regular way (ordinary) and yet is also able to act contrary to this ordinary way. This does not mean that God must perform some particular *ad extra* action. But it does mean that God's *ad extra* act must be ordered to the divine essence and being such that there is correspondence. So, at a minimum, if God chooses, for example, to create, any concrete act of creation and any act of God in relationship to creation must be in accord with the divine essence. God could indeed have done something different, but this something different would also have to correspond to the divine being and essence. Thus, a different act, the result of a different choice, would be possible only if it too were to correspond to God's essence, and just so the range of alternative action is limited.

Hence, for Barth, prior to the act of creation, God could not have decided to just do anything whatsoever; rather God was and continually remains bound and constrained by the divine essence, and thus the range of God's possible choices as regards creation are limited. God must be in act as the one who loves, because God is essentially the one who loves. And so, any possible choice by God to create, while not absolutely necessary, is absolutely bound to God's primal decision to exist in correspondence with the divine essence. Thus, God is not radically self-determining without antecedent. Rather God is self-determining insofar as God is free to act in any way that corresponds to the divine essence. God essentially must be the one who loves but is free to express this divine love in different ways as long as each of these possible ways corresponds to the divine essence. I should note at this point that Barth's phrase "God is the one who loves in freedom" is his way of saying that God exists and acts in correspondence to the divine essence. God is essentially the one who loves, he is free to choose the means, that is, the concrete form of how to live out the love that God essentially is; however, contrary to a

---

24. *CD* II/1, 541 (*KD* II/1, 608–9).

voluntarist notion of freedom, God cannot choose not to be the one who loves.

Barth also rejects the notion that God's will is "absolutely inscrutable," for it would thus be inscrutable even to God. Barth denies that God would have been "just as free" to order the world according to, for example, injustice rather than justice, for this would entail that God's concrete existence is not determined by the eternal and antecedent justice of the divine being.

Thus, Barth rejected theological voluntarism because God's willed activity would otherwise be understood as arbitrary and inconsistent. Against such a concept of divine freedom, writes Barth, "it is entirely correct and important to maintain with Thomas that this (but exactly this!) capacity is most certainly to be understood as free, but to ascribe to him a capacity different from that which he has in fact revealed in his work, and one which contradicts it, is to be entirely rejected."[25] Thus God is free to exercise his omnipotence, but that freedom is not such that God can act unjustly, unlovingly, contrary to the good, and so on.

How, then, does all of this relate to election? In a short section of *Church Dogmatics* II/2, Barth provides a brief sketch of his anti-voluntarist account of divine freedom. Barth recalls his participation at the 1936 *Congrès international de théologie calviniste* where he heard a paper delivered by Pierre Maury.[26] Maury's paper played a significant role in Barth's modification of his doctrine of election. With his revised doctrine of God's gracious election, Barth teaches that God's choice to elect human beings for salvation and Godself for judgment in the person of Christ, God's decision to be God only as the God who does this, is in no way "determined, ordered, or bound" *by anything external to God*. In other words, God is not compelled or influenced by anything external to himself when he elects to do what he does in Jesus. The reason for the divine election to be gracious toward human beings lies entirely within God and is not the result of some external force, pressure, or compulsion. Barth understands God to be free in regard to creation, for the very reason that it is wholly the result of God's prior decision.

Yet, Barth does describe God as determined, bound, and constrained. In fact, his doctrine of election is essentially a defense of the fact that God's will and subsequent act are constrained by necessity on

---

25. *CD* II/1, 541 (*KD* II/1, 609).
26. *CD* II/2, 188–94 (*KD* II/2, 207–14).

all sides. But God can be only self-constrained. Barth maintains that God is constrained out of the concern to show that God's will and act are not arbitrary. God has reasons, apparently antecedent reasons (what else could there be?) for electing—to elect is to choose after all—to be the one who is for human beings in Jesus Christ.

Just so, Barth describes God in analogy to an artisan who molds clay.[27] The artisan does not simply begin to mold arbitrarily without a particular conception of what he will make in the hope that something will appear as he molds. Rather the artisan has a plan and intends to carry out that plan. God's sovereignty is not capricious; it is ordered and always possessed of a particular purpose; just so it can be described, to use Barth's language, as "determined."

Hans Küng, in his classic work on Barth and justification, aptly describes Barth's understanding of God's freedom, and in particular, God's freedom to justify sinful human beings:

> God is not *sub lege*. There is no law and no principle of order over or external to God, to which God would be bound: God is perfectly free. And yet not free in a nominalistic sense: God is not *sub lege* (under the law), and God is just as little *ex lex* (outside of the law); but God is *sibimetipsi lex* (a law unto himself). And God's justice means precisely this: God is true to himself; God's justice is the correspondence of God with himself. In this manner God is justified in justification: he is in the right. Justification is not simply a capricious, arbitrary dispensation of

---

27. Barth writes: "The Bible compares God's will governing creation with the will of the potter towards the clay and also with the considering and planning will of an artisan, but not with the capricious will of a child at play, although this latter comparison would—apparently, but only apparently—better explain the sovereignty of the divine good-pleasure. The sovereignty of God has nothing whatsoever to do with the sovereignty of caprice, chance, and arbitrariness. We have rather to learn from revelation of the sovereignty of God, that the power of caprice, chance, or arbitrariness is not a power, but belongs to the sphere that God rejects and negates as evil, which as such has only the power of impotence. The sovereignty of God and his good-pleasure is therein actual sovereignty, in that it is the sovereignty of the ordering-principle of history which constitutes the content of his eternal will. In that we must understand this eternal, self-ordering will as the will of the living God, as his progressive and always being renewed act of spirit, we understand this in comparison to law, as a letter which can never be reframed or replaced by another, it is at the same time entirely forbidden that we could understand ourselves to be tossed to and fro in boundless exchange of decisions. Just because we recognize this eternal living will to be reliable, we recognize a rule which no dark hidden agendas or ulterior motives can put into question. In relation to this will, we can and should be certain how we stand, at this point we can and should *stop*" (*CD* II/2, 193 [*KD* II/2, 212]; emphasis original).

favor and disfavor; rather God is righteous precisely in his grace and gracious in his righteousness. He remains true to himself in justification too.[28]

God's Self-Correspondence, (Primal-)Decision, and Election

Küng's description of God as "law unto himself" is most useful for it describes Barth's teaching on divine freedom in reference to traditional theories of moral agency. Barth's conception of divine free agency cannot be categorized under the traditional theories of agency such as determinism ("under the law," in the manner of a will bound by external constraints) or voluntarism (unbound by any "law" "in a nominalistic sense").[29] In *Church Dogmatics* II/2, Barth makes statements that affirm this sense of God being a law unto himself:

> The subject of election, *this* election and thus the subject with which the Christian doctrine of election has to reckon, is above all not a "God in general" as he can be conceived and systematically construed from the viewpoint of sovereignty, of omnipotence of a first cause and of the highest necessity.... Even the supplementation of the concept of freedom by that of love is not able to change matters essentially, unless by means of both concepts the decisive thing is understood: the actual God is the one whose freedom and love is entirely foreign to an *abstract* absoluteness, a *naked* sovereignty, who on the contrary has bound and determined himself in his freedom and his love to be God precisely in particular and thus not in general and as such sovereign and omnipotent and the bearer of all other perfections.[30]

---

28. Küng, *Justification*, 54–55; translation revised. See Küng, *Rechtfertigung*, 64–65.

29. Compare this with Thomas: "Since the good as perceived by the intellect is the object of the will, it is impossible for God to will anything except what his wisdom approves. This is, as it were, his law of justice, in accordance with which his will is right and just. Thus, whatever he does according to his will he does justly: as we do justly what we do according to law. But whereas law comes to us from some higher power, God is a law unto Himself" (*ST* Ia, q. 21, a. 1, ad. 2).

30. *CD* II/2, 49 (*KD* II/2, 52); emphasis original. Barth further states, "God ... rules in a determinate sphere with determinate power. But that his reign is determined and bound is precisely what makes him to be the divine Regent: self-determined and self-bound and precisely so really determined and bound—and this not taken in the sense as if his freedom of choice [*Willkür*] as such might be his divine essence and thus the

Hence, for Barth, God's freedom of choice is *concretely* determined and limited by the divine being and essence, that is, by God's being the one who loves in freedom. Küng's third category—*God is a law unto himself*—not only makes the point that Barth is an intellectualist, but it moreover serves to highlight the frequent refrain repeated symphonically throughout *Church Dogmatics* of "God's self-correspondence." Eberhard Jüngel also highlights this theme, writing: "The highest and final statement that it is permissible to say about the being of God is: God corresponds to himself. . . . Barth's *Dogmatics* is basically a thorough exegesis of this statement."[31]

What, then, does self-correspondence mean? It means that God consciously wills to affirm that God's existence (being-in-act) corresponds to the divine essence. God could not have done anything other this make this decision, otherwise God would not be God. But it is still a decision. Barth's use of the reflexive "self" draws out attention to the fact that this decision is "conscious" and "willed"; it is his way of making clear that God is a personal agent, rather than a mechanical operation. God's being-in-act is not an emanation—in some sort of Plotinian sense—of which God is not self-conscious and cognizant. The reflexive language points to the fact that God is able to use his knowledge of his own being to inform every choice to act.

The concept of the divine being as in correspondence to the divine essence is first developed by Barth to support his doctrine that God in his self-revelation to us is the same as what God is in *himself*. And this concept makes a reappearance in the doctrine of election. God corresponds to Godself insofar as God decides to be in correspondence to the divine essence. This decision to correspond to himself is described by Barth as God's "primal decision," and Barth "understands God's primal decision as God's gracious election."[32]

This points to the fact—a subtle one often missed—that Barth makes a technical distinction between a decision and a choice or an

---

principle of his governance of the world, but in such a manner that in a truly kingly way (and thus not in the way of a tyrant) he has concretely determined and bound himself" (*CD* II/2, 50 [*KD* II/2, 53]).

31. Jüngel, *God's Being Is in Becoming*, 36 [*Gottes Sein ist im Werden*, 35].

32. Jüngel writes: "We saw in the sentence, 'God corresponds to himself,' that God's being is substantiated as the one who loves in freedom. But this sentence describes precisely the being of God which repeats itself in the historicality of revelation. This fact brings Barth's speech about the primal decision of God . . . to expression" (*God's Being Is in Becoming*, 83 [*Gottes Sein ist im Werden*, 81]).

election. Election is grounded in God's primal decision. Barth does not use language of "choice"/"election" and "decision" synonymously. A decision is more basic. Election is ordered to an antecedent decision. Barth puts the matter thus: "The primal decision . . . is identical with the *ground* of election and thus the eternal divine essence in its determination and limitation." Moreover, he states that this primal decision is the beginning of "the line" upon which "additional subsequent divine decisions . . . proceed."[33]

In other words, a decision is not actualized until an agent acts in correspondence to a decision. A decision is a punctual determination upon which subsequent choices and acts flow as if on a line. A decision is not in itself executed; a decision signals an agent's self-determination to act toward a particular end, and the agent then makes subsequent choices in pursuit of and just so determined by that end.

For precisely this reason the doctrine of God cannot conclude with an account God's essence and perfections—the subject matter of *Church Dogmatics* II/1. For the end of the story is not the fact that God *is* omnipotent, just, merciful, and so on, but rather God's action: *God does something*. What does God do?—God acts in correspondence with his essence. And what does that look like?—To articulate this is the task of *Church Dogmatics* II/2, which describes what God does—God elects from eternity to be God for us in Jesus Christ.

To reiterate the logic here, when God makes a primal decision, this leads to God's choice (election) to concretely actualize the primal decision. There is in the divine life an order of decisions and choices ordered to an antecedent primal decision.[34] Barth draws our attention to this at the end of §28 and again at the beginning of his doctrine of election in §32. Failure to see God's agency as so ordered leads to the problematic view that God is free to be able to choose to do all sorts of things in such a way that they are not related to a specific antecedent and ultimately a primal determination. It is the failure to recognize that there is a determined order in God's manifold decisions and choices that leads us to

---

33. *CD* II/2, 50 (*KD* II/2, 53).

34. Barth writes: "What God does in his freedom is in order. And as it is done in his freedom [and thus knowable to God and therefore also to us in that God is present in revelation], it can and must be recognized and acknowledged by us that it is done in order, without it first being measured by our conception of order and thereupon acknowledged as orderly. It befits God to teach *us* what order is. But it befits us to measure our conception of order by his decision and thus to learn from *him* what order is" (*CD* II/2, 22 [*KD* II/2, 22]; emphasis original).

conclude (wrongly) that God is absolutely free, free—for example—to be the one who loves or not to be, or free not to be the one who is God with us, and so on. Such an understanding of divine freedom, and the picture of the Creator it depicts, is, simply put, a pastoral disaster. There can be no confidence that we are reconciled to God in Christ for God's freedom entails a state of absolute unconditioned-ness, an attitude of indifference, in regard to human beings and their salvation. This is not Good News.

GOD IS THE ONE WHO LOVES IN FREEDOM

God is the one who loves in freedom. For Barth, the nature of God's freedom turns on its relation to God's love. The current debate among Barth scholars about election and Trinity is at root a debate over the priority of freedom or love. This debate, and the positions taken in it, is in fact a modern version of the medieval intellectualist-voluntarist debate. Those who emphasize freedom over love lean toward voluntarism, those who emphasize love toward intellectualism.

Barth denies that God *chooses* to be the one who loves, as if God could have chosen not to love. Barth makes every effort to make clear that neither divine love nor divine freedom is superior to the other. This is because love and freedom cannot be set in opposition. God cannot be either loving or free, rather God is the one who loves in freedom. Moreover, God's freedom is ordered subsequent to God's loving.[35]

This ordering of divine love and freedom reflects the fact that the triune God essentially *loves*. Just so, there is no abstract freedom prior to and independent of love. That God is the one who loves *in freedom* means that God's love is free from external control. God cannot be prevented from being who God essentially is—the one who loves. No *external* force can affect God such that God does not or cannot be the one who loves. Nevertheless, God is *internally*, yet *consciously*, determined and thus constrained by God's self-knowledge of the divine essence.

---

35. Barth writes: "God's freedom is in fact not less divine than his love. And God's love is in fact divine only in so far as it is his love in freedom. But again, God's love is also no less divine than his freedom. Yet again, God's freedom is also divine only in so far as it is the freedom in which he loves. And not according to quantity and worth, not in the sense of any hierarchy, but entirely in the sense of the order in which God . . . is God, in the sense of the order of his divine life he is first the one who loves and then as such the one who is free" (*CD* II/1, 351 [*KD* II/1, 394–95]).

For Barth, freedom cannot be ordered before love, nor the will before intellect.

A proper concept of God begins with love and articulates God's freedom by ordering it subsequent to love. To order freedom before love would effectively decouple them. God's very existence and essence would thus be a result of will—a choice God makes that could have been otherwise. Moreover, God would thus be self-creating, determinative of his own essence.

That God is the one who loves is not the result of a free choice. But, because God's *love* is *God's*, it is indeed free. God's love is pure grace. It is not owed to the creature. Nor is it compelled by something lovable in the creature. God's love for the creature is the overflow of the love that God already is in the triune life. God's love for another is already fulfilled in the Trinity—in the Father's love for the Son and of the Son for the Father in the Spirit. But, and this is the much debated move Barth seems to make, this intra-Trinitarian love also *already* includes another who is not God, for the Second Person in eternity is already, by anticipation, the person of the hypostatic union, Jesus Christ. God's love for the creature precedes the creature. God already loves it in anticipation of its existence, and this anticipatory love is the "cause" of God's act of creation. God's love is creative. It creates fellowship between God and the creature, and for there to be such fellowship there must be an actual creature, not just its idea.[36]

Why does God create? Why does God do anything that God does? Because God *essentially loves*. God recognizes his love for the other and wills to actualize it through the act of creation and in acting for the reconciliation of sinners in and through Jesus Christ. Apart from these external actions God is already perfect love without us. But, if Barth is right, the God is seemingly not satisfied with the intra-Trinitarian love that God is. God thus determines from eternity to affirm who God is (essentially) and the result is God's being-in-act, an overflowing of intra-Trinitarian love to the other who is not God. God thus elects, because of his primal decision to correspond to his own essence, to create and bring the creature, the human Jesus and the rest of humanity by means of participation in Christ, into the fellowship of the triune life.

---

36. *CD* II/1, 274 (*KD* II/1, 307–8); emphasis original.

CHAPTER 10

"The abasement of the flesh was like a veil, by which the divine majesty was covered"

The Theme of Kenosis in Book 2 of Calvin's *Institutes*

Rinse H. Reeling Brouwer

FAITH IN JESUS CHRIST IN THE SECOND EDITION OF THE *INSTITUTES* OF 1539

The work *Christianae Religionis Institutio* (*Institutes of the Christian Religion*), through which Calvin gained a degree of notoriety in 1536, could be characterized as a catechism on Reformation theology, designed to instruct adults.[1] Its basic structure relates to the apostle Paul's distinction of Law and faith. With reference to the work of the Law, he writes that "those who discard all pride, being aware of their own poverty, reject themselves completely and deem themselves totally worthless, will begin to taste the sweetness of God's mercy in Christ."[2] The knowledge of Christ, then, is received by faith. In a more precise draft of his catechism for the city of Geneva in 1537—itself partly an extract from the 1536 *Institutes*—he then continues as follows: when you ask "what our faith must behold and consider in Christ in order to be confirmed, it is explained in what is called the Symbol (Creed), that is, in what way Christ became for

---

1. The title of this essay is taken from John Calvin on Phil 2:7, in *Calvin's Commentaries*, 248.
2. Calvin, *Opera Selecta* [*OS*], 1:92. In English quoted in Breukelman, *Structure of Sacred Doctrine*, 81.

us wisdom from the Father, and redemption, and life, and righteousness and sanctification (1 Cor 1:30)."[3]

The second (Strasbourg) edition of the *Institutes* (1539) is characterized by a methodological shift away from this initial catechetical framework, which tracks the structure of the Apostles' Creed, to a more systematic and academic organization of his work, a shift which follows the example of the successive editions of the *Loci Communes* of Melanchthon (1521, then 1535).[4] In his explanation of the extensive second article of the creed, however, Calvin actually follows the contents of the Apostles' Creed more precisely in his theological reflections.[5] He does this specifically by unfolding all of his own christological insights and proposals under the headings of the Apostles' Creed. In this context, Calvin's exclusive treatment of the reasons for and the way of the incarnation is fully identified with the article on the conception by the Holy Spirit and the birth from the Virgin Mary.

Already here, two remarks are required. First, a comparison can be made with the way in which Karl Barth describes the virgin birth. Barth distinguishes between the thing (*res*) of the incarnation and the sign (*signum*) of the virgin birth—and then also between the divine mystery and the miracle—and warns the reader neither to identify nor to separate these two dimensions.[6] This distinction was not yet necessary in the days of Calvin when precritical reading of the Bible was practiced. But if we were to resolve to follow Calvin's example now, we would have to reflect on the question whether the surprising and wonderful legendary material found in the Gospels can bear the whole weight of the doctrine of the incarnation of the eternal Son.

Second, Bruce McCormack, in his masterly book *The Humility of the Eternal Son*, appeals to exegetical studies to argue that, in the Gospel

---

3. Calvin, OS 1:396; Breukelman, *Structure of Sacred Doctrine*, 96, 195.

4. Cf. "Establishing the *ordo docendi*," in Muller, *Unaccommodated Calvin*, 118-39; see also Breukelman, *Structure of Sacred Doctrine*, 117-21.

5. In the *Institutes* of 1539, Calvin opens his "Explanation of the Symbol" with a passage about his hermeneutic with regard to the Apostles' Creed (as a painting of salvation history) (*Calvini opera quae supersunt omnia* [*CO*], 1:477-80; Breukelman, *Structure of Sacred Doctrine*, 8). In the editions between 1543 and 1554, this passage represents the beginning of ch. 6; in the division into sections of the edition of 1550 this passage represents §§1-5. For Calvin's own translation of the 1539 edition into French (a landmark in the history of the French language for intellectual communication!), see Calvin, *Institution*, 1:562-67.

6. *CD* I/2, 178-81.

of Luke, the Holy Spirit is said by the angel Gabriel (Luke 1:35) to be the "agent" of the miraculous conception of Jesus—and thus to do what would later be done in the church's dogma by the concept of the "hypostatic union."[7] Despite Calvin's remarkable attention to the work of the Spirit, it seems that for him, nevertheless, in line with ancient Christologies, incarnation is about the eternal Son who becomes Son of man in the unity of the person, that is, about the Logos who takes on human nature. And what then is to be said about the Holy Spirit? Calvin himself does not offer any clarification, as far as I can see, but among later Reformed theologians, we can read a possible response to this question in the disputation on the incarnation by Antonius Thysius, included in the Leiden Synopsis of 1625. First, Thysius stresses that the expression "the Word was made flesh" of John 1:14 has both a passive sense and an active sense. When we take it in an active sense, it is the work of God. After arguing that the incarnation is a divine work (*opus*) and activity (*operatio*) outside of himself (*ad extra*) and common to the whole Trinity, Thysius continues:

> It happens in such a way that the source of the action [*fons actionis*] comes from the Father, and consequently relates to him. The means [*medium*] of the action lies in the Son, who is the "wisdom of the Father," while the outcome [*terminus*] is with the Holy Spirit, inasmuch as he is the strength and power of God most high, through whom the action is carried out.... Therefore, in the Creed it says, "conceived by the Holy Spirit."[8]

I do not conceive this proposal as a final solution to the problem, but it definitely seems to discern the question, and it leaves room for further elaboration on the role of the Holy Spirit. The proposal of McCormack, that we consider the Holy Spirit as the power through which the Logos— in his "wisdom," Thysius would say—could practice a "receptivity"—a better word than the "passivity" (according to the grammatical passive sense) which Thysius references—in relation to his human "nature," could be seen as just such an elaboration.[9]

---

7. McCormack, *Humility of the Eternal Son*, 226; also 147–48.

8. Belt, *Synopsis Purioris Theologiae*, disputation 25, "The Incarnation of the Son of God and the Personal Union of the Two Natures in Christ," thesis 6, 68–70 (Latin), 69–71 (English).

9. Barth quotes thesis 6 of the Leiden Synopsis, but thereafter immediately continues: "True, the whole Trinity is the subject of revelation, of the incarnation.... The result, however, is the incarnate Logos, not the incarnate Trinity" (*Göttingen Dogmatics*,

PART THREE | CONSTRUCTION

THE (LATIN) *INSTITUTES* OF 1559 (AND THE FRENCH EDITION OF 1560)

In the winter of 1558–59, tormented by "the quartan fever,"[10] Calvin took his scissors, rearranged the material of the 1554 edition at hand, and extended it with a range of additions.[11] The overall structure follows that of the Apostles' Creed, and was divided into four parts: the Father, the Son, the Holy Spirit, and the Church. The most significant change — or renewal — is found in the explanation of the second part of the creed, in the discussion of the Son. As already mentioned, in the first edition of the *Institutes* of 1536, the basic plan had been oriented by the distinction between *Law* and *faith* (as in Paul) or *Law* and *Gospel* (as in Luther). But now, given the need that "the fallen human being" (2.1–2.5) ought to seek "redemption in Christ" (2.6), both Law (2.7–2.8) and Gospel (2.12–2.17), as documented by the Old and the New Testaments (2.9–2.11), *together* give testimony to Christ. Therefore, when speaking of Christ (2.12–2.17), the first point of interest will be that "our most merciful Father appointed what was best for us" in order to bring about our redemption.[12]

In this way, the *ordo docendi* of the locus attains a rather systematic-theological character. With his scissors, Calvin takes from the earlier edition 7.8–10 and places it at 2.12.1–2.12.3 (the question *cur deus homo?*); he lifts 7.11–12 and sets it at 2.13.1–2.13.2 (on the true humanity of Christ); and he takes 7.13–16 and posits it at 2.14.1–2.14.4 (on the elements of the Chalcedonian definition). This means that the materials that earlier belonged to the explanation of the conception by the Holy Spirit and of the birth from the Virgin Mary now structure the three chapters on what Scholastics called the person of the Mediator. At the same time, the virgin birth almost lost its character as a subdivision of the explication of the creed. There remains interest only in the "true substance" of the flesh that his mother donated to Jesus Christ (2.13), and the remaining catechetical

---

154). (This sentence on the "result" could be taken from Belt, *Synopsis Purioris Theologiae*, disputation 25, thesis 4.) Barth misses the opportunity to think through a possible inconsistency in the doctrine of Reformed orthodoxy here.

10. Calvin, *Institutes*, 1.3 ("John Calvin to the Reader").

11. Cf. Barth's comment on Calvin's working method in 1559 (*CD* IV/3, 553); "scissors" seems to me to be a better translation of *Schere* than "sifting" as in Bromiley's translation.

12. Calvin, *Institutes*, 2.7.1. McNeill translates *statuit* (here: "appointed") with "decreed." However, Calvin does not appreciate the dictatorial stem *decerno*; instead of *decretum* (decree) he prefers *consilium* (counsel) or *beneplacitum* (good pleasure).

material from 1539 (7.17) has been removed.[13] Earlier we asked: "How justified was Calvin in making the creed's article on Christ's conception and birth bear the whole weight of the doctrine of the incarnation?" But here, instead of bearing the weight of the doctrine, the same article has apparently disappeared. That is a strange affair.

Chapter 2.15 is a revision of the former explanation of the title "Christ"—in his threefold anointing (formerly §§7.2–7.5). This theme formerly dominated the whole treatment of Christology, and remains important, although the "person" is now treated prior to the "work." Chapter 2.16 begins by repeating the earlier explanation of the name of Jesus as "Redeemer" (7.1), and continues by repeating the earlier explication of the symbol in the order of (in terms of Reformation doctrine) the "two states": first the humiliation (2.16.2–2.16.12, formerly 7.[19]22–7.29) and then the exaltation (2.16.13–2.16.19, formerly 7.30–7.37). We can recognize how Calvin prepares the way for Reformed orthodoxy when we compare 2.12–2.16 of the *Institutes* with the *Compendium of Christian Theology* of Johannes Wollebius (1626):[14]

2.12–2.14	The Person of Christ God-and-Man
2.15	The Mediatorial Office of Jesus Christ (*munus triplex*)
2.16	Christ's Two States, with an appendix
2.17	On the Merit of Christ

Throughout, Calvin adds the results of his scriptural study[15] as well as of his reading of the church fathers from the period of the ecumenical

---

13. Millet in Calvin, *Institution*, remarks as an introduction to §7.27, that Calvin returned here, at the end of his treatment of the virgin birth in 1541, to "the sum of our salvation" from a catechetical rather than a theological perspective (626n338). The catechetical perspective practically disappears in 1559, and the theological perspective finds a new place. In their edition of the 1559 *Institutes*, Petrus Barth and Niesel mention this section only in a footnote (*OS* 3:457, lines 30–41).

14. Wollebius, *Christianae Theologiae Compendium*, ch. 16: "The Person of Christ God-and-Man"; ch. 17: "The Mediatorial Office of Christ"; and chs. 18–19: "Christ's State of Exinanition and of Exaltation." Cf. "De christologie van Calvin," in Breukelman, *Theologische Opstellen*, 313–52, 346.

15. Calvin's second edition of the *Institutes* of 1539 was—as the *Loci* of Melanchthon had been in another way—closely orientated to Paul's Letter to the Romans as the basic model for Christian teaching. Therefore, there is a strong interaction between the Strasbourg *Institutes* of 1539 and Calvin's first biblical commentary, that on Romans (1540). From that moment onward, the results of his biblical studies are carried into future editions of the *Institutes*, where they provide clarification of doctrine or ammunition for polemics. Conversely, the *Institutes*—as Calvin remarks in the preface

councils. Most of the sections that are added to this last edition, however, present the fruits of several debates Calvin was involved in during the preceding years: namely with Andreas Osiander (2.12.4–2.12.7), Menno Simons (2.13.3–2.13.4), Michael Servet and Giorgio Biandrata (2.14.5–2.14.8), Sebastian Castellio (2.16.10),[16] and Laelio Sozzini (the whole of the appendix of 2.17), respectively.

In the following, Calvin's position in these debates—as far as the person of Christ is concerned—will be analyzed, looking for clarification from that point of view on the specificity of his thinking on *kenosis*. Thus the research will be limited to the debates in the three chapters on the person of the Mediator (2.12–2.14), leaving aside the debates that are documented in the three chapters on Christ's work (2.15–2.17) and their effects on Calvin's thinking on Christ's person.

Andreas Osiander (2.12.4–2.12.7)

Calvin met the Lutheran theologian Andreas Osiander (1498–1552) at a conference in Worms in 1541, where they did not make a positive impression on one another. Some of Osiander's works subsequently reached Calvin's study. The title of one such work, according to which Christ would still have become human even if no means of redeeming humanity had been required, provoked a response from Calvin, albeit after the death of its author.[17] Calvin remarks that this question had previously been only lightly touched on by a small number of scholars,[18] but that it

---

to the second edition—offers the opportunity to expose the key words and the main topics in biblical language separately, and this helps to avoid long excursuses on these matters in his commentary work. Edmondson presents the interaction between Calvin's commentaries and his *Institutes* in the development of his Christology (*Calvin's Christology*). In what follows, we will encounter in Calvin's *Institutes* of 1559, 2.12–2.14, some of the outcomes from Calvin's commentaries on 1 Corinthians, Philippians, and Colossians.

16. Castellio was a colleague of Calvin in Geneva and a good reader of Scripture. Calvin evidently encountered disagreement in explaining Scripture in the Vénérable Compagnie, in this case on the explanation of the descent to hell. In the eyes of Castellio, Calvin's existential interpretation of the temptation of Christ was too realistic and not stoic enough.

17. Osiander, *An Filius Dei fuerit incarnandus*.

18. Calvin cites Alexander of Hales, Duns Scotus, and Pico della Mirandola, all of whom are mentioned by Osiander (*OS* 3:443, lines 37–43). McNeill's edition of the *Institutes* mentions these names, but refers to the *Opera Selecta* for the exact references (1:470n6).

had received a strongly speculative interest here. Osiander asserts that because Christ as a human being had been foreknown in the mind of God, he was the pattern according to which all human beings were formed.[19] When the one who is God-and-man[20] is said to be our righteousness, this can be with regard only to his divine nature; only in this respect can Christ be Mediator between God and human beings, because the aim of the incarnation is the divinization of human beings, the gathering of humanity into heavenly life.[21] One cannot say that Osiander's position is typical of Lutheran Christology in general, for it was also controversial in his own environment. Nevertheless, one can observe that it belongs to the prehistory of speculation on a synthesis of divinity and humanity as it would be discussed in later German idealism, as well to the prehistory of a theosophical interest in the mystical process by which divine power penetrates human being. And one can also observe that a follower of Calvin would be inoculated against both tendencies, tendencies that would influence kenotic Christology in the nineteenth century. For, Calvin, in his humanistic mood, strongly repudiates any ontological speculation beyond the soteriological witness of Scripture to Christ, who at the cross redeemed the condemned, in an incarnation supposed to be for all creatures, regardless of their obedience. Calvin declares that whosoever desires to know more is apparently "not content with this very Christ, who was given to us as the price of our redemption."[22]

At the same time, Calvin acknowledges that the mediatorship of Christ is not limited to the act of redemption. Already in the state of integrity Christ had been the head of angels and human beings.[23] Even if humanity had remained free from all stain, their condition would have been too lowly for them to reach the majesty of God without a Mediator.[24] For Osiander, Christ is "the firstborn of all creation" (Col 1:15) as the *logos incarnatus*, but Calvin makes a distinction here. Christ is

19. Quoted in Calvin, *Institutes*, 2.12.7 (*OS* 3:445, lines 17-18).
20. Barth explains why for his part he avoids the description of Jesus Christ as *theanthrōpos* (*CD* IV/2, 115).
21. Dorner, *Entwicklungsgeschichte der Person Christi*, 200-204.
22. Calvin, *Institutes*, 2.12.5 (*OS* 3:442, lines 28-30).
23. Calvin, *Institutes*, 2.12.4 (*OS* 3:440, line 24).
24. Calvin, *Institutes*, 2.12.1 (*OS* 3:437, line 24—438, line 2). For this reason, in the year 1560 Calvin would oppose Franscesco Stancaro, for whom the mediatorship of Christ could be limited to his human nature: already as the eternal Son, he is God in his condescension! Cf. "Responsum ad fratres Polonos, quomodo mediator sit Christus, ad refutandum Stancaro errorem," in Calvin, *CO* 9:333-42.

the Mediator of creation as the eternal Son, in the "subsistence"[25] of the Word, always "being with God" (John 1:1); he is the one who reveals the divine life that would otherwise have remained hidden, and he became the Mediator of redemption only after the Fall of Adam. The duality in the structure of the *Institutes* of 1559 finds its expression here: first, "The Knowledge of God the Creator" in book 1, and second "The Knowledge of God the Redeemer"—against the background of the Fall—in book 2, with the historicizing order creation, Fall, redemption. Therefore, with respect to the passage in Colossians quoted by Osiander, Calvin explains: "The apostle in one short passage sets forth two things to be considered: (1) 'through the Son all things have been created,' that he may rule over the angels [v. 16]; (2) he was made man that he might begin to be our Redeemer [v. 14]."[26] One can question, in my opinion, whether this "parallel" order corresponds with the structure of the passage in question. In Col 1 we find a hymn with two stanzas, both beginning with the expression "He is" (vv. 15, 18b). The second stanza, in accordance with the context of the hymn, speaks of redemption and reconciliation. The first stanza, when read independently (without v. 18a), could be conceived as a Hellenistic-Jewish hymn on the Mediator of creation. In context, however, the author of Colossians moves beyond this general consideration, identifying the "firstborn of creation" with the "firstborn from the dead," and therefore with Jesus Christ. In addition, one can remark that "the thrones or dominions or rulers or powers" of verse 16 are not only "angels" in general, but rather ideological and political powers that have been overcome by the dominion of Christ.[27] In short: the Pauline order, in the way it was understood by Karl Barth as well,[28] seems to be an order running from Christ as the head of his church to the same Christ in his cosmic rule. There are also indications in Calvin's writing that he considers the history of the incarnate Christ to give some coloring to the same Christ as the Mediator of creation.[29] If we were to limit ourselves, with

---

25. Calvin, *Institutes*, 1.13.6 (*OS* 3:116, lines 11–16).

26. Calvin, *Institutes*, 2.12.7 (*OS* 3:446, lines 2–5). Cf. Calvin's commentary on Colossians (*CO* 52:84–87).

27. Edmondson remarks that Calvin in his *Institutes* does not explicitly tie this creative work of the Son to his royal office, but such a reference can be found in the aforementioned "Responsum ad fratres Polonos" (*Calvin's Christology*, 145).

28. *CD* IV/3, 756. Barth refers here to Calvin's doctrine of the work of the Holy Spirit in the whole cosmos, as set out by Krusche, *Wirken des Heiligen Geistes nach Calvin*.

29. For example, Calvin writes: "Therefore, let us, first of all, set down this for a

Calvin, to the dual structure of the two dimensions of the Mediation, it would become difficult to recognize the preparation for what McCormack proposed to be the "ontological receptivity" of the eternal Logos that already existed in the Logos prior to the incarnation. In addition, Calvin's exegesis might be mentioned, as it was found in the *Institutes* of 1536 and maintained through the following editions including 1559: "What Christ said about himself—'Before Abraham was, I am' (John 8:58)—was far removed from his humanity . . . he is claiming for himself here what is (exclusively) proper to his divinity."[30] In contrast, Karl Barth says on this point: "This verse, which reaches back to the Prologue [of the Gospel], although it certainly speaks of the eternal Logos, speaks also of the man Jesus."[31] Therefore, in my view, although we must agree with Calvin in his criticism of Osiander, his doctrine concerning the Mediator of creation can be further debated.

Menno Simons (2.8.3–2.8.4)

In the Low Countries, the beginnings of the Reformation were found among groups of Anabaptists. At a later stage, the beginnings of the Reformed churches were characterized by repeated debates with this movement. John à Lasco disputed with the elder Menno Simons (1496–1561) concerning the incarnation, and word of this dispute had certainly reached Calvin by 1554. In 1556, Marten Micron reported on similar disputes in East Frisia, which received a response in turn from Menno,[32] and Micron asked for the help of Calvin (and of Bullinger) in ordering

---

surety, that there was never since the beginning any communication between God and men, save only by Christ; for we have nothing to do with God, unless the Mediator be present to purchase his favour for us" ("Commentary on Acts" [1552], on Acts 7:30, in *CO* 48:144).

30. Calvin, *Institutes*, 2.14.2 (*OS* 3:459, lines 12–14). Cf. in the editions of the *Institutes* between 1539 and 1554, this was at 7.14—for example, *Institution* (1541), 1:623 ("Ce . . . ne se pouvoit entendre de l'humanité"); and cf. the first edition of the *Institutes* (1536), *OS* 1:79.

31. *CD* IV/2, 33.

32. See Calvin, *OS* 3:449, lines 27–32. See also Balke: "Een waerachtigh verhaal der 't zamensprekinghe tusschen Menno Simons en Martinus Micron van der Menschwerdinghe Jesu Christi" (A true story of the conversation between Menno Simons and Martinus Micron about the incarnation of Jesus Christ) and "Een gantsch Duidlyck ende Bescheyden Antwoordt . . . op Martini Microns Antichristische leere" (A very clear and modest response to . . . the antichristian doctrine of Martinus Micron) (*Calvin and the Anabaptist Radicals*, 203).

the arguments. Calvin indeed wrote a letter to Micron,[33] and in 1559 he inserted twenty quotations from this letter—containing his rebuttal of the arguments and the exegetical considerations of Menno—into the thirteenth chapter of *Institutes* book 2.

Already by 1539, polemical works against the thesis that Christ's body was endowed with heavenly flesh—a thesis identified by Calvin as an inheritance from the Manichees[34]—were addressed to Anabaptist groups. Calvin himself stresses by contrast that the flesh that Christ received from Mary made him son of David, son of Abraham (Matt 1:1; Rom 1:3).[35] That is an important element of our subject: if the incarnation concerns the *real history* of Jesus, then the context and past of this history, that is, the history of Israel, are also involved! In this connection, Calvin also inserts into the *Institutes* his explanation of Phil 2:7 from his *Commentary* of 1548, according to which being made "in the likeness of men" does not mean that the Son only *seemed* to take a body—as the neo-Marcionites, and thus the Anabaptists taught. Hence, Calvin notes, Erasmus is right to defend a "tropological," ethical reading of the humiliation and the obedience of Christ, in which he acts as a *real* human being, without being changed in his divinity.[36] The doctrine of the "heavenly flesh" tries to escape the solidarity of Christ with the seed of Adam which was subjected to original sin. Its adherents suggest that without this teaching, the impious would be the brothers and sisters of Christ as well. However, Calvin argues, "when we say that Christ was made man that he might make us children of God, this expression does not extend to all men; *for faith intervenes*, to engraft us spiritually in the body of Christ."[37] Menno asserts by contrast that Christ has not been made *by* woman (*ex muliere*), but only *from* woman (*per mulierem*), as if Matthew were describing Mary as a channel through which Christ flowed. Although Calvin avoids here a medical discussion, he does not adhere, as Menno does, to the Aristotelian view of conception and pregnancy. This view

---

33. "Contra Mennonem," in Calvin, *CO* 10a:167–76.

34. On this point, Bucer and Bullinger were better informed: the thesis was defended by Valentinus, not the Manichees. See also Thysius in Belt, *Synopsis Purioris Theologiae*, disputation 25, antithesis 3.

35. See also the Belgic Confession of 1561, art. 18 (whereas the French Confession of 1559 in its corresponding art. 14 attacked Servetus).

36. "Commentarii in Pauli Epistolas ad Galatas, ad Ephesiso ad Philippenses, ad Colossenses," in Calvin, *CO* 55:27; on Calvin's quoting of Erasmus, see Essary, "Radical Humility of Christ in the Sixteenth Century," 414–15.

37. Calvin, *Institutes*, 2.13.2 (*OS* 3:453, lines 1–4); emphasis added.

was that the woman produced the material for generation but that this material was animated by the seed of the man.[38] Theologically, Calvin stresses that Christ "was made free from all stain because he was sanctified by the Spirit," such that "the generation might be pure and undefiled as would have been true before Adam's fall"—an assertion that does not exclude that Christ *could* have sinned.[39] Therefore, the accusation that "if the Word of God became flesh, then he was confined within the narrow prison of an earthly body," Calvin attests, is "mere impudence." And to prove this point—apparently against an Anabaptist viewpoint, and not primarily against a Lutheran accusation—Calvin then writes his famous sentences on the existence of the eternal Son of God *extra carnem* during his earthly sojourn.[40]

The Enlightenment assumption that Mennonites did not have any interest in doctrinal questions lasted until the second half of the twentieth century, when what we now call the "Melchiorite-Mennist" doctrine of the incarnation was studied in more detail.[41] The doctrine had been proposed by Melchior Hoffman, a furrier and Lutheran lay preacher,[42] who was interrogated around 1533 by the Reformation authorities in Strasbourg, and thereafter imprisoned until his death. It appears that gnostic parallels are only partly helpful in characterizing his doctrine, for in many respects Hoffman learned from the Lutheran teaching he received. The center of his theology is relation to Christ, the Mediator and Reconciler, the source of universal grace and ethical perfection, and this relation is mediated by faith alone. Calvin's remark that faith intervenes to engraft us into the body of Christ could have been endorsed by him. In that sense, his views differ significantly from the spiritualistic currents

---

38. Calvin, *Institutes*, 2.13.3. On the differences between the old Aristotelian and the more modern Lucretian-Hippocratic schools of physicians, see Balke, *Calvin and the Anabaptist Radicals*, 206.

39. Calvin, *Institutes*, 2.13.4 (OS 3:457, lines 12–16). Calvin here follows the Thomistic view, which is distinguished from the Scotist proposal of an *immaculata conceptio* to prevent Mary from original sin; the latter view would not become Roman Catholic dogma until 1854.

40. Calvin, OS 3:458, lines 5–13. Because of this type of quotation, Loofs concludes that the Reformed tradition "never reached the idea of incarnation" in a real kenotic sense ("Kenosis," 10:258).

41. Voolstra, *Het Woord is vlees geworden*.

42. Calvin shows a certain humanistic, (pseudo-)aristocratic disdain for his less educated Anabaptist conversation partners; see Balke, *Calvin and the Anabaptist Radicals*, 206–7. This demonstrates that we cannot neglect the issue of class in interconfessional relationships.

of his time. Reconciliation, satisfaction, and justification are real events, fulfilled by Christ during his life and at the cross, and do not evaporate in the new spiritual reality of our being with him. At the same time, it is true that the incarnation of the eternal Son, which can be identified with the gift of the "bread from heaven" of John 6, has no basis in the history of humanity since Adam's Fall. It is a total renewal, a "new creation" (2 Cor 5:17), an opening of the gate to the Kingdom of God (that will appear very soon!), and an incitement to the missionary work of the community of the reborn brothers and sisters. It is no coincidence that a disciple of Hoffman, Bernhard Rothmann, would play an important role in the violent and extremist Münster rebellion of 1534. Afterward, the Anabaptist movement regrouped around Menno on a pacifist foundation. Nevertheless, Menno defended Hoffman's doctrine of the incarnation, and concentrated on the community as being born "without a spot or wrinkle" (Eph 5:27), increasingly separated from the "world." In the course of several disputes—especially with the Reformed—Menno hesitated to clarify in more detail what was meant by "heavenly flesh" and where it comes from. At the same time, he held unshakably that the incarnate Son in his pureness had never been touched by any splinter of the world of sin.

It seems clear to me that this newly reconstructed, more Reformational, and less spiritualistic, Melchioristic-Mennist doctrine would not have convinced Calvin. For example, the lack of any notion of a justification of the *godless* in it would have remained unacceptable to him. Nevertheless, I see at least two questions to think through in the unfolding of our argument. First, we saw that Calvin, writing against Osiander, rejected all speculation beyond the biblical witness. But in refusing speculation, he himself was in danger of reproducing classical doctrine that perhaps never had been "biblical." Bruce McCormack, among others, mentions the presupposition of divine impassibility in this connection. By contrast, the adherents of the (monothelite) Mennist doctrine asserted that for the eternal, only begotten Son incarnation *must* mean that the perfect God had been made smaller, weakened, and changed.[43] Because of the mystery of divine love, reconciliation in accordance with Phil 2 and John 6 *must* have implied such a kenosis, in which the eternal Son himself suffered and died for our sins. Calvin resisted such considerations in invoking Erasmus's emphasis upon the ethical tendency of

---

43. Voolstra, *Het Woord is vlees geworden*, 168, quoting sentences of the Flemish Mennists De Cuyper and Outerman.

Phil 2:7–8. But did Calvin say enough about the eternal Son with this defense? Second, in the discussion of Calvin's dispute with Osiander, we contrasted "ontological" and "soteriological" intentions. Now, it is clear that the Mennist current brings pressure to bear upon the Reformation understanding of salvation. For Mennists, salvation is being born again, sanctification *besides* justification. In response, we must redefine "soteriology" along the main lines of the third book of the *Institutes* of 1559 as *duplex gratia*.[44] In this sense, it is said in the Netherlands that a Reformed believer, in contrast to a Lutheran, is a twin of the Mennonite.[45]

Michael Servetus (2.14.5–2.14.8)

In my view, Calvin appears deeply shocked by the enthusiastic, extremely direct ecstasy spoken of by Michael Servetus (1509/1511–53), the Spanish Marrano, physician, and provocative thinker. Servetus seems to suggest that any border between divinity and humanity, as well as between creatures, should be erased. Calvin comments that "[Servetus] regards Christ to be a mixture of some divine and some human elements, but not to be reckoned both God and man."[46] Through such confusion and mingling, Servetus tries to achieve an immediate experience of an overflow of divine glory that neglects the need to look forward to the realization of eschatological promise, the need to stand at the "sentry post" of eternity, which for Calvin characterizes the life of a Christian in *this* world.[47]

In chapter 2.14, Calvin seeks to insert his criticisms of Servetus's Christology in the previously written sections on the person of the Mediator, though even in 1539, Servetus was not completely absent. Such an insertion was not a simple operation, because Servetus could hardly be seen as a thinker of the church, who in thinking critically about dogma tries to improve or to vary it. Servetus's whole coordinate system is very different. It is my impression that Calvin tries to make clear how the doctrine of the hypostatic union is *the* instrument by which every attempt to cross boundaries that have been drawn by dogma can be blocked. God

---

44. Calvin, *Institutes*, 3.6.6 (*OS* 4:187, line 30).
45. Noordmans, *Verzamelde Werken*, 464.
46. Calvin, *Institutes*, 2.14.5 (*OS* 3:464, lines 11–13).
47. For this image (derived from Cicero) see Calvin, *Institutes*, 3.9.4; 3.10.6. Calvin's strongly eschatologically motivated criticism of Servetus is instructive: "He pretends that by faith in the gospel we share in the fulfilment of all the promises. As if there were no difference between us and Christ!" (*Institutes*, 2.9.3 [*OS* 3:400, lines 25–27]).

as such cannot be flesh, and the flesh as such cannot be God. There is no connection between (and no separation *in* the connection between) the divine nature and the human nature of Christ in abstraction from the decision and the free act of the triune God, in which the Word becomes flesh. For that reason, it is important that it is said in Phil 2:7 that "Christ could not divest himself of Godhead, but he kept it concealed for a time, that it might not be seen, under the weakness of the flesh," for kenosis must be seen as a covering of divine majesty.[48] No immediacy! No direct accessibility! Esteeming the mystery of the incarnation, and therewith enduring in humility and obedience, has been asked of Jesus Christ and (in him) of all of us as well. In contrast, Servetus willingly renounces that mindset.

For Calvin, as he elaborates in his 1548 commentary, an orthodox, anti-Arian interpretation of Phil 2:6 is necessary: "Being in the form of God, he reckoned it not an unlawful thing for him to show himself in that form." Although Erasmus pretends to be in favor of a Nicene orthodoxy, he denies that this orthodoxy can be confirmed by this verse and proposes to read this verse as referring to the *logos ensarkos* (as he does again vis-à-vis v. 7, in which case Calvin follows him). But then the complaint—perhaps somewhat "fundamentalist" in our perception—follows: "But what am I the better for his orthodox confession, if my faith is not supported by any Scripture authority?"[49] Here in *Institutes* 2.14 we can discover the reason for Calvin's stubbornness. A major part of the dispute with Servetus—including at least eleven of the thirty-four quotations from his works that are cited in this chapter, sixteen of which are located in section 8—is dedicated to the defense of the "orthodox" doctrine of the *eternal generation* of the Son. Servetus rejects the Nicene dogma, but in Calvin's analysis, his basic assumption for that is rather Sabellian than

---

48. Cf. Calvin's explanation of Phil 2:7 as mentioned above, n1. The corresponding sentence in the *Institutes* can partly be found already in the edition of 1543, 7.12; *CO* 1:520 (*OS* 3:451n, lines 27–29); and later in the *Institutes* of 1559, 2.13.2 (*OS* 3:450, line 20: "quia scilicet imaginem servus induit, et ea humilitate contentus, carnis velamina suam diviniaten abscondi passus est" [He took the image of a servant, and content with such lowliness, endured his divinity to be hidden by a "veil of flesh"; translation revised]). How kenosis as *occultatio divinae maiestatis* (governed by the perception of revelation as divine *accommodatio*) pervades Calvin's explanation of the Synoptic Gospels has been sketched in the fine book of Schellong, *Calvins Auslegung der synoptischen Evangelien*.

49. Cf. Essary, "Radical Humility of Christ in the Sixteenth Century," 411. McCormack quotes Calvin's agreement with Erasmus on the interpretation of v. 7 but is silent with regard to Calvin's dissent from Erasmus vis-à-vis v. 6 (*Humility of the Eternal Son*).

Arian in nature. "Before Christ was revealed in the flesh there were only shadow figures in God," Servetus asserts, and continues: "The truth or effect of these appeared only when the Word, who had been destined for this honour, truly began to be the Son of God";[50] and "the Son of God was from the beginning an idea," so that "the figurative representation of Christ took the place of begetting."[51] On this ground, for Servetus, the "being in the form of God" of Phil 2:6 must be read as a "sheer formal" distinction of the persons (and hence, indeed, in the manner of Sabellianism). If the Word becomes Son, then, this takes place not only in Jesus, but at the same time in the fullness of *all* persons and things who were intended in this initial divine idea. Against this tendency, Calvin wants to maintain unwaveringly that "to neither angels nor men was God ever Father, except regarding his only begotten Son; and men, especially, hateful to God because of their iniquity, become God's sons by free adoption because Christ is the Son of God by nature."[52] Therewith, the argument is quite fundamental: if Christ is not the eternal Son, the faith of all ages would have been void. The eternal generation is the actual ground of faith. It is worthwhile keeping in mind the importance of this insight for Calvin, when we ask—as we have already done and will continue to do—concerning the effects of the experiences of Jesus Christ in his history on the eternal Logos.

Giorgio Biandrata (2.14.3; 2.14.4; 2.14.6) and Beyond

After the execution of Servetus, anti-Trinitarian feelings remained present among the Italian community in the city of Geneva. Giorgio Biandrata (latinized as Blandrata, 1515/1516–88), also a physician (Calvin had difficulties with members of this profession), was a searching soul who visited the reformer with persistent questions. After Biandrata had written these questions down, Calvin responded in a series of short, thetic sentences.[53] Most of those theses were used by Calvin in the chap-

---

50. Calvin, *Institutes*, 2.14.5 (*OS* 3:464, lines 14–17).

51. Calvin, *Institutes*, 2.14.8 (*OS* 3:470, lines 8–10, lines 15–16, respectively).

52. Calvin, *Institutes*, 2.14.5 (*OS* 3:465, lines 24–28). A more extensive variant of this reasoning can be found in Calvin's "Defensio orthodoxae fidei de sacra Trinitate," published in 1554, the year after Servetus's execution, in *CO* 8:488 (453–644).

53. "Quaestiones Blandratae," in Calvin, *CO* 17:169–71; "Responsum ad quaestiones Georgii Blandratae," in *CO* 9:321–32. See Tylenda, "Warning That Went Unheeded." An English translation of Biandrata's memorandum and of Calvin's answers are offered in the appendix.

ter on the Trinity in book 1 of the final edition of the *Institutes*, but four questions remained for the chapter in question on the mediatorship of Christ.[54] Generally, one can say that Biandrata was a disciple of Servetus, but gradually, and especially in his later years in Poland and Transylvania, he evolved in the direction of unitarianism and Socinianism. In this way, he personifies a development in anti-Trinitarian thought from an initial ecstatic pantheism toward a more rationalistic deism.

Most of Biandrata's questions suggest that it would be enough to acknowledge the Godhead of the Father. A double procedure the speaking of the Son—equal to the Father as regards divinity, less than the Father as regards the mediatorship of reconciliation—would be unnecessarily complicated.[55] In the New Testament, the name "Lord" should be reserved to Jesus Christ—as in 1 Cor 8:6: "For us there is one God, the Father, from whom are all things and for whom we exist, and one Lord, Jesus Christ, through whom are all things and through whom we exist"—and it is used of the Father only when the work of his Son is meant. However, Calvin answers, "to restrict the word Lord to the person of the Mediator is trifling and silly because the apostles indiscriminately use the word Lord of Yahweh."[56] Then how, Biandrata further asks, does Christ exercise his Lordship "through whom all things exist" in the office of Mediator before the incarnation? In this respect, Calvin's answer is more elaborate than the question anticipates:

> As Mediator he puts himself, with reference to his office, on an inferior level, in order to draw us little by little to the Father. In this respect, the Son himself submits to the Father in the future age because the very perfection of divinity, which is now seen in a mirror according to our capacity, will be then made most clear to us.[57]

---

54. Calvin, *Institutes*, 1.13.20(–27); 2.14.3; 2.14.4; 2.14.6 (*OS* 3:134–35, 142, 144, 462, 466).

55. Cf. the formula in the so-called Athanasian Creed that displeased Biandrata: "equal to the Father as regards divinity, less than the Father as regards humanity."

56. "Responsum ad questions Blandratae," in Calvin, *CO* 9:328; Tylenda, "Warning That Went Unheeded," 59.

57. "Responsum ad questions Blandratae," in Calvin, *CO* 9:326–27; Tylenda, "Warning That Went Unheeded," 56.

Up until now, we have heard Calvin speaking on the mediatorship (of creation) only *before* the incarnation, but now, uninvited, he also speaks of and looks for its *future* state.

> That is, to him was lordship committed by the Father, until such time as we should see his divine majesty face to face. Then he returns the lordship to his Father [1 Cor 15:24-28] so that—far from diminishing his own majesty—it may shine all the more brightly. Then, also, God shall cease to be the Head of Christ, for Christ's own deity will shine of itself, although yet is it covered by a veil.[58]

This reasoning, going beyond the letter of Biandrata's question, is continued in the following chapter in connection with the royal office of the Mediator, which will end with the final judgment as the last act of Christ's reign.[59]

Recently, Rowan Williams has characterized this proposal as a "very eccentric proposition at first sight,"[60] and indeed it is difficult to grasp. Is it meant in the sense of the fourth-century theologian Marcellus of Ancyra, who seems to teach an end of the history of the incarnation at the eschaton, so that the economic Trinity will come to an end and only the immanent Trinity will be left? In any case, Calvin does not seem to deny that "of his kingdom there will be no end" (Luke 1:33), the sentence with which the Council of Constantinople in 381 rejected the doctrine of Marcellus. In the eyes of Calvin, then, there remains some room for an eternal Kingdom of Christ in his divine majesty. But it does seem to be important for Calvin that "the veil, by which the divine majesty was concealed" though the humility of Jesus Christ, according to the hymn on the kenosis of the Son, will be removed, so that we will enjoy a pure vision of the triune God himself in his glory, "and Christ's humanity will then no longer be interposed to keep us back from a closer view of God."[61] In this view, the humanity of Christ is not imperishable.

---

58. Calvin, *Institutes*, 2.14.3 (*OS* 3:462, lines 18-23).

59. Calvin, *Institutes*, 2.15.5 (*OS* 3:478, line 8—479, line 33). In this section, we also find once again §7.7 from the *Institutes* between 1539 and 1554, on the title "Lord" in the Apostles' Creed.

60. Williams, *Christ the Heart of Creation*, 149-50.

61. "Christ will then restore the kingdom which he has received, that we may cleave wholly to God. Nor will he in this way resign the kingdom but will transfer it in a manner from his humanity to his glorious divinity, because a way of approach will then be opened up, from which our infirmity now keeps us back. Thus, then Christ will be subjected to the Father, because the vail [*sic*] being then removed, we shall openly

PART THREE | CONSTRUCTION

In the Netherlands, it was Arnold A. van Ruler (1908-70), professor of dogmatics in Utrecht, who tried to rethink this specific heritage of Calvin for the twentieth century.[62] For him, the work of Christ as Redeemer was undertaken with the aim of restoring creation after the Fall to its original order (and *not* as a "new creation" in the Anabaptist sense). Christ is the Mediator of creation, too, and this work of his is not substitutional. The incarnation was only an "emergency measure" that became necessary because of the sin and the guilt of human beings, but Christian doctrine neither begins nor ends with it. Instead of the "christological concentration" of Karl Barth, one can better speak of a "messianic intermezzo" between the beginning and the end. For it must be said, Ruler argued, that the work of redemption is, indeed, in the center, but it is not the focus of what the incarnation is *for*, namely, the honor of God and the happiness of human beings before God. For that reason, the church certainly has to preach the Gospel, but it must equally—or even more—impose the Law, to Christianize civilizations on earth. Therefore, in my perception it was not by chance that Ruler defended the colonial politics of the Kingdom of the Netherlands in Indonesia after the Second World War on theological grounds.

Of course, Ruler's theology does not offer the only possible interpretation of Calvin's "very eccentric propositions" regarding the eschatological ending of the office of the Mediator of redemption. Precisely in this connection I prefer to give the last word to Karl Barth. In his lectures on the ethics of reconciliation at the end of his academic career (1959-61), and specifically in his reflections on the second petition of the Lord's Prayer, the plea for the swift coming of the Kingdom and its justice, Barth asks whether the Kingdom of the Father must be identified with the Kingdom of the Lord Jesus Christ himself, who prays for it. And in that connection, he too is compelled to offer his reading of the "famous passage" 1 Cor 15:24-28: "Christ at his final Parousia will hand over the kingdom to the Father and having overcome all hostile

---

behold God reigning in his majesty, and Christ's humanity will then no longer be interposed to keep us back from a closer view of God" ("Commentary on 1 Corinthians 15:27" [1546], in Calvin, *CO* 40:549). Cf. "De christologie van Calvin," in Breukelman, *Theologische Opstellen*, 350. For me, it is difficult to grasp how it is possible to combine this vision with the importance of the humanity of Christ as safeguarding our eschatological humanity for God.

62. "Verhouding van het kosmologische en het eschatologische moment in de christologie," in Ruler, *Christus, de Geest en het heil*, 139-65.

forces will himself be subject to God, who has subjected all things to him." Barth writes:

> This passage says that in its future and definitive manifestation, in the form in which we are still to expect it, the kingdom of God will be revealed as the kingdom whose warring, victorious, and triumphant King and Lord is the Son *of God* and therefore Jesus Christ, *the Son* of God, however, who does not advance his own cause as distinct from the Father's, but who subjects himself to the Father, is obedient to him, and acts in his service and in fulfilment of his will and work. If then, he is manifested in the last form of his Parousia in his *subjection* and *servanthood*, if his kingdom is manifested as that of the Servant of the Lord [*ebed* Yahweh], this implies no later restriction but is the authentic interpretation of his action as King and Lord in the kingdom of *God* as his *own* kingdom. His *passion* was itself his action as Kyrios. It is the very thing that *proves* and *confirms* the *identity* of his kingdom with God's. Precisely in his *humility* as the Son of the Father, he has overcome the world and reconciled it to God. Precisely in relation to it, then, there can be no talk of the limitation of his kingdom by God's or of the end of his kingdom. No, in it "God has highly exalted him and bestowed on him the name which is above every name" (Phil 2:9). In it he is the One of whose kingdom there will be no end, for God's kingdom is everlasting.[63]

Read in this way—1 Cor 15:24-28 from the perspective of Phil 2:5-11— the *humility of the eternal Son* is no incident, no intermezzo that will be dissolved, but decisively and forever characterizes this particular God! Perhaps we might even take one step further and suggest a possible reading of Paul's later eschatological perspective, "that God may be all in all." This God does not will to possess a Kingdom only for himself, but in the end, after putting an end to all domination and all enmity, he wills that his humility and his willingness to serve, the characteristics in which he was and remains amid us in his Son, will be common to all creatures, who will then all be servants of one another.[64]

---

63. Barth, *Christian Life*, 263–64, translation slightly corrected. It is delightful to read here Barth's comment regarding Graf N. L. von Zinzendorf, who "took terrible offense at Paul over this, chalked it up as an error, flatly refused to recognize it as binding and ventured the bold hypothesis that because of it Paul was punished with the 'thorn in the flesh' mentioned in 2 Corinthians 12:7."

64. Cf. Reeling Brouwer, "Und seines Königreiches wird kein Ende sein."

PART THREE | CONSTRUCTION

CONCLUSION

The extent to which we can combine Barth's eschatological vision with that of Calvin is surely questionable. But can Calvin's doctrine, as it has been sketched in our analysis, be accepted? For Calvin, neither the preexistence of the Logos as the Mediator of creation nor the eschatological outcome of his divine majesty—that it is no longer covered, but that it can shine without a remnant of the humanity even of the human being Jesus—has been touched by the humility of Christ. Is it, therefore, a doctrine in which kenosis is conceived as a sheer temporary measure? Karl Barth certainly had reasons, when he discovered (by my reckoning at the earliest around 1933–34)[65] that a "pure" Reformed concept of kenosis needed correction. In Barth's context it was a correction that took the Lutheran position into account. We, however, are free to rethink it in our own way.

---

65. Rinse H. Reeling Brouwer, "Jesus Christ," in Jones and Nimmo, *Oxford Handbook of Karl Barth*, 284–85.

CHAPTER 11

"The Princeton Creed"

Expanding the Underlying Romanticism in Bruce McCormack and Karl Barth—on Dogmatics, Trinity, Kenosis

Alexandra Pârvan

"HOPEFULLY, WE ALL HAVE THE ROMANTIC IN OUR BLOOD"[1]

That Barth could still say this at the end of a forty-page chapter where he purposefully argued the contrary—that Reformed theology should leave behind the heritage of romanticism—is testament to his own self-conflicting, underground intellectual romanticism, as well as, perhaps, to the mystifying nature of the artistic phenomenon itself.

Romanticism was a literary movement that erupted in both England and Germany in 1798[2] and spread vigorously throughout the whole of Europe and both Americas, generating relevant works during the following ninety years. Even though it did not appear out of nothing, being prefigured by several decades of pre-romanticism, when it did eventually

---

1. "Uns Allen als Kindern des Zeitalters, an dessen Anfang Novalis stand, der Romantiker, hoffentlich . . . wenigstens der reine Romantiker, auch im Blute sitzt" (Barth, *Protestantische Theologie im 19. Jahrhundert*, 342).

2. The year marks the publication of *Lyrical Ballads* by William Wordsworth and Samuel Taylor Coleridge in England and the periodical *Athenaeum* (1798–1800) in Germany, the primary venue for the works of the early German romantics. The 1798 contributors were the two editors, the brothers Schlegel (August Wilhelm and Friedrich), and Novalis. Aside from these three, between 1799 and 1800 some other contributors were Caroline Schlegel, Friedrich Schleiermacher, August Ludwig Hülsen, Sophie Tieck (Bernhardi), and Dorothea Schlegel.

explode it produced a cultural commotion. It changed the language, content, form, nature, function, and purpose of literature, and through it all the expression of human identity and faculties, thus reshaping the human situation in history, society, and nature. Its earthquake waves spread through the visual arts and music, history, theology, philosophy, economy, social theory, state theory, and jurisprudence, as well as the natural sciences, influencing the way biology, physics, chemistry, and medicine were understood, approached, and practiced.

It was normal for romanticism to be shape shifting, given its geographical and chronological coverage. Traversing time, countries, and continents over a period of intense sociopolitical tumult, it could not incarnate itself in a fixed a-historical, a-national, a-cultural, patterned identity; in addition, such an achievement was never sought and would have gone against romanticism's core innovations and its own fight to define its character precisely in opposition to anything that can be prefixed by an *a*, and hence anything "atemporal" or "impersonal." To the entire movement (in its transnational and transcontinental diverse expressions) could usefully be applied the description given by August Wilhelm Schlegel to the (romantic) work of art as resembling an English park: "Its separate parts" have a "hidden order," as the "succession of landscapes," "their gradation, their alternation, and their opposition, give effect to each other" and acquire unity "in a higher sphere," which retains its mystery when subjected to mere critical dissection.[3]

Throughout its sections this essay singles out, comments on, and develops (in a theologically relevant way) characteristic aspects of romanticism in order to: identify how they appear or are interacted with in the work of Karl Barth and Bruce McCormack; detect problems and ways to amend them in either author; and explain why contemporary theologies cannot move forward while preserving or "repairing" ancient creeds. In addition, because of the two theologians under focus the latter is still alive, here again (as I have done before)[4] the examination of his work is simultaneously intended as the basis of a new theology which only thereby begins. Using Friedrich Schlegel's own description of this method, and replacing "literature" with "theology," I aim for

> [A] criticism that would not be so much the commentary on an already existing, completed, withered [theology], but rather the

---

3. A. W. Schlegel, *Dramatic Art and Literature*, 273, 244.
4. Pârvan, "Eroticism in the Kenotic God."

organon of a [theology] still to be completed, formed, indeed initiated. . . . Thus, a criticism that would consist not merely in explaining and preserving, but would be itself producing, at least indirectly through guidance, arrangement, and excitation.[5]

My broader argument, which will gradually emerge, can also be stated in one (perhaps plural) romantic voice, this time by replacing "philosopher" with "theologian": "The [theologian] must possess as much aesthetic power as the poet."[6] The Romantics gave art central place in the discussion and understanding of the absolute. I hold that insofar as it tries to speak about God—who is not like anything that is given in our reality—insofar as it composes a discourse about one who remains above all possibilities of (regular) speech and, therefore, insofar as it pretends to see (understand) a transcendent reality and communicate it to others as fully as possible, theology needs artistic vision and resources. A good theological creation—like any creation—is artistic.

"CAN WE REQUIRE OF THE BIRD THAT IT FLY IN A TANK OF COMPRESSED AIR?"[7]

The first characteristic of romanticism that I will address is its vehement polemic against the aesthetics of seventeenth-century artistic classicism.[8] As I go on to address the confrontation between romanticism and classicism held on literary ground, I ask my potentially impatient theologian

---

5. F. Schlegel, *Lessings Geist aus seinen Schriften*, 10–11; emphasis added. Throughout the chapter, unless indicated otherwise, all translations into English from German, French, Italian, or Romanian are mine.

6. "Das älteste Systemprogramm des deutschen Idealismus" (1796), in Hölderlin, *Sämtliche Werke*, 310–11. Presumed to be authored by the "Tübingen Three" geniuses—Hegel, Hölderlin, and Schelling—who shared a room while studying theology there; handwritten by the former, believed to be composed by any one of the three or all three, with scholars oscillating mostly between the last two, and favoring Schelling as main author. In 1995, Friedrich Schlegel was also proposed by Martin Oesch as the author of this manifesto.

7. "Mais peut-on exiger de l'oiseau qu'il vole sous le recipient pneumatique?" (Hugo, *Cromwell*, 23).

8. "Classicism"—sometimes alternated in English-language scholarship with the term "neoclassicism"—denotes the aesthetic thinking crystallized and advanced in Europe in the seventeenth century and enduring throughout the eighteenth century. It had proponents and adepts in every country, but its most systematic and normative expression is given in Nicolas Boileau's *L'art poétique* (1674), which made France the radiating center of classicism.

reader to draw in their mind a parallel between these two artistic universes and two forms of doing theology, one that follows closely the tradition (whether classic or Reformed) and one that moves away from it to establish its own, coherent, and distinct ground. Throughout the essay the words "art" and "artistic creation" will refer almost exclusively to poetry and literature.

Classicism was characterized by the strict submission of artistic creation to norms or rules of composition, many of which were set or assumed to be set by Aristotle. The Philosopher is found lacking due to the external comprehension of his object (the arts of rhetoric and poetry); the exclusion from the instruments of understanding of the "imagination or feeling"; and his "anatomical ideas . . . [that came to be] stamped as rules" by "the critics of the dissecting school": "Three unities, five acts: why not seven persons? These rules seem to proceed according to odd numbers."[9] Critics do violence in "hiding themselves behind Aristotle" and condemning innovative work in his name, with the result that "the classic torpedo" has paralyzed even the creative powers of *classic* authors.[10] "To criss-cross the unity of time with the unity of place like the bars of a cage, and force therein, in the name of Aristotle," "real life," which is the subject of a poet's work, "is to mutilate human beings and things, and make history grimace"; the result of such operation carried out by "the dogmatic mutilators" is that "what was alive . . . is [now] dead" and hence "the cage of unities often contains only a skeleton."[11] Instead: "If poetry is the expression of the living nature it must itself be as alive as the object it expresses, as free as the thought that moves it, as daring as the goal that it is addressed to."[12] Not only ancient regularities are not proper to modern writings, but even the Greeks—for whose specific literary forms they were established—did not follow them blindly.[13] That

---

9. A. W. Schlegel, *Dramatic Art and Literature*, 238, 240, 244, 248. On the territory of the drama/tragedy where—along with that of the literary genres—the classic vs. romantic dispute has mostly played out, A. W. Schlegel is very clear on Aristotle's contribution to the obligatory "classic" three unities (of time, place, and action), against which the Romantics typically and fervently protested (cf. lecture 17).

10. Hugo, *Cromwell*. And the best of the *contemporary* classic authors are, according to Berchet, those who display "a great commixture with the romantic" (Berchet, "Lettera").

11. Hugo, *Cromwell*, 20.

12. Berchet, "Lettera."

13. Cf. A. W. Schlegel, *Dramatic Art and Literature*, 259; Hugo, *Cromwell*; Manzoni, "Lettre"; Shelley, preface to *Prometheus Unbound*, 119.

is because it is not the rules that make the poetry; the poet uses them (which also entails modifying them) to give center stage to his intentions, avers Giovanni Berchet—and that is one reason why "had they lived in our time ... Homer, Pindar and Sophocles would have been 'romantic' poets." Hence the poet's invocation: "Why do you not incarnate yourself again good soul of Homer ... to descend in Italy and set ablaze all Poetics, from that of Aristotle to that of Menzini?"[14]

Thus, the Romantics rose vigorously against "the infallibility of Aristotle,"[15] or what Hugo calls "the fundamental law of the pseudo-Aristotelian code."[16] Their voices warn that in "building around itself the Great Wall of China," "this literary orthodoxy ... that is opposed to any fortunate innovation, should in the long term render literature very sterile."[17] Under "the thousand abuses of this little inquisition of the spirit,"[18] "walled in by dogmas and rules,"[19] what was alive dies, because "all these absolute and exclusive rules" are artificial, forged on abstract ideas, which go against reality, experience, nature, and history, and weaken the creative freedom.[20] "I have wished to keep my reader in the company of flesh and blood" is how Wordsworth explains his departure from the classic elevated style, with its prescribed mechanical devices.[21] On the Romanian front, poet Cezar Bolliac rejects explanations of poetry given by Aristotle, Horace, and Boileau, and notes that Shakespeare and Hugo did not have a language forged in Boileau's factory but "a very imperfect language," because "what else is the poet but a reflection of the seen and the unseen nature? And is nature always perfect? ... Why do we demand that poetry be more perfect and consistent than nature?"[22] The mystery of poetry and its revelatory nature are incompatible with rules and canons, clamored the Romantics.[23] The spirit of poetry "cannot be matured by law and precept," writes Keats: "That which is creative must

14. Berchet, "Lettera."
15. A. W. Schlegel, *Dramatic Art and Literature*, 275.
16. Hugo, *Cromwell*, 18.
17. Staël, *Corinne*, bk. 7, ch. 2, 259; ch. 1, 241.
18. Hugo, *Hernani*, 4.
19. Hugo, *Cromwell*, 23.
20. Manzoni, "Lettre." Cf. Berchet, "Lettera."
21. Wordsworth, preface to *Lyrical Ballads*.
22. Bolliac, *Opere*, 23.
23. Cf. A. W. Schlegel, *Vorlesungen über schöne Litteratur*, 261, 93; Staël, *Oeuvres*, bk. 2, ch. 10, 127; Shelley, "Defence of Poetry," paras. 12, 39.

create itself."²⁴ While classic art—with its respect for order, symmetry, clarity, certitude, proportion, good taste, and cultivated expression—was submitted to a rigid and obligatory formal discipline, in romanticism the creative spirit accepts formal convention but only to "move with a becoming liberty, within its proper precincts," acting according to its nature and not artificial, external laws, which only drain out its strength.²⁵ That is to say, the Romantics sought freedom from any conventions that were not sanctioned or installed by the creative spirit itself; they were in pursuit of the naturalness of the artistic process:²⁶ "If Poetry comes not as naturally as the Leaves to a tree it had better not come at all," decides Keats.²⁷ There is no contradiction between art and nature.²⁸ And so Hugo would declaim: "Nature, then! Nature and truth!"; "The poet . . . should take advice only from nature, truth, and inspiration, the latter being itself also a kind of nature and truth."²⁹

For the reigning seventeenth-century poetics—which gave "excessive, and almost exclusive attention to the form," with almost no connection to the work itself³⁰—art was canonical and, in virtue of this constitutional quality, classic art was proclaimed to be the only valid one, regardless of time or space.³¹ Classicism was an art of perfection, and claimed itself to be perfect; it was oriented toward the general, the abstract, the immutable, and I could even say the impossible, insofar as it did not want to stir the spirits, to generate doubt, or to awaken discontent

---

24. "Letter to Hessey, 8 Oct. 1818," in Keats, *Selected Letters of John Keats*, 193.

25. A. W. Schlegel, *Dramatic Art and Literature*, 340, 245; cf. F. Schlegel, *Kritische Fragmente*, #37; Staël, *Oeuvres*, bk. 2, ch. 10, 126; Berchet, "Lettera"; Hugo, *Cromwell*.

26. Cf. A. W. Schlegel, *Dramatic Art and Literature*, 340: the romantic form resembles the growing of a plant, or an embryo; it shapes from the inside to the outside and acquires its determination in the process of its natural development.

27. "Letter to John Taylor, 27 Feb. 1818," in Keats, *Selected Letters of John Keats*, 96; cf. Shelley, "Defence of Poetry," para. 9.

28. A. W. Schlegel, *Dramatic Art and Literature*, 259. "Nature has artistic instinct; hence, to distinguish between nature and art is to blather," writes Novalis (*Gesammelte Werke*, 4:257, #2858).

29. Hugo, *Cromwell*, 24–25.

30. Manzoni, "Lettre."

31. A. W. Schlegel can thus speak of "the great discovery" that not all art is classic, as he pleads for the rights, dignity, and value of romantic art (*Vorlesungen über schöne Litteratur*, 22; cf. *Dramatic Art and Literature*, 234, 237). In his 1802 preface to *Lyrical Ballads*, Wordsworth is acutely conscious that he goes against "a canon of criticism" according to which what he composed cannot even be called poetry.

in audiences.[32] It preferred a preestablished order of things, and all that was asked of the artist was conformity to this order and the skill of a craftsperson,[33] in order to create in accordance with indisputable norms considered impossible of betterment.[34]

"But can we require of the bird that it fly in a tank of compressed air?" The Romantics aimed to liberate the poetic conscience of any restrictions and confinements that would compromise the livingness of art and the autonomy of inspiration.

> To hell with this tomfoolery! Show me a Poetics that precedes the existence of a poet. Show me a true poet educated and formed by the Poetics. Where is it, where is it? I will show you poets whose works have offered material good to fill with petty rules the petty books of thirty petty masters. I will show you thirty thousand pedants, and all of them sons of the Poetics, measurers of syllables, know-it-alls, and blockheads. To hell with the Poetics![35]

The Romantics associated perfection (impeccable form) with limitation. Because it is closed on itself, classic poetry is finite; and it is also descriptively static, marked by fixity.[36] Perfection brings with it determination and confinement (ancient poetry cannot be otherwise): "Yet in the

32. On the classic author's obligation to please the public, see A. W. Schlegel, *Dramatic Art and Literature*, 270–73; Manzoni, "Lettre."

33. For the romantic protest against the reduction of artistic creation to the artificiality of impeccable technique, see A. W. Schlegel, *Dramatic Art and Literature*, 274; A. W. Schlegel, *Vorlesungen über schöne Litteratur*, 264–65; Staël, *Oeuvres*, bk. 2, ch. 10, 125–26; Shelley, preface to *Prometheus Unbound*, 122–23; Hugo, *Cromwell*.

34. Cf. A. W. Schlegel, *Dramatic Art and Literature*, 339. Hugo writes, "The critics of the scholastic school place their poets in a peculiar position. On the one hand they cry incessantly: Copy the models! On the other hand they have the habit of declaring that 'the models are inimitable'" (*Cromwell*, 24). Mihail Kogălniceanu observes, "All those compositions were *imitated* odes, anacreontic verses, hymns and fables, and especially sonnets, the favourite kind of poetry of the Orpheuses that were deafening our ears at that time" (i.e., the time of classic production) (*Scrieri*, 154; emphasis added). Madame de Staël avers that there is no imitation in nature, and hence in art too "imitation is a kind of death because it strips each individual of their natural existence"; on the ground of the ancients, the poet of today can only imitate, not create (*Corinne*, bk. 7, ch. 1, 241–42; bk. 8, ch. 3, 316. For Berchet, the romantic poet places herself in direct dialogue with nature and nature does not speak to her of ancient thoughts and affects, but of modern ones; the poet's object is the ongoing, present, real life, not the imitation of past life ("Lettera").

35. Berchet, "Lettera."

36. Cf. F. Schlegel, *Kritische Fragmente*, #93, #84; A. W. Schlegel, *Dramatic Art and Literature*, lecture 1, lecture 22.

universe of poetry itself nothing is at rest, everything is in becoming, transformation, and harmonious movement."[37] Classic art looks backward, toward the past,[38] as does any system considered perfect, complete in itself, self-sufficient, irreformable, unalterable, and the culmination of all previous efforts throughout the ages. Any *system* is repugnant to the romantic spirit, because it is closed, and thus cannot tend toward the infinite.[39] As a system, classicism involves the mechanical, the simple, the pure, the hierarchical, the conventional, the discursive, all of which are incapable of rendering the spirit of literature; the latter knows no artificial delimitations, traverses all genres, and binds them together to reflect the complex, the real, the natural of both life and art. The Romantics sought to express a reality of less clear contours, one that cannot be strictly delimited, and reached for a different unity in their art, one more fluent, tuneful, more spontaneous, allowing for the unknown, and thus always open and permeable to the infinite and its mystery. This superior unity is not reached in uniformity or simple continuity; rather, as nature's own unity, it encompasses and transcends inner fractures and disorder.

And so, romanticism is "an open model."[40] When the Romantics rejected a prideful stationing within the limits of preestablished formulas, they made permanent renewal to be art's very principle of existence.[41] "Romantic poetry . . . is perpetually striving after new and marvellous

37. F. Schlegel, *Athenaeums-Fragmente*, #434.

38. Combined with its formal and conceptual immobility, as well as with its categorial ideal universality, this turn toward the past makes for an *a-historical viewpoint* in classicism, very different from how the Romantics themselves turned toward and made use of the past. Cf. F. Schlegel, *Gespräch*, 334, 348; A. W. Schlegel, *Dramatic Art and Literature*, lecture 17; Staël, *Oeuvres*, bk. 2, ch. 11, 129–30.

39. Cf. A. W. Schlegel, *Dramatic Art and Literature*, lecture 17; Manzoni, "Lettre." Hugo writes: "Let us take the hammer to theories, poetics, and systems"; they are "bothersome for talent" and comfortable for imitators, such that "the flood of mediocrity" and the "proliferation of poetics" occur simultaneously (*Cromwell*, 24–25). Cf. Sand: "I did not have any system . . . the simplest idea, the most banal circumstance are the only sources of inspiration that works of art should have" (1852 "Notice" to *Mare au diable*); see also her letter "À Gustave Flaubert." On the presumed positive appraisal of the "system" by both F. Schlegel and Novalis, I notice that the synthesis they seek is not static, but dynamic, open, and unlimited, and hence the word "system" is not the right term for it; rather, Novalis's formula of the *System der Systemlosigkeit* is (Novalis, *Werke*, 2:291, #681).

40. Petre Pârvan, *Romantismul*, 184. Viewed through later structuralist theories, romanticism is an open structure with infinite possibilities of reflecting reality within a recognizable conceptual rhetoric (19–20, 182–84).

41. Petre Pârvan, *Romantismul*, 8.

births."⁴² Romantic art is in continuous development, limitless, free, alive as life itself is alive, never perfected or finished such that it could be dissected, as a dead object; it looks ahead, progressing toward a constantly renewed future.

> Romantic poetry is a progressive universal poetry. . . . Other types of poetry are complete and can now be thoroughly dissected. Romantic poetry is still in the becoming; indeed, this is its very essence, that it is forever becoming, and can never be finished. . . . It alone is infinite, just as it alone is free. . . . Romantic poetry is . . . so to speak, poetry itself: for in a certain sense, all poetry is or should be romantic.⁴³

And so, "the romantic spirit is intuitively identified with the poetic," insofar as "a conviction dear to the Romantics" is that

> true art is *becoming*, transformation, spontaneity and novelty. . . . If the essential trait of reality is the becoming, then authentic literature can only be that which captures life in its ceaseless movement, being itself in continuous evolution. [Through] art's dynamic quality . . . the creative spirit is integrated in the general becoming of the real world and mirrors this becoming.⁴⁴

In the words of A. W. Schlegel: "In romantic poetry the striving towards the infinite is expressed not just in individual works of art, but in the entire development of art. Unlimited progressiveness."⁴⁵

The Romantics, then, rebelled against the outdated classical canon, against tradition and authority; they broke the cage of classic, Aristotelian rules of composition that imposed artificiality on the work of art. "At the first shake it cracked, so putrid was that beam of the old scholastic hovel! . . . Reality is the very thing that destroy[ed] it."⁴⁶ The general and the abstract were abandoned for the particular, the individual, the concrete, the historical, the relational, the complex, the alive, the moving. The bird erupted from the compressed air tank and soared into the open space.

---

42. A. W. Schlegel, *Dramatic Art and Literature*, 343.

43. F. Schlegel, *Athenaeums-Fragmente*, #116. Two years later (in 1800), in the same venue (*Athenaeum*, vol. 3), he states that the romantic is not a genre, but an ineluctable element intrinsic to all poetry, and as such "all poetry should be romantic" (*Gespräch*, 335).

44. Petre Pârvan, *Romantismul*, 9.

45. A. W. Schlegel, *Vorlesungen über schöne Litteratur*, 356–57.

46. Hugo, *Cromwell*, 18. Though it did not "crack" quite so quickly, romanticism delivered the blow that would gradually lead to the extinction of the classic art production.

PART THREE | CONSTRUCTION

"WANTING TO DRAW THE BIRD IN FLIGHT NONETHELESS"[47]

My intuition is that the romantic rebellion against regulated ways of thinking and creating has moved from literature into the field of theology from the dusk of romanticism (late nineteenth century) onward, and that it is active and still happening. What I will call "the post-romantic" theologians no longer adopt a strict discipline of doing theology following rules of reasoning often also set by Aristotle and leading to canonical thinking, considered to be the only one valid. They feel comfortable with blurred contours and impure categories. They are not troubled that God could be composite instead of simple, could be mutable and passible, or that humility, death, and suffering can belong to the divinity itself. The thinking about God has been released from technical, long-established, borrowed norms of reasoning or conventions that are set *theoretically* and that are not sufficiently apt to describe the reality under investigation. Words like revelation, livingness, the real, the concrete, replace the descriptively static and fixed accounts of God. This (romantic) God can no longer be dissected (to use a Schlegelian term) or held down in the cage of ruling theoretical systems; his actions in the world, his movements, are to be observed like the bird in flight.

Interestingly, Karl Barth, to whom the above image belongs, declared himself averse to attempts to "draw the bird in flight."[48] That is:

---

47. Barth, "Christ in der Gesellschaft," 565: "den Vogel im Fluge *doch* zeichnen zu wollen."

48. In English this phrase was translated as "to paint the bird in flight," but I do not see any reason to force the image by embellishing it. Barth uses exclusively a language standing for "drawing" and "photography," which makes sense given that he wants to imply "haste" (since the object is in movement) and "fixity" (what is captured no longer moves). His verbs are *zeichnen*, *abbilden* (drawing, sketching, making an image of); his nouns are *Augenblicksbild*, *Momentbild* (snapshot, momentary image or picture). I thank my friend, the eminent German scholar Christof Müller, for telling me that *Augenblicksbild* (the older version of the current *Momentaufnahme*) could also be acceptably translated as "drawing" or "sketch," albeit, clearly, the temporal dimension, the momentariness of the act would be weakened; and that the connotation of a "subjective view/picture" and not merely that of "objective" photo capture should also be rendered by the translation. All this is consistent with Barth's use of the image to protest against the subjective, erroneous human possibility of religion. And there is more: in order to photograph it, the object has to be present; in contrast, one is more likely to paint a moving object, such as a bird, from memory and not in the moment (also because painting is usually done with less speed than drawing). The direct exposure, the act of rendering the object in ongoing contact with it, is thus lost, and this was something important for Barth, who wants us to have "eyes to see" and "ears to hear" the Word

to theoretical structures (methodologies),[49] or any human possibility of religion—which includes the work of theologians, priests, prophets, philosophers as well as events in the lives of believers, such as praying, feeling, experiencing[50]—none of which can capture the flight of the bird. This image (*Vogel im Flug*) denotes the movement that is God's history (*die Bewegung der Gottesgeschichte*),[51] or "the impossibility of God" (*die Unmöglichkeit Gottes*)[52] in relation to human endeavors, or the turn (*Wendung*) from the old human to the new human in Christ.[53] Movement escapes descriptions, whether the latter isolate a singular position (*Augenblicksbild, Momentbild*), or take them as a series of contrasting positions (*eine Reihe widersprechenden Momentbildern*), because in either case the movement itself is lost, and that which moves is turned into a fixed, abstract thing, which is precisely what the flight is not.[54] The paradox is that while Barth failed to grasp something essential to art—which is that it preserves and emphasizes the intrinsic mobility or freedom of the reality it depicts—his solution to the impossible situation of the theologian who has to pin down God in discourse was precisely to "draw the bird in flight." Unwittingly, and perhaps even unwillingly, in doing theology he recruited some of the capacities and resources characteristic of art and especially of romantic poetry, as a way not to annihilate or lose his object/subject in researching it. In that he kept on drawing the bird's flight throughout his life, namely in the progressiveness or continuous renewal of his intellectual production, Barth was romantic in the deepest sense.

Just like romantic literature, post-romantic theology is free and creative insofar as it rejects the prideful stationing within limited, well-defined, preestablished formulas, and accepts a constant development or a state of perpetual becoming. Barth writes:

> Thus the real results of dogmatics, even though they have the form of the most positive statements, can themselves only be new questions.... If questioning ceased, if dogma itself came on

of God that speaks today, a living God. Cf. Barth, "Christ in der Gesellschaft," 564–65; *Römerbrief (Zweite Fassung) 1922*, 254–55, 274.

49. Barth, "Christ in der Gesellschaft," 565.
50. Barth, *Römerbrief (Zweite Fassung) 1922*, 256.
51. Barth, "Christ in der Gesellschaft," 564.
52. Barth, *Römerbrief (Zweite Fassung) 1922*, 256.
53. Barth, *Römerbrief (Zweite Fassung) 1922*, 274.
54. Barth, "Christ in der Gesellschaft," 564; *Römerbrief (Zweite Fassung) 1922*, 274.

the scene instead of dogmas and dogmatic propositions ... then dogmatics would be at an end along with the *ecclesia militans*, and the Kingdom of God would have dawned.[55]

This attitude was ingrained in Barth long before *Church Dogmatics* I/1. In a lecture he gave in the summer of 1922 in Schulpforta, Germany, he speaks against theologies as systems, rejecting the notion that his is a "new type" of theology, instead of simply a viewpoint. He defines his work in a thoroughly romantic manner, as my parentheses indicate: His is just a "marginal note" (*Randbemerkung*, the romantic *fragment*), a "wandering" thinking (*theologia viatorum*) that rejects staying put alongside other venerable theologies (the romantic *Heimlosigkeit*; the Romantics were *die Heimatlosen*, Barth is *theologus viator*), an "illumination" (*Beleuchtung*) of existing theologies "from outside" (the Romantic as a stranger [*Fremdling*] among his fellow humans, possessing illuminating knowledge), a viewpoint characterized by the openness and the "not knowing" of the question "What now?" (*Was nun?*, the ongoing, not finished, progressive romantic production).[56] In the second edition of *Romans* completed the year before, Barth had mentioned the obligation not to adopt any viewpoint without a deep commitment to abandon it as quickly as the tactical goal for its adoption had been achieved, for the viewpoint will unquestionably be "shown to be finally inadequate. [The prophet] will never build up without at the same time making preparations to demolish what he has built; and he will always guard against any stability of his which would militate against the freedom of God."[57]

Bruce McCormack notes that in 1924, during his preparations for what would become known in the English-speaking world as the *Göttingen Dogmatics*, Barth immersed himself in reading the ancients (the Western and Eastern church fathers), along with Aquinas, and nineteenth-century German-language theologians.[58] I notice that the language Barth uses to reflect on the theologies of the past and his conclusions display the extraordinary mobility of the romantic artist. Guidance from the Church *in the past* has to be sought neither in Aquinas nor in the fathers, neither in Luther nor in Calvin, but in the post-Reformation theologians, yet "a return to this orthodoxy (in order to *stand still with*

---

55. *CD* I/1, 268-69.

56. Barth, "Not und Verheissung der christlichen Verkündigung, 1922," 67, 68-69, 73.

57. Barth, *Epistle to the Romans*, 336.

58. McCormack, *Karl Barth's Critically Realistic Dialectical Theology*, 334.

them and to do things the same way!)" is deemed impossible.[59] Faithful to the principles he had already set out by that time, in the *Göttingen Dogmatics* Barth advances points of view "which are almost immediately . . . set aside by the emergence of a new perspective," thus attesting to the "rapid evolution"[60] of his thinking—and of romantic blood, I would add. The same attitude is reiterated in *Church Dogmatics* I/2, where he holds that dogmatics can never be shaped into a *true* system.[61] In *Church Dogmatics* IV/1, he continues to maintain the view that dogmatics exists not to repeat (or, in romantic language "not to copy the models"), and should not work under a "back to" imperative.[62] In addition, he continues to understand dogmatic theology in an utterly romantic way: as a never-ending, provisional, fragmentary activity, because dogmas are inherently reformable.[63]

Despite his eventual turn toward an architectural composition in theology (from *Church Dogmatics* IV/1 onward), I believe Barth held on to his intrinsic romanticism insofar as he did not think that his own dogmatics was irreformable or that he had finally brought his object under epistemic control and had stopped the flight of the bird. A clear indication that this is the case is given by Barth himself, in a documentary made in the year before his death.[64] There, addressing revelation, he says that the God who spoke his Word in Jesus Christ is a living God who *speaks today* (*der lebendige Gott der heute spricht*), not a dead God, and therefore we could be in continuous hearing (*könnten wir ihn beständig hörend*) of his Word; the greatest mistake, which he associates with dictatorship (i.e., Hitler), is to think, "Now I've got it!" (*Jetzt hab ich!*); instead, we should exercise *total openness* (*alle Offenheit*) toward the beauty of the world and the events of history, as well as in how we look for God where he has spoken for himself unambiguously (*wo Gott unzweideutig für sich selber geschprochen*), in Jesus Christ. *Constant listening* and *total openness* for the Word of God spoken *today* is anything but a plea for a closed

---

59. Karl Barth, "Zum Geleit," quoted in McCormack, *Karl Barth's Critically Realistic Dialectical Theology*, 336; emphasis added.

60. McCormack, *Karl Barth's Critically Realistic Dialectical Theology*, 337.

61. *CD* I/2, 861, 868.

62. *CD* IV/1, 372.

63. See McCormack for an argument that, contrary to appearances, in *CD* IV Barth had *not*, in fact, "violated his own protest against *system*" ("Karl Barth's Contribution to Constructive Theology Today," 119).

64. Knorr, "JA und NEIN." The interview with Barth from which I quote is posted at Geiste und Psyche, "Karl Barth—ein Interview (1967)."

system, which would indeed convey: "Now I've got it!" In fact, already in his 1922 Schulpforta lecture Barth was aware that every wanderer, like himself, had ended up constructing their cathedral or fortress, but he seemed less bothered by that than by the fact that that architecture had come to be understood as their "new theology" instead of remaining a gloss, the latter of which Barth deemed as the true identity of such wandering thinking.[65] Hence, both early and late, Barth prompts us not to take his architectural construction as the lifeblood of his theology; the latter opposes the immobile "Now I have it!" position, which is to say that it refuses to be finished or to expire. In romantic spirit, Barth's work does not stand for a theology that pours content into preexisting forms, nor for one interested in building the walls of new comprehensive formulas that others after him can continue to fill in indefinitely.

By the very romantic attitude that rejects "any stability," the postromantic theology looks toward the future, not the past; it too, like romanticism, is an "open model" because, as Bruce McCormack frequently says, "there is no irreformable teaching." The walls of dogmatic constructions are mobile; romantically built, they possess inner vitality (progressiveness), and therefore do not contain or hide only a skeleton. This kind of constructing is eminently illustrated in the scholarship of McCormack, who proves to "have the Romantic in his blood."[66] He has worked for thirty years to produce his "system," and then, even before its first volume was published (thus threatening to cage a chunk of his thinking), he was already immersed in revising it.[67] I am a live witness to this ongoing process which now spreads simultaneously backward (into that first volume) and onward (toward the second one). This extraordinary mobility is typical of the way the Romantic pursues his goal. Only "a system of the most diverse unity, of infinite expansion, a compass of freedom," only "the lack of system brought into a system . . . can avoid the errors of the system."[68] A system that is free, infinite, and finds its unity in openness and variety looks like a work of art.

65. Barth, "Not und Verheissung der christlichen Verkündigung, 1922," 69.

66. For my argument that McCormack's theology is romantic in character but held back by his bondage to classic, traditional ways of thinking which are incompatible with his core theses and his innovations in kenoticism, all of which remain entangled in a net of unsolvable paradoxes, see Pârvan, "Romanticism in the Kenotic God."

67. McCormack, "Response to Alexandra Pârvan," containing revisions to McCormack, *Humility of the Eternal Son*. Though the article appeared after the book was published, it was written well before.

68. Novalis, *Werke*, 2:293, #681; 2:291, #681.

This points precisely to my broader argument: the intrinsic mobility of theoretical compositions only comes with aesthetic quality and power. Because: How does one *draw* the bird in flight? The flying bird is real, the flying bird that my eyes see is less real than the one in the sky, and my description of what I see is yet another step removed from the reality under observation. In fact, my description of the bird has no reality outside the one it itself creates, because the flying bird can never be equated with it. Barth insists that we should use our ears and eyes to receive the God that speaks today. I say that artistic resources are needed both for that and for our descriptions of that reception. It is so because of the distinct powers that art has both to capture and render the object at once as *given in* and as *lifted beyond* direct perception. That is to say artistic capacities exercised both in reception and description meet the "spirit," not the "letter" of the object. This is possible due to a number of characteristics that the artistic process involves. First, the "total openness" that Barth called for in seeking to hear and see the God that is present to us now is a quality typical to the artist. The openness "creates" anew, so to speak, the organ of reception, preparing it to receive the object in a way that does not lend itself to simple perception. It is easy to imagine that if we had before us the actual "shoes" that Van Gogh painted in the 1886 work by this title, we would not see the *Shoes* he showed us in his depiction. Artistic openness creates the eye that sees and the vision: to "see" the spirit of the object rather than its direct appearance, reception or perception has to become insight. This is facilitated by a second specific trait of the artistic act: "movement" is central to both reception and description of the object. Art does not seek to contain that which it depicts; the artist both captures and shows the object in its proper and constant movement, thus setting it free to perpetually reveal itself under our eyes, to speak to us again and again. Instead of arresting, freezing, or making the object static and, in that sense, already dead, art releases its life, renders the object *with intrinsic movement*. When you see Van Gogh's *Shoes* you see the walking being alive in them, they literally look like they are moving and even "speaking" about the life they lived; when you read a play by Shakespeare or a poem by Eminescu you will never get to the end of what they are able to communicate. Each time they will meet you differently. Mere descriptions will kill the object; only in art does the object keep moving, and that is why to draw the bird in flight—to give a proper description of a reality that is alive and present—one needs aesthetic power. This brings me to a third characteristic of the artistic engagement: the object of art is always a subject. Retaining its life and proper movement, the reality described never becomes a passive object under the inspection of the writer or the audience. And fourth, the same liveliness or constant movement inside the subject-object which accounts for its unending revelation also accounts for its similarly inexhaustible veiling, as it impedes the complete grasp of the subject-object.[69] And so, a theological creation that relies on artistic power in its very composition would present an intrinsic mobility that is appropriate to its subject-object; and by depicting the latter's spirit it would show something that, outside the theological description, cannot be accessed with naked eyes or ears, but that is not confined to the description either, moving beyond it at all times.

"EXPRESSION: THE INNER [LIFE] IS PRESSED OUT"[70]

The Romantics opposed the classic use and classic theory of language as a mere instrument, as an analytic inventory of technical devices that underline the oratorical message, and advanced the idea of poetic language as expression.[71] "Poetry is . . . free rule—victory over raw nature in every word—its spirit [*Witz*] is the expression of a free, independent activity—flight."[72] Expression is the only form of communication that surpasses the divide between life and speech, due to the following qualities. It does not merely render or represent something already fully shaped; expression is formative, and constitutes the reality of what is communicated.

> We know something only insofar as we express it, *id est*, insofar as we can *make* it. The more complete and diverse we can produce or carry out something, the better we know it. We know it

---

69. I discussed this coincidence of veiling and revealing in my erotic theory. The erotic body is veiled even when it is in full sight, available or accessible to the erotic receiver, just because it is not static; like a bird in flight, it moves, and by that very movement and by all that it entails, it shows you something different every time the eye catches it (Pârvan, "Eroticism in the Kenotic God").

70. "[Der] Ausdruck: das Innere wird . . . herausgedrückt" (A. W. Schlegel, *Vorlesungen über schöne Litteratur*, 91).

71. A. W. Schlegel, *Vorlesungen über schöne Litteratur*, 91–94, 264. Novalis writes, "Language is the expression of spirit. . . . Transparent, conductive expression" (*Werke*, 3:58, #936). For Madame de Staël, "To write is to express one's character and thought" (*Oeuvres*, bk. 2, ch. 10, 125, 126; cf. also *Corinne*, bk. 7, ch. 1, 239). Berchet says that "poetry is expression," and it expresses a living object ("Lettera").

72. Novalis, *Werke*, 2:195, #412.

fully, when we can generate it everywhere and communicate it in all ways—when we can produce an individual expression of it in each organ.[73]

Thus, expression makes be; it is not limited to what is or can be spoken in words; and with or without words expression is multidimensional—it includes the affective, the cognitive, the volitional, the axiologic, the aesthetic, the corporal, or the somatic. Because it covers these multiple dimensions and values of that which is communicated, expression makes possible a reception that is immediate, powerful, deep, truthful, and, for all these reasons, I would add—most complete. It is my view that the Romantics' expressive use of language is intent on communicating truthfully a lived state of being *that is relational par excellence*. The poem communicates the poet's self in its process of communicating with the other (human or nonhuman) and attaining through this uniting a higher, supersensible reality.

Based on this, I want to propose a new term and speak of the triune God in his three *life-expressions*, rather than in three persons or three "modes of being." In the latter concept, used by Barth (*Seinweisen*), there are three *classic* terms: "mode," "being," and "mode of being," all of which carry a heavy philosophical heritage, in their origin, nature, and history, and in their varied meanings assumed over centuries. They are more cumbersome than they are helpful. The way I see it, expression is God's self-constitution as triune: it makes be; it is not a partial bringing out (limited by the possibilities of speech) of something that is already there. Father, Son-Jesus, and Spirit do not formulate or express partially or imperfectly an ontological content that lies deeper and remains "silent," that preexists or is more basic than their expression. In God, life and word are identical, there is no divide between his Word and his godly reality; this reality is efficiently and fully communicated in godly Word. As triune, God is relation, and therefore self-communication between the related terms, and therefore expression; he "presses himself out"—which is the Latin meaning of the word "expression" ("to take out by pressing," *exprimo*). God is in himself a pressing out, a "life extended towards" his own self but also the other, the human Jesus who, in this movement, is made Godself. A person can rest in oneself; expression cannot.

Furthermore, expression is intentional, and as such entails involvement, commitment; its creator is not indifferent, rather she wants

---

73. Novalis, *Werke*, 3:94, #1043.

to influence the audience and guides it toward her intended meaning. Moreover, in expression her own attitude toward that which is communicated as well as her own individuality are also communicated.[74] And because expression is not reducible to the transmission of informational content or data, it can never become an object possessed, controlled, altered, or fully explained by the receivers. It remains alive, active, and independent, and continues to work in the receiver pushing her to seek deeper, to discover new aspects of that expression, new ways of looking at it. Borrowing some of Solomon Marcus's terms—which Marcus uses to define poetical language in opposition to scientific language—expression is immeasurable, its meanings are unquantifiable, its semantic openness is given in relation with its receivers and not independently from them; it is never just a vehicle of a meaning independent from it, rather it adheres organically to all its meanings, forming an indivisible whole with them; it is not explicable but ineffable, and knows no synonymy—there are no equivalent formulations that can replace it.[75] Through all this, expression retains intrinsic vitality, as the mystery of the poet's word is both eminently conveyed and preserved, at once revealed and veiled. I would say that expression reveals; expression is revelation, makes known what it communicates in a way that no other means can.[76]

All these aspects apply to God's expressing of himself. His self-constitution as expression is unique, not replicable; it has no equivalent; it reveals in perpetuity; there is no end to its meanings which emerge anew in relation to the receivers; it is therefore inconsumable, at once self-veiling and self-revealing; it is intentional, not indifferent, committed to the purpose of revealing both what is expressed and the one expressing it (which in God are one and the same); it seeks to make its content accessible, "visible," understandable, in the way its Creator wants or intends it; it is oriented toward its addressee, and guides the receiver toward the conveyed and intended meaning, even as this remains ultimately unconquerable; it is both fully graspable and impregnable. And it has all the dimensions entailed by expression, including the corporal, because God is also flesh; he is the human Jesus no less than he is all else that he makes

---

74. Petre Pârvan, *Cercetări de poetică și stilistică*, 6–7.

75. Cf. Marcus, *Poetica matematică*, 31–67.

76. A. W. Schlegel uses the verb *offenbaren* (to reveal) in connection with the power of paralinguistic expression to make known immediately, intuitively, one's inner events (the inwardness), without requiring of the receiver any prior knowledge (*Vorlesungen über schöne Litteratur*, 91).

himself be; God expresses himself as human body too and therefore has something to communicate that involves this level as well.

Understanding God's self-constitution as expression collides with Barth's view on God's self-revealing by way of *dicere* (speech). That is because Barth limits God's Word to reason alone, to the communication of God's thoughts. The content of God's self-revealing by *dicere* is "word, *logos*, communication of the *spirit*, a revelation of *reason*. And our being addressed by God is in the most concise sense *knowledge*, appropriation of the *word*, reflection [*Nachdenken*] on the *thought* of God communicated to us."[77] The truth of God is restricted to intellectual content, and God's Word is reduced to communicate only such content: "[The] content [of revelation] . . . is the truth, and thus it comes to us in a form that corresponds to the truth: . . . in the form of the *Word* which seeks to be *known* . . . spirit speaking to the spirit."[78]

There are innumerable problems with the claim that God is word or speech or truth that wants to be known by thinking. First, *incarnation is made useless*, and the flesh of God irrelevant because divine reason can communicate directly with human reason without taking up human flesh. Second, in incarnation *Jesus is made incapable of being the one in whom God self-reveals*, for the following two reasons. First, the divine truth is reason and is spiritual only, according to Barth; but Jesus's own human truth (as that of any other human) cannot be defined by reason alone. Jesus is *not* a "revelation of reason"; his life and teaching are not a gospel of reason. That reason cannot even communicate the truth of *human* life, let alone the truth of superhuman life, is something that the Romantics have amply and eminently shown (see below). Second, Barth himself thinks that the Word of God is distinct from the physical events (including Jesus's corporeality) with which it associates itself, and that this association is for our sake only, and not because that is how he exists in and for himself.[79] But if God is not also flesh in Jesus, then in Jesus he self-reveals in and as something other than himself, and that cannot properly be called self-revelation. This entails that the separation

---

77. Barth, *Göttingen Dogmatics* (trans. Thomas Herwig), §3, "Deus dixit." The same is repeated in later works: "The Word of God is . . . speech from reason to reason, Logos, which is based on knowledge and involves knowledge . . . it is spirit that speaks to spirit" (*Christliche Dogmatik im Entwurf*, 87-88). "Speech, including God's speech, is the form in which reason communicates with reason . . . it is the divine reason communicating with the human reason" (*CD* I/1, 135).

78. Barth, *Göttingen Dogmatics*, §3.

79. Cf. *CD* I/1, 133-38.

between the divine and the human in Jesus Christ is not that of two natures belonging to the same godly entity but between two entities: God as divine-only and Jesus, the human. If the latter is thus separated from God, then Jesus *is not* Lord, and the first base of Barth's Trinitarian doctrine collapses.

Of course, for Barth—given that he explains things as he does—"God could . . . be God without speaking to us";[80] but then Jesus is in no way defining for his godness. The immediate implication is that the Trinity is not Christian, is not the Trinity of a Christian God, if Jesus is not proper to it and, again, if Jesus is not proper to God then how can God *self*-reveal in him? The sentence "God's revelation is Jesus Christ, the Son of God"[81] is made to mean in Barth's line of thought that the Son of God is the spiritual Logos, without Jesus.[82] That "God's revelation is *Deus dixit*"[83] or "the Word became flesh"[84] means, in this argumentative context, that *dixit* (the Word) affirms and communicates only the divine, because God is just that: "The Word, *the Logos*, is the revelation."[85]

Consequently, when Barth holds that *Deus dixit* speaks only of the divine, is meant to reveal only the divine, and is directed only to human persons—and hence that through Jesus God speaks only of a divine Trinity—the implications are these: Jesus is made a mere medium for a strictly divine revelation, and not part of the Trinity itself, and God's revelation cannot actually be *self*-revelation in Jesus, if the Trinity is wholly divine. The way I see it, if we accept that God self-reveals in Jesus, then this entails that God speaks not only *of* the divine and not only *to* human persons. God expresses himself *as* the human Jesus too, and he speaks *to* Jesus too. There is expressivity inside the Trinity, because each of the three members communicates themselves to the other two, and Jesus reveals God as also human and as relation to the human.

---

80. *CD* I/1, 138.
81. *CD* I/1, 138.
82. Barth is consistent in this view from his first treatment of *Deus dixit* to the last: "Revelation is God's Word itself, God's own speaking . . . in which no flesh is involved even only verbally, but *he* and he *alone*." Therefore, he contends, "To revere . . . even . . . the human being Jesus of Nazareth, is denial of revelation, for it forgets the *Deus dixit* [God has spoken], *the divine nature in Christ* which alone deserves honor and worship." It is so because "the truly holy is spirit" only, thus "God's own and exclusive reality" excludes Jesus (*Göttingen Dogmatics*, §3; emphasis added).
83. *CD* I/1, 115.
84. *CD* I/1, 119.
85. Barth, *Göttingen Dogmatics*, §3; emphasis added.

Summarizing all the points made thus far, Barth's position is that "the encounter of God and man takes place primarily, pre-eminently and characteristically in this sphere of *ratio*."[86] But Jesus is not needed at all for this kind of encounter. And if things were indeed so, then Jesus would be only a medium conducting God's rational content, not part of it. As we have seen, communicating rational content is typical of *non-expressive* scientific language, which acts only as a vehicle (or an infinitely replaceable "conductor") for a content that goes through it and can be conveyed in innumerable *equivalent* forms, thus being independent of its vehicle. Instead, as expression, God is not a medium traversed by a content that is independent of him and can be communicated otherwise, and this means that "what he is" and "what he expresses" cannot be separated, and hence he could not use a medium other than himself to convey himself, i.e., for either self-expression or self-revelation. Expression adheres organically to its content; the two form an indivisible whole. When that content is Jesus, God's *self*-revelation is one of himself as *not only* divine yet still as fully God.

A third problem with Barth's equivalence of God's *dicere* with the speech of reason is this: if revelation is divine reason communicating with human reason, that *makes God himself irrelevant*, because human reason does not need a God—a professor of philosophy will suffice. The idea of "truths of reason" that can be reached by reason only when its own processes are removed by divine intervention is itself absurd. Those could be called truths of "inspiration" or "intuition" (and it is no accident that these two notions are central in romanticism), either of which, by definition, goes beyond reason and its possibilities, and eminently involves "emotion" and "relationality" (two other key romantic notions).

McCormack has had a lifelong commitment to Barth's *dicere*. The arguments already assembled should be sufficient to show him why he needs to let it go. But there are two more considerations which go to the very heart of his christological proposal. Retention of Barth's *dicere* would mean that *the Son's receptivity is* both *pushed outside the person* and *made impossible*. If God is not also Jesus, then in being ontologically receptive to Jesus, the Son is permeated by a foreign entity that is not his own self. And, if restricted to reason, Logos, thought, then the divine Son, *the* Word of God as Word of Reason, cannot receive Jesus's feelings and life events. To borrow a sentence from Viktor Frankl, the creator of

---

86. *CD* I/1, 135.

logotherapy (therapy through finding meaning): "*Logos* is deeper than logic."[87] In McCormack's kenotic model, through receptivity, the Son lives with Jesus always, before and after he is born and even in his death, as the otherness of human life *in its entirety* is allowed to be not only with the Son but *within* his divinity. This speaks of the Son's uprootedness, anticipating, reaching toward the other to receive the other inside himself yet without losing himself; it speaks of his self-humbling, self-limitation, and even suffering that even leads the divine to experience death as his own. No word of reason can ever explain all this.

In his *dicere* passages, Barth is interested in rejecting any "anti-intellectualism"[88] or "anti-spiritualism,"[89] and, less explicitly, any trace of romanticism, in the rather distorted idea that Barth has of this literary movement (see below). To me, the two main results of this are two catastrophic losses: first, in stripping God's Word of the expressivity it possesses in Jesus, in God the Son, and in Scripture, Barth loses the Christian God altogether in his *dicere* argument. And second, he furthermore loses the effective (or even legitimate) capacity to speak of God, as a theologian. Because, coming back to my larger point: It is a work of art to speak with sense about God. Reason alone is not enough for such a task. It is not just that one needs talent to describe God (to draw the bird's flight); but both to grasp and to render what and how God is, one needs imagination (another pivotal romantic term) far more than one needs the forensic powers of reason—which, to *schlegelize*, would merely make one a critic of "the dissecting school." And who has ever dissected a flight? To communicate to others the object/subject that is God, as closely as possible to his own reality, the object/subject has *to be created for the others' vision*, in order for their eyes to be able to see it. If you simply explain God by way of lists of properties and intellectual conditions of existence, you succeed as much as you would from conveying what a house is by way of analyzing the chemical composition of its bricks. Just because—as Barth insists—the human word can never be the same as God's Word, we need to make our word expressive. His is.

---

87. Frankl, *Man's Search for Meaning*, 188.
88. Barth, *Göttingen Dogmatics*, §3.
89. *CD* I/1, 134.

"THE PRINCETON CREED"

"THE MIND IS BUT A WINDOW WHEREBY THE SUN OF A NEW LIGHT ENTERS INTO THE HEART"[90]

The immensely valuable thing the Romantics teach us is that reason is opaque. Consider for a moment the difference between reasoning about love and living it. The Romantics sought to know not just with their intellect, but with their entire being. Imagination, feeling, enthusiasm, "vivid and great illusions, strong and varied passions," beauty, the poetic, are needed not alongside "cold reason" but in order for the latter to function in the first place and not be "itself an illusion"; to be able to analyze (ideas, the human being, the whole system of nature, the universal system of beings), and not end up with half-truths or short of insights, reason needs *experiential* knowledge of "the most hidden secrets" of imagination and the heart.[91]

The way I see it, the romantic distinct epistemic method was centered around what I call *passive and possible receptivity*, and I identify this as *the romantic kenosis*. This is an intensely exploratory state (experienced in contemplation, sleeping, laziness, idleness, or the sense of death or dying), which pulverizes the ego, the self-centering, the limits of the self and the focus on the self's acting, and therefore the self's expressing of itself alone and not also of the other, of something more and different than the self. In these passive-receptive states the Romantics sought to know also with the unknown in them, with the most obscure territories and faculties of being; they sought a knowing that is more characteristic of life, more natural, pure—one that bore the creative, magic force of life

---

90. "Da! . . . orice descoperire mare purcede de la inimă și apelează la inimă. . . .—mintea nu mai e decât o fereastră prin care pătrunde soarele unei lumini nouă, și pătrunde în inimă" (Eminescu, *Fragmentarium*, 549, #2287).

91. Leopardi, *Zibaldone*, 4 Oct. 1821. Novalis writes, "Intelligence, imagination, reason: these are the poor compartments of our inner universe. Not a word about their wonderful mixtures, configurations, and transitions. It has occurred to no one to search for new, unnamed forces, to trace their convivial relations. Who knows what marvellous associations, what fabulous generations are still in store for us within!" (*Werke*, 4:271, #2924). Madame de Staël identifies "[Human] nature's most beautiful gifts: imagination, sentiment, and thought" (*Corinne*, bk. 2, ch. 1, 43; cf. Shelley, "Defence of Poetry," para. 37). One could say that the Romantics seek a "kenosis of reason," namely, to use it in a voluntary self-limitation that results in its ultimate expansion. Thus, the best thing about reason is a negative quality, or, in Keats's notorious phrase, the "Negative Capability" to "[be] in uncertainties, Mysteries, doubts, without any irritable reaching after fact and reason" ("Letter to George and Tom Keats. 21/27 Dec. 1817," in *Selected Letters of John Keats*, 60).

itself and would thus both reveal and "save" in uniting them with the organic whole of life. I have discussed in published work how in McCormack, the Son knows Jesus more fully than just by intellect—McCormack speaks of the "self-illumination" brought about by the Son's *experience* of what Jesus knows, wills, does, and lives, and I myself have used the word "transformation."[92] Consider, for instance, that receptivity allows him to have corporal knowing even though he does not have a body, insofar as the body belongs to Jesus. The Son too walks into the unknown, on foreign, perilous territory up to his own experience of death; and this explorative and receptive enterprise transforms his strictly divine regime of experience. In his eternal reception of Jesus, the Son knows also in the "not knowing," just as the Romantics attempted.[93]

The connection of romantic passive receptivity with McCormack's theory of the Son's ontological receptivity to Jesus is impossible to miss, and I have addressed it elsewhere, introducing various topics that I will only briefly list here:[94] that being passible, receptivity is also *passive* (both in the Romantics and McCormack's kenosis), and that passivity—excluded from classic divine metaphysics—should be instated and revaluated; that there is a fundamental element of passivity in love too (love being a receptive state and not sheer activity), and hence that God, as love, is not rendered affective just by the Son's receptivity, but already possesses intrinsic and *complex* affectivity; that "the romantic kenosis" (the combination of passivity, receptivity, and passibility) is transgressive in that it generates self-transcendence/transformation, creativity, and freedom; that romantic freedom consists in making oneself part of a greater activity *through self-giving*, and is therefore achieved *in relation*, in the passive attentiveness of the self-offering to otherness where the transgression of the self's bounds occurs. I have shown that the elements of romantic kenosis, its method, and its finality are recognizable in McCormack's kenotic model too, but the latter would benefit from deepening and developing them, especially by exploring the meaning of the Son's passivity in reception and the responsive engaging on the part of Jesus of that receptivity. Without the latter's response, I claimed, there is no uniting, no forming of a single life-expression (or person).

---

92. McCormack, *Humility of the Eternal Son*, 260; Pârvan, "Eroticism in the Kenotic God," 41–43.

93. Pârvan, "Eroticism in the Kenotic God," 35–41.

94. Pârvan, "Romanticism in the Kenotic God."

In romanticism, what gives access to this knowledge in and with the unknown, what makes one see within the unseen, is feeling: "Not the idea, but something else, that lies deeper, is *the primordial*. . . . The affects are the fountainhead."[95] Without passibility, the crepuscular states of passive receptivity would remain as epistemically dry and blind as the clear reason is. The Romantics immerse in feeling as into a dimension that opens the gates of vision, makes one visionary. "The resurrecting life-blood of thinking is passion."[96] Approached in the romantic method, intense emotion makes one see because its purpose is always beyond itself and never in the actual object. "The poet needs . . .—no fixation on *one* particular object, no passion in the full meaning—a many-sided receptivity."[97] Thus, a well-ingrained fear of theologians—which in Barth becomes a charge against theological romanticism—can be dispelled: romantic feeling is not a sinking into a purely psychological, strictly individual experience that closes the subject into one's self and away from the secure, certain and objective path of reason.[98] In the *Deus dixit* passages Barth positions himself firmly against locating revelation (other than in reason, where it belongs) in "feeling or experience or what is called inwardness," or in "pathos, enthusiasm," or the "heart,"[99] thinking that this would mean to entrap God in the human person, who would thus claim to take possession or control of God. Barth thinks that this is the error to which the romantic artists have led us: to make the "I" the foundation of reality to the point where edification is sought by letting each individual say how they felt the hand of God, in what way, and how this has benefited him, and her, and him, and her, each of them in particular.[100] The charge is invalidated by precisely the poet that Barth considers to be its perfect illustration and the foremost influence in introducing this

---

95. Eminescu, *Fragmentarium*, 90, #2257. Coleridge writes, "[A] metaphysical solution that does not tell you something in the heart is grievously to be suspected as apocryphal" ("Letter to Southey," quoted in introduction to Coleridge, *Biographia literaria*, xxxiii).

96. Eminescu, *Fragmentarium*, 88, #2289; 549–50, #2287. Leopardi writes, "The great truths . . . are discovered only by means of an enthusiasm of reason" (*Zibaldone*, 8 Sept. 1823); while F. Schlegel notes that "the beginning of all poetry is to cancel the course and laws of the reason that thinks rationally" (*Gespräch*, 319).

97. "Paralipomena zum *Heinrich von Ofterdingen*," 1.8, in Novalis, *Heinrich von Ofterdingen*, 180.

98. Cf. Barth, *Protestantische Theologie im 19. Jahrhundert*, 313, 315, 321, 327, 339.

99. Barth, *Göttingen Dogmatics*, §3.

100. Barth, *Protestantische Theologie im 19. Jahrhundert*, 302–42.

tendency in theology—Novalis. For Novalis writes, "The first step is to direct the look inward. . . . Whoever stops there only half-succeeds. . . . No one will achieve anything excellent in his depiction, so long as he will portray nothing more than his own experiences."[101]

The Romantics understood that only affective unity defeats the conceptual separation between beings of distinct kinds or between beings and things and can bring about ontological unity: "Let us restore the unity [between human being and nature]. In unmediated feeling *already* lies the unity."[102] Romantic feeling is the intentional, golden path toward that superintellectual *and supersensible* knowledge that cannot be possessed merely by reason and hence is not strictly theoretical but constitutes an experience of *lived life*, at its purest and most complete level: through affective unity with the other (human, natural, or superphysical), the Romantic reaches a higher level of being-together, i.e., a being-together with the all-pervasive spirit of life. A similar dynamic is present in McCormack's kenosis, where the unity of the Christic person, secured in the Son's receptivity, is not achieved rationally, but *affectively*. There is ontological unity inside the Second Person because there is affective unity, and *through* affective unity. For McCormack receptivity is possibility, and it is in possibility (in feeling) that ontological unity is achieved. That is why he specifically states that "taking all that Jesus did and experienced and therefore is 'up' into his [the Son's] own life" has an effect precisely on the level of affectivity and *through that* on the level of ontology: "Receptivity renders the being of God affective. It is, therefore, an 'ontological receptivity.'"[103] And I would say that here too, in the Christic uniting, a higher level of unity is accessed, namely the unity that is God's life in the entire Trinity, because the co-living of the Son-Jesus is at the same time *godly living*. That is, the life of God is present in each of its three expressions (persons).

---

101. Novalis, *Werke*, 2:15, #24, #25. There is no solipsist sinking into a self-created reality in the Romantics because that would lead to the creation of as many realities as there are poets, and never to the conviction so dear to them—as voiced by A. W. Schlegel—that "the great truth that one is all and all is one" (*Vorlesungen über schöne Litteratur*, 93). The self-centeredness and the horizontality (or lack of transcendence) of the inner-outer relation are precisely *anti-romantic* also because they render the expression void: if the "pressing outward" becomes "sinking inward," this makes art (and individuals themselves) ultimately incommunicable to another, i.e., inexpressible.

102. Eminescu, *Fragmentarium*, 90, #2257.

103. McCormack, *Humility of the Eternal Son*, 258.

"THE PRINCETON CREED"

The romantic spiritualized affection[104] that gives access to the highest level of reality brings about a larger and fuller rationality, one that exceeds the confines of reason. "For Conception can only comprise each object separately, but nothing in truth can ever exist separately and by itself; *Feeling perceives all in all at one and the same time*."[105] Being boundless, feeling is a medium far more capable than the limited reason to both capture and express the infinite.[106] And the fact that this all-consuming feeling *is expressed*—namely, communicated in the way it can be best *received in others*—is another indication that it frees the Romantic from the cage of subjectivity, and makes possible an experience that far transcends personal biography.[107] All romantic creative powers (passivity, imagination, expression) carry the ego beyond itself. All romantic goals—transformation, creation, transsubjective union—are self-decentered and oppose a reduction to the individual self or personal experience.

"THE LYRE OF HIS SOUL EOLIAN TUN'D"[108]

Before reaching the closing section, let us take a moment to notice that Barth's entire *dicere* argument and his stress on reason and, through it, on objectivity in knowing God, though openly anti-romantic, turn back

---

104. F. Schlegel writes that romanticism is not about the ill-famed, usual meaning of "sentimental," namely, all that is moving and tearful in a trite way; in romantic sensibility there prevails a feeling that is "not sensual, but spiritual" (*Gespräch*, 333). Elsewhere, he writes: "Feeling that is aware of itself becomes spirit" (*Athenaeums-Fragmente*, #339).

105. A. W. Schlegel, *Dramatic Art and Literature*, 343; emphasis added.

106. A. W. Schlegel writes, "The feeling, so far as it is not merely sensual and passive, is our sense, *our organ for the Infinite*, which forms itself into ideas for us" (*Dramatic Art and Literature*, 244; emphasis added). For Madame de Staël, "Enthusiasm is the incense that rises up from the earth and unites it with heaven" (*Oeuvres*, bk. 2, ch. 10, 124).

107. Novalis identifies poetry's "great purpose of all purposes: the elevation of humans above their own selves" (*Werke*, 3:25, #818). Madame de Staël writes, "I am a poet when I admire, I scorn, I hate not out of personal sentiments, not for my own cause, but for the dignity of the human species" (*Corinne*, bk. 3, ch. 3, 95). For Keats, "A Poet . . . has no Identity; he is continually . . . filling some other Body" ("Letter to Richard Woodhouse, 27 October 1818," in *Selected Letters of John Keats*, 95). Coleridge observes, an artist "know[s] no self but that which is reflected not only from the faces of all around us" but from plants, animals and nature's elements too (*Philosophical Lectures 1818–1819*, lecture 5, 179; cf. Shelley, "Defence of Poetry," para. 26).

108. Keats, *Endymion*, bk. 2, 866.

on him at a deeper level and reflect a thoroughly romantic *ars theologica*. There can be no possession or control of God's Word by the word of human persons: the two remain distinct, and God alone can make his Word present to individuals. This for Barth entails that a theologian should start with and from God's own subjectivity: in order that God's Word is not altered, objectified, owned, or perverted (made into the subjective word of human persons), the theologian has to make himself *the receptacle* of God's Word, be open to *receive* it, "hear" it and then communicate it as it comes to him or as it passes through him. That is why "what [the theologian] does comes under the concept of prophecy: One has heard the witness in such a way that one has to accept it and pass it on."[109] That is also why, as the receiver and communicator of this Word, Barth can forget that he is not the author.[110] The analogy with the image of the "Aeolian lyre," which stands for the romantic *ars poetica* and which expresses precisely this surrendering to and nonpossession of inspiration and consequently the sense that one is both the author and not the author is conspicuous.[111] And it is not an accident that the comparisons between poet and prophet or between poet and priest emerge quite naturally in romantic texts, Schleiermacher included.

With such views Barth once again reinforces my argument for the required aesthetic capability of the theologian both for reception and rendition of what is received. This idea too is captured in romantic reflections on the Aeolian harp: the poet—writes Shelley—is a *"lyre [that] could accommodate its chords to the motions of that which strikes them."*[112] In attuning herself to that which is received the poet also "creates" the latter for the others' reception or their receptive capacities, and in that very process she passes it on, or expresses it for others, or—if you wish—"draws the flight."

109. Barth, *Göttingen Dogmatics*, §10, "Freedom."

110. Barth, preface in *Epistle to the Romans*, 8.

111. George Sand writes to a young Flaubert who struggles with method: "The wind plays in my old harp as he likes.... I do not care, as long as the emotion comes.... If we were nothing but instruments, this is already ... a sensation like no other—that of feeling oneself vibrate. So, let the wind run a little in your chords" ("À Gustave Flaubert"). The wind harp is a central symbol and reference in the Romantics for obvious reasons: it produces music when the wind touches its chords, which means by way of *reception in passivity* and also *completely naturally*, this being another core romantic idea—the non-artificiality of creation. In addition, the wind lyre image captures something essential for the romantic method as well as for Barth's own: the *relationality* of receptive, inspired writing, the imperative laying oneself open in and for relation.

112. Shelley, "Defence of Poetry," para. 2; emphasis added.

"THE PRINCETON CREED"

The romantic "freedom in relation" that is released in receptivity is also present in Barth. The hearing and "prophetizing," or communicating the word, "has to happen *without authority* . . . in freedom."[113] That the spirit that is received is freer (in self-possessing its life-form) than the one dedicated to its reception, and that it remains free in being received and ultimately impossible either to capture or to express fully, is again something which the poets have long known about inspiration and artistic expression and which is also made evident by the image of the wind harp. All these ideas are also conveyed in Barth's seemingly paradoxical insistence, first on the "identification between me and the author" of a biblical text that communicates God's Word, and hence Barth's positioning against those who "fail to recognise the existence . . . of any Word in the words" of human receivers;[114] and second on the ultimate distance between the speeches involved: Barth's word is not that of the apostle Paul and neither of the two is identical with the Word of God ("I say this, not the Lord" [1 Cor 7:12]);[115] the latter alone has absolute freedom. The free (and clearly *passive*, in the romantic sense) reception is "meaningless" if "detached from the freedom of God itself" and hence "unconnected."[116] Obviously, in receptivity there can be talk of a freedom only in relation.

What is typical to Barth in all this is something that I find untenable and that also backfires. As we have seen in the *dicere* pieces, he pretends to restrict "the hearing" and the receiving to reason alone; emotion, enthusiasm are explicitly excluded.[117] Yet, at the same time he stresses the immediacy of reception (and, in truth, reception, as it appears in the Romantics and Barth alike, can only be immediate!). But reasoning done with immediacy is no longer reasoning properly speaking; it is *intuition*, and intuition necessarily involves emotion and, by definition, overrides reason. That is why Barth too acknowledges that in "a real hearing of the Word . . . I do not only observe, I not only think. No, *now*, the witness to revelation appears to me in *this* very special light. . . . Conceptual abstraction [is] overcome, and the witness becomes for me a *Word, the* Word."[118]

---

113. Barth, *Göttingen Dogmatics*, §10.
114. Barth, preface in *Epistle to the Romans*, 9.
115. Barth, *Göttingen Dogmatics*, §10.
116. Barth, *Göttingen Dogmatics*, §10.
117. Barth writes, "There must also be no talk of enthusiasm or the like without offending the character of the Word as a living reality" (*Göttingen Dogmatics*, §10). See the discussion below.
118. Barth, *Göttingen Dogmatics*, §10.

The very idea of "hearing" entails immediacy and "relationality" and therefore rules out a process of pure reasoning. First, because the hearing cannot mediate a speech from reason to reason, or from spirit to spirit, to the exclusion of precisely those elements that would make any hearing possible—passivity and passibility. Second, because hearing entails (as the wind harp figure makes clear) placing oneself in relation, something not needed for pure reasoning, which can be done by the mind on its own. If "the hearing" of God's Word occurs in reception, passivity, and relationality, one cannot climb back to God on the stairs of reason, of scientific, technical, logical, or objective speech. And this uncovers a further point. The Barthian "hearing" reveals something of which the Romantics were aware but which he ignores: that the starting point of knowledge is *in the middle*. If it is placed in God alone, then the hearing, the attentive listening, the lying open in receptivity, the engaging of the relation with (God as) the other, the standing in the situation of being addressed by God's *dicere*—all of which Barth cares deeply about—are canceled. I too, and not just God, have to come to the meeting point; I have to enter a relation with God's Word; I too have to be there, and not just God, if I am to know anything. And the knowledge gained through hearing is mine, not God's; my knowledge of God is in me, not in God (which would be absurd), even as God founds it (God is its foundation) in my receptivity. And therefore, knowledge of God does not start in God, but *in between*, just as the music of the Aeolian harp does not start in the wind, but in the coming together of wind and harp. Just like that lyre, all Barth's talk of God (however prophetic) goes through Barth, and there are at all times two irreducible subjectivities involved: that of God and my [Barth's] own.

"WE WORSHIP THE LIVING [GOD] ACCORDING TO DEAD MEN'S FORMS AND CREEDS"[119]

Bruce McCormack wants to repair Chalcedon. But Chalcedon cannot be repaired. Chalcedon remains forever in AD 451, closed there, in its time, and nothing one could do to it now could still be called "Chalcedon." It would be something else. And whenever a specialist uses the name "Chalcedon," they are referring to the fifth-century council that took place there, and not, say, to a book published in 2021, by a scholar who wants to revise or rewrite parts of *that* creed. Chalcedon's life is closed

---

119. Hawthorne, *House of the Seven Gables*, 161.

on itself, restricted to the affirmations that it chose to contain then and there. But Jesus Christ's life is not closed and it is not in the past; it is perpetually now. Revelation is not restricted to the life of Jesus Christ in his historical time plus the next five centuries; it happens now too; it is also for us, *now*. Revelation is ongoing; it cannot be frozen in old creeds, in what the ancients made of it, or in ancient understanding. The Bible, Jesus Christ, the church, and revelation are all now, not sixteen hundred years ago.

It is both God's own freedom and that which is expected of us in relation with him that stop revelation from being arrested in old creeds. This was Karl Barth's "feeling" too:

> The equation of God's Word and God's Son makes it radically impossible to say anything doctrinaire in understanding the Word of God. In this equation, and in it alone, a real and effective barrier is set up against . . . a fixed sum of revealed propositions which can be systematised like the sections of a corpus of law. The only system is revelation, i.e., Jesus Christ.[120]

Because of this, our standing in a relation with God's Word—in the correlation of address (i.e., revelation, *Deus dixit*) and being addressed—needs to be "always again and foundationally a *question* as certainly as we are human," just as it was "for the prophets and apostles themselves":

> If there were not one question left here, if this question were not always again vital for us, if there would be a security in *us*, in *ourselves*, if the question would be accomplished and now irrelevant, then the correlate of our faith would certainly *not* be revelation, certainly *not* the "Deus dixit" [God has spoken].[121]

That is why we are to remain open, to think anew, to allow for permanent dogmatic reformulation, reformation, progression. "'Back to . . .' is never a good slogan"[122]; dogmas are "human words" and who can say "Now I have it!" about God's Word? "God's faithfulness to His Church consists in His availing Himself of His freedom to come to us Himself in His Word and in His reserving to Himself the freedom to do this again and

---

120. *CD* I/1, 137.
121. Barth, *Göttingen Dogmatics*, §3.
122. *CD* IV/1, 372.

again."[123] In the year before his death, Barth was reminding us that it is crucial to "have ears to hear . . . to have eyes to see."[124]

To *this* Barth I say: Yes! But if we are not to get trapped in human words, nor let the human word halt its continuous openness to God's Word, Scripture, revelation, and Jesus Christ, if God's faithfulness to the Church consists in his Word *coming to us again and again*, then why do we keep the church creeds frozen? Why do we reformulate doctrines but not the creeds? *A creed is not the Word of God; it is human words.* And is a creed not also a compendium of dogmas? Are creeds not also systems which are never to be equated with the only "system," which is God's Word, or, as Barth prefers to put it, Jesus Christ? We are to always question our words pronounced in this relation, in which we are addressed by God's Word, and we are never to find security that we have pinned down God's Word, but at the same time we can remain bound to old creeds? If so, then the result is that theologies such as that of Barth or McCormack do not align with the creeds. Their and our understanding of God moves disjointedly from the *content* of the affirmation of faith, which does not move but stays put. Placing ourselves in the *appropriate*, permanently self-questioning relation with God's Word leads to massive changes in the God concept, but all the while we are left with the same old creeds. We are trying to move forward, while carrying at the core of our progression, as the lifeblood of our arguments, contents of faith that are no longer aligned with *the actual faith* conveyed in our present understanding of God's Word. Can theology move at all and be revisable if the creeds are non-revisable?

"The Church is the subject of a creed," McCormack said to me in the summer of 2022, resisting any departure from "the old," not realizing the deep incompatibility of the past creeds and the belief that his theology actually affirms. Upon delivery of this chapter as a lecture in Princeton, he himself and other scholars close to him thought that for him to walk too far on the romantic path I opened here would be equivalent to leaving the Church. My answer to McCormack was this: the Church is now. The Church is not in the past, but the creeds are. "The case is just as if a young giant were compelled to waste all his strength in carrying about the corpse of the old giant, his grandfather, who died a long while ago, and only needs to be decently buried. Just think a moment, and it will

---

123. *CD* I/1, 138.
124. Knorr, "JA und NEIN."

startle you to see what slaves we are to bygone times,—to Death, if we give the matter the right word!"[125] God is not caged in past creeds, living somewhere in *human* antiquity, in human *past* understanding. And God cannot be understood by dead people. We are "dead" if we surrender our understanding to the now-closed understanding of people from the past. The Word of God comes toward us (in its expressivity, its pressing out), and we do not engage it if we borrow our words from the dead. Giovanni Berchet's assessment holds for theology's classic creeds too: he deems classicism the "poetry of the dead" and romanticism "the poetry of the living," because the former is relevant to the past, the latter to the present.[126] Compared to poetry, the situation in theology is made sadder by the fact that Christianity is founded on a regenerating God. Jesus Christ brings new life but apparently not to our creeds.

When you actually watch a bird in flight, you notice that you cannot observe it for a long time: the bird disappears from your view precisely because it moves; other people elsewhere, at different moments, will witness its flight. Should they—instead of observing the flight—look at old pictures taken by people from other moments in space and time and then describe the flight according to those pictures, and not according to what they witness themselves? Even if God stays the same, or moves only within himself, our accounts of God cannot stay the same over the course of millennia if we are to draw the bird in flight, and not render the same fixed image over and over again, an image that we do not witness ourselves but borrow from old watchers. Those would not be accounts of "the living God that speaks today," for whom Barth urges us to keep our ears and eyes open. Once again the Romantics were eloquent on this point too: "The soul is [not] moved into liveliness . . . by things ancient, belonging to other people, and that we get notice of only through books and history."[127] Or again, painters cannot "feel what they paint" if artists are "transported in Antiquity and compelled to get their inspiration from books and statues"; life itself should be the source of art.[128] The same holds for theologians: God's reality and not old accounts of it should be the source of their productions.

The necessity of a new creed became clear to me while reading McCormack's book dedicated to "the repair of Chalcedon." The God of

---

125. Hawthorne, *House of the Seven Gables*, 161.
126. Berchet, "Lettera."
127. Berchet, "Lettera."
128. Staël, *Corinne*, bk. 8, ch. 3, 316.

Chalcedon was built in the classical tradition, and McCormack departs drastically from it: his God is not simple, not impassible, not outside time, history, suffering and death, not unrelated to the world; he is always also human; he actually has flesh (he *is* Jesus's body), and also receives the humanity *within* his divinity. Bruce McCormack's God concept cannot be referred back to Chalcedon or to any ancient creed that, by necessity, is submitted to a conception of God built on Greek metaphysics. The voice of some ancient Greek philosopher runs through all past creeds, artistic or Christian. "The literature of the ancients," wrote Madame de Staël, "is in the moderns a transplanted literature," whereas the new, romantic literature, which is proper to and at home with the moderns, is the only one that can still renew itself and rise to new life."[129] The reality of art cannot be trapped in ancient times; can that of God? If not, then why stop at past attempts to give accounts of it in old sets of formulations of belief? Is that not trapping God? Is that anything like drawing the bird in flight? The direct exposure necessary in order to capture movement is surrendered.

McCormack wants to "repair" Chalcedon because he wants continuity with the history of the church. But continuity is found in keeping with the *spirit* of the tradition. Understanding with the understanding of others (the "transplant" method) is not to understand (cf. Augustine's *De Magistro*), and hence it is not to keep with or honor the tradition. Also, pushing old forms into new ones (the "repairs" method) is equally mutilating as it is to force new forms into old ones. Doing such repairs mutilates "the old" in content (the revisions) and in form (the spirit that constructed it). Again, this is a discovery which the Romantics made over two hundred years ago, and which holds true for theology as well, an obvious fact when we replace in the following quote "poetic beauty," "nature," "parchments," and "Greek and Roman literature" with "drawing the bird's flight (theological descriptions of God)," "God's revealed reality," "old creeds," and "classic theology": "When you understand these [romantic] doctrines . . . you will learn that the boundaries of poetic beauty are as broad as those of nature, and that the touchstone by which this kind of beauty is to be judged is nature itself and not a pile of parchments—and thereby you will learn how the literature of the Greeks and the Romans should truly be respected."[130] Instead of mutilating past

---

129. Staël, *Oeuvres*, bk. 2, ch. 11, 129, 130.
130. Berchet, "Lettera."

creeds, past *human words*, let us respect their spirit by producing our own effort today.

In calling for the formulation of the "Princeton Creed"—as I named it in the Princeton "Barth" conference of June 2022—I understand this phrase symbolically as denoting the reason and nature (the spirit!) of all future efforts to define our faith. That is to say, the Princeton Creed is a creed constructed as an open model, possessing infinite inner movement: in refusing to be satisfied with old forms, it both accepts and surpasses its own limitation. It too will be old, a "frozen picture" for upcoming generations, but—just like romantic poetry—in defining itself in openness and movement, or in the act of renewing the old, this creed can endure in its spirit (its core intention), not in its letter (the robust text).

A new creed does not mean a new church or a new God and, as explained, it does not mean to break connection with the past (only with its "literal" terms and construals). Nothing eternal ever lies in the past; that is why Barth rejects looking for God under a "back to" imperative. Put in a romantic voice which resounded well before Barth's: "God is the future! He who . . . divinely pulled . . . would not free himself from the chains of the past and be completely absorbed in the future does not head towards God."[131] The Romantics did not *invent* literature, and similarly, the formulation of a new creed would not mean the affirmation of a new God or the invention of one every fifty years. But as God is constantly revealed to every epoch through the Bible and in Jesus Christ, we must constantly find new ways to come to God's truth. God is expression, and therefore is presenting us with an infinite self-formulation and self-pressing-out, while we are limited in our reception, grasp, and rendition of his expression. Hence, "it must be possible for us to press forward to the goal via more than one path."[132]

The God of the Princeton Creed is no longer opposed by the notions of corporality, relationality, receptivity, suffering, passivity, history, time, complex affectivity, out pressing, transformation, death; this *alive* God *speaking today* does not stand still within the cage bars of abstract, classic, ancient, dogmatic concepts. As should be obvious, this God does not belong to McCormack or any romantic reconstruction of his theology; he is shared by many in their actual, current belief. This God is also not outside the church, not least because the church is founded on Jesus

---

131. Arnim, *Clemens Brentanos Frühlingskranz*, ch. 33.
132. F. Schlegel, *Gespräch*, 320.

Christ. He is simply outside of any existing church creed. For the moment he is recognized only in the unwritten Princeton Creed. Pronouncing this new creed will mean to acknowledge that the church's statements need the "romantic" transfusion to disentangle themselves from old conceptual and linguistic ties and find coherent, non-inert, life-imbued realization in the actual, lived belief of Christians. Because: "Can the bird fly in a tank of compressed air?"

CHAPTER 12

"Doch was geht uns die Kirche an?"

A Response to Alexandra Pârvan

Bruce McCormack

I should note at the outset that if the reader has not already read Alexandra Pârvan's essay in this volume with great care, they should not read the essay I present here. Our collaboration (which stretches back to 2015) is dialogical in nature. To hear only one voice in the back-and-forth of the encounter would make in-depth understanding of even that one voice highly doubtful. I should also point out, before launching into my material, that the focus of Pârvan's chapter in this volume falls more nearly on Barth than on my Christology. To stay near negotiated word limits, she was forced to eliminate a considerable amount of material. And so, I too focus to a larger degree than originally anticipated on Barth. But I am speaking to Pârvan throughout.

WHAT IT MEANS TO BE A "POST-ROMANTIC THEOLOGIAN"—ILLUSTRATED IN THE WRITINGS OF THE EARLY KARL BARTH

It is customary among English-language interpreters of Barth's famous Tambach lecture (1919) to lift from it but a single line. No, not even a line but just several phrases from a line which are then, quite understandably, made the springboard for a wider canvassing of Barth's so-called

PART THREE | CONSTRUCTION

"Socialist Speeches" for an explanation of his political views at the time. But it is worth placing this line in a larger context to appreciate the caveat by which it is surrounded and delimited—most conspicuously through Barth's characterization of those views as a "parable." The larger context consists in the *second* of three movements in thought (which occupy the final three sections of this lecture): the movement in thought which Barth characterizes as "antithesis"—the opposition to powers and systems which are themselves opposed to the Kingdom of God. The first and third movements are, not surprisingly, referred to as "thesis" and "synthesis."[1]

> Faced with God in our secure creatureliness, we *have no choice* but to disrupt the equilibrium. No longer *may* we make appeal to "reality" when what should concern us is the *Reality* which wants to break through "reality." We *must* ourselves become aware of the gravity of the situation, of the sheer power of the attack which is, at one and the same time, directed against us and led by us. How terrible it would be if, among all institutions, it is the *Church* which does not see this, but puts all of its effort into *maintaining* the equilibrium in existence which humans are supposed to *lose*! And yet, what does the Church matter to us? [*Doch was geht uns die Kirche an?*] . . . But *have we really* understood what we think we have understood? That a new orientation of the *whole* of our life on God is what is called for in our day, [and] not just an entering into opposition to some or many details.[2]

This is the larger context in which Barth goes on to say that of course the details are also important, even if only of penultimate importance. In fact, we can only demonstrate that we have truly understood the revolution which God is for all things human by becoming "hopeful and complicit comrades *within* the *Sozialdemokratie*, in which the problem of opposition to the status quo has now been posed in *our* time."[3] Indeed, he says,

---

1. Barth, "Christ in der Gesellschaft," §3, 576–85; §5, 593–98, respectively (English translation [ET], "The Christian in Society," in Barth, *Word of God and Theology*, 52–59; 64–69).

2. Barth, "Christ in der Gesellschaft," 591–92 ("The Christian in Society," in Barth, *Word of God and Theology*, 63–64).

3. Barth, "Christ in der Gesellschaft," 592 ("The Christian in Society," in Barth, *Word of God and Theology*, 64). *Sozialdemokratie* is the name originally given to the socialist movement in Germany prior to its split into communist (KPD) and reformist (SPD) wings. In using this word, he is declaring that he feels no need to choose between them. See on this point McCormack, *Karl Barth's Critically Realistic Dialectical Theology*, 200.

it is in the *Sozialdemokratie* that "the parable of the Kingdom" is to be found.[4] *That* is the phrase interpreters love to celebrate. But notice! The powers opposed by the socialists have only a penultimate significance. Human opposition to the existing political and economic order is not, Barth is saying, *the Opposition* which takes place in that the Reality of God breaks through all that we call reality. Our oppositions are but witnesses to the Opposition, to the divine Other who breaks through "from above" to reorder the world from the ground up.

Now there is nothing wrong with reading Barth *also* as a political theologian. He was that too. But even more important is the fact that he understood himself to be a witness to the movement of *God*—which, he insisted, cuts through all movements of opposition to the status quo (including the political) "senkrecht von oben her [perpendicularly from above]" and is identical with none of them. "Our place in the situation is really a moment in a *movement*, comparable to a freeze frame image of a bird in flight—wholly and completely meaningless, incomprehensible and impossible. By that, I most certainly mean neither the socialist, nor the religious-socialist, nor the general, somewhat questionable movement of so-called Christianity but rather *the* movement, which passes through all of these movements perpendicularly from above as their hidden, transcendent meaning and motor."[5] *The* movement does not have its origin in time and space; it is not a "movement alongside of others."[6] What Barth has in view is the "history of God"—whose "power and significance has been unveiled in the resurrection of Jesus from the dead."[7]

I mention all of this because what we catch sight of in Barth's depiction of the movement from above are romantic impulses in his thinking and in his way of being in the world at this time. It is impossible to read Alexandra Pârvan's close description of romantic opposition to classicism in literature without seeing clearly that every point she makes here is mirrored theologically in the Barth who wrote (at a minimum!) the

---

4. Barth, "Christ in der Gesellschaft," 592 ("The Christian in Society," in *Word of God and Theology*, 64).

5. Barth, "Christ in der Gesellschaft," 564 ("The Christian in Society," in *Word of God and Theology*, 42).

6. Barth, "Christ in der Gesellschaft," 564 ("The Christian in Society," in *Word of God and Theology*, 42).

7. Barth, "Christ in der Gesellschaft," 564 ("The Christian in Society," in *Word of God and Theology*, 42).

Tambach lecture, "Biblical Questions, Insights and Vistas" (1920),[8] the second edition of *Romans*,[9] and the three great occasional lectures given in the summer and autumn of 1922.[10] The protest against disengaged, nonparticipatory ways of knowing; the protest against every abstraction from life, from lived *existence*; the contempt for fixed "systems"; the protest against every preestablished order, against the identification of any single fixed method or conventions of writing/creating as "perfect"— such that it now suppresses to the point of elimination all capacity for real thinking (which is always new); the death of fresh insight and eventually of the soul which slavery to the past imbues in those caught in it; the elevation of "permanent renewal" as art's "very principle of existence," the joy experienced in "perpetually striving after new and marvellous births";[11] the rebellious spirit that seeks freedom from convention; the active tearing down of the cages created by those who want everything to remain as it is—all of these elements find expression in Barth's way of theologizing, most fulsomely in his second *Romans*. To "stir the spirits, to generate doubt, or awaken discontent"—oh my, yes. That is the Barth of *Romans II*, as Pârvan has rightly recognized—and brought to my/our attention.

Think, for example, how Barth explains the relation of revelation to our history in the second edition of *Romans*: "Jesus Christ our Lord. . . . In this name, two worlds encounter each other and separate themselves, two planes intersect, the one known and the other unknown. . . . The point on the line of intersection itself, however, has, like the whole of the unknown plane whose presence it announces, no extension whatsoever on the plane known to us."[12] The "point of intersection" is a mathematical point—without "before" or "after," without (that is) "visibility" to the one

---

8. "Biblische Fragen, Einsichten und Ausblicke, 1920," in Barth, *Vorträge und kleinere Arbeiten, 1914–1921*, 662–701 (ET, "Biblical Questions, Insights and Vistas, 1922," in *Word of God and Theology*, 71–100).

9. Barth, *Römerbrief (Zweite Fassung) 1922* (ET, *Epistle to the Romans*).

10. Barth: "Not und Verheissung der christlichen Verkündigung, 1922" (ET, "Need and Promise of Christian Proclamation, 1922," in *Word of God and Theology*, 101–29); "Das Problem der Ethik in der Gegenwart, 1922," in *Vorträge und kleinere Arbeiten, 1922–1925*, 98–143 (ET, "Problem of Ethics Today, 1922," in *Word of God and Theology*, 131–69); "Das Wort Gottes als Aufgabe der Theologie, 1922," in *Vorträge und kleinere Arbeiten, 1922–1925*, 144–75 (ET, "Word of God as the Task of Theology, 1922," in *Word of God and Theology*, 171–98).

11. A. W. Schlegel, *Dramatic Art and Literature*, 343, quoted in Pârvan, "Princeton Creed," 230–31.

12. Barth, *Römerbrief (Zweite Fassung) 1922*, 48–49 (*Epistle to the Romans*, 29).

called to know it. It does not and cannot become our "object"—which means that in the revelation relation established in the movement of God, God is and remains the subject of that relation and human beings the object and never the reverse. Human beings know God only insofar as they are known by him (Gal 4:9).

Commenting upon the curious human practice of marking the turning of years on a calendar with festive celebration, an earlier, more clearly romantic theologian wrote:

> The average individual recognizes nothing but his transient existence, and its irresistible decline from sunny heights into a dread night of annihilation.... And could men also explain in mechanistic fashion the entire nexus of such a life, they would regard themselves as having reached the summit of humanity and of self-comprehension. But in thinking thus they mistake the reflected image of their activity for the whole activity itself, those outer contact points, wherein the energies of the self meet with external things, for their most inward essence.... *The point which cuts through a line is not a part of it; it relates more properly and immediately to the Infinite than to it*, and everywhere in it you can posit such a point. The moment you divine the course of life and cut through it [as occurs in the turning of the year on our calendars] should be no part of temporal life. You should regard it otherwise and in it become conscious of your immediate relation to the Eternal and Infinite.[13]

Both theologians speak of a vertical line dissecting the horizontal line, though the image is being employed for an apparently different purpose in each case. I say "apparently" because the two stand in a closer relationship than will be thought possible by many. Friedrich Schleiermacher seeks to find that which most truly makes a human individual to be who and what they are in an "experience" which does not belong to the horizontal line on which psychic and spiritual experiences occur, an "experience" which cuts through all normal, everyday "experiences," grounding and transforming them.

Karl Barth, on the other hand, seeks to "awaken" (what is this if not an "experience"—however extraordinary it may be?) his readers to

---

13. Schleiermacher, *Monologen* (Kritische Ausgabe), 10–11; emphasis added (ET, *Schleiermacher's Soliloquies*, 11–12). It should be noted that Schleiermacher was himself a Romantic. He participated in the romantic movement and wrote for *Athenaeum*. Barth did not participate in the movement—which is why I will refer to Schleiermacher as romantic and Barth as "post-romantic."

an awareness of a relation that joins them to an Origin that is no longer directly available but must be reestablished, moment by moment, from the side of that Origin. It bears mentioning in this context that Barth inherited two "targets" of neo-Kantian epistemology from Hermann Cohen, "historicism" and "psychologism" (the latter of which he quite wrongly equated with Schleiermacher). The day would come when he would do justice to the grain of truth contained in all "historicizing"[14]; the same cannot be said, however, of "psychologizing"—since his real model for the latter was never really Schleiermacher, as he thought, but rather contemporary theologians like Georg Wobbermin and contemporary readings by advocates of Schleiermacher which committed the same errors in interpreting him that Barth does.[15] Barth would always be closer to Schleiermacher than he could allow himself to admit. What is important here, however, is that Barth too, has a grounding and transforming "experience" up and running. And like Schleiermacher, he locates it "beyond" (above? beneath?) the merely psychic and spiritual. Listen to what Barth says in the second edition of *Romans* about that "righteousness" of God by which the ungodly—who remain ungodly!—are "justified": "The righteousness of God is the *standpoint in midair*, outside of all possible standpoints known to us; there, where we are only still held by God, by God himself, by God alone, there where we are in his hand, for weal or woe."[16] The "standpoint" of faith, Barth is saying, is no "standpoint" at all. His talk of a "standpoint in midair" is meant to underscore the thought that, although the righteousness of God establishes a new, positive relationship with a human individual, that relation is *never* a "given," never something we can take for granted as we might a finished or completed state of affairs. A standpoint in midair, on the other hand, is an impossible place to stand. Suspended in midair, one can only fall. And if one does *not* fall, if one is held by God, then the miracle of "faith" has occurred—however true it may be that this "faith" is never the secure possession of the human. My point is this: even the miracle of "faith" is an experience, albeit a grounding and transforming one, an utterly unique one which does not find its place on the timeline of our ordinary, mundane psychic and spiritual experiences.

14. I have treated this problem at considerable length. See "Karl Barth's Historicized Christology," in McCormack, *Orthodox and Modern*, 201–33.

15. See on this problem, "What Has Basel to Do with Berlin?," in McCormack, *Orthodox and Modern*, 63–88.

16. Barth, *Römerbrief (Zweite Fassung) 1922*, 68 (*Epistle to the Romans*, 94).

The person who has been suspended in midair in this way, however momentarily, is a person who now knows herself (and all others!) to belong to two worlds, this world of time and an eternal world that is always in-breaking: "Homeless in this world, not yet at home in the next, we human beings are wanderers between two worlds. But precisely as wanderers, we are also children of God in Christ."[17] To homelessness must be added "perpetually striving" as a leading characteristic of a human existence rightly understood, a seeking of manifestations of the world "above" in all things, great and small. One's attachment to the great achievements of others, not to mention one's own achievements, can only be "loose" to the point of disregard. "Permanent renewal" must be the watchword of any theologian who has understood this. And that applies too to Christian theology. Perhaps most especially to Christian theology![18]

Pârvan rightly makes appeal on precisely this point to Barth's July 1922 lecture, "The Need and Promise of Christian Proclamation." There Barth speaks of the profound embarrassment created for him by talk of "his theology." What he himself thinks of as "his theology" is, when he looks at it, nothing more than a standpoint on which one cannot stand; a mathematical point only, a "*view*point." He tells his listeners *not* to

17. Barth, *Konfirmandenunterricht, 1909–1921*, 372. The image of the "wanderer between two worlds" would be employed in the so-called "Göttingen Dogmatics" by Barth as a basic description of the human in all of his/her/their questionability in this world. See Barth, *Unterricht in der christlichen Religion*, 1:153; cf. 89, 93 (ET, *Göttingen Dogmatics*, 59). It is also a piece of self-description employed by Barth and his friend Thurneysen. See Thurneysen, letter to Barth, October 6, 1921, in Barth and Thurneysen, *Barth–Thurneysen*, 1:524.

18. I should make mention here of the fact that Barth takes on a series of "sacred cows" in his Tambach lecture, i.e., orders of life or institutions which have been allowed over time to acquire a kind of ultimacy, being seen as ends in themselves. And Barth openly applauds all voices of protest which had been calling these orders and institutions into question: "How is it that, in spite of all of our *penultimate* objections, we are *not* able to find any *final* [ultimate] reason to close ourselves off to the protest which Kierkegaard raises against marriage and the family, which Tolstoy brings against the state, education and art, which Ibsen brings against the approved bourgeois morality, which Kutter brings against the church, which Nietzsche brings against Christianity as such, which socialism directs against the entire spiritual and material existence of society with a power that contains all other protests in itself?" ("Christ in der Gesellschaft," 589 ["The Christian in Society," in *Word of God and Theology*, 61–62]). Cf. with this what Barth says about the "shaking of so many 'things in themselves' [*Dinge an sich*]": "authority in itself," "the family in itself," "art in itself," "work in itself" and "religion in itself." The greatest danger of all, he concludes is that we would consider God a "thing-in-himself" ("Christ in der Gesellschaft," 571–73 ["The Christian in Society," in *Word of God and Theology*, 48–49]).

conceive of my contribution to the [current] theological discussion . . . as an undertaking that stands in competition with positive, liberal, Ritschlian or history of religion theology, but as a kind of *marginal comment* and gloss which tolerates and does not tolerate all of them; which, according to my conviction, loses its meaning in the moment in which it wants to be more than that, in which it wants to take up space alongside the others as a new theology. Insofar as Thurneysen, Gogarten and I really should have, in the customary sense of the words, formed a school, we are finished.[19]

It was just twenty-one months later that Barth would launch a series of lectures on Christian dogmatics, the so-called "Göttingen Dogmatics." This was a move that was not well understood by anyone—with the honorable exception of Eduard Thurneysen. One-time allies would depart from him, or remain for a time while maintaining a critical stance over against him.[20] In truth, however, no great change in outlook had occurred. True, revelation would now be conceived of in a way that allowed one to see it as extended along our timeline, taking its place in our human history. But the "dialectic of veiling and unveiling" elaborated by Barth in his first dogmatics would do all the *critical* work that had, up to that point in time, been done by his talk of the mathematical point, the line of intersection, and the standpoint in midair. Theology remained for Barth what it had been, the attempt to "sketch" the bird in flight by means of an attentive and faithful following after of the movement of God—and necessarily so! since *the* "veil" of the divine self-revelation (i.e., the human Jesus) does not cease to be a "veil" even in God's use of it to bear witness to God's self. The "veil" being, in itself, a *barrier*, the anti-bourgeois tendency of Barth's early theology is preserved. Therefore, the situation remains the same: there can be no direct access to revelation.

It is for this reason, I think, that Barth's turn to dogmatics can aptly be described as a shift that took place within a "post-romantic" outlook—a shift from a volcanic, continuously destabilizing mode of presentation to the measured breathing of a dogmatics. But the lessons learned in *Romans* were not left behind. This is quite evident in Barth's still-present allergy to "systems" of theology:

19. Barth, "Not und Verheissung der christlichen Verkündigung, 1922," 67–68 ("Need and Promise of Christian Proclamation, 1922," in *Word of God and Theology*, 103–4).
20. See Barth, *Christliche Dogmatik im Entwurf*, 7–9.

> It is quite evident that there can be no dogmatic system. Rightly understood, it is the material principle of dogmatics [i.e., the Word of God itself] which destroys at its root the very notion of a dogmatic system. . . . There is no point in dogmatic thinking and speaking if, in it, all systematic clarity and certainty is not challenged by the fact that the content of the Word of God is God's work and activity, and therefore God's free grace, which as such escapes our comprehension and control, upon which, reckoning with it in faith, we can only meditate, and for which we can only hope. . . . The focal point and foundation themselves determine that in dogmatics strictly speaking there are no comprehensive views, no final conclusions and results. There is only the investigation and teaching which take place in the act of dogmatic work and which, strictly speaking, in every point, must constantly begin again at the beginning [*immer wieder mit dem Anfang anfangen*].[21]

To be sure, Barth's turn to dogmatics entailed great risk. The risk consisted in the fact that Barth's intentions would be misunderstood. And that has most certainly been the case. His *Church Dogmatics* especially has frequently been read by English-language Barth interpreters as if it were an ordinary, "bourgeois" theology—a theology of "having," of "possessing," of holding in his hands the key that unlocks the door to every dogmatic problem. This is not the place to demonstrate the failure of such a reading of his dogmatics; I think myself to have already accomplished that task anyway.[22] I content myself here to say that Paul Lehmann said it best when he described Barth—early and late!—as a "theologian of permanent revolution."[23]

PÂRVAN'S CRITIQUE OF BARTH

To Begin: On Art and Theology

Karl Barth and Alexandra Pârvan walk very different paths. The differences are conspicuous. Barth's account of revelation was informed by his Reformed theological heritage and the neo-Kantian philosophies

---

21. *CD* I/2, 868 (*KD* I/2, 971).

22. That was, in fact, almost the entire point of my treatment of Karl Barth's theological development. See McCormack, *Karl Barth's Critically Realistic Dialectical Theology*—when read in its entirety.

23. Lehmann, "Karl Barth, Theologian of Permanent Revolution."

of Hermann Cohen and Paul Natorp at Marburg.[24] Pârvan's theological reflections in her chapter are informed by the thought and art produced within the romantic movement. And yet both share an outcome that makes them allies in my eyes. Both understand theology as fragmentary, provisional, open ended. That they can come to this conclusion in such different ways is of great interest to me; I find myself drawn to both.

I begin with Barth. Even when the mathematical point had been replaced by the dialectic of divine unveiling in and through a veil which remains a veil—a "salutary barrier,"[25] Barth says—there can be no capture or control of revelation by the human recipient, precisely because revelation remains hidden in the veil. And so, for example, a disciple of Jesus who walked the dusty roads of ancient Judea with him might well see the *effects* of the relation which joins the eternal Son to Jesus but the relation itself would remain (in the Kantian phrasing employed by him in those years) unintuitable, lacking any sense data. This would still be true even if one then added a "communication" of human attributes to the christological subject (as Barth was tempted to do in *Church Dogmatics* IV/1). The subject, as defined by him (i.e., the Logos), would remain unintuitable. Peter could not have discerned that "communication"; to the extent that he had any knowledge of it, it was only because he was taught by the Father in the power of the Spirit (Matt 16:17). "Flesh and blood did not reveal this to you." Only the contrary movement—if were there one!—a "communication" of divine attributes directly to the human "nature" would result in a direct revelation of the divine to the disciples of Jesus. But the Gospel portrayals of the disciples' understanding of Jesus give no hint of that either. And so: "unintuitability" is a constant in Barth's reflections on revelation. But I must return to the early Barth . . .

Revelation heals, for Barth, but it heals only by creating "unrest,"[26] by setting its recipients in motion, by turning the complacent inhabitants of a city into those who have no lasting city (Heb 13:14). And if it should come about that we can, after all, sketch the bird in flight, this should be understood as a divine possibility, not as a human possibility. To sketch the movement of God, one must be caught up in it. "*In spite of* the unapproachability of God, there *must* be a way from there to here."[27] And: "We

---

24. The definitive study of Barth's reception of Marburg neo-Kantianism is Lohmann, *Karl Barth und der Neukantianismus*. But see also Fisher, *Revelatory Positivism?*

25. Barth, *Unterricht in der christlichen Religion*, 1:69 (*Göttingen Dogmatics*, 59).

26. Barth, *Unterricht in der christlichen Religion*, 1:569 (*Göttingen Dogmatics*, 46).

27. Barth, *Unterricht in der christlichen Religion*, 1:568 (*Göttingen Dogmatics*, 568).

are no disengaged observers. We *are* moved by God. We know God. The history of God is happening in us and to us."²⁸ Therefore: "This awakening of the soul is the movement in which we stand, the movement of the history of God or of the knowledge of God, the movement in life towards Life."²⁹ And so: Barth's protest against attempts to "sketch the bird in flight" was actually a highly specific protest against every methodological attempt to explain how humans can, starting from themselves, attain to the knowledge of God. It is the fateful preoccupation with method (still with us!) that is the target of Barth's talk of the impossibility of sketching the bird in flight. It is not an absolute impossibility; it becomes impossible when one thinks oneself to possess a method for it. The one who would sketch the bird in flight must be caught up in a divine activity and ... follow after it.

Alexandra Pârvan's way to the conclusion that theology is always fragmentary, incomplete, open to fresh insights and movement, comes about by asking what theology can learn from poetry. Poetry, she says, "is formative, and constitutes the reality of what is communicated."³⁰ This much is said only to ensure that readers understand that poetry does not adhere to a fully formed "poetics" (an abstract description complete with rules) but is a creative act. The crucial point is: that which is communicated *lives*; it is redolent with life. In part, this is due to the fact that art creates an "object" which cannot be "seen" with the naked eye. Insofar as great art gives to the viewer the "eye" to "see," what the viewer sees can change with each new viewing—or, in the case of poetry, each new reading. The viewer/reader is set free from "the cage of subjectivity."³¹ An experience takes place that "transcends personal biography."³²

Pârvan wants theology to become more artistic. Her contention is that a theology more open to artistic capacities of comprehension and expression will necessarily understand its "products" as arising out of a

---

28. Barth, *Unterricht in der christlichen Religion*, 1:575 (*Göttingen Dogmatics*, 51).
29. Barth, *Unterricht in der christlichen Religion*, 1:570 (*Göttingen Dogmatics*, 47).
30. Pârvan, "Princeton Creed," 239.
31. Pârvan, "Princeton Creed," 249.
32. Pârvan, "Princeton Creed," 249. I know this to be true. I have visited any number of museums here in the United States and around the world with a singular purpose in view, to stand before the paintings of Van Gogh. Many I have visited multiple times. And each time, I see something different, feel something different. And I cannot explain that solely in terms who I was on the day; Vincent painted in a way that was intended to evoke precisely such expressions. His paintings have depths and emotions in themselves; they are alive and they *move*.

lived relation and therefore as fragmentary, provisional, and so on. The many reasons I am drawn to this way of thinking about theology will become clear as I proceed.

Encountering the Word "in the Middle"

I turn in this section to the knotty problem of the believer's reception of God's self-revelation in Christ. In doing so, I turn to pneumatology. The issue is not that of the Son-Jesus relation, which I treated in my Christology, but the believer's relation to the Son-Jesus. Because incarnation is made possible and necessary only by the Son-Jesus relation, the relation of the believer to Christ differs qualitatively (not merely quantitatively) from that foundational relation. That means, as we shall now see, that it must be understood on its own terms. It cannot be collapsed back into the Son-Jesus relation, so that every characteristic of the latter relation is now made to be characteristic of the former as well. This time, I begin with Pârvan.

Pârvan understands Barth to reduce the "hearing" of the Word to a merely intellectual activity on our side.[33] I think there is a lot of truth in that. She finds in Barth himself a "qualifier" to his "intellectualism"—though she is convinced that he fails to think it through with any consistency at all. The qualifier lies in the affirmation of an "immediacy of reception."[34] In a "real hearing of the Word," Barth says, "I do not only observe, I not only think. No, *now*, the witness to revelation appears to me in *this* very special light. . . . conceptual abstraction [is] overcome, and the witness becomes for me a *Word*, the Word."[35] Missing here, for me, is any mention of the work of the Holy Spirit in this event (as the third "moment" in the self-revelation of God for Barth). But Pârvan is certainly right to insist that "reasoning done with immediacy is no longer reasoning properly speaking; it is *intuition*, and intuition necessarily involves emotion and, by definition, overrides reason."[36]

But let us explore this a bit more before turning to Pârvan's central concern. Why immediacy? I would say that the answer lies in the fact that the work of the Spirit has no presuppositions on our side other than

---

33. Pârvan, "Princeton Creed," 251.
34. Pârvan, "Princeton Creed," 251.
35. Barth, *Göttingen Dogmatics*, §10, quoted in Pârvan, "Princeton Creed," 252.
36. Pârvan, "Princeton Creed," 251–52.

the mere fact that *we are there*. And being there requires no "spiritual capacities" for reception beyond the natural capacities that are proper to every human being. And it is characteristic of Barth (early and late) to insist that revelation does not add capacities to its recipients beyond those already present in the human *as human*. What changes in revelation is *not* our natural way(s) of knowing—and by this, I mean as Pârvan does, a knowing of the whole person and not the intellect alone; what changes is that God breaks into our circle of self-enclosedness (Luther); the Spirit "bears witness to our spirits" that we are children of God (Rom 8:16). This is the aforementioned "immediacy." A third factor has entered in—between God in Christ and ourselves. And that third factor, according to Barth, is the Spirit of God. That the Spirit of freedom spoken of in 2 Cor 3:17–18 is the Spirit of Christ also means, however, that the Spirit who works immediately in us without the need to change us is a power that flows from Christ himself (John 20:22). And with that said, I come to Pârvan's important concern to say that we meet God in revelation "in the middle."

The account Pârvan offers here is complex. As a Reformed theologian, there are phrases in her description with which I could quibble. But most of it fits with Barth, the Reformed tradition and, therefore, me, quite well.

> The very idea of "hearing" entails immediacy and "relationality" and therefore rules out a process of pure reasoning.... Second, because hearing entails (as the wind harp figure makes clear) placing oneself in relation, something not needed for pure reasoning, which can be done by the mind on its own. If "the hearing" of God's Word occurs in reception, passivity, and relationality, one cannot climb back to God on the stairs of reason, of scientific, technical, logical, or objective speech.[37]

"Placing oneself in relation" is a phrase I would need to ask questions about. But the third sentence in the above passage could have been written by Karl Barth. But, then Pârvan adds:

> The Barthian "hearing" reveals something of which the Romantics were aware but which he ignores: that the starting point of knowledge is *in the middle*. If it is placed in God alone, then the hearing, the attentive listening, the lying open in receptivity, the engaging of the relation with (God as) the other, the standing in

37. Pârvan, "Princeton Creed," 252.

the situation of being addressed by God's *dicere*—all of which Barth cares deeply about—are canceled. I too, and not just God, have to come to the meeting point; I have to enter a relation with God's Word; I too have to be there and not just God, if I am to know anything. And the knowledge gained through hearing is mine, not God's; my knowledge of God is in me, not in God (which would be absurd), even as God founds it (God is its foundation) in my receptivity. And, therefore, knowledge of God does not start in God, but *in between*. . . . There are . . . two irreducible subjectivities involved: that of God and my [Barth's] own.[38]

To all of this, I feel confident that Barth would have responded: Of course! The Holy Spirit does not do our believing for us in that he awakens us to faith and obedience. It is we who believe and obey. But the meeting "in the middle" has to do with the relation to Christ which is *actualized* in the revelation event by the Spirit. And so I can say that, in one sense, the starting point of knowledge of God is in God alone because the dialectic of unveiling in and through the veil of creaturely flesh finds its origin on the Son's side, in the Son's receptivity in relation to Jesus. But in that it is given to me to "see" what is hidden in flesh, to "hear" what the testimony of Scripture has to say about this event, I am there—*as I am*. How, after all, is the knowledge of God "delivered"? It is not dropped like a parcel into my hands (although many conservative Reformed thinkers would express themselves this way). It is not "poured" into me. These "physical" analogies do harm to the spiritual nature of the encounter. Knowledge taking place "in the middle" means for me as a Reformed theologian that it takes place in an encounter between the Spirit of Christ and me, an encounter in which the ontological difference between the Spirit and myself is preserved—which is absolutely needful if I am to remain me. What happens? The Spirit makes Christ present through an act of "illumination." And "illumination" engages the whole person: mind, yes, but also "heart" (feeling, imagination, and so on), so that I am enabled to pass on what has been communicated to others.

Do I place myself in relation to revelation? Do I make myself ready to receive, to listen attentively? My own answer would be: Once I have been awakened from the dead, that is, once revelation in its illuminating power has been bestowed upon me once, I can indeed do these things

---

38. Pârvan, "Princeton Creed," 252.

... in my seeking of more illumination. But not in the initiating moment that Protestants call "regeneration."

Divine Self-Revelation

What we have before us in section 4 of Pârvan's chapter is what I would like to call a *lived* theory of communication—one, that is, which seeks to overcome the "divide between life and speech."[39] Why is this needed? Because language is often thought of in reductive ways, as the mere instrument of already fully formed ideas or concepts. Such an understanding of communication betrays the fact that the knowing of that which would be communicated has already taken place though the employment of reason; what are communicated are, therefore, rationally formed concepts—at least, ideally. The clearest example, in that case, would be scientific investigation and the report that follows upon that investigation. But the human act of knowing cannot be reduced in this way. In fact, communication is already basic to the act of knowing itself, even if only to ourselves. Pârvan appeals here to Novalis, who said, "We know something only insofar as we express it.... We know it fully when we can generate it everywhere and communicate it in all ways—when we can produce an individual expression of it in each organ."[40] Clearly, knowing is a deeply personal, self-involving act of the whole person, not of the reason alone, an act which cannot be divided or kept separate from communication. Not surprisingly, then, "expression" (whether in the form of words or wordlessly) "includes the affective, the cognitive, the volitional, the axiologic, the aesthetic, the corporal, or the somatic."[41] Knowing is thus *by* the whole person; communication is *of* the whole person. And, Pârvan adds, communication is only complete when received by an other, making communication to be "a lived state of being *that is relational par excellence*."[42]

All of this sets the stage for close consideration of the act of divine self-revelation, a consideration with implications for the doctrine of the Trinity. I will reverse Pârvan's order of treatment here, beginning with her forceful critique of Barth's understanding of the divine self-revelation

---

39. Pârvan, "Princeton Creed," 239.
40. Novalis, *Werke*, 3:94, #1043, cited in Pârvan, "Princeton Creed," 239.
41. Pârvan, "Princeton Creed," 239.
42. Pârvan, "Princeton Creed," 239.

as speech or a speaking (*dicere*) and come back to the doctrine of the Trinity. She lists three major shortcomings of Barth's understanding and concludes by showing why his understanding collides with the christological model I developed in my recent book.[43]

First, incarnation is of no value if God can be known through rational communication in words.[44] If that were true, says Pârvan, then divine reason could communicate "directly" with human reason "without taking up human flesh."[45] It is impossible to dispute that many do in fact think this when, even today, supporters of the "orthodox" Protestant view of the "verbal inspiration" of Scripture equate revelation with God-given *words*.

Second, "in incarnation *Jesus is made incapable of being the one in whom God self-reveals*."[46] If the first criticism spoke to the undermining of the need for incarnation, this second line of critique looks to demonstrate its impossibility. Two reasons are given in support of this critique. The first reason has to do with the fact that the physical side of the incarnation is suppressed and quite possibly eliminated by Barth. Pârvan has in mind a passage like the following:

> Speech, including God's speech, is the form in which reason communicates with reason and person with person. To be sure, it is the divine reason communicating with the human reason and the divine person with the human person. The utter inconceivability of this event is obvious. But reason with reason, person with person, is primarily analogous to what happens in the spiritual realm of creation, not the natural and physical realm.[47]

Barth says this of what he calls "the threefold form of the Word" when seen in its entirety.[48] It is intended, then, to include the primary form of revelation, namely, Jesus Christ. The problem here, however—and in this Pârvan demonstrates an unerring instinct—is that in claiming that the revelation consists in a speaking of divine reason to human reason, the ostensibly primary form has been sidelined, made subservient to the second form especially (the words of the Bible). The first form—even while

---

43. McCormack, *Humility of the Eternal Son*.
44. Pârvan, "Princeton Creed," 241.
45. Pârvan, "Princeton Creed," 241.
46. Pârvan, "Princeton Creed," 241.
47. *CD* I/1, 135.
48. *CD* I/1, 88–124.

being defined as the fullness of material content!—is being treated *only* as a "barrier" to human knowing, *the* "veil" which grounds and generates the dialectic of veiling and unveiling. Mind you, I think this negative function is a hugely important contribution to Christian theology on Barth's part; it is something I would want to retain. But missing here is a well-worked-out understanding of the positive significance of the first and supposedly primary form of revelation. I will have more to say about this in a moment.

The second reason that incarnation is made impossible is this: if the self-revelation of God can take place independently of a physical event, then the body of Jesus is "his" in the primary form of revelation only in a figurative (merely "possessive") sense. And *that* is a *huge* problem. Pârvan is right that Barth winds up (at least some of the time) in a situation—similar, I would say to Thomas Aquinas's more self-consistent performance—in which he posits a Son whose identity is complete in itself, to which nothing can be "added." But if that were the case, then it would be true to say that "the separation between the divine and the human in Jesus Christ is not that of two natures belonging [really belonging, not merely figuratively!] to the same godly entity but between two entities: God as divine-only and Jesus, the human."[49] At his best, I would say, Barth understands the eternal Son and Jesus the human as two hypostases *becoming* one, joined eternally by a teleologically ordered relation in which that becoming is grounded. But Barth is anything but consistent as he moves from the christological sections of *Church Dogmatics* IV/1 to those found in IV/2. Pârvan's critical reflections on Christology are completely congruent with my own.[50] So obviously I have no objections to bring against her diagnosis.

Third, a revelation which could take place by means of reason alone makes God unnecessary to revelation. While this might seem surprising to some, Pârvan's reasoning here is unassailable. She writes:

> The idea of "truths of reason" that can be reached by reason only when its own processes are removed by divine intervention is itself absurd. Those could be called truths of "inspiration" or "intuition" (and it is no accident that these two notions are central in romanticism), either of which, by definition, goes beyond

---

49. Pârvan, "Princeton Creed," 242.
50. Pârvan, "Princeton Creed," especially 241–42.

reason and its possibilities, and eminently involves "emotion" and "relationality" (two other key romantic notions).[51]

How could this not be right? But if it is, then we need an enlarged, positive understanding of the role of incarnation in divine self-revelation.

Pârvan calls upon me to let go of Barth's reduction of revelation to speaking (*dicere*). Revelation reduced to a speaking of reason with reason would make the eternal Son (as its subject) to be divine only. The reason is clear: restricted to rational communication, God's Word cannot "receive Jesus's feelings and life events" as my christological model has the Word doing.[52] A divine reason that has been abstracted from divine life is unable to explain how God "knows" the suffering of Jesus in any other way than from the comforts of a "skybox" (that is, as an interested observer, perhaps, but not as an affective subject).

PÂRVAN'S CRITICAL REFLECTIONS ON MY THEOLOGY

Trinity

Pârvan's proposal is to differentiate the "three" members of the Trinity as "life-expressions" of the triune God rather than as "persons" (with the tradition) or as "modes of being" (with I. A. Dorner and Karl Barth). In doing so, she is applying romantic epistemology and communication theory to questions surrounding the self-communication of God. But lest there be any misunderstanding, she is quite clear in saying that God's

> self-constitution as expression is unique, not replicable; it has no equivalent; it reveals in perpetuity; there is no end to its meanings which emerge anew in relation to the receivers; it is therefore inconsumable, at once self-veiling and self-revealing; it is intentional, not indifferent, committed to the purpose of revealing both what is expressed and the one expressing it (which in God are one and the same); it seeks to make its content accessible, "visible," understandable, in the way its Creator wants or intends it; it is oriented toward its addressee, and guides the receiver toward the conveyed and intended meaning, even as this remains ultimately unconquerable; it is both fully graspable and impregnable. And it has all the dimensions entailed by

51. Pârvan, "Princeton Creed," 243.
52. Pârvan, "Princeton Creed," 244.

expression, including the corporal, because God is also flesh; he is the human Jesus no less than he is all else that he makes himself to be; God expresses himself as human body too and therefore has something to communicate that involves this level as well.[53]

I have presented this paragraph in full because I think it needs to be heard loud and clear by Barth scholars above all. Pârvan is *not* simply tailoring her proposal for the doctrine of the Trinity to a preformed communication theory. Her broad understanding of the Trinity rests rather upon a foundation laid in a revised (with her help!) version of my Christology— a Christology which, like Barth's, takes its starting point in the narrated history of God's self-revelation in Jesus Christ. She is not doing "natural theology" even though she would not personally be averse to that. She remains within the limits of the kind of analogical thinking practiced by me (on the basis of Barth) because her only interest here lies in making my model be the best it can be.

The place to begin is with her most fundamental and far-reaching claim: "Expression is God's self-constitution as triune."[54] Pârvan proves able to think more deeply about the divine self-constitution as triune than did the ancients, since she has more to say about the *how* of it. She is able to do that because her doctrine of the Trinity is *concrete*. It is not forced by a contentless abstraction called the utterly simple "essence" of God to treat the building blocks of the Trinity as so many "rune stones" as Barth once put it,[55] which resist material definition.

The concreteness of Pârvan's thinking emerges clearly in the following passage:

> As triune, God is relation, and therefore self-communication between the related terms, and therefore expression; he "presses himself out"—which is the Latin meaning of the word "expression" ("to take out by pressing," *exprimo*). God is in himself a pressing out, a "life extended towards" his own self but also the other, the human Jesus who, in this movement, is made Godself. A person can rest in oneself; expression cannot.[56]

---

53. Pârvan, "Princeton Creed," 240–41.

54. Pârvan, "Princeton Creed," 239.

55. Barth, letter to Thurneysen, May 28, 1924, in Barth and Thurneysen, *Barth–Thurneysen*, 2:253.

56. Pârvan, "Princeton Creed," 240.

PART THREE | CONSTRUCTION

Readers of these lines will immediately grasp that Pârvan is supportive of the idea that God has an *eternal* relation to the world in Jesus Christ, a relation that is grounded in the "expression" known as the second "member" of the Trinity. And that means, then, that the self-communication of God is not limited to a strictly internal activity of the Father in generating and spirating: that is, to the giving of the "being" of the Father in its entirety to Son and Spirit (as the tradition had it). It includes that, of course! But "self-communication" in what was traditionally called the "processions" is ordered by her (and by me as well) to the self-revelation of God in Christ in the power of the Spirit. The purposive nature of God includes the incarnation and the outpouring of the Spirit in time. And "expression" is Pârvan's way of explaining this.

The advantages of Pârvan's proposal are, as I see it, three in number. First, three "life-expressions" does a better job than "modes of being" ever could in making it clear that the three are what they are in a "communication"—and not "in and for themselves." There is no Son *an sich* or Spirit *an sich*. There never was. Barth's "modes of being" (*Seinsweisen*), on the other hand, seeks only to refer to "an eternal repetition in eternity"[57] of the divinity proper to the Father in new and different forms. And that is to have a far too limited aspiration. The eternality of the relation joining the Son to Jesus—which Barth affirmed in some contexts and which leaves us with highly significant but as yet unresolved questions—is left out of account where the static term *Seinsweisen* is employed. But the phrase "life-expressions" was coined by Pârvan in order to call our attention to that eternal relation by embodying it linguistically.

Second, where Christology is concerned, a triunity of "life-expressions" allows us to think deeply about the uniting activity by which the Son and Jesus become one without prejudice in favor of either term in this relation. I will say no more about this here; it will be thoroughly explored in a book of essays I am co-authoring with Pârvan.[58] Certainly, it was Pârvan's reflections on the how of uniting that has forced me to some revisions of my Christology.

Third, because the *Life* of God is basic to the concept of "life-expressions," materially defined (and not merely formal) "personal properties"

---

57. CD I/1, 350 (KD I/1, 369).

58. The book is still on the drawing board. It is tentatively titled *Eroticism, Romanticism, and Kenosis: Elements for a Psychological Ontology of Trinitarian Life*. It will include a thirty-two-thousand-word version of the essay Pârvan has written for this volume and an altogether new response from me.

become thinkable for the first time. This had never been possible where the divine essence had been defined as utterly simple *before* any reflection on Three-ness had taken place. Against this background, the absolutization of the idea of "inseparable operations" was a wholly unavoidable conclusion. The meaning was this: if one member of the Trinity does something, they all do it (*opera trinitatis ad extra sunt indivisa*). But then it became necessary to develop alongside this basic commitment a doctrine of "appropriations." It was held that individual operations could be "appropriated" to one member of the Trinity by virtue of a decision of the Three in favor of it. So, in principle, any of the Three could have become incarnate. And so it came about that it was *decided* that only the "Son" would be. But because incarnation was "assigned" as it were to the Son and, by definition, might not have been, the incarnation has no significance for the Trinity. More specifically, no material definition of the Trinitarian "persons" was possible on this basis. But if, now, Pârvan holds that the *Life* of God "goes all the way down" (that is, that there is no concept more basic, and if that divine Life can only be fleshed out as a particular kind of love), then the activities proper to each "life-expression" can only be appealed to collectively (as three materially defined expressions) in the attempt to envision the living divine Subject—*in motion*, as it were. Put another way, what God is "essentially" is still emerging and will continue to do so. In any event, I think Pârvan to be exactly right in her insistence that there is nothing that lies "deeper" than the Three (Father, Son, and Spirit), nothing that is prior (even if only logically) to these three "life-expressions." And for this reason, "life-expressions" must be understood as materially diverse.

Romantic Kenosis

Here, I must be brief. Much of what I would like to say will have to await the aforementioned book of essays, since the extensions I envision to my christological model require a great deal of space to explain.[59] I will content myself here with but a single observation.

In my view, Pârvan's response to Barth's charge that romanticism leads necessarily to "psychologism" is both convincing and much needed.

---

59. The language of "affective unity" was devised by Pârvan to expand on the "how" of my talk of "ontological receptivity." In the expansion of these essays for our forthcoming book, I will enlarge on this conceptuality most especially.

I have already made mention above of Barth's one-sided treatment of "psychologism." A full treatment of this problem must await a later essay.

What Does the Church Matter to Us?

In her final section, Pârvan turns her attention from Karl Barth to my recently published Christology, though it now becomes clear that her sections 2 and 3, while on Barth, were aimed at me all along. This is not guesswork on my part; her presentation in Princeton at the 2022 Barth conference on which the present paper is based consisted in a dialogue with me. I begin by, once again, registering my gratitude to her for engaging my work so closely and critically. Alexandra Pârvan is the kind of critic every scholar would like to have. She is not a "glad-hander"—someone whose praise, if given at all, has not been earned. And her criticisms rest on real wrestling with the subject matter treated by another and thorough understanding. Above all, she asks, on the basis of sound understanding, how my work might be made better. For all of these reasons, dialogue with her is a pleasure.

Two elements above all seem to have convinced Pârvan that I failed to follow through consistently in the task I set for myself. The first is the word "repair"; the second is the place of honor given willy-nilly to the Church in the past as an implied "authority" where Chalcedon is "returned to" again and again as a sort of touchstone by which all future advance is to be measured. I am convinced that it is the first—the use of the word "repair"—which invites the second; that, and the unfortunate, off-the-cuff response I gave to a colleague's question after hearing Pârvan's paper (referred to by her here) as well.

I want to begin by saying that I agree completely with the theological principle repeated several times in this final section. "Back to . . . " is indeed always a bad slogan.[60] Every piece of theologizing which sets out to speak freely, not constrained by a need for acceptance by others or a desire for commercial success, will inevitably be a "new creed" if the writer has any capacity for genuinely original work. So yes, my Christology certainly constitutes a "new creed"—which, in fact, is still evolving (thanks in large measure to ongoing dialogue with Pârvan). I have always been keenly aware of the "deep incompatibility"[61] of my work with past

---

60. Pârvan, "Princeton Creed," 254.
61. Pârvan, "Princeton Creed," 255.

creeds. What, after all, did I retain of Chalcedon's conceptual apparatus? Only the word "hypostasis"—which I was taught by Brian Daley to equate with "thatness." Surely a neutral term! But the rest of that apparatus I dispensed with. "Person" was surrendered due to its ambiguities in the ancient world: Is it what moderns would call the "subject" or is it the outward appearance only? "Natures" was even more explicitly left behind. What then did I retain? This only: that, like me, the bishops at Chalcedon thought that they were addressing a problem bequeathed to us all by the New Testament itself. Whether, in fact, their problem was *that* problem or had become a completely different problem in the course of the christological developments that took place in the first four centuries is a question that will never go away.

I had my own answer to that question, of course. My answer was that I do not think that the bishops were still addressing a New Testament problem at all. Not that I think it was a mistake to read the New Testament canonically, i.e., to read passages like Rom 1:3–4 together with John 1:1–18; Col 1:15–20; and Heb 1:1–4 in order to form a synthetic picture. The New Testament writers did not themselves engage in metaphysical reflection, though I do think it is possible to construct a metaphysical Christology responsible to the limits established by their (collective) commitments. And yet, I do *not* believe that those commitments included the understanding that God is utterly simple and impassible.

The conviction that God is impassible was common among the Apologists by the mid-second century. The idea of "simplicity" only entered into the stream of Christian theology in the late second and early third centuries. It was borrowed by Clement and Origen from the writings of Numenius of Apamea, a neo-Pythagorean philosopher[62]—which might have been appropriate had either idea had any biblical warrant whatsoever. But neither did. The net effect of this borrowing was to introduce a qualitative change into the problem under discussion. It is no longer the same problem. Where the Logos is thought to be simple and impassible, a becoming "one" with anything that is not himself is an absolute impossibility. All talk of becoming "one" with Jesus in the incarnation, then, could only be a figure of speech. It could not be realistically conceived. And so it came about that the two elements composing Christ (divinity and humanity) threatened constantly to be torn asunder. That was as true of the Cyrillines as it was of the Nestorians. And so it came

---

62. Dillon, *Middle Platonists*, 361–79.

about that the "unity" of the "person" of Christ became the central problem. "Incarnation" now entailed (even if only in principle and not yet in rhetorical formulation) the "hypostasizing" of a human "nature" in the eternal hypostasis of the Logos. But such a solution could achieve only a single end; that, namely, of protecting the simplicity and impassibility of the Logos. It was a "unity" that erased humanness. Moreover, since these were not biblical commitments, the problem now being addressed could not possibly be the problem received from the New Testament—which was to explain how a single human could be "fully divine" while being "fully human."

What Pârvan is challenging is my use of the word "repair." I could not possibly be repairing Chalcedon, she says, since I am addressing a different problem than they did. I agree; I am addressing a different problem. So why did I use that word at all? My answer is: it was meant to be an expression of good will, advanced in the kinds of grassroots ecumenical efforts that I have engaged in over the last twenty years or so. I recognized that those with whom I have been in dialogue think Chalcedon to be "biblical." Rather than addressing that conviction head on, I said to myself: Let us assume for the moment that Chalcedon's problem was the problem bequeathed to the churches by the New Testament writers. What then? I tried to show that the solution of the bishops at Chalcedon does not work *on its own grounds*. It is a failure. In doing so, I was also trying to show my conversation partners what a "fix" of Chalcedon would require, namely, starting over without simplicity and impassibility, a root-and-branch reconstruction. In the process, they would have to recognize that the New Testament problem is *not* the Chalcedonian problem. Whether I was wise to adopt this strategy, I will leave others to decide.

CONCLUSION

The Romantics have long been under suspicion in Barth circles—in large measure because Friedrich Schleiermacher was placed under suspicion by Barth himself. It seems to me that such reactions have been anything but thoughtful and well informed. Much of it reflects a kind of tribal loyalty that has no place in academic research and which Barth himself despised. The way forward, it seems to me, might well lie through widespread reconsideration of Barth's relationship to Schleiermacher. That is something I hope to contribute to moving forward.

Bibliography

Aleinikova, S. M. *"Russkii Mir": Belorusskii Vzgliad* [Russian world: A Belarussian perspective]. Minsk: RIVSh, 2017.

Anatolios, Khaled. *Retrieving Nicaea: The Development and Meaning of Trinitarian Doctrine.* Grand Rapids: Baker Academic, 2018.

Anderson, Clifford B. "Jesus and the 'Christian Worldview': A Comparative Analysis of Abraham Kuyper and Karl Barth." *Cultural Encounters* 2 (2006) 61–80.

Aquinas, Thomas. *Summa Theologiae* [*ST*]. Rev. ed. Translated by Fathers of the English Dominican Province. London: Benziger Brothers, 1920.

Armstrong, Meg. "'The Effects of Blackness': Gender, Race, and the Sublime in Aesthetic Theories of Burke and Kant." *Journal of Aesthetics and Art Criticism* 54 (1996) 213–36.

Arnim, Bettine von. *Clemens Brentanos Frühlingskranz.* Projekt Gutenberg, n.d. 2nd ed. Gutenberg 16. ttps://www.projekt-gutenberg.org/arnimb/kranz/kranz31.html.

Baker, Matthew. "'Offenbarung, Philosophie, und Theologie': Karl Barth and Georges Florovsky in Dialogue." *Scottish Journal of Theology* 68 (2015) 299–326.

Balke, Willem. *Calvin and the Anabaptist Radicals.* Translated by William Heynen. Eugene, OR: Wipf & Stock, 1999.

Balthasar, Hans Urs von. *Epilogue.* Translated by Edward T. Oakes. San Francisco: Ignatius, 2005.

———. *Theo-Drama: Theological Dramatic Theory.* Translated by Graham Harrison. Vol. 3, *The Dramatis Personae: Persons in Christ*. San Francisco: Ignatius, 1993.

———. *Theo-Logic: Theological Logical Theory.* Translated by Adrian J. Walker. Vol. 2, *The Truth of God*. San Francisco: Ignatius, 2004.

———. *The Theology of Karl Barth: Exposition and Interpretation.* Translated by Edward T. Oakes. Communio. San Francisco: Ignatius, 1992.

Barth, Karl. *Barth in Conversation.* Edited by Eberhard Busch. Translated by Translation Fellows of the Center for Barth Studies. Vol. 3, *1964–1968*. Louisville: Westminster John Knox, 2019.

———. *Briefe des Jahres 1933.* Edited by Eberhard Busch et al. Zurich: TVZ, 2004.

———. "The Christian Community and the Civil Community." In *Community, State, and Church: Three Essays*, edited by Will Herberg, translated by Ronald Gregor Smith, 149–89. Garden City, NY: Anchor, 1960.

———. *The Christian Life.* Translated by G. W. Bromiley. Edinburgh: T&T Clark, 1981.

———. "Der Christ in der Gesellschaft, 1919." In *Vorträge und kleinere Arbeiten 1914–1921*, edited by Hans-Anton Drewes, 546–98. Zurich: TVZ, 2012.

———. *Die christliche Dogmatik im Entwurf 1927*. Edited by Gerhard Sauter. Vol. 1, *Die Lehre vom Wort Gottes: Prolegomena zur christlichen Dogmatik*. Zurich: TVZ, 1982.

———. *The Church and the War*. Translated by Antonia H. Froendt. Eugene, OR: Wipf & Stock, 2008.

———. *The Early Barth—Lectures and Shorter Works*. Edited by Hans-Anton Drewes and Hinrich Stoevesandt with Herbert Helms. Translated and edited by Darrel L. Guder et al. Vol. 1, *1905–1909*. Louisville: Westminster John Knox, 2022.

———. *The Epistle to the Romans*. 6th ed. Translated and edited by Edwyn C. Hoskyns. London: Oxford University Press, 1968.

———. *Ethics*. Edited by Dietrich Braun. Translated by Geoffrey W. Bromiley. Edinburgh: T&T Clark, 1981.

———. *Evangelical Theology: An Introduction*. Translated by Grover Foley. Grand Rapids: Eerdmans, 1979.

———. "Farewell." In *The Essential Karl Barth: A Reader and Commentary*, edited by Keith L. Johnson, 81–92. Grand Rapids: Baker Academic, 2019.

———. *Fides Quaerens Intellectum*. Edited by Eberhard Jüngel and Ingolf Dalferth. Zurich: TVZ, 1981.

———. "The First Commandment as the Axiom of Theology." In *The Way of Theology in Karl Barth: Essays and Comments*, edited by H. Martin Rumscheidt, 63–78. Allison Park, PA: Pickwick, 1986.

———. *Für die Freiheit des Evangeliums*. Theologische Existenz heute 2. Munich: Kaiser, 1933.

———. *The Göttingen Dogmatics*. Edited by Hannelotte Reiffen. Translated by Geoffrey W. Bromiley. Vol. 1, *Instruction in the Christian Religion*. Grand Rapids: Eerdmans, 1991.

———. *The Göttingen Dogmatics*. Translated by Thomas Herwig. Vol. 1, *Instruction in the Christian Religion*. Grand Rapids: Eerdmans, forthcoming.

———. *Konfirmandenunterricht, 1909–1921*. Edited by Jürgen Fangmeier. Zurich: TVZ, 1987.

———. "Letter to Friedrich Gogarten, July 28, 1931." In Karl Barth Archive, Basel.

———. *A Letter to Great Britain from Switzerland*. Translated by E. H. Gordon and George Hill. Eugene, OR: Wipf & Stock, 2004.

———. *Letters 1961–1968*. Edited by Jürgen Fangmeier and Hinrich Stoevesandt. Translated by Geoffrey W. Bromiley. Grand Rapids: Eerdmans, 1981.

———. *Die Menschlichkeit Gottes*. Theologische Studien 48. Zollikon, Switz.: Evangelisch, 1956.

———. "Nachwort." In *Schleiermacher-Auswahl*, edited by Heinz Bolli, 290–312. Munich: Siebenstern, 1968.

———. "No! A Reply to Emil Brunner." In *Natural Theology: Comprising "Nature and Grace" by Professor Dr. Emil Brunner and the Reply "No!" by Dr. Karl Barth*, translated by Peter Fraenkel, 65–128. London: Centenary, 1946.

———. "Not und Verheissung der christlichen Verkündigung, 1922." In *Vorträge und kleinere Arbeiten 1922–1925*, edited by Holger Finze, 65–97. Zurich: TVZ, 1990.

———. *Die protestantische Theologie im 19. Jahrhundert: Ihre Vorgeschichte und ihre Geschichte*. Zollikon, Switz.: Evangelisch, 1947.

———. *Protestant Theology in the Nineteenth Century*. Translated by Brian Cozens and John Bowden. Rev. ed. London: SCM, 2001.

———. *Reformation als Entscheidung*. Theologische Existenz heute 3. Munich: Kaiser, 1933.

———. *Der Römerbrief (Erste Fassung) 1919*. Edited by Hermann Schmidt. Zurich: TVZ, 1985.

———. *Der Römerbrief (Zweite Fassung) 1922*. Edited by Cornelis van der Kooi and Katja Tolstaja. Zurich: TVZ, 2010.

———. "Sermon on Romans 15:5–13." In *The Essential Karl Barth: A Reader and Commentary*, edited by Keith L. Johnson, 308–19. Grand Rapids: Baker Academic, 2019.

———. *The Teaching of the Church Regarding Baptism*. Translated by Ernest A. Payne. London: SCM, 1948.

———. *Theological Existence To-Day! (A Plea for Theological Freedom)*. Translated by R. Birch Hoyle. Eugene, OR: Wipf & Stock, 2011.

———. *Die Theologie Schleiermachers*. Edited by Dietrich Ritschl. Zurich: Theologisch, 1978.

———. *Die Theologie Zwinglis: Vorlesung Göttingen 1922/23*. Edited by Matthias Freudenberg. Zurich: TVZ, 2004.

———. *Theologische Existenz heute! (1933)*. Edited by Hinrich Stoevesandt. Theologische Existenz heute 219. Munich: Kaiser, 1984.

———. *The Theology of John Calvin*. Translated by Geoffrey W. Bromiley. Grand Rapids: Eerdmans, 1995.

———. *The Theology of Schleiermacher*. Edited by Dietrich Ritschl. Translated by Geoffrey W. Bromiley. Edinburgh: T&T Clark, 1982.

———. *The Theology of the Reformed Confessions*. Translated by Darrell L. Guder and Judith J. Guder. Louisville: Westminster John Knox, 2002.

———. *Unterricht in der christlichen Religion*. Edited by Hannelotte Reiffen. Vol. 1, *Prolegomena, 1924*. Zurich: TVZ, 1990.

———. *Unterricht in der christlichen Religion*. Edited by Hinrich Stoevesandt. Vol. 2, *Die Lehre von Gott/Die Lehre vom Menschen, 1924/1925*. Zurich: TVZ, 1990.

———. *Unterricht in der christlichen Religion*. Edited by Hinrich Stoevesandt. Vol. 3, *Die Lehre von der Versöhnung/Die Lehre von der Erlösung*. Zurich: TVZ, 2003.

———. *Vorträge und kleinere Arbeiten, 1909–1914*. Edited by Hans-Anton Drewes and Hinrich Stoevesandt. Zurich: TVZ, 2004.

———. *Vorträge und kleinere Arbeiten, 1914–1921*. Edited by Hans-Anton Drewes. Zurich: TVZ, 2012.

———. *Vorträge und kleinere Arbeiten, 1922–1925*. Edited by Holger Finze-Michaelsen. Zurich: TVZ, 1990.

———. *Vorträge und Kleinere Arbeiten, 1930–1933*. Edited by Michael Beintker et al. Zurich: TVZ, 2013.

———. *The Word of God and Theology*. Translated by Amy Marga. London: T&T Clark, 2011.

Barth, Karl, and Emil Brunner. *Karl Barth–Emil Brunner Briefwechsel, 1916–1966*. Edited by Eberhard Busch. Zurich: TVZ, 2000.

Barth, Karl, and Eduard Thurneysen. *Karl Barth–Eduard Thurneysen Briefwechsel*. Vol. 1, *1913–1921*, edited by Eduard Thurneysen. Zurich: TVZ, 1973.

———. *Karl Barth–Eduard Thurneysen Briefwechsel*. Vol. 2, *1921–1930*, edited by Eduard Thurneysen. Zurich: TVZ, 1974.

BIBLIOGRAPHY

———. *Karl Barth-Eduard Thurneysen Briefwechsel.* Vol. 3, *1930–1935*, edited by Caren Algner. Zurich: TVZ, 2000.

———. *Revolutionary Theology in the Making: Barth-Thurneysen Correspondence 1914-25.* Translated by James D. Smart. London: Epworth, 1964.

Bavinck, Herman. *Gereformeerde Dogmatiek.* Vol. 2. 2nd rev. ed. Kampen: Bos, 1908.

———. *Reformed Dogmatics.* Edited by John Bolt. Translated by John Vriend. Vol. 2, *God and Creation.* Grand Rapids: Baker, 2004.

Beintker, Michael. "Barths Abschied von *Zwischen den Zeiten*: Recherchen und Beobachtungen zum Ende einer Zeitschrift." *Zeitschrift für Theologie und Kirche* 106 (2009) 201–22.

Beiser, Frederick C. *The Romantic Imperative: The Concept of Early German Romanticism.* London: Harvard University Press, 2003.

Belt, Henk van den, ed. *Synopsis Purioris Theologiae/Synopsis of a Purer Theology.* Translated by Riemer A. Faber. Vol. 2, *Disputations 24–42.* Studies in Medieval and Reformation Traditions 204/8. Texts and Sources 204/8. Leiden: Brill, 2016.

Benedict XVI. *Deus Caritas Est: God Is Love; First Encyclical Letter.* London: CTS, 2006.

Berchet, Giovanni. "Sul 'Cacciatore feroce' e sulla 'Eleonora' di Goffredo Augusto Bürger: Lettera semiseria di Grisostomo al suo figliuolo." Wikisource, 1816. https://it.wikisource.org/wiki/Lettera_semiseria_di_Grisostomo_al_suo_figliuolo.

Betz, John R. "Erich Przywara and Karl Barth: On the *Analogia Entis* as a Formal Principle of Catholic Theology." In *The Analogy of Being: Invention of the Antichrist or Wisdom of God*, edited by Thomas J. White, 35–87. Grand Rapids: Eerdmans, 2011.

Bolliac, Cezar. *Opere.* Vol. 2. Bucharest: ESPLA, 1956.

Bonhoeffer, Dietrich. *Letters and Papers from Prison.* Edited by Eberhard Bethge. London: SCM, 1971.

Bowens, Lisa M. *African American Readings of Paul: Reception, Resistance and Transformation.* Grand Rapids: Eerdmans, 2020.

Bremer, Thomas. "Diffuses Konzept: Die Russische Orthodoxe Kirche und die 'Russische Welt.'" *Osteuropa* 66 (2016) 3–18.

———. "Mythos 'Russische Welt': Russlands Regime, die ROK und der Krieg." *Osteuropa* 73 (2023) 261–74.

Breukelman, Frans H. *The Structure of Sacred Doctrine in Calvin's Theology.* Edited by Rinse H. Reeling Brouwer. Translated by Martin Kessler. Grand Rapids: Eerdmans, 2009.

———. *Theologische Opstellen.* Kampen: Kok, 1999.

Bridges, AnnMarie M. "Blindness, Imagination, Perception: Calvin's 1559 *Institutes* and Early Modern Visual Instability." PhD diss., Harvard University, 2020.

Brooten, Bernadette. "'Junia . . . Outstanding Among the Apostles' (Romans 16:7)." In *Women Priests: A Catholic Commentary on the Vatican Declaration*, edited by Leonard Swidler and Arlene Swidler, 41–44. New York: Paulist, 1977.

Brunner, Emil. "Die andere Aufgabe der Theologie." *Zwischen den Zeiten* (1929) 255–76.

Bulgakov, Sergius. *The Lamb of God.* Translated by Boris Jakim. Grand Rapids: Eerdmans, 2008.

Busch, Eberhard. "Dem Vater Luther als Widerhaken gesetzt: Von Karl Barths Reserve gegenüber Ulrich Zwingli." *Kirchenblatt für die reformierte Schweiz* 140 (1984) 244–46.

———. *Karl Barth: His Life from Letters and Autobiographical Texts*. Translated by John Bowden. London: SCM, 1976.

Byron, John, and Joel N. Lohr, eds. *"I (Still) Believe": Leading Bible Scholars Share Their Stories of Faith and Scholarship*. Grand Rapids: Zondervan, 2015.

Calvin, John. *Calvini opera quae supersunt omnia [CO]*. Edited by W. Baum et al. 59 vols. Brunswick, Germ.: Schwetschke, 1863–1900.

———. *Calvin's Commentaries*. Translated by T. H. L. Parker. Vol. 11, *Galatians, Philippians and Colossians*. Grand Rapids: Eerdmans, 1974.

———. *Commentary on the Gospel According to John*. CCEL, 1847. Translated by William Pringle. Vol. 1. https://ccel.org/ccel/calvin/calcom34/calcom34.i.html.

———. *Institutes of the Christian Religion*. Translated by Lewis Ford Battles. 2 vols. Library of Christian Classics. Louisville: Westminster John Knox, 1961.

———. *Institution de la religion chrétienne (1541)*. Edited by Olivier Millet. 2 vols. Geneva: Droz, 2008.

———. *Opera Selecta [OS]*. Edited by Petrus Barth and Guilelmus Niesel. 5 vols. Eugene OR: Wipf & Stock, 2018.

Carter, J. Kameron. "Anarchē; or, The Matter of Charles Long and Black Feminism." *American Religion* 2 (2021) 103–35.

Chapnin, Sergey. "A Church of Empire: Why the Russian Church Chose to Bless Empire." *First Things*, Nov. 1, 2015. https://www.firstthings.com/article/2015/11/a-church-of-empire.

Clark, Stuart. *Vanities of the Eye: Vision in Early Modern European Culture*. Oxford: Oxford University Press, 2007.

Cochrane, Arthur C. *Reformed Confessions of the 16th Century*. Philadelphia: Westminster, 1966.

Coleridge, Samuel Taylor. *Biographia Literaria*. Edited by John Shawcross. Vol. 1. Oxford: Clarendon, 1907.

———. *Philosophical Lectures 1818–1819*. Edited by Kathleen Coburn. London: Pilot, 1949.

Cone, James H. *God of the Oppressed*. Rev. ed. Maryknoll, NY: Orbis, 1997.

Congar, Yves. *Tradition and Traditions*. 2 vols. Paris: Arthème Fayard, 1960–63.

Copenhaver, Brian P. *Magic in Western Culture: From Antiquity to the Enlightenment*. Cambridge: Cambridge University Press, 2015.

Courvoisier, Jacques. "Zwingli et Karl Barth." In *Antwort: Karl Barth zum siebzigsten Geburtstag am 10. Mai 1956*, edited by Ernst Wolf et al., 369–87. Zollikon, Switz.: Evangelisch, 1956.

Daley, Brian E. *God Visible: Patristic Christology Reconsidered*. Changing Paradigms in Historical and Systematic Theology. Oxford: Oxford University Press, 2018.

Dallmayr, Fred, ed. *The Legacy of the Barmen Declaration: Politics and the Kingdom*. Faith and Politics: Political Theology in a New Key. Lanham, MD: Lexington, 2019.

De Boer, Martinus. "Karl Barth, Theological Exegesis, and the Apocalyptic Interpretation of Paul." *Zeitschrift für dialektische Theologie* 73 (2021) 11–37.

Demura, Akira. "Zwingli in the Writings of Karl Barth: With Special Emphasis on the Doctrine of the Sacraments." In *Probing the Reformed Tradition: Historical*

Studies in Honor of Edward A. Dowey, Jr., edited by Elsie Anne McKee and Brian G. Armstrong, 197–219. Louisville: Westminster John Knox, 1989.

Denysenko, Nicholas. *The Church's Unholy War: Russia's Invasion of Ukraine and Orthodoxy*. Eugene, OR: Wipf & Stock, 2023.

———. "Fractured Orthodoxy in Ukraine and Politics: The Impact of Patriarch Kyrill's 'Russian World.'" *Logos: A Journal of Eastern Christian Studies* 54 (2013) 33–67.

Derrida, Jacques. *Margins of Philosophy*. Translated by Alan Bass. Chicago: University of Chicago Press, 1984.

Dewan, Lawrence. "The Existence of God: Can It Be Demonstrated?" *Nova et Vetera* 10 (2012) 731–56.

Dillon, John. *The Middle Platonists: 80 B.C. to A.D. 220*. Ithaca, NY: Cornell University Press, 1977.

Dorner, Isaak August. *Divine Immutability: A Critical Reconsideration*. Translated by Robert R. Williams and Claude Welch. Fortress Texts in Modern Theology. Minneapolis: Fortress, 1994.

———. *Entwicklungsgeschichte der Lehre von der Person Christi von den ältesten Zeiten bis auf die neuesten*. Stuttgart: Liesching, 1839.

———. "Ueber die richtige Fassung des dogmatischen Begriffs der Unveränderlichkeit Gottes." In *Gesammelte Schriften*, 188–377. Berlin: Hertz, 1883.

Dowey, Edward A. *The Knowledge of God in Calvin's Theology*. New York: Columbia University Press, 1952.

Edmondson, Stephen. *Calvin's Christology*. Cambridge: Cambridge University Press, 2004.

Eminescu, Mihai. *Fragmentarium*. Edited by Magdalena D. Vatamaniuc. Bucharest: Ştiinţifică şi Enciclopedică, 1981.

Epp, Eldon J. *Junia: The First Woman Apostle*. Minneapolis: Fortress, 1995.

Essary, Kirk. "The Radical Humility of Christ in the Sixteenth Century: Erasmus and Calvin on Philippians 2:6–7." *Scottish Journal of Theology* 68 (2015) 398–420.

Fisher, Simon. *Revelatory Positivism? Barth's Earliest Theology and the Marburg School*. Oxford: Oxford University Press, 1988.

Frankl, Viktor E. *Man's Search for Meaning*. New York: Pocket, 1963.

Freudenberg, Matthias. *Karl Barth und die reformierte Theologie*. Neukirchen, Germ.: Neukirchen-Vluyn, 1997.

———. "Nach Gottes Wort Reformiert: Anmerkungen zu Karl Barths Rezeption der reformierten Theologie." *Communio Viatorum* 39 (1997) 35–59.

———. *Reformierter Protestantismus in der Herausforderung*. Berlin: LIT, 2012.

Friedman, Russell L. *Intellectual Traditions at the Medieval University: The Use of Philosophical Psychology in Trinitarian Theology Among the Franciscans and Dominicans, 1250–1350*. 2 vols. Studien und Texte zur Geistesgeschichte des Mittelalters 108. Leiden: Brill, 2012.

———. *Medieval Trinitarian Theology from Aquinas to Ockham*. Cambridge: Cambridge University Press, 2013.

Gallaher, Brandon. *Freedom and Necessity in Modern Trinitarian Theology*. Oxford: Oxford University Press, 2016.

———. "The Pure Signifier of Power: Remembering, Repeating and Working Through the Significance of the Papacy and Pope Francis for Eastern Orthodoxy." In *The Geopolitics of Pope Francis*, edited by Jan De Volder, 169–98. Annua Nuntia Lovaniensia. Leuven: Peeters, 2019.

———. "The Road from Rome to Moscow." *Tablet* (2016) 8–9.

———. "A Tale of Two Speeches: Secularism and Primacy in Contemporary Roman Catholicism and Russian Orthodoxy." In *Primacy in the Church: The Office of Primate and the Authority of the Councils*, edited by John Chryssavgis, 2:807–37. Crestwood, NY: St. Vladimir's Seminary Press, 2016.

Gallaher, Brandon, and Pantelis Kalaitzidis. "A Declaration on the 'Russian World' (*Russkii Mir*) Teaching." *Mission Studies* 39 (2022) 269–76. https://publicorthodoxy.org/2022/03/13/a-declaration-on-the-russian-world-russkii-mir-teaching/.

———. "A Declaration on the 'Russian World' (*Russkii Mir*) Teaching." Orthodox Christian Studies Center, Mar. 13, 2022. Cover letter. https://mailchi.mp/8199f7740b4c/ocsc-spring-updates-14172292?e=8f8689449a.

Gaventa, Beverly Roberts. "The Paradox of Power: Reading for the Subject in Romans 14:1–15:6." *Journal of Theological Interpretation* 5 (2011) 1–12.

———. "'That Grace Should Come Into Its Own': Romans 12:1–8 in and with Karl Barth's *Römerbrief*." In *The New Perspective on Grace: Paul and the Gospel After "Paul and the Gift*," edited by Edward Adams et al., 251–63. Grand Rapids: Eerdmans, 2023.

Gavrilyuk, Paul. "Hitler and Putin: 1938 and 2022." *Public Orthodoxy*, Feb. 23, 2022. https://publicorthodoxy.org/2022/02/23/hitler-and-putin/.

———. "The Moral Defeat of the Russian World: Putin, Kirill, and the Tribunal of History." *Public Orthodoxy*, May 13, 2022. https://publicorthodoxy.org/2022/05/13/moral-defeat-of-russian-world/.

Geiste und Psyche. "Karl Barth—ein Interview (1967)." YouTube, Dec. 15, 2019. From "JA und NEIN, Karl Barth zum Gedächtnis," directed by Heinz Knorr. https://www.youtube.com/watch?v=RgSTyEPqmSY.

Gogarten, Friedrich. *Einheit von Evangelium und Volkstum*. Hamburg: Hanseatisch, 1933.

———. "Karl Barths Dogmatik." *Theologische Rundschau* 1 (1929) 60–80.

———. *Politische Ethik: Versuch einer Grudlegung*. Jena: Diederichs, 1932.

———. "Predigt über Joh. 15:26–27." *Zwischen den Zeiten* 11 (1933) 465–72.

———. "Schöpfung und Volkstum: Vortrag gehalten auf der Berliner Missionswoche am 3 October 1932." *Zwischen den Zeiten* 10 (1932) 481–504.

———. "Die Selbständigkeit der Kirche." *Deutsches Volkstum* 15 (1933) 445–51.

Gorski, Philip S., and Samuel L. Perry. *The Flag and the Cross: White Christian Nationalism and the Threat to American Democracy*. New York: Oxford University Press, 2022.

Grant, Hardy. "Geometry and Politics: Mathematics in the Thought of Thomas Hobbes." *Mathematics Magazine* 63 (1990) 147–54.

Griffin, Sean. "Putin's Holy War of the Fatherland: Sacred Memory and the Russian Invasion of Ukraine." *Russian Review* 83 (2024) 79–92.

———. "Russian World or Holy World War? The Real Ideology of the Invasion of Ukraine." *Public Orthodoxy*, Apr. 12, 2023. https://publicorthodoxy.org/2022/04/12/russian-world-or-holy-world-war.

Gundiaev, Patriarch Kirill. "Address at the Grand Opening of the Third Assembly of the Russian World (November 3, 2009)." Translated by Stephen D. Shenfield. *Russian Politics and Law* 49 (2011) 57–64.

———. "His Holiness Patriarch Kirill Calls on the Faithful to Pray for Peace and Unity of the Church." Russian Orthodox Church, Feb. 27, 2022. http://www.patriarchia.ru/en/db/text/5904398.html.

———. "Molitva o vosstanovlenii mira [Prayer for the restoration of peace]." Russian Orthodox Church, Mar. 3, 2022. http://www.patriarchia.ru/db/text/5905833.html.

———. "'Patriarshaia propoved' v Nedeliu 15-iu po Piatidesiatnitse posle Liturgii v Aleksandro-Nevskom skitu [Patriarchal sermon on the 15th Sunday after Pentecost following the liturgy at the Alexander Nevsky Skete]." Russian Orthodox Church, Sept. 25, 2022. http://www.patriarchia.ru/db/text/5962628.html.

———. "'Patriarshaia propoved' v Nedeliu syropustnuiu posle Liturgii v Khrame Khrista Spasitelia [Patriarchal sermon on Cheesefare Week after the liturgy at the Cathedral of Christ the Savior]." Russian Orthodox Church, Mar. 6, 2022. http://www.patriarchia.ru/db/text/5906442.html.

———. "'Patriarshaia propoved' v prazdnik Vozdvizheniia Kresta Gospodnia posle Liturgii v Khrame Khrista Spasitelia [Patriarchal sermon on the Feast of the Exaltation of the Holy Cross following the liturgy at the Cathedral of the Christ the Saviour]." Russian Orthodox Church, Sept. 27, 2022. http://www.patriarchia.ru/db/text/5963304.html.

———. *Sem' Slov' o Russkom Mire*. Edited by A. V. Shchipkov and Anastasiiā Klimova. Moscow: Vsemirnyi Russkii Harodnyi Sobor [Russian People's Council], 2015.

———. "Sviateshii Patriarkh Kirill rasskazal delegatsiiam Pomestnykh Pravoslavnykh Tserkvei o situatsii na Ukraine [His Holiness Patriarch Kirill told the delegates of the local Orthodox churches concerning the situation in Ukraine]." Orthodox Information Agency, Feb. 1, 2019. https://rusk.ru/newsdata.php?idar=83406.

———. "Vystuplenie Sviateishego Patriarkha Kirilla na otkryitii IV Assamblei Russkogo mira [Address of His Holiness Patriarch Kirill at the opening of the Fourth Assembly of the Russian World]." Russian Orthodox Church, Nov. 3, 2010. http://www.patriarchia.ru/db/text/1310952.html.

Hancock, Angela Dienhart. *Karl Barth's Emergency Homiletic 1932–1933: A Summons to Prophetic Witness at the Dawn of the Third Reich*. Grand Rapids: Eerdmans, 2013.

Hawthorne, Nathaniel. *The House of the Seven Gables*. Electronic Classics. N.p.: Pennsylvania State University, 2008. Ebook.

Hector, Kevin W. "Barth on Theological Method." In *The Wiley Blackwell Companion to Karl Barth*, edited by George Hunsinger and Keith L. Johnson, 83–94. Wiley Blackwell Companions to Religion. Oxford: Wiley-Blackwell, 2020.

———. "Karl Barth." In *The Routledge Companion to Modern Christian Thought*, edited by Chad Meister and James Beilby, 152–62. Routledge Religion Companions. London: Routledge, 2013.

———. *The Theological Project of Modernism: Faith and the Conditions of Mineness*. Oxford: Oxford University Press, 2015.

———. "Theology as an Academic Discipline: Reconciling Theological Encyclopedia and Evangelical Theology." In *Karl Barth and the Making of "Evangelical Theology": A Fifty-Year Perspective*, edited by Clifford B. Anderson and Bruce L. McCormack, 91–118. Grand Rapids: Eerdmans, 2015.

Hegel, G. W. F. *Faith and Knowledge*. Translated by Walter Cerf and H. S. Harris. New York: SUNY Press, 1977.

———. *Lectures on the Philosophy of Religion: The Lectures of 1827*. Edited by Peter C. Hodgson. Translated by Robert F. Brown et al. Single vol. ed. Oxford: Clarendon, 2006.

———. *Phänomenologie des Geistes*. Hamburg: Meiner, 1988.

Heppe, Heinrich, ed. *Reformed Dogmatics*. Revised by Ernst Bizer. Translated by G. T. Thomas. London: Wakeman Great Reprints, n.d.

Hitler, Adolf. "Proclamation to the German Nation, February 1, 1933." In *My New Order*, edited by Raoul de Roussy de Sales, 142–47. New York: Reynal & Hitchcock, 1941.

Hobbes, Thomas. *Leviathan: With Selected Variants from the Latin Edition of 1668*. Edited by Edwin Curley. Hackett Classics. Indianapolis: Hackett, 1994.

Hölderlin, Friedrich. *Sämtliche Werke*. Edited by Friedrich Beissner. Kleine Stuttgarter Ausgabe 4. Stuttgart: Cotta, 1962.

Hong Kong Pastors Network. "Hong Kong 2020 Gospel Declaration." Hong Kong Pastors Network, 2020. https://hkpastors.net/hk2020gospeldeclaration/en/. URL no longer active.

Hovorun, Cyril. "Interpreting the 'Russian World.'" In *Churches in the Ukrainian Crisis*, edited by Andrii Krawchuk and Thomas Bremer, 163–71. Basingstoke: Palgrave Macmillan, 2016.

Hugo, Victor. *Cromwell—Préface*. Académie des écrivains publics de France, 1827. https://ecrivains-publics.fr/wp-content/uploads/2016/10/preface_de_cromwell_-_hugo.pdf.

———. *Hernani*. Wikisource, last updated Nov. 1, 2023. https://fr.wikisource.org/wiki/Hernani_(Hetzel,_1889).

Iantsen, V. V. "Pisma Russkikh Myslitelei v Bazel'skom Archive Fritsa Liba." In *Issledovaniia Po Istorii Russkoi Mysli*, edited by M. A. Kolerov, 227–563. Moscow: Tri Kvadrata, 2002.

Jehle, Frank. "Karl Barths Zwinglivorlesung 1922/23." *Zwingliana* 44 (2017) 501–9.

Jennings, Willie James. *Acts*. Belief: Theological Commentary on the Bible Series. Louisville: Westminster John Knox, 2017.

———. *The Christian Imagination: Theology and the Origins of Race*. New Haven, CT: Yale University Press, 2010.

John Paul II. *Fides et Ratio*. Dublin: Veritas, 1998.

———. *Novo Millennio Ineunte*. London: CTS, 2001.

Johnson, Keith L., ed. *The Essential Karl Barth: A Reader and Commentary*. Grand Rapids: Baker Academic, 2019.

———. *Karl Barth and the* Analogia Entis. T&T Clark Studies in Systematic Theology. London: T&T Clark, 2010.

———. "Reconsidering Barth's Rejection of Przywara's *Analogia Entis*." *Modern Theology* 26 (2010) 632–50.

Jones, Paul Dafydd, and Paul T. Nimmo, eds. *The Oxford Handbook of Karl Barth*. Oxford Handbooks. Oxford: Oxford University Press, 2019.

Journet, Charles. *Les septs paroles du Christ au croix*. Paris: Seuil, 1954.

Jüngel, Eberhard. *God's Being Is in Becoming: The Trinitarian Being of God in the Theology of Karl Barth*. Translated by John Webster. Grand Rapids: Eerdmans, 2001.

———. *Gottes Sein ist im Werden: Verantwortliche Rede vom Sein Gottes bei Karl Barth: Eine Paraphrase*. Tübingen: Mohr Siebeck, 1965.

Kant, Immanuel. *Critique of the Power of Judgment*. Edited by Paul Guyer. Translated by Paul Guyer and Eric Matthews. Cambridge Edition of the Works of Immanuel Kant. Cambridge: Cambridge University Press, 2000.

Kasper, Walter. *The Absolute in History: The Philosophy and Theology of History in Schelling's Late Philosophy*. Translated by Katherine E. Wolff. New York: Paulist, 2018.

———. *The God of Jesus Christ*. Translated by Matthew J. O'Connell. New York: Crossroad, 1989.

Keats, John. *Endymion*. Poems by John Keats, n.d. http://keats-poems.com/endymion-book-2/.

———. *Selected Letters of John Keats*. Edited by Grant F. Scott. Rev. ed. Cambridge, MA: Harvard University Press, 2005.

Kent, Bonnie. *Virtues of the Will*. Washington, DC: Catholic University of America Press, 1995.

Kogălniceanu, Mihail. *Scrieri*. Bucharest: Tineretului, 1978.

Knorr, Heinz, dir. "JA und NEIN, Karl Barth zum Gedächtnis." [Stuttgart?]: Calwer, 1967.

Krusche, Werner. *Das Wirken des Heiligen Geistes nach Calvin*. Forschungen zur Kirchen- und Dogmengeschichte 7. Göttingen: Vandenhoeck & Ruprecht, 1957.

Küng, Hans. *Justification: The Doctrine of Karl Barth and a Catholic Reflection*. Translated by Thomas Collins et al. Philadelphia: Westminster, 1964.

———. *Rechtfertigung: Die Lehre Karl Barths und eine Katholische Besinnung*. Einsiedeln, Switz.: Johannes, 1957.

Lamm, Julia A. *The Living God: Schleiermacher's Theological Appropriation of Spinoza*. University Park: Pennsylvania State University Press, 1996.

Lehmann, Paul. "Karl Barth, Theologian of Permanent Revolution." *Union Seminary Quarterly Review* 28 (1972) 67–81.

Leinsle, Ulrich G. *Introduction to Scholastic Theology*. Translated by Michael J. Miller. Washington, DC: Catholic University of America Press, 2010.

Leong, Elaine, and Alisha Rankin, eds. *Secrets and Knowledge in Medicine and Science, 1500–1800*. Surrey: Ashgate, 2011.

Leopardi, Giacomo. *Zibaldone*. Edited by M. Caesar and F. D'Intino. Translated by Kathleen Baldwin et al. New York: Macmillan, 2015.

Lettsome, Raquel S. "Mary's Slave Song: The Tensions and Turnarounds of Faithfully Reading *Doulē* in the Magnificat." *Interpretation* 75 (2021) 6–18.

Leustean, Lucian N. "Russia's Invasion of Ukraine: The First Religious War in the 21st Century." LSE Religion and Global Society, Mar. 3, 2022. https://blogs.lse.ac.uk/religionglobalsociety/2022/03/russias-invasion-of-ukraine-the-first-religious-war-in-the-21st-century/.

Lichtenfeld, Manacnuc. "Georg Merz: Pastoraltheolgie zwischen den Zeiten." *Lutherische Kirche: Geschichte und Gestalten* 18 (1997) 174–212.

Lietzmann, Hans. *An die Römer*. 4th ed. Tübingen: Mohr Siebeck, 1933.

Linebaugh, Jonathan A. "Relational Hermeneutics and Comparison as Conversation." In *The Word of the Cross: Reading Paul*, 77–96. Grand Rapids: Eerdmans, 2022.

Locher, Gottfried W. *Die Theologie Huldrych Zwinglis im Lichte seiner Christologie*. Part 1, *Die Gotteslehre*. Zurich: Zwingli, 1952.

———. *Zwingli's Thought: New Perspectives*. Translated by Milton Ayler and Stuart Casson. Studies in the History of Christian Traditions 25. Leiden: Brill, 1981.

BIBLIOGRAPHY

Lohmann, Johann Friedrich. *Karl Barth und der Neukantianismus: Die Rezeption des Neukantianismus im "Römerbrief" und ihre Bedeutung für die weitere Ausarbeitung der Theologie Karl Barths*. Theologische Bibliothek Töpelmann. Berlin: de Gruyter, 1995.

Long, Charles H. "Indigenous People, Materialities, and Religion: Outline for a New Orientation to Religious Meaning." In *Religion and Global Culture: New Terrain in the Study of Religion and the Work of Charles H. Long*, edited by Jennifer Reid, 167–80. Lanham, MD: Lexington, 2003.

Loofs, Friedrich. "Kenosis." In *Realencyklopädie für protestantische Theologie und Kirche*, edited by Albert Hauck, 10:246–63. 3rd ed. Leipzig: Hinrichs, 1901.

Lyden, John. "The Influence of Hermann Cohen on Karl Barth's Dialectical Theology." *Modern Judaism* 12 (1992) 167–83.

Lyons, John D. *Before Imagination: Embodied Thought from Montaigne to Rousseau*. Stanford: Stanford University Press, 2005.

MacDonald, Neil B., and Carl Trueman, eds. *Calvin, Barth, and Reformed Theology*. Colorado Springs: Paternoster, 2008.

Mackey, Louis. *Peregrinations of the Word*. Ann Arbor: University of Michigan Press, 1997.

Makkreel, Rudolf. "The Role of Judgment and Orientation in Hermeneutics." *Philosophy and Social Criticism* 34 (2008) 29–50.

Manzoni, Alessandro. "Lettre à M. C[hauvet] sur l'unité de temps et de lieu dans la tragédie." Wikisource, last updated Oct. 28, 2023. From 1820/1823. https://fr.wikisource.org/wiki/Lettre_%C3%A0_M.C.***_sur_l%E2%80%99unit%C3%A9_de_temps_et_de_lieu_dans_la_tragedie.

Marcus, Solomon. *Poetica matematică*. Bucharest: Academiei, 1970.

Marshall, Bruce. "The Absolute and the Trinity." *Pro Ecclesia* 13 (2014) 147–64.

Matherne, Samantha. "Kant and the Art of Schematism." *Kantian Review* 19 (2014) 181–205.

McCormack, Bruce L. *The Humility of the Eternal Son: Reformed Kenoticism and the Repair of Chalcedon*. Cambridge: Cambridge University Press, 2021.

———. "Karl Barth's Christologically-Grounded Understanding of the Ecumenical Task." *Studia Universitatis Babeș-Bolyai, Theologia Catholica* 1–2 (2017) 111–25.

———. "Karl Barth's Contribution to Constructive Theology Today." *Theologische Zeitschrift* 71 (2015) 114–25.

———. *Karl Barth's Critically Realistic Dialectical Theology: Its Genesis and Development 1909–1930*. New York: Oxford University Press, 1995.

———. *Orthodox and Modern: Studies in the Theology of Karl Barth*. Grand Rapids: Baker Academic, 2008.

———. "Response to Alexandra Pârvan." *International Journal of Systematic Theology* 24 (2022) 47–55.

Merz, Georg. "Abschied." *Zwischen den Zeiten* 11 (1933) 551–54.

———. "Letter to Karl Barth, January 24, 1933." In Karl Barth Archive, Basel.

Montaigne, Michel de. *The Complete Essays*. Translated by M. A. Screech. Penguin Classics. London: Penguin, 1987.

Moyse, Ashley John, et al., eds. *Correlating Sobornost: Conversations Between Karl Barth and the Russian Orthodox Tradition*. Minneapolis: Fortress, 2016.

Muller, Richard A. "The Barth Legacy: New Athanasius or Origen Redivivus? A Response to T. F. Torrance." *Thomist* 54 (1990) 673–704.

———. *Divine Will and Human Choice: Freedom, Contingency, and Necessity in Early Modern Reformed Thought*. Grand Rapids: Baker, 2017.

———. *The Unaccommodated Calvin: Studies in the Foundation of a Theological Tradition*. Oxford: Oxford University Press, 2000.

Myers, Benjamin. "Karl Barth as Historian: Historical Method in the Göttingen Lectures on Calvin, Zwingli and Schleiermacher." *Zeitschrift für dialektische Theologie* 23 (2007) 96–109.

Namee, Matthew. "The 'Bulgarian Question' and the 1872 Council of Constantinople, Part 1." *Orthodox History*, Nov. 29, 2012. https://orthodoxhistory.org/2012/11/29/the-bulgarian-question-and-the-1872-council-of-constantinople-part-1/.

———. "The 'Bulgarian Question' and the 1872 Council of Constantinople, Part 4." *Orthodox History*, Dec. 4, 2012. https://orthodoxhistory.org/2012/12/04/the-bulgarian-question-and-the-1872-council-of-constantinople-part-4/.

Newman, John Henry. *An Essay on Development of Christian Doctrine*. South Bend, IN: Notre Dame University Press, 1989.

Newman, William R. "From Alchemy to 'Chymistry.'" In *Early Modern Science*, edited by Katharine Park and Lorraine Daston, 497–517. Vol. 3 of *The Cambridge History of Science*. Cambridge: Cambridge University Press, 2006.

Newman, William R., and Anthony Grafton, eds. *Secrets of Nature: Astrology and Alchemy in Early Modern Europe*. Boston: MIT Press, 2011.

Niesel, Wilhelm. *The Theology of Calvin*. London: Lutterworth, 1953.

Noordmans, Oepke. *Verzamelde Werken*. Vol. 2. Kampen: Kok, 1979.

Norris, Kathleen. *Dakota: A Spiritual Geography*. New York: Ticknor and Fields, 1993.

Novalis. *Gesammelte Werke*. Vols. 1–5. Edited by C. Seelig. Zurich: Herrliberg/Bühl, 1945.

———. *Heinrich von Ofterdingen*. Stuttgart: Reclam, 1965.

Nummedal, Tara. *Alchemy and Authority in the Holy Roman Empire*. Chicago: University of Chicago Press, 2007.

Orthodox. "The Head of the OCU Asked the Ecumenical Patriarch to Deprive the Head of the Russian Orthodox Church, Kirill, of the Patriarchal Throne." Religious Information Service of Ukraine, Aug. 20, 2022. https://risu.ua/en/the-head-of-the-ocu-asked-the-ecumenical-patriarch-to-deprive-the-head-of-the-russian-orthodox-church-kirill-of-the-patriarchal-throne_n131676.

Osiander, Andreas. *An Filius Dei fuerit incarnandus, si peccatum non introvisset in mundum*. Königsberg, 1550.

Paert, Irina. "How Do Orthodox Christians Pray in the Year 2022? The Official Prayers of the Russian Orthodox Church During Russia's War Against Ukraine." Khristiane protiv voiny, Feb. 15, 2023. https://shaltnotkill.info/how-do-orthodox-christians-pray-in-the-year-2022-the-official-prayers-of-the-russian-orthodox-church-during-russias-war-against-ukraine/.

Partee, Charles. "The Soul in Plato, Platonism, and Calvin." *Scottish Journal of Theology* 22 (1969) 278–95.

Pârvan, Alexandra. "Eroticism in the Kenotic God: On the Psychological Ontology of the Christic Person." *International Journal of Systematic Theology* 24 (2022) 15–46.

———. "Reformed and Romantic Kenoticism." Lecture delivered at the Annual Karl Barth Conference, Princeton University, June 22, 2022. https://youtu.be/yCI4rexDV54?si=kZo7VjWySBQHDvth.

———. "Romanticism in the Kenotic God: Receptivity, Engaging, Affective Unity, and the Psychological Ontology of the Christic Person." *International Journal of Systematic Theology* 27.2 (2025) 221-47.

Pârvan, Alexandra, and Bruce L. McCormack. "Immutability, (Im)passibility and Suffering: Steps Towards a 'Psychological' Ontology of God." *Neue Zeitschrift für Systematische Theologie und Religionsphilosophie* 59 (2017) 1-25.

Pasnau, Robert. *Theories of Cognition in the Later Middle Ages.* Cambridge: Cambridge University Press, 1997.

Paulin, Roger. *The Life of August Wilhelm Schlegel: Cosmopolitan in Art and Poetry.* Cambridge: Open Book, 2016.

Perrie, Maureen. "Apocalypse Delayed: Patriarch Kirill on Restraining the Antichrist in Ukraine." *Public Orthodoxy*, Jan. 23, 2023. https://publicorthodoxy.org/2023/01/23/apocalypse-delayed-restraining-antichrist/.

Persh, George. "War and Eschatology." *Public Orthodoxy*, Jan. 27, 2023. https://publicorthodoxy.org/2023/01/27/war-and-eschatology/.

Petre Pârvan, L. *Cercetări de poetică și stilistică.* Pitești: Calende, 1994.

———. *Romantismul. Studiu stilistic.* Pitești: Pygmalion, 1995.

Pieper, Moritz. "Russkiy Mir: The Geopolitics of Russian Compatriots Abroad." *Geopolitics* 25 (2020) 756-79.

Pinchuk, Andrii. "Open Appeal of the Priests of the UOC-MP to the Primates of Local Orthodox Churches." *Public Orthodoxy*, Apr. 26, 2022. https://publicorthodoxy.org/2022/04/26/open-appeal-of-uoc-priests/.

Pipkin, H. Wayne. "The Positive Religious Values of Zwingli's Eucharistic Writings." In *Huldrych Zwingli, 1484-1531: A Legacy of Radical Reform*, edited by E. J. Furcha, 107-43. Montreal: McGill University Press.

———. "Resonating with Zwingli." In *Huldrych Zwingli, 1484-1531: A Legacy of Radical Reform*, edited by E. J. Furcha, 99-106. Montreal: McGill University Press, 1985.

Poe, Marshall. "Moscow, the Third Rome: The Origins and Transformations of a 'Pivotal Movement.'" *Jahrbücher für Geschichte Osteuropas* 49 (2001) 412-29.

Presbyterian Church (USA). *Book of Confessions.* Louisville: Office of the General Assembly, 1999.

Przywara, Erich. *Analogia Entis: Metaphysics: Original Structure and Universal Rhythm.* Translated by John Betz and David Bentley Hart. Grand Rapids: Eerdmans, 2014.

Putin, Vladimir. "Address by the President of the Russian Federation." Kremlin, Feb. 24, 2022. English: http://en.kremlin.ru/events/president/news/67828. Russian: http://kremlin.ru/events/president/news/67828.

———. "On the Historical Unity of Russians and Ukrainians." Kremlin, July 12, 2021. English: http://en.kremlin.ru/events/president/news/66181. Russian: http://kremlin.ru/events/president/news/66181.

———. "Presidential Address to the Federal Assembly." Kremlin, Dec. 8, 2014. English: http://en.kremlin.ru/events/president/news/47173. Russian: http://kremlin.ru/events/president/news/47173.

Rahner, Karl. *Foundations of Christian Faith: An Introduction to the Idea of Christianity.* Translated by W. V. Dych. New York: Seabury, 1978.

Ratzinger, Joseph. *"In the Beginning . . .": A Catholic Understanding of the Story of Creation and the Fall.* Translated by Boniface Ramsey. Grand Rapids: Eerdmans, 1998.

———. *Introduction to Christianity*. Translated by J. R. Foster. San Francisco: Ignatius, 2000.

Reeling Brouwer, Rinse H. *Karl Barth and Post-Reformation Orthodoxy*. Aldershot, UK: Ashgate, 2015.

———. "'Und seines Königreiches wird kein Ende sein.' Ein klassischer Widerspruch: Lukas 1:33 oder 1 Korinther 15:28?" In *Unless Someone Guide Me . . . : Festschrift for Karel A. Deurloo*, edited by Janet W. Dyk, 293–301. Maastricht: Shaker, 2001.

Re Manning, Russell, ed. *The Oxford Handbook of Natural Theology*. Oxford Handbooks. Oxford: Oxford University Press, 2013.

Rose, Matthew. "Karl Barth's Failure." *First Things*, June 1, 2014. https://www.firstthings.com/article/2014/06/karl-barths-failure.

Ruler, A. A. van. *Christus, de Geest en het heil*. Verzameld Werk 4-A. Zoetermeer: Boekencentrum, 2011.

Russian Orthodox Church [in Russian]. "Molitva o Sviatoi Rusi." Russian Orthodox Church, Sept. 25, 2022. http://www.patriarchia.ru/db/text/5962654.html.

Russkii Mir [in Russian]. https://russkiymir.ru/.

Sanchez, Michelle C. *Calvin and the Resignification of the World*. New York: Cambridge University Press, 2019.

Sand, George. "À Gustave Flaubert, à Croisset." Wikisource, last updated June 30, 2018. From *Correspondance 1812–1876*, letter 620, Nov. 29, 1866. https://fr.wikisource.org/wiki/Correspondance_1812-1876,_5/1866/DCXX.

———. *La Mare au Diable*. Bibliothèque électronique du Québec, 1852. https://beq.ebooksgratuits.com/vents/Sand-mare.pdf.

Schellong, Dieter. *Calvins Auslegung der synoptischen Evangelien*. Munich: Kaiser, 1969.

Schlegel, A. W. *Course of Lectures on Dramatic Art and Literature*. Translated by John Black. New York: AMS, 1965.

———. *Vorlesungen über schöne Litteratur und Kunst*. Vol. 1, *Die Kunstlehre* [1801–1802]. Heilbronn: Henninger, 1884. Nendeln/Liechtenstein: Kraus Reprint, 1968.

Schlegel, Friedrich. *Athenaeums-Fragmente*. Zeno, 1798. http://www.zeno.org/Literatur/M/Schlegel,+Friedrich/Fragmentensammlungen/Fragmente.

———. *Gespräch über die Poesie*. Stuttgart: Metzler, 1968.

———. *Kritische Fragmente*. Zeno, 1797. http://www.zeno.org/Literatur/M/Schlegel,+Friedrich/Fragmentensammlungen/Kritische+Fragmente.

———. *Lessings Geist aus seinen Schriften, oder dessen Gedanken und Meinungen*. Leipzig: Hinrichs, 1810.

Schleiermacher, Friedrich. *The Christian Faith*. Translated by H. R. Mackintosh and J. S. Stewart. Edinburgh: T&T Clark, 1928.

———. *Der Christliche Glaube*. 2nd ed. Berlin: de Gruyter, 1960.

———. *Ethik 1812/13*. Edited by Hans-Joachim Birkner. Hamburg: Meiner, 1981.

———. *Kurze Darstellung des theologischen Studiums (1811/1830)*. Kritische Gesamtausgabe I/6. Edited by Dirk Schmid. Berlin: de Gruyter, 1998.

———. *Monologen*. Edited by Günter Meckenstock. Kritische Gesamtausgabe 1/3. Berlin: de Gruyter, 1998.

———. *Monologen*. Kritische Ausgabe. Leipzig: Dürr'sch, 1902.

———. *Schleiermacher's Soliloquies*. Translated by Horace Leland Friess. Westport, CT: Hyperion, 1979.

———. *Schriften aus der Berliner Zeit, 1796–1799*. Kritische Gesamtausgabe 1/2. Edited by Günter Meckenstock. Berlin: de Gruyter, 1984.

———. *Schriften aus der Berliner Zeit, 1800–1802*. Kritische Gesamtausgabe 1/3. Edited by Günter Meckenstock. Berlin: de Gruyter, 1988.

Scholder, Klaus. *The Churches and the Third Reich: Preliminary History and the Time of Illusions*. Vol. 1, *1918–1934*. Minneapolis: Fortress, 1988.

Schroeder, Joy A., and Marion Ann Taylor. *Voices Long Silenced: Women Biblical Interpreters Through the Centuries*. Louisville: Westminster John Knox, 2022.

Sergeitsev, Timofey. "RIA NOVOSTI Has Clarified Russia's Plans Vis-à-Vis Ukraine and the Rest of the Free World in a Program Like Article: What Russia Should Do with Ukraine?" *Centre for Civil Liberties*, Apr. 4, 2022. English: https://ccl.org.ua/en/news/ria-novosti-has-clarified-russias-plans-vis-a-vis-ukraine-and-the-rest-of-the-free-world-in-a-program-like-article-what-russia-should-do-with-ukraine-2/. Russian: https://ria.ru/20220403/ukraina-1781469605.html.

Shaw, Gregory. "Neoplatonic Theurgy and Dionysius the Areopagite." *Journal of Early Christian Studies* 7 (1999) 573–99.

Shelley, Percy Bysshe. "A Defence of Poetry." Saylor, n.d. From *English Essays: Sidney to Macaulay*, edited by Charles W. Eliot (New York: Collier & Son, 1910). https://resources.saylor.org/wwwresources/archived/site/wp-content/uploads/2011/01/A-Defense-of-Poetry.pdf.

———. *Prometheus Unbound*. Edited by L. J. Zillman. Seattle: University of Washington Press, 1959.

Shishkov, Andrey. "Some Reflections on the Declaration on the 'Russian World.'" *Public Orthodoxy*, Apr. 13, 2022. https://publicorthodoxy.org/2022/04/13/some-reflections-on-the-declaration-on-the-russian-world-teaching/.

Shumylo, Serhii. "'Ordinary Fascism' or The Russian World of Patriarch Kirill." *Wheel*, Apr. 10, 2024. https://www.wheeljournal.com/blog/2024/4/10/serhii-shumylo-ordinary-fascism-or-the-russian-world-of-patriarch-kirill.

Skinner, Quentin. *From Humanism to Hobbes: Studies in Rhetoric and Politics*. Cambridge: Cambridge University Press, 2018.

Sluhovsky, Moshe. "Calvinist Miracles and the Concept of the Miraculous in Sixteenth-Century Huguenot Thought." *Renaissance and Reformation* 19 (1995) 5–25.

Smith, Christian. *The Bible Made Impossible: Why Biblicism Is Not a Truly Evangelical Reading of Scripture*. Grand Rapids: Brazos, 2012.

Söhngen, Gottlieb. "The Analogy of Faith: Likeness to God from Faith Alone?" Translated by K. Oakes. *Pro Ecclesia* 21 (2012) 56–76.

———. "The Analogy of Faith: Unity in the Science of Faith." Translated by K. Oakes. *Pro Ecclesia* 21 (2012) 169–94.

Solberg, Mary M. *A Church Undone: Documents from the German Christian Faith Movement 1932–1940*. Minneapolis: Fortress, 2015.

Staël, Madame de. *Corinne ou l'Italie*. Vol. 1. Paris: Librairie Stéréotype, chez Nicolle, 1807.

———. *Oeuvres de Madame la Baronne de Staël-Holstein*. Vol. 3, *De l'Allemagne*. Paris: Lefèvre, 1858.

Stamatopoulos, Dimitris. "Orthodox Ecumenicity and the Bulgarian Schism." *St. Vladimir's Theological Quarterly* 54 (2013) 305–23.

Stang, Charles M. "From the Chaldean Oracles to the Corpus Dionysiacum: Theurgy Between the Third and Sixth Centuries." *Journal for Late Antique Religion and Culture* 5 (2011) 1–13.

Stapel, Wilhelm. *Der christliche Staatsmann: Eine Theologie des Nationalismus.* Hamburg: Hanseatisch, 1932.

Stephens, W. Peter. *The Theology of Huldrych Zwingli.* Oxford: Clarendon, 1986.

Suslov, M. "The Russian Orthodox Church and the Crisis in Ukraine." In *Churches in the Ukrainian Crisis,* edited by Andrii Krawchuk and Thomas Bremer, 133–62. Basingstoke: Palgrave Macmillan, 2016.

Taylor, Marion, ed. *Handbook of Women Biblical Interpreters.* Grand Rapids: Eerdmans, 2012.

Thompson, John L. *Reading the Bible with the Dead: What You Can Learn from the History of Exegesis That You Can't Learn from Exegesis Alone.* Grand Rapids: Eerdmans, 2007.

Tietz, Christiane. *Karl Barth: A Life in Conflict.* Translated by Victoria J. Barnett. Oxford: Oxford University Press, 2021.

Todorov, Tzvetan. "The Historiographical Rethinking of the Bulgarian Schism (1872) Through the Postsecular Perspective—Reasons and Consequences." *Études Balkaniques* 52 (2016) 242–64.

Torrance, Thomas F. "The Problem of Natural Theology in the Thought of Karl Barth." *Religious Studies* 6 (1970) 121–35.

Tylenda, Joseph N. "The Warning That Went Unheeded: John Calvin on Giorgio Biandrata." *Calvin Theological Journal* 12 (1977) 24–72.

Valliere, Paul. "The Influence of Russian Religious Thought on Western Theology in the Twentieth Century." In *The Oxford Handbook of Russian Religious Thought,* edited by Caryl Emerson et al., 661–64. Oxford Handbooks. Oxford: Oxford University Press, 2020.

Van der Kooi, Cornelis. *As in a Mirror: John Calvin and Karl Barth on Knowing God.* Translated by Donald Mader. Leiden: Brill, 2005.

Vatican Council I. *Dei Filius.* Vatican, Apr. 24, 1870. https://www.vatican.va/archive/hist_councils/i-vatican-council/documents/vat-i_const_18700424_dei-filius_la.html.

Vial, Theodore. *Modern Religion, Modern Race.* Oxford: Oxford University Press, 2015.

Voigtländer, Johannes. *Ein Fest der Befreiung: Huldrych Zwinglis Abendmahllehre.* Neukirchen, Germ.: Neukirchen, 2013.

Voolstra, Sjouke. *Het Woord is vlees geworden: De melchioritisch-mennniste incarnatieleer.* Kampen: Kok, 1982.

Waddell, Mark A. *Magic, Science, and Religion in Early Modern Europe.* New Approaches to the History of Science and Medicine. Cambridge: Cambridge University Press, 2021.

Wandel, Lee Palmer. "Calvin and Montaigne on the Eye." In *Early Modern Eyes,* edited by Lee Palmer Wandel and Walter Melion, 139–53. Intersections 13. Leiden: Brill, 2009.

Waswo, Richard. *Language and Meaning in the Renaissance.* Princeton, NJ: Princeton University Press, 1997.

Weber, Max. *The Protestant Ethic and the Spirit of Capitalism.* Routledge Classics. London: Routledge, 2021.

Webster, Charles. *From Paracelsus to Newton: Magic and the Making of Modern Science.* Cambridge: Cambridge University Press, 1982.

Webster, John. *Barth's Earlier Theology: Four Studies.* London: T&T Clark, 2005.

———. "Karl Barth." In *Reading Romans Through the Centuries: From the Early Church to Karl Barth*, edited by Jeffrey P. Greenman and Timothy Larsen, 205–23. Grand Rapids: Brazos, 2005.
White, Thomas J. "The *analogia fidei* in Catholic Theology." *International Journal of Systematic Theology* 22 (2020) 512–37.
———. "The Crucified Lord: Thomistic Reflections on the Communication of Idioms and the Theology of the Cross." In *Aquinas and Barth: An Unofficial Catholic Protestant Ecumenical Dialogue*, edited by Bruce L. McCormack and Thomas Joseph White, 157–92. Grand Rapids: Eerdmans, 2013.
———. "*Dyotheletism* and the Consciousness of Christ." *Pro Ecclesia* 17 (2008) 396–422.
———. *Incarnate Lord: A Thomistic Study in Christology*. Washington, DC: Catholic University of America Press, 2017.
———. "On the Ecumenical Work of Reforming Christology: *Sacra Doctrina, Analogia Entis*, and Kenosis." *Nova et Vetera* 20 (2022) 649–72.
———. *Wisdom in the Face of Modernity*. 2nd ed. Naples: Sapientia, 2016.
Whitehead, Andrew L., and Samuel L. Perry. *Taking America Back for God: Christian Nationalism in the United States*. New York: Oxford University Press, 2020.
William of Ockham. *Opera philosophica et theologica*. 17 vols. Edited by Gedeon Gál et al. St. Bonaventure: Franciscan Institute, 1967–88.
Williams, Rowan. *Christ the Heart of Creation*. London: Bloomsbury Continuum, 2018.
———. "Language, Reality, and Desire in Augustine's *De Doctrina*." *Journal of Literature and Theology* 3 (1989) 138–50.
Winzeler, Peter. "Zwingli und Karl Barth." *Zwingliana* 17 (1987) 298–314.
Wollebius, Johannes. *Christianae Theologiae Compendium*. Basel: Genathi, 1626.
Woodard-Lehman, Derek A. "Reason After Revelation: Karl Barth on Divine Word and Human Words." *Modern Theology* 33 (2016) 92–115.
Wordsworth, William. Preface [1800, 1802] to *Lyrical Ballads*. In *Prefaces and Prologues to Famous Books*, edited by Charles W. Eliot, 274. Harvard Classics 39. New York: Collier & Son, 1910. https://www.myharvardclassics.com/downloads/20120213_24.
World Russian People's Council 2024 [in Russian]. "Nakaz XXV Vsemirnogo russkogo narodnogo sobora 'Nastoiashchee i budushchee Russkogo mira [Order of the XXV World Russian People's Council 'The Present and Future of the Russian World']." Russian Orthodox Church, Mar. 27, 2024. http://www.patriarchia.ru/db/text/6116189.html.
Wynter, Sylvia. "Unsettling the Coloniality of Being/Power/Truth/Freedom: Towards the Human, After Man, Its Overrepresentation—an Argument." *CR: The New Centennial Review* 3 (2003) 257–337.
Zantop, Susanne. *Colonial Fantasies*. Durham, NC: Duke University Press, 1997.
Ziegler, Philip G. "On the Present Possibility of *Sola Scriptura*." *International Journal of Systematic Theology* 24 (2022) 565–83.
Zuber, Mike A. *Spiritual Alchemy: From Jacob Boehme to Mary Anne Atwood*. Oxford Studies in Western Esotericism. Oxford: Oxford University Press, 2021.
Zwahlen, Regula. "Da ili Net—Sofiologiia Sergiia Bulgakova v Kontekste Protestantskoi 'Dialekticheskoi Teologii' 'v 1930-kh gg." In *Russkaia Emigratsiia: Tserkovnaia zhizn' i bogoslovsko-filosofskoe nasledie*, 29–48. Moscow: PSTGU, 2022.

———. "Over a Beer with Barth and Bulgakov: Cosmodicy." *Public Orthodoxy*, July 18, 2022. https://publicorthodoxy.org/2022/07/18/over-a-beer-with-barth-and-bulgakov-cosmodicy/.

Zwingli, Huldrych [Huldreich, Ulrich]. *Commentary on True and False Religion*. Edited by Samuel Macauley Jackson and Clarence Nevin Heller. Translated by Henry Preble. Eugene, OR: Wipf & Stock, 2015.

———. *The Latin Works of Huldreich Zwingli*. Vol. 2. Edited by William John Hinke. Translated by Henry Preble. Philadelphia: Heidelberg, 1922.

———. *"On Providence" and Other Essays*. Edited by William John Hinke. Translated by Henry Preble. Eugene, OR: Wipf & Stock, 1999.

Zwingli, Huldrych [Huldreich, Ulrich], and Heinrich Bullinger. *Zwingli and Bullinger*. Edited and translated by Geoffrey W. Bromiley. Louisville: Westminster John Knox, 2006.

www.ingramcontent.com/pod-product-compliance
Lightning Source LLC
Chambersburg PA
CBHW021649230426
43668CB00008B/568